Encyclopedia of MATLAB: Science and Engineering

Volume VI

Encyclopedia of MATLAB: Science and Engineering Volume VI

Edited by **Louis Young**

CLANRYE INTERNATIONAL

New Jersey

Published by Clanrye International,
55 Van Reypen Street,
Jersey City, NJ 07306, USA
www.clanryeinternational.com

Encyclopedia of MATLAB: Science and Engineering
Volume VI
Edited by Louis Young

International Standard Book Number: 978-1-63240-194-6 (Hardback)

Printed in the United States of America.

Contents

Permissions

List of Contributors

Preface

This book has been an outcome of determined endeavour from a group of educationists in the field. The primary objective was to involve a broad spectrum of professionals from diverse cultural background involved in the field for developing new researches. The book not only targets students but also scholars pursuing higher research for further enhancement of the theoretical and practical applications of the subject.

Proportional-integral-derivative (PID) controllers are widely regarded as the most important tool for a control engineer. However, in today's era of computer science, MATLAB has acquired the position of an essential tool for the modern system engineering. This book has been written in a manner to serve as a practical guide for both practicing engineers and engineering students. Numerous applications use MATLAB as the working framework which shows that it is an effective, comprehensive and handy technique for performing technical computations. This book discusses various prominent applications in which MATLAB is used: from pure algebraic computations to data acquisition in real-life experiments and control strategies.

It was an honour to edit such a profound book and also a challenging task to compile and examine all the relevant data for accuracy and originality. I wish to acknowledge the efforts of the contributors for submitting such brilliant and diverse chapters in the field and for endlessly working for the completion of the book. Last, but not the least; I thank my family for being a constant source of support in all my research endeavours.

Editor

Part 1

Applied Mathematics

Effect of the Guess Function & Continuation Method on the Run Time of MATLAB BVP Solvers

Fikri Serdar Gökhan

Gazikent University, Faculty of Engineering and Architecture,
Department of Electrical and Electronic Engineering, Gaziantep
Turkey

1. Introduction

The MATLAB computing environment is a package used extensively throughout industry, research and education by users of a complete range in proficiency. MATLAB provides then an ideal platform to introduce such an item of Boundary Value Problem (BVP) software and indeed, Kierzenka and Shampine (Kierzenka & Shampine, 2001) developed the core BVP Ordinary Differential Equation (ODE) software bvp4c to solve a large class of two-point boundary value problems of the form;

$$y'(x) = f(x, y(x), p) \tag{1}$$

$$g(x_L, x_R, y(x_L), y(x_R), p) = 0 \tag{2}$$

where f is continuous and Lipschitz function in y and p is a vector of unknown parameters. Their view was that a user solving a BVP of form (1) in MATLAB would be most interested in the graphical representation of a solution, and as such a solver with a MIRK4-based Simpson Method would be appropriate for graphical accuracy.

If information is specified at more than one point the problem (1) becomes a Boundary Value Problem. The most common types of BVP are those for which information given at precisely two points. These are known as two-point boundary value problems.

The MATLAB BVP solver of bvp4c is introduced as a Residual control based, adaptive mesh solver. An adaptive mesh solver is an alternative approach to that of a uniform mesh, which would specify a uniform grid of data points x_i over the interval $[x_i, x_{i+1}]$ and solve accordingly. The adaptive solver will adjust the mesh points at each stage in the iterative procedure, distributing them to points where they are most needed. This can lead to obvious advantages in terms of computational and storage costs as well as allowing control over the grid resolution. The concept of a residual is the cornerstone of the bvp4c framework; being responsible for both errors control and mesh selection (Hale, 2006).

The most difficult part for the solution of BVPs is to provide an initial estimation to the solution. In order to direct the solver for the solution of interest, it is necessary to assist the solver by informing it with a guess. Not only for the computation of the solution of interest but also whether any solution is achieved or not depends strongly on the initial guess. Therefore, depending of the guess function, BVPs may have no solution or a single solution, or multiple solutions. Moreover, the quality of the initial guess can be critical to the solver performance, which reduces or augments the run time. However, coming up with a sufficiently good guess can be the most challenging part of solving a BVP. Certainly, the user should apply the knowledge of the problem's physical origin (MATLAB Documentation).

In MATLAB, when solving BVPs the user must provide a guess to assist the solver in computing the desired solution (Kierzenka & Shampine, 2001). MATLAB BVP solvers call for users to provide guesses for the mesh and solution. Although MATLAB BVP solvers take an unusual approach to the control of error in case of having poor guesses for the mesh and solution, especially for the nonlinear BVP, a good guess is necessary to obtain convergence (Shampine *et al.*, 2003).

Whatever intuitive guess values/functions are imposed, eventually the BVP solver fails for some parameters or for some lengths. If any guess values works for the range of length, the rest of the length may be extended using *continuation*. The method of continuation exploits the fact that the solution obtained for one input will serve as the initial guess for the next value tried. In case of any difficulty in finding a guess for the interval of interest, generally it will be easier to solve the problem on a shorter interval. Then the solution of the sequence of BVPs on the shorter interval will be used as a guess for the next section. With modest increases in the interval, this will continue until the interval of interest is spanned (Shampine *et al.*, 2003).

The cost of the continuation method is the increased run time. How the guess value good is, the less computation time it takes with the continuation method. This is due the fact that, the remaining length depends of the convergence length (based on the guess value) which its higher value reduces the computation time.

2. Initial setup

The first step in solving a problem is defining it in a way the software can understand. The bvp4c framework uses a number of subfunctions which make it as simple as possible for the user to enter the ODE function, initial data and parameters for a given problem. By way of the following example we see exactly how a problem is supplied and solved by bvp4c. For the evaluation of the guess value /function, the steady-state Brillouin equation is exploited. The coupled ODEs for the evolution of the intensities of pump I_p and Stokes I_s can be written as (Agrawal, 2001),

$$\frac{dIp}{dz} = -g_B I_p I_s - \alpha I_p \tag{3}$$

$$\frac{dIs}{dz} = -g_B I_p I_s + \alpha I_s \tag{4}$$

where $0 \leq z \leq L$ is the propagation distance along the optical fiber of the total length L, α is the fiber loss coefficient, g_B is the Brillouin gain coefficient, respectively. Here, it is assumed that, Stokes wave is launched from the rear end of the fiber. Then the known values of the input pump power $I_p(0)$ and the Stokes wave power I_s (L) are referred as the boundary values.

The first task is to define the ODEs in MATLAB as a function to return these equations. Similarly the user then rewrites the boundary conditions to correspond to this form of the problem. We may code the ODEs for scalar evaluation and boundary conditions, respectively as,

```
function dydx = bvpode(x,y)
global alpha_s gb K

dydx =   [ -gb *y(1)*y(2)-alpha_s*y(1)
            -gb *y(1)*y(2)+alpha_s*y(2) ];

-------------------------------------------------------

function res = bvpbc(ya,yb)
 global Ip0 IsL

 res = [ya(1)- Ip0
         yb(2)- IsL ];
```

The next step is to create an initial guess for the form of the solution using a specific MATLAB subroutine called bvpinit . The user passes a vector x and an initial guess on this mesh in the form bvpinit (x, Yinit), which is then converted into a structure useable by bvp4c. Aside from a sensible guess being necessary for a convergent solution the mesh vector passed to bvpinit will also define the boundary points of the problem, i.e. $x_L = x[1]$ and $x_R = x[end]$.

The initial guess for the solution may take one of two forms. One option is a vector where Yinit(i) is a constant guess for the i-th component y(i,:) of the solution at all the mesh points in x. The other is as a function of a scalar x, for example bvpinit(x,@yfun) where for any x in [a, b], yfun(x) returns a guess for the solution y(x). It must be pointed out that even when a function is supplied that approximates the solution everywhere in the interval; the solver uses its values only on the initial mesh. The guess can be coded as a function of a scalar x as,

```
function v = guess(x)

global alpha_s L gb k Pp0 PsL Aeff
a=alpha_s*L;
k=gb/Aeff*Pp0*L;
epsilon=PsL/Pp0;
kappa=-log(gb/Aeff*PsL*L);
T=log(kappa*(1-kappa/k));
c0=-(PsL + PsL*k - 1)/((PsL*k^2)/2 + 1);
A=c0./(1-(1-c0).*exp(-c0*k.*x));
B=c0*(1-c0)./(exp(c0*k.*x)-1+c0);
w=(A.^(exp(-a))).*exp(-a.*x);
u=(B.*exp(a.*(x-1)));

v=[w*Pp0; u*Pp0];
```

The next subroutine to look at is bvpset, that specifies which options bvp4c should be use in solving it. The function is called options = bvpset('name1',value1,...) and since MATLAB documentation gives an in depth account of each of the options only a brief outline of those notable is given here (Hale, 2006).

```
options = []; % default
%options = bvpset('Stats','on','RelTol',1e-5,'abstol',1e-4);
%options = bvpset(options,'Vectorized','on');
%options = bvpset(options,'FJacobian',@odeJac);
%options = bvpset(options,'BCJacobian',@bcJac);
```

RelTol - Relative tolerance for the residual [positive scalar 1e-3]
The computed solution $S(x)$ is the exact solution of $S'(x) = F(x, S(x)) + res(x)$. On each subinterval of the mesh, component i of the residual must satisfy norm

$$norm\left(\frac{res(i)}{\max(abs(F(i)),\ AbsTol(i)\ /\ RelTol)}\right) \le RelTol$$

AbsTol - Absolute tolerance for the residual [positive scalar or vector 1e-6]
Elements of a vector of tolerances apply to corresponding components of the residual vector. AbsTol defaults to 1e-6.
FJacobian \ BCJacobian - Analytical partial derivatives of ODEFUN \ BCFUN
Computation of the Jacobian matrix at each mesh point can be a very expensive process. By passing an analytic derivative of the ODE and BC functions the user can greatly reduce computational time. For example when solving $y' = f(x, y)$, setting FJacobian to @FJAC where $\partial f / \partial y$ = FJAC(x, y) evaluates the Jacobian of f with respect to y.
Stats - Display computational cost statistics [on — off]
Vectorized - Vectorized ODE function [on — off]
As will be discussed in section 6, bvp4c is able to accept a vectorised function which can markedly increase the efficiency of calculating local Jacobians over using finite differences with the odenumjac subroutine. Hence in the following programs, we will define

```
options = bvpset('Stats','on','RelTol',1e-5,'abstol',1e-4);
solinit = bvpinit(linspace(0,L,2), @guess);
```
And call the bvp4c routine with:
```
sol = bvp4c(@ode,@bc,solinit,options);
```

The above essentially ends the user input in solving the BVP system and the rest is left to bvp4c. Within the framework there are several notable steps which should be expounded.

3. Derivation of the guess

In this chapter, four guess functions are derived for the assistance of the MATLAB BVP solvers with the help of MATLAB symbolic toolbox.

3.1 1st Guess
If the constant guess is used as the initial values i.e., for the pump "Ip0" and for the Stokes "IsL" and L = 10000;

```
solinit = bvpinit(linspace(0,L,2),@guess);
options = bvpset('Stats','on','RelTol',1e-5);
function v = guess(x)
global Ip0   IsL
v=[Ip0 ; IsL];
```

It prompts as, "Unable to solve the collocation equations -- a singular Jacobian encountered". However, if the computation length is decreased as, L = 1000, the solver *is able* to solve coupled equations with these poor guesses v=[Ip0 ; IsL]. Therefore, with these guess values the convergence length (the maximum length which the solver is able to converge) is 1000 meter. The evolution of the guess values (estimate) with the real solution is shown in Fig. 1

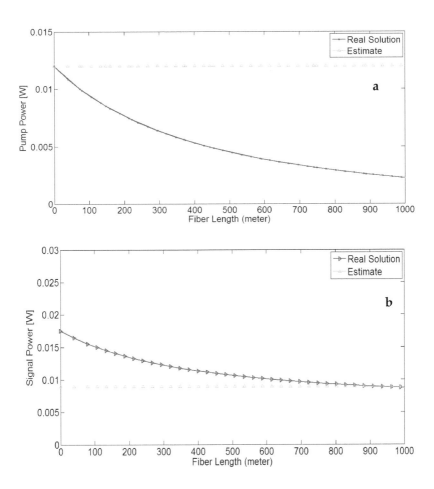

Fig. 1. Evolution of the guess values and real solution according to 1st guess

3.2 2nd Guess

If we guess that I_p and I_s is linearly changing as,

```
Ip ~ Ip0+A*z ;
Is ~ Is0+B*z ;
```

Exploiting with the MATLAB Symbolic Toolbox using the following script,

```
syms Is Ip Is0 Ip0 IsL gb L alpha A B z

 Ip = Ip0+A*z ;
 Is = Is0+B*z ;

 eqn1 = collect(diff(Ip,'z') + (gb)*Ip*Is+alpha*Ip);
 eqn2 = collect(diff(Is,'z') + (gb)*Ip*Is-alpha*Is);

 eqn3=collect(taylor(eqn1,1,0),z)
 eqn4=collect(taylor(eqn2,1,L),z)
```

The below output is produced;

```
eqn3 =   A + Ip0*alpha + (Ip0*Is0*gb)
eqn4 =   B - Is0*alpha - L*(B*alpha - (gb*(A*Is0 + B*Ip0))) +
         (Ip0*Is0*gb) + (A*B*L^2*gb)

Is0=IsL-B*L;
```

Here, there are two equations and two unknowns A and B. With the substitution of Is0, It can be solved simultaneously by the below script,
eqn=

```
solve(A + Ip0*alpha + (Ip0*(IsL-B*L)*gb),...
    B - (IsL-B*L)*alpha - L*(B*alpha - (gb*(A*(IsL-B*L) + B*Ip0)))+
    (Ip0*(IsL-B*L)*gb) + (A*B*L^2*gb),...
    'A','B')
eqn =

    A: [1x1 sym]
    B: [1x1 sym]
```

Here A and B can be obtained as,

```
A=-(Ip0*alpha_s + Ip0^2*IsL*L*gb^2 + Ip0*IsL*gb -
    Ip0*IsL*L*alpha_s*gb)/(Ip0*IsL*L^2*gb^2);

B=(IsL*alpha_s + Ip0*IsL^2*L*gb^2 - Ip0*IsL*gb +
    Ip0*IsL*L*alpha_s*gb)/(Ip0*IsL*L^2*gb^2)

Ip ~ Ip0+A.*x ;
```

```
Is ~ (IsL-B.*L)+B.*x ;
```

The evolution of the 2nd guess values with the real solution is shown in Fig. 2

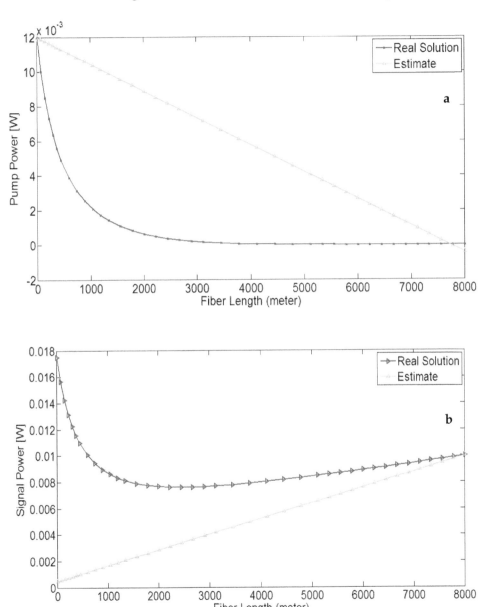

Fig. 2. Evolution of the guess values and real solution according to 2nd guess

3.3 3rd Guess

If it is guessed that I_p and I_s is exponentially changing as,

```
Ip ~ Ip0*exp(gamma1*z) ;
Is ~ Is0*exp(kappa1*z) ;
```
with using the following script,
```
syms Ip Is Is0 Ip0 gb z L IsL alpha gamma1 kappa1

Ip = Ip0*exp(gamma1*z) ;
Is = Is0*exp(kappa1*z) ;

eqn1 = collect(diff(Ip,'z') + (gb)*Ip*Is+alpha*Ip);
eqn2 = collect(diff(Is,'z') + (gb)*Ip*Is-alpha*Is);

eqn3=taylor(eqn1,1,0)
eqn4=taylor(eqn2,1,L)
```

The below output is produced;

```
eqn3 =Ip0*alpha + Ip0*gamma1 + (Ip0*Is0*gb)
eqn4 =Is0*kappa1*exp(L*kappa1) - Is0*alpha*exp(L*kappa1) +
      (Ip0*Is0*gb*exp(L*gamma1)*exp(L*kappa1))
```

gamma1 and kappa1 can be obtained as;
```
eqn5=solve(Ip0*alpha + Ip0*gamma1 + (Ip0*Is0*gb),'gamma1')
gamma1= -(alpha + Is0*gb)
```
using the same way;
```
kappa1 = (alpha - Ip0*gb*exp(L*gamma1));
```

Here, Is0 can be readily found by,

```
Is(z) = Is0*exp(kappa1*z) ;
For z=L
IsL= Is0*exp(kappa1*L);
Is0= IsL/exp(kappa1*L);
```

Therefore,

```
Ip ~ Ip0*exp(gamma1*z) ;
Is ~ IsL/exp(kappa1*L)*exp(kappa1*z) ;
```

The evolution of the 3rd guess values with the real solution is shown in Fig. 3

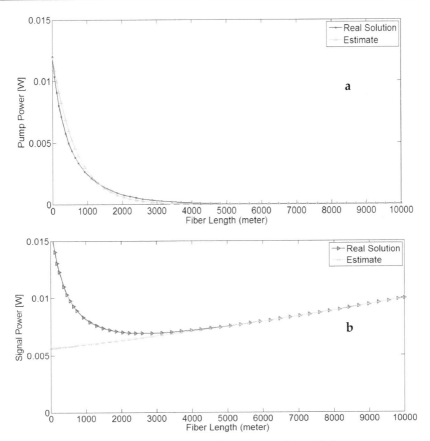

Fig. 3. Evolution of the guess values and real solution according to 3rd guess

3.4 4th Guess

Highly intuitive guess function may be derived the using the solution of lossless system, i.e., with eliminating the α coefficient in the Eq (3) and Eq. (4),

$$\frac{dIp}{dz} = -g_B I_P I_S \tag{5}$$

$$\frac{dIs}{dz} = -g_B I_P I_S \tag{6}$$

With neglecting the attenuation coefficient, the solution of the Eq.(5) and Eq.(6) is found as (Kobyakov et al., 2006),

$$A(\zeta) = c_0 [1 - (1 - c_0)\exp(-c_0 k\zeta)]^{-1} P_P(0) \tag{7}$$

$$B(\zeta) = c_0 (1 - c_0)[\exp(c_0 k\zeta) - 1 + c_0]^{-1} P_P(0) \tag{8}$$

where,

$$c_0 \approx \frac{1}{k}\left\{\Lambda + \ln\left[\Lambda(1-\frac{\Lambda}{k})\right]\right\}, \ k = \frac{g_B}{A_{eff}}P_P(0)L, \ \zeta = \frac{z}{L} \tag{9}$$

where,

$$\Lambda = -\ln(\frac{P_{SL}}{P_{p0}}k) = -\ln[\frac{g_B}{A_{eff}}P_{SL}L], \ \frac{P_{SL}}{P_{p0}}k \ll 1 \tag{10}$$

Exploiting the solution of Eq.(7) and Eq. (8), general expression of $P_P(z)$ and $P_S(z)$ can be derived as,

$$P_P(z) = A(z)\cdot[1 - a\cdot(A\cdot x + B\cdot x^2)] \tag{11}$$

$$P_S(z) = B(z)\cdot[1 - a\cdot(C\cdot x + D\cdot x^2)] \tag{12}$$

If a→0, then $P_P(z) = A(z)$ and $P_S(z) = B(z)$

```
syms z k A B C D a AA BB c0 x

AA=c0/(1-(1-c0)*exp(-c0*k*z));
BB=c0*(1-c0)/(exp(c0*k*z)-1+c0);
w=(AA*(1-a*(A*x+B*x^2)));

u=(BB*(1-a*(C*x+D*x^2)));
eqn1 = collect(diff(w,1,'z') + (k*u*w)+a*w)
eqn2 = collect(diff(u,1,'z') + (k*u*w)-a*u)
The output produces,

eqn1 =
...+ ((c0^2*k*(A*a + C*a)*(c0 - 1))/(((c0 - 1)/exp(c0*k*z) + 1)*(c0 +
exp(c0*k*z) - 1)) - (A*a^2*c0)/((c0 - 1)/exp(c0*k*z) + 1) -
(2*B*a*c0)/((c0 - 1)/exp(c0*k*z) + 1) - (A*a*c0^2*k*(c0 -
1))/(exp(c0*k*z)*((c0 - 1)/exp(c0*k*z) + 1)^2))*x ...
+ (a*c0)/((c0 - 1)/exp(c0*k*z) + 1) - (A*a*c0)/((c0 - 1)/exp(c0*k*z)
+ 1) + (c0^2*k*(c0 - 1))/(exp(c0*k*z)*((c0 - 1)/exp(c0*k*z) + 1)^2)
- (c0^2*k*(c0 - 1))/(((c0 - 1)/exp(c0*k*z) + 1)*(c0 + exp(c0*k*z) -
1))


 eqn2 =
... + ((2*D*a*c0*(c0 - 1))/(c0 + exp(c0*k*z) - 1) - (C*a^2*c0*(c0 -
1))/(c0 + exp(c0*k*z) - 1) + (c0^2*k*(A*a + C*a)*(c0 - 1))/(((c0 -
1)/exp(c0*k*z) + 1)*(c0 + exp(c0*k*z) - 1)) -
(C*a*c0^2*k*exp(c0*k*z)*(c0 - 1))/(c0 + exp(c0*k*z) - 1)^2)*x ...
+ (a*c0*(c0 - 1))/(c0 + exp(c0*k*z) - 1) + (C*a*c0*(c0 - 1))/(c0 +
exp(c0*k*z) - 1) - (c0^2*k*(c0 - 1))/(((c0 - 1)/exp(c0*k*z) + 1)*(c0
+ exp(c0*k*z) - 1)) + (c0^2*k*exp(c0*k*z)*(c0 - 1))/(c0 +
exp(c0*k*z) - 1)^2
```

We are interested in the behavior as $z \to 0$ and so, the higher the power of x, the less effect it has in these expansions. Our goal is to satisfy the equations as well as possible, so we want to choose coefficients that make as many successive terms zero as possible, starting with the lowest power. To eliminate the constant terms, we see from the expansions that we must take

```
A= 1; C=-1;
B= -(a - a/exp(c0*k*z) + (a*c0)/exp(c0*k*z) - (c0*k)/exp(c0*k*z) +
    (c0^2*k)/exp(c0*k*z))/((2*c0)/exp(c0*k*z) - 2/exp(c0*k*z) + 2)
D=  (a - a/exp(c0*k*z) + (a*c0)/exp(c0*k*z) - (c0*k)/exp(c0*k*z) +
    (c0^2*k)/exp(c0*k*z))/((2*c0)/exp(c0*k*z) - 2/exp(c0*k*z) + 2)
```

The evolution of the 4rd guess values with the real solution is shown in Fig. 4

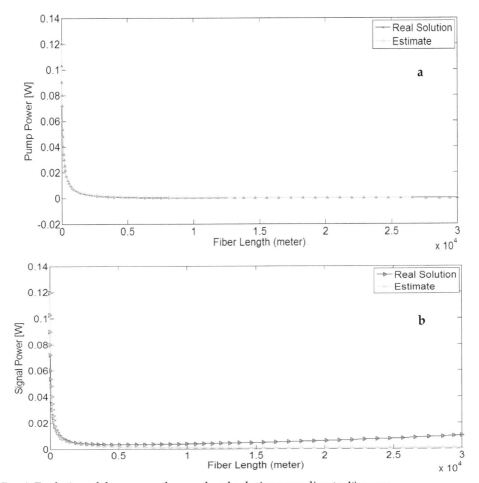

Fig. 4. Evolution of the guess values and real solution according to 4th guess

Guess	Length(mt) /mesh	Convergence length/mesh	Computation Time (with bvp4c) at 8000 meter
1st Guess - values (Ip0,IsL)	8000/ 40	8000/40	~1.18 sec
2nd Guess - functions (linear)	8000/ 40	9000/453	~1.13 sec
3rd Guess -functions (exponential)	8000/ 40	15000/56	~1.13 sec
4th Guess functions (modified exponential)	8000/ 35	30000/61	~1.0 sec

Table 1. Guess values/functions versus convergence length/mesh and run time.

As can be seen from Table 1 and Fig.4 the best estimation is the 4th guess. Because its' convergence length (30000) is more than the others (15000, 9000, 8000, respectively). The performance of the 2nd guess is approximately same as the first one. Because it hardly converge the solution using 453 points at 9000 meter. However, its performance is same as the first one with 40 points at 8000 meter.

4. Continuation

The method of continuation exploits the fact that generally the solution of one BVP is a good guess for the solution of another with slightly different parameters. If you have difficulty in finding a guess for the solution that is good enough to achieve convergence for the interval of interest, it is frequently the case that the problem is easier to solve on a shorter interval. The idea is then to solve a sequence of BVPs with the solution on one interval being used as a guess for the problem posed on a longer interval. Of course, this technique cannot be used to extend the interval *ad infinitum*; no matter how good the guess is, eventually the solver will not be able to distinguish the different kinds of solutions (Shampine *et al.*, 2003).
For the range of interested lengths bigger than the convergence lengths, the continuation process can be applied. Some types of snippets of continuation are illustrated below,

```
=================#1#========================
options = bvpset('FJacobian',@sampleJac,...
                 'BCJacobian',@sampleBCJac,...
                 'Vectorized','on');

sol = bvpinit([-1 -0.5 0 0.5 1],[1 0]);

c = 0.1;
for i=2:4
    c = c/10;
    sol = bvp4c(@sampleODE,@sampleBC,sol,options);
end

=================#2#========================

infinity = 3;
maxinfinity = 6;

solinit = bvpinit(linspace(0,infinity,5),[0 0 1]);
sol = bvp4c(@fsode,@fsbc,solinit);
```

```
eta = sol.x;
f = sol.y;

for Bnew = infinity+1:maxinfinity

    solinit = bvpinit(sol,[0 Bnew]); % Extend solution to Bnew.
    sol = bvp4c(@fsode,@fsbc,solinit);
    eta = sol.x;
    f = sol.y;
```

================#3#=====================

```
L=30000;
for i = 1:1000:L
D = 5*i/1000; d = 1/D;
if i == 1
solinit = bvpinit(linspace(1,i,10),@guess);
else
solinit = bvpinit(sol,[d,D]);
end

sol = bvp4c(@odes,@bcs,solinit);
end
```

================#4#=====================

```
function Boundary_value_increment
global a b

a= XL;      %[a
b= XR;      %   b]
sol = bvpinit(linspace(0,L,2),[Boundary values for each pump and
signal power]);

options = bvpset('Stats','on','RelTol',1e-5);

for k=1:Desired_Power
b=b+k;
sol = bvp4c(@bvpode,@bvpbc,sol,options);
end
```

If the interested length is bigger than the convergence length then continuation can be applied with the **bvpxtend** function. In the recent version of MATLAB, bvpinit function is simplified to a new function **bvpxtend**. Besides offering new possibilities, this function permits extension of length of interval to only one end point at a time (Kierzenka & Shampine, 2008). Briefly,

`solinit = bvpxtend(sol,xnew,ynew)` uses solution sol computed on [a,b] to form a solution guess for the interval extended to xnew. The extension point xnew must be outside the interval [a,b], but on either side. The vector ynew provides an initial guess for the solution at xnew.

For example, if it is assumed that the convergence and interested lengths are 15 and 30 km, respectively, the continuation can be applied via the below codes (Gokhan & Yilmaz, 2011a),

================#5#=====================

```
L= 15000;
Interested=30000;
solinit = bvpinit(linspace(0,L,2),[Guess expression running with 15
km]);
sol = bvp4c(@bvpode,@bvpbc,solinit,options);
.
for Bnew=L:2000:Interested
    solinit=bvpxtend(sol,Bnew);
    sol = bvp4c(@bvpode,@bvpbc,solinit,options);
end
```

In the above codes, 2000 is the step size which is the modest increment range. In case of bigger step size, the solver may fail but the computation time reduces. On the other hand, if this increment is kept little, it takes more time to reach the end of the computation. Therefore, selecting the step size is important factor for the efficiency of the computation for continuation. One advantage of using bvpxtend function is the reduced computation time. Because, bvp solvers try to use mesh points as few as possible, the step size is incremented automatically depending on the previous mesh points. In bvpxtend, after obtaining convergence for the mesh, the codes adapt the mesh so as to obtain an accurate numerical solution with a modest number of mesh points. Here it must be emphasized that, for BVPs the most difficult part is providing an initial approximation to the solution.

5. Effect of the step size on the run time

Using the snippets 5 and the 1st Guess of Table 1, the performance of the continuation over step size is illustrated in Table 2.

Convergence Length (km)	Computation Length (km)	Linspace (0,L,N) Optimal N	Step Size (mt.)	Computation Time at Convergence Length (with bvp4c)	Total Computation time	Mesh number (between) (with bvp4c)
40	50	10	50	~3.2 sec	~110.0 sec	482-541
40	50	10	100	~3.2 sec	~60.0 sec	482-541
40	50	10	200	~3.2 sec	~32.8 sec	482-553
40	50	10	300	~3.2 sec	~25.3 sec	482-560
40	50	10	400	~3.2 sec	~23.6 sec	482-663
40	50	10	500	~3.2 sec	~44.5 sec	482-1984
40	50	10	600	Computation fails.		

Table 2. The performance of continuation method versus step size

If the step size is increased over the 600 meter, the computation fails with the below warning message;
```
Warning: Unable to meet the tolerance without using more than 5000
mesh points.
```

The last mesh of 4106 points and the solution are available in the
output   argument.

The maximum residual is 0.00018931, while requested accuracy is 1e-
005.
As can be seen on Table 2, for some step size over the modest increment, computation blows
up (i.e. 600 m). When the step size is between 50 and 400, the number of used mesh is
slightly different from each other. However, when it is 500 m, abruptly increase in the
number of used mesh is a sign of lack of confidence.
In Fig.5, it can be seen that the distance between some mesh points, especially near the
boundaries are denser than the others. This is because the solver tries to control the residual
of the interpolating polynomial: $r(x) = S'(x) - f(x,S(x))$. The behavior of this residual
depends on the behavior of some high derivatives of the solution (that the solver does not
have access to). In the solver, the residual is estimated at each mesh subinterval, and
additional mesh points are introduced if the estimate is bigger than the tolerance.
The mesh selection algorithm is 'localized', which means that if the residual is just above the
tolerance, the interval will be divided into two (and likely on each of those subintervals, the
residual will be much smaller than the tolerance). Also, the algorithm for removing mesh
points is quite conservative, so there could be regions where the residual will be quite a bit
smaller that the tolerance (i.e., the mesh could be quite a bit denser than necessary)(
Kierzenka & Shampine, 2001).

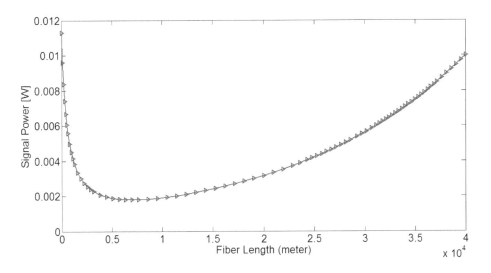

Fig. 5. Evolution of mesh density along the computation

5.1 Effect of the constructing an initial guess with bvpinit function on the run time

As can be seen from Table 3, when constructing an initial guess using `bvpinit(linspace(0,L,N)`, starting with a mesh of 5-10 points could often result in a more efficient run. It must be pointed out that with adaptive collocation solvers, using that many points (N=50,100) with a poor guess could often be counterproductive. In the case of N=100, the solver still achieved the sufficient accuracy as it is between 2 and 10.

Linspace (0,L,N) Optimal N	Computation Time (with bvp4c)	Mesh number (with bvp4c)	Maximum Residual
2-4	Singular Jacobian encountered		
5	~3.20 sec	498	9.791e-006
6	~2.85 sec	475	9.967e-006
7	~3.10 sec	483	9.983e-006
8	~2.75 sec	487	9.913e-006
9	~2.87 sec	464	9.848e-006
10	~2.68 sec	469	9.817e-006
50	~2.81 sec	478	9.938e-006
100	~3.10 sec	485	9.959e-006

Table 3. Performance of equally spaced N points for the mesh of a guess

6. Speeding up the run time of BVP solvers

The first technique which is used to reduce run time is vectorizing the evaluation of the differential equations. Vectorization is a valuable tool for speeding up MATLAB programs and this greatly reduces the run time (Shampine *et al.*, 2003). By vectorization, the function $f(x,y)$ is coded so that when given a vector $x=[x_1,x_2,...]$ and a corresponding array of column vectors $y=[y_1,y_2,...]$, it returns an array of column vectors $[f(x_1,y_1),f(x_2,y_2),...]$). By default, bvp4c and bvp4c approximate a Jacobian using finite differences. The evaluation of the ODEs is vectorized by changing the vectors to arrays and changing the multiplication to an array multiplication. It can be coded by changing scalar quantities like $y(1)$ into arrays like $y(1,:)$ and changing from scalar operations to array operations by replacing * and ^ with .* and .^, respectively. When vectorizing the ODEs, the solver must be informed about the presence of vectorization by means of the option `'Vectorized', 'on'`.

```
options = bvpset('Stats','on','RelTol',1e-3,'Vectorized','on');
```

The second technique is that of supplying analytical partial derivatives or to supply a function for evaluating the `Jacobian` matrix. This is because, in general, BVPs are solved much faster with analytical partial derivatives. However, this is not an easy task since it is too much trouble and inconvenient, although MATLAB Symbolic Toolbox can be exploited when obtaining analytical Jacobians. The third technique is to supply analytical partial derivatives for the boundary conditions. However, it has less effect on the computation time compared with supplying analytical Jacobians and vectorization. The solver permits the user to supply as much information as possible. It must be emphasized that supplying more information for the solvers results in a shorter computation run time (Gokhan & Yilmaz, 2011b).

The set of equations (3) and (4) is vectorized by changing the vectors to arrays and changing the multiplication to an array multiplication as seen below,

```
function dydx = bvpodevectorized(x,y)
global alpha_s gb K

dydx =   [ -gb *y(1,:).*y(2,:)-alpha_s*y(1,:)
           -gb *y(1,:).*y(2,:)+alpha_s*y(2,:) ];
```

Using vectorized ODEs with N=8, the performance of the vectorization is illustrated in Table 4.

Length (mt)	Computation Time with scalar evaluation (with bvp4c)	Computation Time with vectorization (with bvp4c)
5000	~1.83 sec	~1.79 sec
10000	~2.26 sec	~2.15 sec
20000	~2.60 sec	~2.45 sec
30000	~2.70 sec	~2.58 sec
40000	~3.00 sec	~2.85 sec

Table 4. Comparison of the computation time with scalar evaluation and with vectorization

The code bvp4c permits you to supply analytical partial derivatives for either the ODEs or the boundary conditions or both. It is far more important to provide partial derivatives for the ODEs than the boundary conditions. The solver is informed that a function is written for evaluating $\partial f/\partial y$ by providing its handle as the value of the FJacobian option. Similarly, the solver can be informed of a function for evaluating analytical partial derivatives of the boundary conditions with the option BCJacobian (Shampine et al., 2003). FJacobian and BCJacobian can be introduced as with the below codes,

```
%options = bvpset(options,'FJacobian',@odeJac);
%options = bvpset(options,'BCJacobian',@bcJac);
```

The MATLAB Symbolic Toolbox has a function jacobian that can be very helpful when working out partial derivatives for complicated functions. Its use is illustrated with a script for the partial derivatives of the ODEs of this example.

```
syms res y1 y2 y1 y2 alpha_s gb

res = [ -gb*y1*y2 - alpha_s*y1
        -gb*y1*y2 + alpha_s*y2];
dFdy = jacobian(res,[y1; y2])

dFdy =
```

```
[ - alpha_s - gb*y2,          -gb*y1]
[             -gb*y2, alpha_s - gb*y1]
```

The performance of the insertion of analytical partial derivatives and vectorization, and both are compared in Table 5. As can be seen from Table 5, with vectorization and analytical partial derivatives, the computation time is reduced approximately 15 %. The calculations are simulated using the MATLAB 7.9 (R2009b) on an Intel Core i5 2.53 GHz laptop computer.

Length (mt)	Computation Time with scalar evaluation (with bvp4c)	Computation Time with only vectorization (with bvp4c)	Computation Time with only analytical partial derivatives (with bvp4c)	Computation Time with both vectorization & analytical partial derivatives (with bvp4c)
5000	~1.83 sec	~1.79 sec	~1.69 sec	~1.59 sec
10000	~2.26 sec	~2.15 sec	~2.05 sec	~1.80 sec
20000	~2.60 sec	~2.45 sec	~2.26sec	~1.96sec
30000	~2.70 sec	~2.58 sec	~2.40 sec	~2.04 sec
40000	~3.00 sec	~2.85 sec	~2.60 sec	~2.18 sec

Table 5. Comparison of the computation time of bvp4c with vectorization, with analytical partial derivatives and with both

In Table 6, the performance of the bvp5c is illustrated. In terms of scalar evaluation, the performance of bvp5c solver is better than bvpc4 and it is evident as the length is increased. This improvement is about 47 % at 40 km. As in the case of bvp4c, the performance can be increased with vectorization and analytical partial derivatives or with both. Compared with the scalar evaluation, only with vectorization and only with analytical partial derivatives this improvement is 8% and 13 %, respectively. If both is used this improvement is about 24 %.

Length (mt)	Computation Time with scalar evaluation (with bvp5c)	Computation Time with only vectorization (with bvp5c)	Computation Time with only analytical partial derivatives (with bvp5c)	Computation Time with both vectorization & analytical partial derivatives (with bvp5c)
5000	~1.32 sec	~1.32 sec	~1.30 sec	~1.23 sec
10000	~1.38 sec	~1.38 sec	~1.35 sec	~1.27 sec
20000	~1.44 sec	~1.42 sec	~1.38sec	~1.30sec
30000	~1.55 sec	~1.50 sec	~1.43 sec	~1.34 sec
40000	~1.60 sec	~1.52 sec	~1.47 sec	~1.36 sec

Table 6. Comparison of the computation time of bvp5c with vectorization, with analytical partial derivatives and with both

If the comparison among two solvers has made, it could be expressed that bvp5c "looks" exactly like bvp4c. However, bvp5c controls scaled residual and true error but bvp4c controls residual in a different norm. And, bvp5c is more efficient at stringent tolerances.

Also, bvp5c solves singular BVPs, but not multipoint BVPs. Moreover, bvp5c handles unknown parameters in a different way. And also, bvp5c was added to MATLAB at R2007b (Shampine, 2008)

7. Conclusion

Within the chapter, in order to analyze the effect of guess functions on the computation time, four guess functions are derived. For better understanding, while exploiting physical origin, guess functions are derived with the help of MATLAB Symbolic toolbox. Continuation method with functional snippets is presented to cope with poor guesses. Effect of the step size and bvpinit function on the computation time is analyzed. Speeding up the run time with vectorization and analytical partial derivatives are discussed and the comparison between bvp4c and bvp5c has been made.

As a conclusion, it is illustrated that, intuitive guess values/functions improves the convergence length, leads the computation with fewer mesh points and consequently lessens the computation time. On the other hand, regarding with the continuation, adjusting the step size is important for the reduction of run time. It is illustrated that, over the modest step size, the solver fails and below the optimum step size, the computation time is increased. Moreover, it is showed that when constructing an initial guess using bvpinit(linspace(0,L,N), starting with a mesh of 5-10 points could often result in a more efficient run. Another outcome of the chapter is the illustration of the efficiency of the vectorization and analytical partial derivatives. It is showed specifically with an example and with bvp4c that, with the application of vectorization and analytical partial derivatives, the computation time is reduced approximately 15 %. The performance of the bvp4c and bvp5c is also compared. In terms of scalar evaluation, the performance of bvp5c solver is better than bvpc4 and it is evident as the computation length is increased. Compared with the scalar evaluation, for the bvp5c, only with vectorization and only with analytical partial derivatives this improvement is 8% and 13 % respectively. If both is used this improvement is about 24 %.

8. Acknowledgments

The author gratefully acknowledges the financial support from the head of scientific research projects commission of Gazikent University.

9. References

Kierzenka J. & Shampine Lawrence F. (2001), *A BVP Solver Based on Residual Control and the MATLAB PSE*, ACM TOMS, vol. 27, No. 3, pp. 299-316.

Hale N.P., (2006), *A Sixth-Order Extension to the MATLAB bvp4c Software of J. Kierzenka and L. Shampine*, Msc Thesis. Accessed 06.04.2011, Available from:
< http://people.maths.ox.ac.uk/hale/files/hale_mastersthesis.pdf >

MATLAB Documentation, *Continuation*, Accessed 06 April 2011, Available from:
< http://www.mathworks.com/help/techdoc/math/f1-713877.html>

Shampine, L.F., Gladwell, I. & Thompson, S. (2003), *Solving ODEs with MATLAB*, 1st ed., Cambridge University Press, ISBN, 978-0-521-82404-4, New York

Agrawal G. P. (2001), *Nonlinear Fiber Optics*, 3rd ed. Academic, Chap. 9.

Kobyakov A., Darmanyan S., Sauer M. & Chowdhury D (2006), *High-gain Brillouin amplification: an analytical Approach*, Opt.Lett. 31 1960

Kierzenka, J. & Shampine, L.F. (2008), *BVP solver that controls residual and error*, Journal of Numerical Analysis, Industrial and Applied Mathematics (JNAIAM), Vol. 3 Nos 1/2, pp. 27-41, available at: www.jnaiam.org/downloads.php?did=44 (Accessed 06 April 2011).

Gokhan F. S., & Yilmaz G, (2011a), *Solution of Raman fiber amplifier equations using MATLAB BVP solvers*, COMPEL: The International Journal for Computation and Mathematics in Electrical and Electronic Engineering, Vol. 30 Iss: 2, pp.398 – 411

Gokhan F. S., & Yilmaz G, (2011b), *Novel Guess Functions for Efficient Analysis of Raman Fiber Amplifiers*, COMPEL: The International Journal for Computation and Mathematics in Electrical and Electronic Engineering, *accepted in 2010*

Shampine L.F, (2008). *Control of Residual and Error*, In: CAIMS-Canadian Mathematical Society, Accessed 06 April 2011,
Available from: < http://faculty.smu.edu/shampine/Montreal.pdf>

2

Matrix Based Operatorial Approach to Differential and Integral Problems

Damian Trif
Babes-Bolyai University of Cluj-Napoca
Romania

1. Introduction

Many problems of the real life lead us to linear differential equations of the form

$$\sum_{k=0}^{m} P_k(x)\frac{d^k y}{dx^k} = f(x), \quad x \in [a,b] \tag{1}$$

with the general conditions

$$\sum_{j=1}^{m} \alpha_{ij}^{(1)} y^{(j-1)}(x_{ij}^{(1)}) + \cdots + \sum_{j=1}^{m} \alpha_{ij}^{(m)} y^{(j-1)}(x_{ij}^{(m)}) = \beta_i, \quad i = 1,...,m \tag{2}$$

where $x_{ij}^{(k)} \in [a,b]$, $\forall i,j,k = 1,...,m$. These multipoint conditions include (for $m = 2$, for example)
- initial value conditions, $y(a) = \beta_1$, $y'(a) = \beta_2$,
- boundary value conditions $\alpha_{11}y(a) + \alpha_{12}y'(a) = \beta_1$, $\alpha_{21}y(b) + \alpha_{22}y'(b) = \beta_2$,
- periodic conditions $y(a) - y(b) = 0$, $y'(a) - y'(b) = 0$.
Eigenvalue problems for linear differential operators

$$\sum_{k=1}^{m} P_k(x)\frac{d^k y}{dx^k} + (P_0(x) - \lambda w(x))y = 0, \quad x \in [a,b]$$

$$\sum_{j=1}^{m} \alpha_{ij}^{(1)} y^{(j-1)}(x_{ij}^{(1)}) + \cdots + \sum_{j=1}^{m} \alpha_{ij}^{(m)} y^{(j-1)}(x_{ij}^{(m)}) = 0, \quad i = 1,...,m$$

are also included in this general form. Moreover, nonlinear problems where the r.h.s. $f(x)$ is replaced by $f(x,y(x),y'(x),...,y^{(m-1)}(x))$ can be solved using Newton's method in the functional space $C^m[a,b]$ by solving a sequence of linear problems (1)+(2).
MATLAB uses different methods to solve initial condition problems (ode family) or boundary value problems (bvp4c or bvp5c) based on Runge-Kutta, Adams-Bashforth-Moulton, BDF algorithms, etc.
One of the most effective methods for solving (1)+(2) is to shift the problem to the interval $[-1,1]$ and then to use the *Chebyshev spectral methods*, i.e. to approximate the solution y by a finite sum of the Chebyshev series

$$y(x) = \frac{1}{2}c_0 T_0(x) + c_1 T_1(x) + c_2 T_2(x).... \tag{3}$$

Here $T_k(x) = \cos(k \cos^{-1}(x))$, $k = 0, 1, ...$ are the Chebyshev polynomials of the first kind and the coefficients c_k, $k = 0, 1, ...$are unknown. A spectral method is characterized by a specific way to determine these coefficients. The Chebyshev spectral methods could be implemented as
- Galerkin and tau methods, where we work in the spectral space of the coefficients $\mathbf{c} = c_0, c_1, c_2, ...$ of y or as
- spectral collocation (or pseudospectral) methods, where we work in the physical space of the values of y at a specific grid $\mathbf{x} = x_1, x_2, ... \in [-1, 1]$.
The well known MATLAB packages which use spectral methods, *MATLAB Differentiation Matrix Suite (DMS)* (Weideman & Reddy, 2000) and *Chebfun* (Trefethen et al., 2011), are based on the pseudospectral methods. Usually, these methods are implemented in an operatorial form: a differentiation matrix D (or linear operator) is generated so that $Y' = DY$ where the vector Y' contains the values of the derivative y' at the specific grid while Y contains the values of y at the same grid. The equation (1) becomes

$$\left(\sum_{k=0}^{m} diag(P_k(\mathbf{x}))D^k \right) Y = f(\mathbf{x}) \text{ i.e. } AY = F$$

and the conditions (2) are enclosed in the matrix A and in the vector F. The numerical solution of the differential problem is now $Y = A^{-1}F$. We note that MATLAB capabilities of working with matrices make it an ideal tool for matrix based operatorial approach.
There is a price to pay for using pseudospectral methods: the differentiation matrix D is full (while for finite differences or finite element methods it is sparse) and, more importantly, D is very sensitive to rounding errors. We give here a comparison between *DMS*, *Chebfun* and our proposed package *Chebpack* (based on the tau spectral method) for an eigenvalue problem suggested by Solomonoff and Turkel. Let us consider the evolution problem

$$u_t = -xu_x, \ u(x, 0) = f(x), \ x \in [-1, 1],$$

with the exact solution $u(x, t) = f(xe^{-t})$. Here $x = \pm 1$ are outflow boundaries so that no boundary conditions are required. Using a Chebyshev spectral method to discretize the spatial part of the equation, the stability of time integration depends on the eigenvalues of that spatial part

$$- xu_x = \lambda u, \ x \in [-1, 1]. \tag{4}$$

The exact (polynomial) eigenvectors are the monomials x^n and the corresponding eigenvalues are $\lambda_n = -n$, $n = 0, 1, ...$.
The commands for the *DMS* package

```
[x,D]=chebdif(64,1);L=eig(-diag(x)*D);
```

for *Chebfun*

```
N=chebop(@(x,u)  -x.*diff(u),[-1,1]);L=eigs(N(66),64,'LR');
```

and for *Chebpack*

```
X=mult(64,[-1,1]);D=deriv(64,[-1,1]);L=eig(full(-X*D));
```

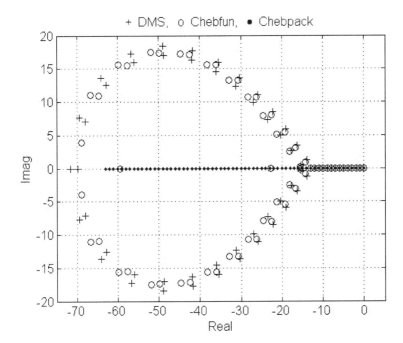

Fig. 1. Eigenvalues for the problem (4)

give the 64 approximated eigenvalues successively in the vector L and they are represented in Fig. 1. We see that *DMS* and *Chebfun* calculate accurately only a small number of eigenvalues, while *Chebpack* gives exactly all 64 eigenvalues.

The proposed package *Chebpack*, which is described in this chapter, is based on the representation (3) of the unknown functions and uses the *tau method* for linear operators (such as differentiation, integration, product with the independent variable,...) and the pseudospectral method for nonlinear operators – nonlinear part of the equations.

The tau method was invented by Lanczos (1938, 1956) and later developed in an operatorial approach by Ortiz and Samara (Ortiz & Samara, 1981). In the past years considerable work has been done both in the theoretical analysis and numerical applications.

Chebpack is freely accessible at `https://sites.google.com/site/dvtrif/` and at (Trif, 2011). All the running times in this chapter are the elapsed times for a 1.73GHz laptop and for MATLAB 2010b under Windows XP.

2. Chebpack, basic module

The package contains, at the basic module – level0, the tools which will be used in the next modules. Let us start with the Chebyshev series expansion of a given function y (Boyd, 2000):

THEOREM 1. *If y is Lipschitz continuous on [-1, 1], it has a unique representation as an absolutely and uniformly convergent series*

$$y(x) = \frac{c_0}{2} T_0(x) + c_1 T_1(x) + c_2 T_2(x) + ...,$$

and the coefficients are given by the formula

$$c_k = \frac{2}{\pi} \int_{-1}^{1} \frac{y(x)T_k(x)}{\sqrt{1-x^2}} dx, \ k = 0, 1, 2, ...$$

Let y_{N-1} be the truncation of the above Chebyshev series

$$y_{N-1}(x) = \frac{c_0}{2} T_0(x) + c_1 T_1(x) + c_2 T_2(x) + \cdots + c_{N-1} T_{N-1}(x) \tag{5}$$

and $dom = [-1, 1]$ be the working interval. Any interval $[a, b]$ can be shifted and scaled to $[-1, 1]$ by using the shifted Chebyshev polynomials

$$T_k^*(x) = T_k(\alpha x + \beta), \ \alpha = \frac{2}{b-a}, \ \beta = -\frac{b+a}{b-a}, \ x \in [a, b].$$

First of all, we need a set of N collocation points $x_1, ..., x_N \in dom$ in order to find a good transformation between the above spectral approximation (5) of y and its physical representation $y(x_1), y(x_2), ..., y(x_N)$. Let

$$p_{N-1}(x) = \frac{a_0}{2} T_0(x) + a_1 T_1(x) + ... + a_{N-1} T_{N-1}(x) \tag{6}$$

be the unique polynomial obtained by interpolating $y(x)$ through the points $x_1, ..., x_N$, see (Trefethen, 2000) for more details on the coefficients a_k versus c_k. The next theorem of (Boyd, 2000) estimates the error:

THEOREM 2. *Let y have at least N derivatives on dom. Then*

$$y(x) - p_{N-1}(x) = \frac{1}{N!} y^{(N)} (\xi) \prod_{k=1}^{N} (x - x_k)$$

for some ξ on the interval spanned by x and the interpolation points. The point ξ depends on the function y, upon N, upon x and upon the location of the interpolation points.

Consequently, the optimal interpolation points are the roots of the Chebyshev polynomial $T_N(x)$, (**Chebyshev points of the first kind**)

$$x_k = -\cos \frac{(2k-1)\pi}{2N}, \ k = 1, ..., N. \tag{7}$$

For these points **x**, the polynomials $\{p_{N-1}\}$ are generally nearly as good approximations to y as the polynomials $\{y_{N-1}\}$ and if y is *analytic* on *dom*, then both $\|y - y_{N-1}\|$ and $\|y - p_{N-1}\|$ decrease geometrically as $N \to \infty$. This is the *spectral convergence property*, i.e. the convergence of $\|y - y_{N-1}\|$ and $\|y - p_{N-1}\|$ towards zero is faster than any power of $\frac{1}{N}$ as $N \to \infty$.

Numerical integration and Lagrangian interpolation are very closely related. The standard formulas for a continuous function f on $[-1, 1]$ are of the type

$$\int_{-1}^{1} f(x)dx \approx \sum_{k=1}^{N} w_k f(x_k), \tag{8}$$

where w_k are the quadrature weights

$$w_k = \int_{-1}^{1} \prod_{j=1, j \neq k}^{N} \frac{x - x_j}{x_k - x_j} dx, \ k = 1, 2, ..., N.$$

The *Gauss quadrature formulas* are based on the optimal Legendre points x_k, $k = 1, ..., N$ and these formulas are exact for polynomials f up to degree $2N - 1$. The idea of *Clenshaw-Curtis quadrature* is to use Chebyshev points $\mathbf{x}$ instead of the above optimal nodes. By using the Chebyshev points of the first kind (7) one obtains the "classical" Clenshaw-Curtis formula while by using the zeros of the first derivative of a Chebyshev polynomial plus the endpoints ± 1, i.e. the Chebyshev extrema

$$x_k = -\cos\frac{(k-1)\pi}{N-1}, k = 1, ..., N \tag{9}$$

in $[-1, 1]$ (the so called **Chebyshev points of the second kind**) one obtains the "practical" Clenshaw-Curtis formula. Both formulas have all the good properties of the Gaussian quadrature, see (Trefethen, 2008) for more details.

Consequently, we may use Chebyshev points of the first kind or of the second kind both for quadrature formulas and for physical representation of a function y on $[-1, 1]$. Any interval $[a, b]$ may be scaled to $[-1, 1]$ and we obtain the corresponding formulas. Moreover, by using the mapping $x = \cos\theta$ and $T_k(x) = \cos k\theta$ we see that the following two series

$$y(x) = \frac{c_0}{2}T_0(x) + c_1 T_1(x) + c_2 T_2(x) + ...$$

$$y(\cos\theta) = \frac{c_0}{2} + c_1 \cos\theta + c_2 \cos 2\theta + ...$$

are equivalent. A Chebyshev series is in fact a Fourier cosine series so that the FFT and iFFT may be used to transform the spectral representation of y into the physical one and conversely, the physical representation into the spectral representation. The quadrature weights $\mathbf{w}$ could also be calculated by a fast algorithm given in (Waldvogel, 2006).

The first code of level0, inspired from `chebpts.m` of *chebfun* (Trefethen et al., 2011) is

$$[\text{x},\text{w}] = \text{pd}(\text{N},\text{dom},\text{kind})$$

(pd means "**p**hysical **d**omain"). It calculates the grid $\mathbf{x} = [x_1, ..., x_N]^T$ (column vector) and the quadrature weights $\mathbf{w} = [w_1, ..., w_N]$ (row vector) for the quadrature formula

$$\int_a^b f(x)dx \approx \sum_{j=1}^N w_j f(x_j) \equiv \mathbf{w} \cdot f(\mathbf{x}).$$

The input parameters are N – the dimension of the vectors $\mathbf{x}$ and $\mathbf{w}$, *dom* – the computational domain $[a, b]$ and *kind* which can be 1 or 2 in order to calculate $\mathbf{x}$ as the Chebyshev points of the first or of the second kind.

Some short tests show the performances of this code. Let us approximate

$$\int_0^1 x \sin\frac{1}{x}dx = \frac{cos(1) + sin(1) + Si(1)}{2} - \frac{\pi}{4} \approx 0.37853001712416130988...$$

for $N = 10, 10^2, ..., 10^6$. Here we use Chebyshev points of the first kind and hence we have no problems with the singularity at the origin. We have instead problems with the highly oscillatory behavior of the integrand near the origin. The code is `Chebpack\examples\ex_level0\quad_ex1.m` and the result for $N = 10^6$ is

```
Elapsed time = 0.938258074699438 seconds
err = 1.9568e-11.
```

A more efficient code is

```
[int,gridpts] = quadcheb(myfun,n,dom,kind,tol,gridpts,I)
```

in the folder Chebpack\examples\ex_level0 which uses pd into a recursive procedure. Precisely, starting from the initial interval $dom = [a, b]$, pd is used with n points in $[a, b]$ and on two subintervals $[a, c]$ and $[c, b]$ where $c = (a + b)/2$. If the results differe by more than a tolerance ε, the interval $[a, b]$ is divided to that subintervals . Now quadcheb is called again for each subinterval and at each step we sum the results. For $N = 128$ we obtain
```
Elapsed time = 0.013672 seconds.
err = 4.907093620332148e-010
```
Of course, this non-optimized quadrature calculation is only a collateral facility in *Chebpack* and it does not work better than the basic quadrature command quadgk from MATLAB, which is designated for highly oscillatory integrals.
The next codes of level0

$$v = \text{t2x}(c, \text{kind}) \text{ and } c = \text{x2t}(v, \text{kind})$$

are inspired by chebpolyval.m and chebpoly.m from *chebfun* (Trefethen et al., 2011). These codes perform the correspondence between the spectral representation **c** of a function f and its physical representation $\mathbf{v} = f(\mathbf{x})$ on Chebyshev points of the first or second kind. It is important to remark that linear operators are better represented in the spectral space, while the nonlinear operators are easily handled in the physical space.
In t2x and x2t, **c** and **v** are matrices of the same dimension, each column represents the coefficients or the values for some other function, the number of rows is the above dimension N, while *kind* specifies the type of Chebyshev points used in **v**. For example, the code
```
n=16;dom=[0,1];kind=2;x=pd(n,dom,kind);
vs=sin(x);vc=cos(x);ve=exp(x);c=x2t([vs,vc,ve],kind);
```
gives in the columns of **c** the coefficients of the Chebyshev series (6) of $\sin(x)$, $\cos(x)$ and $\exp(x)$ calculated by using the values of these functions on Chebyshev points of the second kind on $[0, 1]$. We remark here that, taking into account the term $c_0 T_0/2$, the coefficient c_0 is doubled.
Another code from level0, inspired from bary.m of *chebfun* (Trefethen et al., 2011) and useful for graphical representation of the functions is

$$\text{fxn} = \text{barycheb}(\text{xn}, \text{fk}, \text{xk}, \text{kind})$$

It interpolates the values **fk** of a function f at the Chebyshev nodes **xk** of the first or second kind in *dom* by calculating the values **fxn** at the new (arbitrary) nodes **xn** in *dom*. The barycentric weights are calculated depending on kind.
Precisely, cf. (Berrut & Trefethen, 2004), the barycentric formula is

$$f(x) = \frac{\sum_{k=1}^{N} \frac{w_k}{x - x_k} f_k}{\sum_{k=1}^{N} \frac{w_k}{x - x_k}}, \quad w_k = \frac{1}{\prod_{j \neq k} (x_k - x_j)}, \quad k = 1, ..., N.$$

For Chebyshev points one can give explicit formula for barycentric weights **w**. For the Chebyshev points of the first kind we have

$$x_k = -\cos\frac{(2k-1)\pi}{2N}, \quad w_k = (-1)^k \sin\frac{(2k-1)\pi}{2N}, \quad k = 1, ..., N$$

and for the Chebyshev points of the second kind we have

$$x_k = -\cos\frac{(k-1)\pi}{N-1}, \quad w_k = (-1)^k \delta_k, \quad \delta_k = \begin{cases} \frac{1}{2}, & k = 1, N \\ 1, & \text{otherwise} \end{cases}, \quad k = 1, ..., N.$$

We remark that for a general interval $dom = [a, b]$ and if the sign changes for all x_k and w_k the weights must be multiplicated by $\pm 2^{N-1}(b-a)^{1-N}$. This factor cancels out in the barycentric formula so that it is no need to include it.

Let us calculate now the differentiation matrix D such that if $\mathbf{f}$ is the column of the Chebyshev coefficients of a function f, then $D\mathbf{f}$ is the column of the Chebyshev coefficients of the derivative function $\frac{df}{dx}$. On $[-1, 1]$ the derivatives of T_i satisfy

$$T_0 = T_1', \quad T_1 = \frac{T_2'}{4}, ..., T_i = \frac{T_{i+1}'}{2(i+1)} - \frac{T_{i-1}'}{2(i-1)}, \quad i \geq 2$$

from where

$$\frac{T_0'}{2} = 0, \quad T_i' = 2i\left(T_{i-1} + T_{i-3} + ... + T_1\right), \quad i \text{ even}$$

$$T_i' = 2i\left(T_{i-1} + T_{i-3} + ... + 0.5T_0\right), \quad i \text{ odd}.$$

Consequently, D is a sparse upper triangular matrix with

$$D_{ii} = 0, \quad D_{ij} = 0 \text{ for } (j - i) \text{ even and } D_{ij} = 2j \text{ otherwise}.$$

Of course, the differentiation could be iterated, i.e. the coefficients of $f^{(p)}$ are $D^p\mathbf{f}$. The corresponding code from level0 is

```
D=deriv(n,dom)
```

where n is the dimension of the matrix D. For $dom = [a, b]$ the above matrix D is multiplied by $2/(b-a)$.

Similarly, the code

```
[J,J0]=prim(n,dom)
```

calculates the sparse integration matrix J such that the coefficients of $\int^x f(t)dt$ are $J\mathbf{f}$. *Here the first coefficient of the result $J\mathbf{f}$ may be changed in order to obtain the coefficients for a specific primitive of f. For example, the coefficients of the primitive which vanishes at $a = dom(1)$ are obtained by using $J_0\mathbf{f}$.*

The basic formulas for $dom = [-1, 1]$ are

$$\int \frac{T_0}{2}dx = \frac{T_1}{2}, \quad \int T_1 dx = \frac{T_0/2}{2} + \frac{T_2}{4}, \quad \int T_k dx = \frac{1}{2}\left(\frac{T_{k+1}}{k+1} - \frac{T_{k-1}}{k-1}\right), \quad k \geq 2$$

from where

$$J_{k,k} = 0, \quad J_{0,1} = \frac{1}{2}, \quad J_{k,k-1} = \frac{1}{2k} = -J_{k,k+1}, \quad k = 1, 2, ...$$

For a general $dom = [a, b]$ the above matrix J is multiplied by $(b-a)/2$.

As an important example, let us calculate the coeficients of a specific primitive $F(x)$ of the function $f(x)$. We must then solve the initial-value problem

$$\frac{dF}{dx} = f(x), \ y(-1) = \alpha, \ x \in [-1,1].$$

If $\mathbf{c}$ are the Chebyshev coefficients of F and $\mathbf{f}$ are the coefficients of f, the equation is discretized in spectral space as $D\mathbf{c} = \mathbf{f}$. In order to implement the initial condition, we remark that

$$y(-1) = c_0 \frac{T_0}{2} + c_1 T_1(-1) + c_2 T_2(-1) + \dots + c_{N-1} T_{N-1}(-1) = \alpha$$

can be written as $T\mathbf{c} = \alpha$ where

$$T = \left[\frac{T_0}{2}, T_1(-1), T_2(-1), \dots, T_{N-1}(-1) \right].$$

This means that we can replace the last row of D by T and the last entry of $\mathbf{f}$ by α, thus obtaining a new matrix $\tilde{D}$ and a new vector $\tilde{f}$. Finally, $\mathbf{c} = \tilde{D}^{-1}\tilde{f}$ are the coefficients of the specific primitive.

The following code from level0

```
T=cpv(n,xc,dom)
```

(chebyshev polynomial values) implements such conditions. Here $\mathbf{x}_c$ is an arbitrary vector in $dom = [a,b]$ and cpv calculates the values of the Chebyshev polynomials $T_k, k = 0, 1, .., n-1$ at the column of nodes ζ

$$T = [T_0/2, T_1(\zeta), T_2(\zeta), \dots, T_{N-1}(\zeta)], \ \zeta = \frac{2\mathbf{x}_c}{b-a} - \frac{b+a}{b-a}, \ 1 \leq \zeta \leq 1.$$

The code is based on the recurrence formulas of Chebyshev polynomials on $[-1,1]$

$$T_0(x) = 1, \ T_1(x) = x, \ T_k(x) = 2x T_{k-1}(x) - T_{k-2}(x), \ k \geq 2.$$

The test code Chebpack\examples\ex_level0\quad_ex3 performs these calculations for the special case $y' = \cos x$, $y(0) = 0$, with the solution $y = \sin(x)$. The coefficients $\mathbf{c}$ are obtained by using the differentiation matrix, $\mathbf{cc}$ are the coefficients of the exact solution, $\mathbf{ccc}$ are obtained by using the integration matrix J and $\mathbf{cccc}$ are obtained by using the integration matrix J_0.

We also remark that if T=cpv(n,x,dom),

$$f(x) = 0.5c_0 T_0^*(x) + c_1 T_1^*(x) + \dots + c_{N-1} T_{N-1}^*(x) \tag{10}$$

and $\mathbf{c} = (c_0, \dots, c_{N-1})^T$, we have $f(\mathbf{x}) = T\mathbf{c}$, for $\mathbf{x} \in [a,b]$. The code cpv could be used to transform between the spectral representation $\mathbf{f}$ of the function f and the physical representation $\mathbf{v} = f(\mathbf{x})$ of values at the Chebyshev grid $\mathbf{x}$,

$$\mathbf{v} = T\mathbf{f}, \ \mathbf{f} = T^{-1}\mathbf{v}.$$

These transforms are performed by FFT in the codes x2t and t2x, but for a small dimension N we may use this direct matrix multiplication.

As another example, let us calculate the values at the grid points $\mathbf{x}$ of the specific primitive which vanishes at $a = dom(1)$

$$F(x_i) = \int_a^{x_i} f(t)dt, \quad i = 1, ..., n$$

Starting with the values $\mathbf{f} = f(\mathbf{x})$ we have the Chebyshev coefficients $T^{-1}\mathbf{f}$, then $J_0 T^{-1}\mathbf{f}$ are the Chebyshev coefficients of the specific primitive on $[a, b]$ and finally,

$$F(\mathbf{x}) = T J_0 T^{-1}\mathbf{f}. \tag{11}$$

Another code from level0

```
X=mult (n,dom)
```

calculates the sparse multiplication matrix X such that if $\mathbf{f}$ is the column vector of the Chebyshev coefficients of a function $f(x)$, then $X\mathbf{f}$ is the column vector of the coefficients of the function $xf(x)$. The code is based on the formulas

$$xT_0 = T_1, \quad xT_1(x) = \frac{T_0}{2} + \frac{T_2}{2}, ..., \quad xT_k(x) = \frac{T_{k-1}(x)}{2} + \frac{T_{k+1}(x)}{2}, \quad k \geq 2$$

for $x \in [-1,1]$. Consequently,

$$X_{k,k} = 0, \quad X_{k,k-1} = X_{k,k+1} = \frac{1}{2}, \quad k = 2, 3, ..., N-1,$$

$$X_{1,1} = 0, \quad X_{1,2} = 1, \quad X_{N,N-1} = \frac{1}{2}.$$

Then, in general, the coefficients of $x^p f(x)$ are given by $X^p\mathbf{f}$ and the coefficients of $a(x)f(x)$ are given by $a(X)\mathbf{f}$ for analytical functions $a(x)$, where $a(X)$ is the matricial version of the function a. Moreover, if $\dfrac{f(x)}{x^p}$ has no singularity at the origin, then its coefficients are $X^{-p}\mathbf{f}$.

Of course, X is a tri-diagonal matrix, X^2 is a penta-diagonal matrix and so on but, generally, the matrix version funm(full(X)) of the scalar function $a(x)$ or $X^{-p} = [inv(X)]^p$ are not sparse matrices. For a general interval $dom = [a, b]$, X is replaced by $\frac{b-a}{2}X + \frac{b+a}{2}I_N$ where I_N is the sparse unit matrix speye(N).

Another method to calculate $a(X)$ is to pass from the values $a(\mathbf{x})$ at the Chebyshev grid $\mathbf{x}$ to the Chebyshev coefficients $\mathbf{a}$ using x2t and to approximate

$$a(x) \approx \cdot\frac{a_0}{2} + \sum_{k=1}^{m-1} a_k T_k(x). \tag{12}$$

Here m must be chosen sufficiently large, but $m \leq N$ so that the known function $a(x)$ is correctly represented by $a_0, a_1, ..., a_{m-1}$.

In order to calculate the coefficients of the product

$$a(x)f(x) = \left(\frac{a_0}{2} + \sum_{k=1}^{m-1} a_k T_k(x) \right) \left(\frac{f_0}{2} + \sum_{j=1}^{n-1} f_j T_j(x) \right)$$

we may use the formula

$$T_j(x)T_k(x) = \frac{T_{j+k}(x) + T_{|j-k|}(x)}{2}, \ \forall j, k.$$

The needed coefficients are given by $A\mathbf{f}$ where the matrix $A \approx a(X)$ is given by the code

```
A=fact(a,m)
```

from level0.
The test code `Chebpack\examples\ex_level0\fact_ex1.m` calculates `cosh(X)` using `fact` and `funm` from Matlab. We remark that X is a sparse matrix, so that `funm` must be applied to `full(X)`.

3. Chebpack, linear module

At the first level – level1, the package contains subroutines to solve
- initial and boundary value problems for high order linear differential equations
- initial value problems for first order linear differential systems
- linear integral equations
- eigenvalues and eigenfunctions for differential problems.
The main method used is the so called tau-method, see (Mason & Handscomb, 2003) or (Canuto et al., 1988) for more theoretical details. It is based on
- discretization using the differentiation matrix D
- discretization using the integration matrix J
- splitting the interval $dom = [d_1, d_2, ..., d_p]$.

3.1 Discretization using the differentiation matrix D
The corresponding code is `Chebpack\level1\ibvp_ode.m`

```
[x,solnum]=ibvp_ode(n,dom,kind)
```

where $n, dom, kind$ have the same significance as above, $\mathbf{x}$ is the Chebyshev grid and **solnum** is the numerical solution in the physical space calculated at the grid $\mathbf{x}$.
The structure of `ivp_ode` is
```
function [x,solnum]=ibvp_ode(n,dom,kind)
x=pd(n,dom,kind);X=mult(n,dom);D=deriv(n,dom);
myDE;myBC;sol=A\b;solnum = t2x(sol,kind);myOUT;
end
```
where `myDE`, `myBC` and `myOUT` must be written by the user and describe the differential equation, the boundary conditions and the output of the program.
For example, for the problem

$$y''' - xy = (x^3 - 2x^2 - 5x - 3)e^x, \ x \in [0,1]$$
$$y(0) = 0, \ y'(0) = 1, \ y(1) = 0$$

we have
```
function myDE
A=D^3-X;b=x2t((x.^3-2*x.^2-5*x-3).*exp(x),kind);end
function myBC
T=cpv(n,dom,dom);A(n-2,:)=T(1,:);b(n-2)=0;
```

```
A(n-1,:)=T(1,:)*D;b(n-1)=1;A(n,:)=T(2,:);b(n)=0;end
```
The program is called by
```
[x,solnum]=ibvp_ode_test(32,[0 1],2);
```
Other examples are coded in `Chebpack\examples\ex_level1\ibvp_ode_ex*.m`
The general form for initial/boundary value problems for high order linear differential equations is (1) and its discrete form is

$$Ac \equiv \left(\sum_{k=0}^{m} P_k(X)D^k \right) c = b$$

where the unknown y is represented in the spectral space by its Chebyshev coefficients c, while b are the Chebyshev coefficients of the r.h.s. $f(x)$.
We remark that the coefficients $P_k(X)$ of the equation can be defined in `myDE`
- directly, for example $P_k(x) = -x$ gives $P_k(X) = -X$
- using $funm$, for example $P_k(x) = \sin x$ gives $P_k(X) = funm(full(X), @sin)$, i.e. using the Taylor series of $\sin X$
- using $fact$, for example $P_k(x) = \cos x$ gives $P_k(X) = fact(x2t(\cos(x), kind), m)$, i.e. using the Chebyshev series of $\cos X$
- if $P_k(x)$ is a constant, say P_k, then $P_k(X) = P_k \cdot speye(N)$.
The boundary conditions of the general type (2) are implemented using `cpv`. For example, for $y(x_{1c}) - y'(x_{2c}) + 2y''(x_{3c}) = y_c$ we calculate `T=cpv(N,[x1c,x2c,x3c],dom)`. One of the last rows of A is replaced by `T(1,:)-T(2,:)*D+2*T(3,:)*D^2` and the corresponding entry of the vector b is replaced by y_c.

3.2 Discretization using the integration matrix J
The corresponding code is `Chebpack\level1\ibvp_ode_int.m`

$$[x,solnum]=ibvp\_ode\_int(n,dom,kind)$$

We remark that the discretization using the differentiation matrix D does not work well for large N. For example, this type of discretization for the problem

$$\varepsilon y'' + xy\prime = -\varepsilon \pi^2 \cos(\pi x) - \pi x \sin(\pi x), \ x \in [-1,1], \ \varepsilon = 10^{-5}, \tag{13}$$
$$y(-1) = -2, \ y(1) = 0$$

with $N = 2048$ and an error about 5.46×10^{-11} leads us to a sparse system $Ac = b$ but with a sparsity factor about 25% that increases the computational time to 6.4 sec, see the example `ibvp_ode_ex.m` in the folder `Chebpack\examples\ex_level1`. A better idea is to integrate two times the above equation using the much more sparse integration matrix J. This integration make the coefficients c_0 and c_1 arbitrary and we may fix their values by using the boundary conditions, this time at the first two rows of A and b.
Precisely, the first and the second integration of the equation (13) gives

$$\varepsilon y' + xy - \int^x y = \int^x \left[-\varepsilon \pi^2 \cos(\pi x) - \pi x \sin(\pi x) \right]$$
$$\varepsilon y + \int^x xy - \int^x \int^x y = \int^x \int^x \left[-\varepsilon \pi^2 \cos(\pi x) - \pi x \sin(\pi x) \right].$$

The discrete form is $\left(\varepsilon I_N + JX - J^2 \right) c = J^2 f$ where c are the Chebyshev coefficients of the solution y and f are the Chebyshev coefficients of the r.h.s. The new code `ibvp_ode_int_ex.m` in the same folder as above gives the same accuracy for the same $N = 2048$, but needing only 0.12 sec. The new matrix A has now a sparsity factor of about 0.2439% for the dimension 2048.

This higher sparsity qualifies the integration method to be used for splitting the interval $dom = [a, b]$ into $dom = [a, d_1] \cup [d_1, d_2] \cup ... \cup [d_{m-1}, b]$ as well as for differential systems, where the dimension N of matrices is multiplied by the number of subintervals or by the number of differential equations in the system.

We give the formulas for first order equations and a general formula. For the first order we have in myDE

$$P_1(x)y' + P_0(x)y = F \implies P_1(x)y - \int P_1'(x)y + \int P_0(x)y = \int F,$$

$$Ac \equiv \left[P_1(X) + J \left[P_0(X) - P_1'(X) \right] \right] c = Jf \equiv \mathbf{b}.$$

Generally, if we denote the differentiation operator on functions P by dP, the identity operator by I and the formal k power of the operator $I - Jd$ by $[\ ]^{(k)}$, we obtain, after m integrations, $Ac = \mathbf{b}$ where

$$A = \sum_{k=0}^{m} J^{m-k} [I - Jd]^{(k)} P_k(X), \quad \mathbf{b} = J^m \mathbf{f}. \tag{14}$$

For example, for $m = 3$ we have

$$\iiint P_0(x)y(x) \rightarrow J^3 P_0(X)\mathbf{c}, \quad \iiint P_1(x)y'(x) \rightarrow J^2 \left[P_1(X) - JP_1'(X) \right] \mathbf{c},$$

$$\iiint P_2(x)y''(x) \rightarrow J \left[P_2(X) - 2JP_2'(X) + J^2 P''(X) \right] \mathbf{c},$$

$$\iiint P_3(x)y'''(x) \rightarrow \left[P_3(X) - 3JP_3'(X) + 3J^2 P_3''(X) - J^3 P_3'''(X) \right] \mathbf{c}.$$

It is important to remark that the absolute value of the Chebyshev coefficients gives us some information about the necessary dimension N of the discretized problem in order to capture the correct behavior of the solution. For example, let us consider the problem `ibvp_ode_int_ex2.m` in the folder `Chebpack\examples\ex_level1`

$$\varepsilon y'' + (x^2 - w^2)y = 0, \quad y(-1) = 1, y(1) = 2, \quad x \in [-1, 1]$$

for $w = 0.5, \varepsilon = 1.e - 6$. The command
`[x,solnum]=ibvp_ode_int_ex2(1024,[-1 1],2);`
gives the results in Fig. 2. We see that up to a dimension about $N = 400$, the algorithm cannot resolve y accurately, due to its highly oscillatory behavior. After that, the Chebyshev series begins to converge rapidly. For $N = 1024$ the elapsed time is about 0.05 sec.

3.3 Discretization using the integration matrix J and splitting the interval

The corresponding code is `Chebpack\level1\ibvp_ode_split.m`

```
[x,solnum]=ibvp_ode_split(n,dom,kind)
```

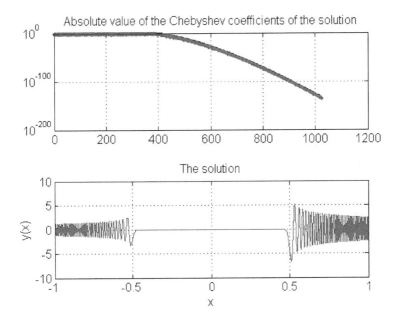

Fig. 2. The Chebyshev coefficients and the numerical solution for ex2

Sometimes, the solution of a differential problem has a different behavior in different subintervals. For example, for small ε the solution of the problem (13) has a shock near the origin and we need a very large N in order to capture its correct behavior. In these cases it is better to split the working interval $dom[a, b]$ into disjoint subintervals $[d_1, d_2] \cup [d_2, d_3] \cup ... \cup [d_{p-1}, d_p] = [a, b]$ adapted to the behavior of the solution. The great advantage is to use a small N for each subinterval. The partial solutions on each subinterval are connected by some level of smoothness.

Precisely, let us consider for example a second order differential problem on $[a, b]$ and let us split the interval as $[a, b] = [d_1, d_2] \cup [d_2, d_3] \cup [d_3, d_4]$. This splitting is given by $dom = [d_1, d_2, d_3, d_4]$ on input. If we calculate the basic ingredients $\mathbf{xs}$, Xs, Ds, Js for the standard interval $[-1, 1]$, then for each subinterval $[d_i, d_{i+1}]$, $i = 1, 2, 3$ the corresponding ingredients become

$$\mathbf{x} = len * \mathbf{xs} + med, \quad X = len * Xs + med * I_N, \quad D = \frac{Ds}{len}, \quad J = len * Js$$

where $len = \frac{d_{i+1} - d_i}{2}$, $med = \frac{d_{i+1} + d_i}{2}$.

Using the matrix J for the discretization we obtain on each subinterval $i = 1, 2, 3$ the discretized form $A^{(i)} c^{(i)} = b^{(i)}$ where the matrix $A^{(i)}$ and the vector $\mathbf{b}^{(i)}$ are given by (14) as above, while $c^{(i)}$ are the Chebyshev coefficients of the solution $y^{(i)}$ on that subinterval i. Now, using the Kronecker product and the reshape command of Matlab, we build a large (but very sparse) system $A\mathbf{c} = \mathbf{b}$

$$\begin{pmatrix} A^{(1)} & O & O \\ O & A^{(2)} & O \\ O & O & A^{(3)} \end{pmatrix} \begin{pmatrix} c^{(1)} \\ c^{(2)} \\ c^{(3)} \end{pmatrix} = \begin{pmatrix} \mathbf{b}^{(1)} \\ \mathbf{b}^{(2)} \\ \mathbf{b}^{(3)} \end{pmatrix}.$$

The boundary conditions are now the given boundary conditions say at d_1 and d_4 supplemented by smoothness conditions at d_2, d_3

$$y^{(1)}(d_2 - 0) = y^{(2)}(d_2 + 0), \; \frac{dy^{(1)}}{dx}(d_2 - 0) = \frac{dy^{(2)}}{dx}(d_2 + 0), \tag{15}$$

$$y^{(2)}(d_3 - 0) = y^{(3)}(d_3 + 0), \; \frac{dy^{(2)}}{dx}(d_3 - 0) = \frac{dy^{(3)}}{dx}(d_3 + 0).$$

Of course, for a higher order equation (say m) we have coincidence conditions (15) until the derivatives of order $m - 1$. The given boundary conditions are implemented in the first m rows of the first block-row of the matrix A and in the first entries of the first block of the vector $\mathbf{b}$, while the coincidence conditions are implemented in the first m rows of each of the following block-rows of A and in the first m entries of each following block of $\mathbf{b}$. The sparsity structure of A with 4 subintervals is given in Fig. 3. Here we have 16 blocks of size 64×64, the

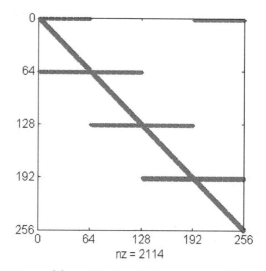

Fig. 3. The sparsity structure of the matrix A with boundary conditions implemented for 4 subintervals

4 diagonal segments come from the matrices $A^{(i)}$, $i = 1, 2, 3, 4$, the first horizontal segments come from the given boundary conditions while the next 3 pairs of horizontal segments come from connectivity conditions. Each block acts on the corresponding block coefficients $\mathbf{c}^{(i)}$, $i = 1, 2, 3, 4$.

Using this technique for the problem (13) for example, the command

`[x,solnum]=ibvp_ode_split_ex(64,[-1 -0.05 0 0.05 1],2);`

from the folder `Chebpack\examples\ex_level1` gives the numerical solution with an accuracy of about 6×10^{-15} with four subintervals with $N = 64$ in only 0.014 sec. The new matrix A has now a sparsity factor of about 3.2257% and the dimension 256.

3.4 Linear first-order systems

Let us consider a first order linear differential system for $x \in [a, b]$

$$P_1(x)y_1' + P_{11}(x)y_1 + \ldots + P_{1m}(x)y_m = f_1(x), \; y_1(a) = y_{1a},$$
$$P_2(x)y_2' + P_{21}(x)y_1 + \ldots + P_{2m}(x)y_m = f_2(x), \; y_2(a) = y_{2a},$$
$$\ldots\ldots\ldots\ldots\ldots\ldots\ldots\ldots\ldots\ldots$$
$$P_m(x)y_m' + P_{m1}(x)y_1 + \ldots + P_{mm}(x)y_m = f_m(x), \; y_m(a) = y_{ma}.$$

If we denote by $\mathbf{c} = (c^{(1)}, \ldots, c^{(m)})^T$ the Chebyshev coefficients of $y_1(x), \ldots, y_m(x)$ and by $\mathbf{f}^{(1)}, \ldots, \mathbf{f}^{(m)}$ the coefficients of $f_1, \ldots, f_m$ then the discretized version of the system is $\mathbf{Ac} = \mathbf{b}$ where

$$\mathbf{A} = \begin{pmatrix} P_1(X)D + P_{11}(X) & \cdots & P_{1m}(X) \\ \vdots & \ddots & \vdots \\ P_{m1}(X) & \cdots & P_m(X)D + P_{mm}(X) \end{pmatrix}, \; \mathbf{b} = \begin{pmatrix} \mathbf{f}^{(1)} \\ \vdots \\ \mathbf{f}^{(m)} \end{pmatrix}.$$

The initial conditions are implemented like in (15): the last row of each block in the above matrix is replaced by T or zeros for the corresponding columns and the last entry of each block in the r.h.s. is replaced by y_{ka} such that $[O, \ldots, T, \ldots, O]\mathbf{c} = y_{ka}$ for each k. The corresponding code from level1 is

```
[x,solnum]=ibvp_sys(n,dom,kind,y0)
```

where $\mathbf{y0}$ is the column vector of the initial values $[y_{1a}, \ldots, y_{ma}]^T$. Of course, we may use the integration matrix J instead of D for discretization, obtaining again a system $\mathbf{Ac} = \mathbf{b}$ where

$$\mathbf{A} = \begin{pmatrix} P_1(X) - JP_1'(X) + JP_{11}(X) & \cdots & JP_{1m}(X) \\ \vdots & \ddots & \vdots \\ JP_{m1}(X) & \cdots & P_m(X) - JP_m'(X) + JP_{mm}(X) \end{pmatrix}, \; \mathbf{b} = \begin{pmatrix} J\mathbf{f}^{(1)} \\ \vdots \\ J\mathbf{f}^{(m)} \end{pmatrix}$$

with the implementation of the initial conditions on the first row of each block, see `ibvp_sys_ex3_int.m`, or we may consider systems of higher order, see `ibvp_sys_ex2x2.m` from the folder `Chebpack\examples\ex_level1`.

3.5 Linear integral equations

Let us consider a Fredholm integral equation

$$y(x) = \int_a^b K(x, t)y(t)dt + f(x) \equiv A(y)(x) + f(x), \; x \in [a, b]. \tag{16}$$

The Fredholm integral operator $A(y)$ becomes after discretization with shifted Chebyshev polynomials

$$A(y)(x) = \int_a^b K(x, t) \sum_{k=0}^{N-1} c_k T_k^*(t)dt = \sum_{k=0}^{N-1} c_k \int_a^b K(x, t)T_k^*(t)dt =$$

$$\sum_{k=0}^{N-1} c_k \cdot I_k(x) = \sum_{k=0}^{N-1} c_k \sum_{j=0}^{N-1} k_{jk}T_j^*(x) = \sum_{j=0}^{N-1} \left[\sum_{k=0}^{N-1} k_{jk}c_k \right] T_j^*(x).$$

Consequently, if $\mathbf{c} = (c_0, ..., c_{N-1})^T$ are the coefficients of y, then $K\mathbf{c}$ are the coefficients of $A(y)$, given by the matrix $K = (k_{jk})_{j,k=0,...,N-1}$.

The matrix K can be calculated starting from the physical values

$$I_k(x_s) = \int_a^b K(x_s, t)T_k^*(t)dt = \sum_{i=0}^{N-1} w_i K(x_s, x_i) T_k^*(x_i), \quad s, k = 0, ..., N-1.$$

In matrix form, this means

$$(I_k(x_s))_{k,s=0,...,N-1} = (K(x_s, x_i))_{s,i=0,...,N-1} \cdot diag((w_i)_{i=0,...,N-1}) \cdot T$$

where T=cpv(n,x,dom) and then we apply x2t, see also (Driscoll, 2010).

The Fredholm integral equation (16) becomes $(I_N - K)\mathbf{c} = \mathbf{f}$ where $\mathbf{f}$ are the Chebyshev coefficients of f and we obtain the solution by solving this linear system. The corresponding model code from the folder Chebpack\level1 is

$$[\text{x, solnum}]=\text{fred\_eq}(\text{n, dom, kind})$$

Similarly, for a Volterra integral equation

$$y(x) = \int_a^x K(x, t)y(t)dt + f(x) \equiv A(y)(x) + f(x), \quad x \in [a, b]$$

we obtain, using (11), for the Volterra integral operator

$$A(y)(x) = \int_a^x K(x, t)y(t)dt = \left[TJ_0T^{-1}.* K(x_i, x_j) \right] \mathbf{y},$$

where $\mathbf{y}$ are the values of $y(x)$ at the grid points $\mathbf{x}$. Consequently, the physical representation of the Volterra integral operator is the matrix $V_{phys} = TJ_0T^{-1}.* K(x_i, x_j)$, see again (Driscoll, 2010) while its spectral representation is $V_{spec} = T^{-1}V_{phys}T$. The Volterra integral equation becomes in physical representation $(I_N - K)\mathbf{y} = \mathbf{f}$ where $\mathbf{f}$ are now the values of f at the grid points $\mathbf{x}$.

The corresponding model code from *Chebpack* is

$$[\text{x, solnum}]=\text{volt\_eq}(\text{n, dom, kind})$$

from the folder Chebpack\level1. The folder Chebpack\examples\ex_level1 contains some examples in the files fred_eq_ex* and volt_eq_ex*.

Of course, these codes work well only if the kernel $K(x, t)$ is sufficiently smooth such that it can be spectrally represented by an acceptable number of Chebyshev polynomials.

3.6 Eigenvalues/eigenfunctions for Sturm-Liouville problems

Let us consider now the second order spectral problem

$$P_2(x)y'' + P_1(x)y' + P_0(x)y = \lambda R(x)y$$

with homogeneous boundary value conditions as above. Using tau method, we get the following N – dimensional matrix eigenproblem

$$(P_2(X)D^2 + P_1(X)D + P_0(X))\mathbf{c} = \lambda R(X)\mathbf{c}$$

of the form $A\mathbf{c} = \lambda B\mathbf{c}$. The conditions give $T\mathbf{c} = 0$ and combining these equations we derive the generalized eigenproblem

$$\begin{pmatrix} T \\ A \end{pmatrix} \mathbf{c} = \lambda \begin{pmatrix} \dfrac{1}{\lambda^*}T \\ B \end{pmatrix} \mathbf{c} \text{ i.e. } \tilde{A}\mathbf{c} = \lambda \tilde{B}\mathbf{c}$$

where we retain only the first N rows of the matrices to obtain $\tilde{A}$ and $\tilde{B}$. Here λ^* is chosen by the user as a large and known value. We remark that for $\lambda \neq \lambda^*$ we get $T\mathbf{c} = 0$ as above but now the matrix $\tilde{B}$ behaves well. Consequently, the eigenproblem has instead of two infinite eigenvalues two known λ^* eigenvalues that can be eliminated. The same procedure is applied for higher order problems.

The corresponding model code from the folder Chebpack\level1 is

```
[lam,phi,x]=eig_ode2(n,dom,kind,numeigval)
```

The folder Chebpack\examples\ex_level1 contains some other examples in the files eig_ode2_ex*, eig_ode3_ex and eig_ode4_ex. An older package *LiScEig* is also freely accessible at (Trif, 2005).

4. Chebpack, nonlinear module

At the second level – level2, we have subroutines to solve
- initial and boundary value problems for nonlinear differential equations
- nonlinear integral equations.

Here the codes of the first level are used at each step of the Newton method applied in the functional space. Another method could be the successive iteration method.

4.1 Successive iteration method

Let us consider, as an example, the nonlinear Emden boundary value problem

$$xy'' + 2y' = -xy^5, \ y'(0) = 0, \ y(1) = \frac{\sqrt{3}}{2}, \ x \in [0,1].$$

If the starting spectral approximation of y is, for example, $Y_0 = 1$ then the discretization of the problem is $AY = F$. Here $A = XD^2 + 2D$ and $F = F(x, Y_0)$ are the coefficients of the r.h.s. modified by using the boundary value conditions. We apply successively

$$Y_{n+1} = A^{-1}F(x, Y_n), \ n = 0, 1, 2, ..., n_{max}.$$

If Y_n converges, then it converges to a solution of the bvp.

The Matlab codes are ibvp_ode_succapprox.m from the folder Chebpack\level2 or ibvp_ode_ex1.m from the folder Chebpack\examples\ex_level2.

Of course, the discretization could be performed using the integration matrix J instead of D. Let us consider, for example, the Lotka-Volterra system

$$y_1' - Ay_1 = -By_1y_2, \ y_2' + Cy_2 = By_1y_2, \ t \in [0, 100]$$
$$y_1(0) = y_2(0) = 0.5, \ A = 0.1, \ B = 0.2, \ C = 0.05.$$

We transform this system to integral form

$$y_1 - A \int y_1 dt = -B \int y_1 y_2 dt, \quad y_2 + C \int y_2 dt = B \int y_1 y_2 dt$$

and the discretized form in spectral representation is

$$\begin{pmatrix} I_n - AJ & 0 \\ 0 & I_n + CJ \end{pmatrix} \begin{pmatrix} Y_1^{new} \\ Y_2^{new} \end{pmatrix} = \begin{pmatrix} -BJF \\ BJF \end{pmatrix}$$

where F is the column vector of the coefficients of $y_1^{old}(t) y_2^{old}(t)$ obtained by using t2x.m and x2t.m. In this discretized form we implement the initial conditions as usually and we must solve this system which has a sparsity factor of about 6% for $n = 32$ and about 3% for $n = 64$. For a long interval dom given as $dom = [d_0, d_1, ..., d_m]$, we apply the successive approximations method at each subinterval. The initial approximation for the following subinterval is given by the final values of the solution for the current subinterval. To test the numerical solution, we remark that the Lotka-Volterra system has as invariant $\Lambda = By_1 + By_2 - C \log y_1 - A \log y_2$. The code is used by the command

[x,solnum]=ibvp_sys_succapprox(32,[0:10:100],2,[0.5,0.5]);

and the result is given in Fig. 4, with the value of the invariant $\Lambda = 0.3039720770839$.

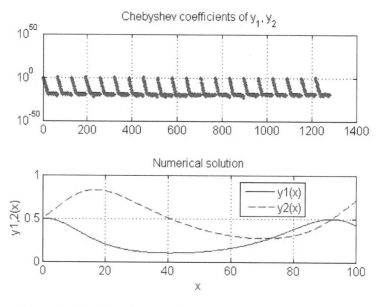

Fig. 4. The solution of the Lotka-Volterra problem

In the case of nonlinear integral equations, for example

$$y(x) = f(x) + \int_0^b K(x, t, y(t)) dt,$$

we perform successive iterations (if this method works)

$$y^{new}(x) = f(x) + \int_0^b K(x, t, y^{old}(t)) dt$$

starting with a suitable y^{old}. For each $x = x_s$ in the grid and at each iteration, the integral is evaluated as

$$\int_0^b K(x_s, t, y^{old}(t))dt \approx \sum_{k=1}^n w_k K(x_s, t_k, y^{old}(t_k)),$$

where $\{t_k, k = 1, ..., n\}$ is the Chebyshev grid on $[0, b]$ and $\{w_k, k = 1, ..., n\}$ are the corresponding weights. Consequently, we obtain

$$y^{new}(x_s) = \sum_{k=1}^n w_k K(x_s, t_k, y^{old}(t_k)), \ s = 1, ..., n.$$

Taking into account the nonlinearities, all the calculations are performed into the physical space. Next, $y^{old} \longleftarrow y^{new}$ until $\left\| y^{new} - y^{old} \right\| < \varepsilon$. The corresponding code is ibvp_int_succapprox.m from the folder Chebpack\level2.

4.2 Newton method

Let us consider again a nonlinear differential problem of the form

$$Ly(x) = f(x, y(x)), \ x \in [a, b]$$

where L is a linear differential operator, such as $Ly(x) = xy''(x) + 2y'(x)$ and f is the nonlinear part. We have also the boundary or initial conditions BC/IC. If we denote by

$$P(y)(x) = Ly(x) - f(x, y(x)), \ BC/IC$$

the problem is of the form $P(y)(x) = 0$ where P is the operator of the problem and y is the unknown.

The Newton method works as follows. Starting with an initial approximation $y_0(x)$ verifying the initial or boundary conditions, we must solve at each step n the linear problem

$$P'(y_n)(y_{n+1} - y_n)(x) = -P(y_n)(x),$$

for $y_{n+1} - y_n$, with the corresponding homogeneous IC/BC. Next, $y_{n+1} = y_n + (y_{n+1} - y_n)$ and we perform these iterations until $\|y_{n+1} - y_n\| < \varepsilon$. For our problem, the linear step is

$$\left[L - \frac{\partial f(x, y_n(x))}{\partial y} \right] (y_{n+1} - y_n)(x) = - \left[Ly_n(x) - f(x, y_n(x)) \right].$$

The corresponding code is ibvp_ode_newton.m from the folder Chebpack \level2. It starts with $y_0(x)$ verifying or not the IC/BC and solves at each step the above linear problem for y_{n+1} with the nonhomogeneous IC/BC.

A nonlinear system (of order 2 for example)

$$y_1' + a_{11}y_1 + a_{12}y_2 = f_1(x, y_1, y_2), \ x \in [a, b]$$
$$y_2' + a_{21}y_1 + a_{22}y_2 = f_2(x, y_1, y_2), \ y_1(a) = y_{1a}, y_2(a) = y_{2a}$$

is in matrix form

$$Y'(x) + A(x)Y(x) = F(x, Y).$$

At the linear step it becomes

$$[Z' + [A(x) - JacF(x, Y_n)] Z = - [Y_n' + AY_n - F(x, Y_n)]$$

where $Z = Y_{n+1} - Y_n$ is the correction, $Y_n \equiv Y(x_n)$ and

$$JacF(x, Y_n) = \begin{vmatrix} \dfrac{\partial f_1(x, y_{1n}, y_{2n})}{\partial y_1} & \dfrac{\partial f_1(x, y_{1n}, y_{2n})}{\partial y_2} \\ \dfrac{\partial f_2(x, y_{1n}, y_{2n})}{\partial y_1} & \dfrac{\partial f_2(x, y_{1n}, y_{2n})}{\partial y_2} \end{vmatrix}.$$

As above, $Y_{n+1} = Y_n + Z$ until $\|Z\| < \varepsilon$.
We remark that in the linear step we use the integration

$$Z + \int [A(x) - JacF(x, Y_n)]\, Z = - \int [Y_n' + AY_n - F(x, Y_n)]$$

which becomes in the discrete form

$$[I_n + J(A(X) - JacF(X, Y_n))]\, Z = -[Y_n + JA(x)]Y_n + JF(x, Y_n).$$

i.e $AZ = B$. In the l.h.s the matrix $J(A(X) - JacF(X, Y_n))$ is calculated using the code `fact.m`. This code uses the physical values of $A(x) - JacF(x, Y_n)$ and converts them into spectral coefficients. In the r.h.s the code also starts with the physical values and converts them into their spectral coefficients. The initial conditions are implemented now in the rows $1, n+1, \ldots$. Of course, this code `ibvp_sys_newton.m` from the folder `Chebpack\level2` can be used in a long-term integration algorithm that starts with the initial values y_{a1}, y_{b1}, calculates the solution on $[a, b]$, extracts the final values y_{b1}, y_{b2} which become initial values for the same code on a new interval $[b, c]$ and so on.
A short comparison between the successive approximations method (SA) and the Newton method (N) for the example from `ibvp_sys_newton_ex1` shows that, for the same $n = 64$, $dom = [0, 1, 2 : 2 : 200]$ and $M = 8$,
- SA: 2910 iterations, 3.4 sec elapsed time, 12940 Chebyshev coefficients calculated
- N : 490 iterations, 6 sec elapsed time, 6475 Chebyshev coefficients calculated.
In the case of a nonlinear integral equation (of Fredholm or Volterra) type

$$P(y) \equiv y(x) - \int_a K(x, t, y(t))dt - f(x) = 0,$$

we start with an initial approximation y_0 (in physical space) and at each Newton step we obtain the linear equation for the correction z

$$z(x) - \int_a \frac{\partial K}{\partial y}(x, t, y_0(t))z(t)dt = -y_0(x) + \int_a K(x, t, y_0(t))dt + f(x).$$

We solve this equation in spectral form as in the previous section and the corrected value of y is $y_0 + z$. We repeat this step until convergence, i.e. until $\|z\| < \varepsilon$. There are many examples in the folder `Chebpack\examples\level2`.

5. Chebpack, experimental module

Finally, the package contains an experimental level – level3, in progress, for
- partial differential equations of evolution type
- fractional differential equations (i.e. differential equations of non-integer order).

5.1 Partial differential evolution equations

Let us consider, as a simple example, a problem from (Trefethen et al., 2011)

$$u_t = u_{xx}, \; x \in [-4, 2], \; t > 0$$
$$u(x, 0) = u^{(0)}(x) \equiv \max(0, 1 - abs(x)),$$
$$u(-4, t) = 1, \; u(2, t) = 2.$$

First, we discretize in time by a backward finite difference on the grid $0 = t_0 < t_1 < ... < t_K$ starting with $u^{(0)}(x)$

$$\frac{u^{(k+1)}(x) - u^{(k)}(x)}{dt} = u_{xx}^{(k+1)}(x),$$

where $u^{(k)}(x) = u(x, t_k)$, $u_{xx}^{(k)}(x) = u_{xx}(x, t_k)$. We obtain the second order boundary value problems in x

$$\left(I - dt \frac{\partial^2}{\partial x^2}\right) u^{(k+1)}(x) = u^{(k)}(x), \; u^{(k+1)}(-4) = 1, \; u^{(k+1)}(2) = 2.$$

These problems, for each $k = 1, 2, ..., K$, are also discretized by the spectral Chebyshev method with some N, $dom = [-4, 2]$, $kind$ as

$$\left(I_n - dt D^2\right) c^{(k+1)} = c^{(k)}, \; u^{(k+1)}(-4) = 1, \; u^{(k+1)}(2) = 2.$$

Here $c^{(k)}$ are the Chebyshev spectral coefficients $\left(c_0^{(k)}, c_1^{(k)}, ..., c_{N-1}^{(k)}\right)$ of $u^{(k)}(x)$ corresponding to the grid $x_1, ..., x_N$ in dom. This way we may obtain the solution $u(x_j, t_k)$ on the computational grid $\left(x_j, t_k\right)_{j=1,...,N}^{k=1,...,K}$. The corresponding code is pde_lin.m from the folder Chebpack\level3.

Similarly, for nonlinear equations of the form $u_t = Lu + Nu$ where L is a linear operator and N a nonlinear one, for example for the Burgers equation

$$u_t = vu_{xx} - \left(\frac{u^2}{2}\right)_x, \; x \in [-1, 1], \; t > 0, \; v = \frac{0.01}{\pi},$$
$$u(x, 0) = \sin \pi x, \; u(0, t) = u(1, t) = 0,$$

we may take the backward Euler finite difference for the linear part while the forward Euler finite difference for the nonlinear part.

$$\frac{u^{(k+1)}(x) - u^{(k)}(x)}{dt} = Lu^{(k+1)}(x) + Nu^{(k)}(x),$$

We obtain

$$(I - dt\,L)\,u^{(k+1)}(x) = u^{(k)}(x) + dt\,Nu^{(k)}(x), \; u^{(k+1)}(0) = u^{(k+1)}(1) = 0$$

which is implemented in pde_nonlin.m.

Of course, we may take the approximating solution in the physical representation on the grid $x_1, ..., x_n$ and the semidiscrete problem becomes $u'(\mathbf{x}, t) = \tilde{D}u(\mathbf{x}, t)$ where $\tilde{D} = TD^2T^{-1}$ is the physical second order derivative. The boundary value condition imposes $u(x_1, t) = \alpha$,

$u(x_n, t) = \beta$ and therefore at these points we don't need to satisfy the equation. Consequently, if $\hat{D} = \tilde{D}(2 : n - 1, 2 : n - 1)$ is obtained by eliminating the first and last rows and columns from $\tilde{D}$, the problem becomes

$$\hat{u}'(t) = \hat{D} * \hat{u}(t) + \tilde{D}(2 : n - 1, [1, n]) * BC, \ \hat{u}(0) = \hat{u}^{(0)},$$

where $BC = (\alpha, \beta)^T$, i.e. $\hat{u}'(t) = \hat{D} * \hat{u}(t) + b, \ \hat{u}(0) = \hat{u}^{(0)}$ with the solution

$$\hat{u}(t) = expm(t\hat{D}) \cdot \hat{u}^{(0)} + \hat{D}^{-1} \cdot \left(expm(t\hat{D}) - I_{n-2}\right) \cdot b.$$

Here $expm(A)$ is the matricial exponential function of A. The code `pde_lin_matr.m` uses this procedure.

The same thing may be performed in spectral space. The problem

$$u' = L \cdot u, \ u(0) = u_0, \ BC = T \cdot u$$

(where L is a linear differential operator with constant coefficients and T is given by `cpv` from `level0`) may be expanded as

$$\begin{pmatrix} \hat{u}' \\ BC \end{pmatrix} = \begin{pmatrix} \hat{L} & \hat{\hat{L}} \\ \hat{T} & \hat{\hat{T}} \end{pmatrix} \cdot \begin{pmatrix} \hat{u} \\ \hat{\hat{u}} \end{pmatrix}.$$

Therefore, successively,

$$\hat{u}' = \hat{L}\hat{u} + \hat{\hat{L}}\hat{\hat{u}}, \ BC = \hat{T}\hat{u} + \hat{\hat{T}}\hat{\hat{u}}, \ \hat{\hat{u}} = \hat{\hat{T}}^{-1}\left(BC - \hat{T}\hat{u}\right), \tag{17}$$

$$\hat{u}' = \left(\hat{L} - \hat{\hat{L}}\hat{\hat{T}}^{-1}\hat{T}\right)\hat{u} + \hat{\hat{L}}\hat{\hat{T}}^{-1}BC, \ \hat{u}' = \tilde{L} \cdot \hat{u} + \tilde{\tilde{L}} \cdot BC.$$

The exact solution of the last equation is given by

$$\hat{u}(t) = e^{t\tilde{L}} \cdot \hat{u}_0 + \frac{e^{t\tilde{L}} - I}{\tilde{L}}\tilde{\tilde{L}} \cdot BC$$

and, using (17), $u = (\hat{u}, \hat{\hat{u}})^T$.

This procedure is coded in `pde_lin_ex2.m` from the folder `Chebpack\examples\ex_level3`.

In the case of a nonlinear problem

$$u' = L \cdot u + Nu, \ u(0) = u_0, \ BC = T \cdot u$$

the same procedure leads to

$$\hat{u}(t) = e^{t\tilde{L}} \cdot \hat{u}_0 + \frac{e^{t\tilde{L}} - I}{\tilde{L}}\left(\tilde{\tilde{L}} \cdot BC + \widehat{Nu}\right)$$

and to the same $\hat{\hat{u}}$ given by (17). This fixed point equation must now be solved using successive iterations method (for t sufficiently small) or using Newton method. It is coded in pde_nonlin_ex4.m in the folder Chebpack\examples\ex_level3 for the Korteweg-de Vries problem

$$u_t + 6u\, u_x + u_{xxx} = 0, \ x \in [-20, 20], \ t \in [0, 4]$$

$$u(x, 0) = 2\operatorname{sech}(x)^2, \ u(-20, t) = u(20, t) = u_x(20, t) = 0.$$

This problem of the form $u_t = Lu + N(u)$ is numerically solved in spectral space $c'(t) = Lc(t) + N(c(t))$ by using the so called implicit exponential time differencing Euler method

$$c^{(k+1)} = e^{Ldt}c^{(k)} + \frac{e^{Ldt} - I}{L}N(c^{(k+1)}),$$

applied in a symmetric form

$$c = e^{Ldt/2}c^{(k)} + \frac{e^{Ldt/2} - I}{L}N(c), \quad c^{(k+1)} = e^{Ldt/2}c + \frac{e^{Ldt/2} - I}{L}N(c).$$

Here, the first fixed point problem is solved using successive iterations starting with $c^{(k)}$, where $c^{(k)}$ are the Chebyshev coefficients of the numerical solution at the time level k.

5.2 Fractional differential equations

The fractional derivative $D^q f(x)$ with $0 < q < 1, 0 < x \leq b$, in the Riemann-Liouville version, is defined by (Podlubny, 1999)

$$D^q f(x) = \frac{1}{\Gamma(1-q)} \frac{d}{dx} \int_0^x f(t)(x-t)^{-q} dt$$

while the Caputo fractional derivative is

$$D_*^q f(x) = \frac{1}{\Gamma(1-q)} \int_{0}^x f'(t)(x-t)^{-q} dt$$

and we have

$$D^q f(x) = \frac{f(0)x^{-q}}{\Gamma(1-q)} + D_*^q f(x).$$

Let us consider a function $f : [0, b] \rightarrow \mathbb{R}$, with the spectral representation

$$f(x) = \sum_{k=0}^{n-1} c_k T_k(\alpha x + \beta), \ \alpha = \frac{2}{b}, \ \beta = -1$$

Using the spectral derivative matrix D, we have

$$f'(x) = \sum_{k=0}^{n-1} (Dc)_k T_k(\alpha x + \beta)$$

and using the linearity of the fractional derivative of order $q \in (0, 1)$, we obtain

$$D_*^q f(x) = \frac{1}{\Gamma(1-q)} \int_0^x \frac{f'(t)dt}{(x-t)^q} = \frac{1}{\Gamma(1-q)} \sum_{k=0}^{n-1} (Dc)_k \int_0^x \frac{T_k(\alpha x + \beta)}{(x-t)^q} dt.$$

By calculating the physical values of the above integrals in the columns k of a matrix I, each row corresponding to a sample of x from the Chebyshev grid, the formula for the fractional derivative is

$$D_*^q f(x) = \frac{1}{\Gamma(1-q)} \cdot I \cdot D \cdot T^{-1} f(x)$$

where T is the matrix given by `cpv.m`. This means that the Caputo fractional differentiation matrix $\mathbf{D}$ in physical form is given by

$$\mathbf{D}_{phys} = \frac{1}{\Gamma(1-q)} \cdot I \cdot D \cdot T^{-1}$$

i.e. $\mathbf{D}_{phys}$ times the vector of physical values of f gives the vector of physical values of $D_*^q f$. For the spectral form,

$$\mathbf{D}_{spec} = \frac{1}{\Gamma(1-q)} \cdot T^{-1} \cdot I \cdot D,$$

i.e. $\mathbf{D}_{spec}$ times the vector $T^{-1} f(x)$ of the coefficients of f gives the vector of the coefficients of $D_*^q f$.

If $q > 1$ then let ex be $[q]$ and q will be replaced by $q - [q]$. In this case, the differentiation matrix will be

$$\mathbf{D}_{spec} = \frac{1}{\Gamma(1-q)} \cdot T^{-1} \cdot I \cdot D^{(ex+1)}.$$

In order to avoid the singularity of the fractional derivative $D^q f$ if $f(0) \neq 0$, **we suppose that** $f(0) = 0$. The problem of computing the integrals

$$I_k(x) = \int_0^x \frac{T_k(\alpha x - 1)}{(x-t)^q} dt$$

for each x of the grid may be solved iteratively, see (Piessens & Branders, 1976). Indeed, we have, by direct calculation, using the recurrence formula for Chebyshev polynomials, as well as for the derivatives of the Chebyshev polynomials, for $k = 3, 4, ..$

$$I_k(x) \cdot \left(1 + \frac{1-q}{k}\right) = 2(\alpha x - 1) \cdot I_{k-1}(x) + \left(\frac{1-q}{k-2} - 1\right) \cdot I_{k-2}(x) - \frac{2(-1)^k}{k(k-2)} x^{1-q}$$

and

$$I_0(x) = \frac{x^{1-q}}{1-q}/2, \; I_1(x) = \frac{\alpha x^{2-q}}{(2-q)(1-q)} - \frac{x^{1-q}}{1-q},$$

$$I_2(x) = \frac{4\alpha^2 x^{3-q}}{(3-q)(2-q)(1-q)} - \frac{4\alpha x^{2-q}}{(2-q)(1-q)} + \frac{x^{1-q}}{1-q}.$$

This recurrence is as stable as the recurrence which calculates the Chebyshev polynomials. The calculation of the fractional derivative matrix $\mathbf{D}_{spec}$ is coded in `deriv_frac.m` from the folder `Chebpack\level3`. Next, if needed, $\mathbf{D}_{phys} = \frac{1}{\Gamma(1-q)} \cdot I \cdot D^{(ex+1)} \cdot T^{-1} = T \cdot \mathbf{D}_{spec} \cdot T^{-1}$. Using an idea of Sugiura & Hasegawa (Sugiura & Hasegawa, 2009), let $J(s; f)$ be

$$J(s; f) = \int_0^s f'(t)(s-t)^{-q} dt$$

and, approximating $f(t)$ by a combination $p_n(t)$ of Chebyshev polynomials on $(0,1)$ we have the approximations $|J(s; f) - J(s; p_n)| \sim O(n\rho^{-n})$, for some $\rho > 1$.
Of course, this method is not suitable for the functions with a singularity in $[0,1]$ or singularities of lower-order derivatives, like $x^{0.1}$ for example. In this case, n must be excessively large.
For the initial value problems for fractional differential equations, let us consider the problem

$$D_*^q y(x) = x^2 + \frac{2}{\Gamma(3-q)} x^{2-q} - y(x), \quad y(0) = 0, \ q = 0.5, \ x \in [0,1].$$

The physical discretization is

$$A\mathbf{y} = \mathbf{b}, \ A = T \cdot DF \cdot T^{-1} + I_N, \ \mathbf{b} = x^2 + 2/\Gamma(3-q) \cdot x^{2-q}$$

where, in order to implement the initial condition, the first row of A is replaced by $[1, 0, ..., 0]$ and $\mathbf{b}(1)$ is replaced by 0. The solution is now $y(x) = A^{-1}B$. The example is coded in `deriv_frac_ex1.m` from the folder `Chebpack\examples\ex_level3`.
If we use the spectral representation, for example for the problem

$$D^q y(x) + y(x) = 1, \ y(0) = 0, \ y'(0) = 0, \ q = 1.8, \ x \in [0,5],$$

with the exact solution $yex = x^q E_{q,q+1}(-x^q)$, the spectral discretized form becomes

$$Ay \equiv (D^q + I_n) y = T^{-1} \cdot \mathbf{1} = B,$$
$$A(n-1,:) = T(1,:), \ B(n-1) = 0, \ A(n,:) = T(1,:) * D, \ B(n) = 0,$$

see `deriv_frac_ex2.m`
For nonhomogeneous initial conditions like $y(0) = c_0$, $y'(0) = c_1$, we perform a function change $y(x) = c_0 + c_1 x + z(x)$ where z verifies the same equation but with homogeneous initial conditins ($c_0 + c_1 x$ disappears by differentiation), see `deriv_frac_ex3.m`. Examples for discontinuous data, boundary value problems or eigenproblems are also given.

6. Conclusion

The new package *Chebpack* (Trif, 2011) is a large and powerful extension of *LiScEig* (Trif, 2005). It is based on the Chebyshev tau spectral method and it is applied to linear and nonlinear differential or integral problems, including eigenvalue problems. An experimental module contains applications to linear or nonlinear partial differential problems and to fractional differential problems. Each module is illustrated by many examples. A future version will handle also piecewise functions as well as functions with singularities.
The following comparisons with MATLAB codes *bvp4c*, *bvp5c* as well as with *DMS* or *Chebfun* prove the efficiency of *Chebpack*. The elapsed time was evaluated after three code executions. The first test problem (`test1.m` in the folder `Chebpack\tutorial`) is

$$-u'' - \frac{1}{6x} u' + \frac{1}{x^2} u = \frac{19}{6} x^{1/2}, \ u(0) = u(1) = 0, \ x \in [0,1]$$

with the exact solution $u_{ex}(x) = x^{3/2} - x^{5/2}$. The elapsed time and the errors are presented in Table 1. Here *Chebpack* uses the differentiation matrix.
The second test problem (`test2.m` in the folder `Chebpack\tutorial`) is (13) with $\varepsilon = 10^{-4}$. The elapsed time and the errors are presented in Table 2. Here *Chebpack* uses the integration matrix.

	bvp4c RelTol=1.e-5	bvp5c RelTol=1.e-4	dms N=64	Chebfun N=98	Chebpack N=80
elapsed time (sec)	0.737	0.744	0.004	0.192	0.005
errors	3.2e-7	9.2e-8	2.3e-7	1.8e-7	4.6e-7

Table 1. Test 1

	bvp4c default	bvp5c default	dms N=1024	Chebfun N=[13,114,109,14]	Chebpack N=1024
elapsed time (sec)	0.131	0.244	3.471	1.053	0.041
errors	8.6e-5	6.6e-6	8.4e-13	1.0e-12	1.e-14

Table 2. Test 2

7. References

Berrut, J. P. & Trefethen, L. N. (2004). Barycentric Lagrange interpolation, *SIAM Review* Vol.46(No.3): 501–517.

Boyd, J. P. (2000). *Chebyshev and Fourier Spectral Methods*, Dover Publications, Inc.

Canuto, C., Hussaini, M. Y., Quarteroni, A. & Zang, T. A. (1988). *Spectral Methods in Fluid Dynamics*, Springer-Verlag, Berlin.

Driscoll, T. A. (2010). Automatic spectral collocation for integral, integro-differential, and integrally reformulated differential equations, *J. Comp. Phys.* Vol.229: 5980–5998.

Mason, J. & Handscomb, D. (2003). *Chebyshev Polynomials*, Chapman & Hall/CRC.

Ortiz, E. L. & Samara, H. (1981). An operational approach to the tau method for the numerical solution of non-linear differential equations, *Computing* Vol.27: 15–25.

Piessens, R. & Branders, M. (1976). Numerical solution of integral equations of mathematical physics, using Chebyshev polynomials, *J. Comp. Phys. (1976)* Vol.21: 178–196.

Podlubny, I. (1999). *Fractional Differential Equations*, Academic Press.

Sugiura, H. & Hasegawa, T. (2009). Quadrature rule for Abel's equations: Uniformly approximating fractional derivatives, *J. Comp. Appl. Math.* Vol.223: 459–468.

Trefethen, L. N. (2000). *Spectral Methods in MATLAB*, SIAM, Philadelphia.

Trefethen, L. N. (2008). Is Gauss quadrature better than Clenshaw–Curtis?, *SIAM Review* Vol.50(No.1): 67–87.

Trefethen, L. N. et al. (2011). *Chebfun Version 4.0*, The Chebfun Development Team. URL: *http://www.maths.ox.ac.uk/chebfun/*

Trif, D. (2005). LiScEig, MATLAB Central. URL: *http://www.mathworks.com/matlabcentral/fileexchange/8689-lisceig*

Trif, D. (2011). Chebpack, MATLAB Central. URL: *http://www.mathworks.com/matlabcentral/fileexchange/32227-chebpack*

Waldvogel, J. (2006). Fast construction of the Fejér and Clenshaw–Curtis quadrature rules, *BIT Numerical Mathematics* Vol.46: 195–202.

Weideman, J. A. C. & Reddy, S. C. (2000). A MATLAB differentiation matrix suite. URL: *http://www.mathworks.com/matlabcentral/fileexchange/29-dmsuite*

3

Revisiting the Ceschino Interpolation Method

Alain Hébert
École Polytechnique de Montréal
Canada

1. Introduction

The Ceschino polynomial expansion method is a generalization of the Taylor polynomial expansion method where higher derivatives of a function are predicted in addition to the value of the function itself. This technique was first introduced by (Ceschino, 1956), but was largly forgotten afterward. An unsuccessfull atempt was tried in 1975 to apply the Ceschino coupling relations to the solution of an elliptic space–dependent differential equation, but the resulting spatial discretization was found to be less accurate than competing finite-element approaches, as presented by (Pageau, 1975). No further published work was reported after the Pageau thesis.

Here, we propose to apply the Ceschino coupling relations to the basic interpolation problem, as an alternative to existing univariate interpolation schemes, such as the cubic spline approach. The interpolation problem consists to evaluate a functional $\mathcal{I}\{f(x); \xi\}$ of a continuous function (or dependent variable) $f(x)$ at a specific point ξ in the case where function $f(x)$ is only known at tabulated abscissa (or independent variables) $\{x_{m+1/2}; \, m = 0, M\}$. We also introduce the concept of interpolation factors (a. k. a., *terp factors*) that are useful for interpolating large databases with respect to a small number of independent variables, as presented by (MacFarlane, 1984). The Ceschino polynomial expansion method is the core component of the multiparameter reactor database system used in the reactor physics code DRAGON for performing cross section interpolation (Hébert, 2009). We will show that Ceschino polynomial expansion theory is an attractive choice for computing such interpolation factors and propose sample Matlab scripts for performing this task.

2. Ceschino polynomial expansion theory

The polynomial expansion theory is first applied over the one-dimensional domain depicted in Fig. 1. A continuous function $f(x)$ is defined over this domain and is known at specific abscissa points $x_{m+1/2}$. A $(J+1)$–th order Taylor series expansion of $f(x)$ around $x = x_{m-1/2}$ is written

$$f_{m+1/2} = \sum_{j=0}^{J} (\Delta x_m)^j \, M_{m-1/2}^{(j)} + \mathcal{O}(\Delta x_m)^{J+1} \tag{1}$$

where the mesh width is equal to

$$\Delta x_m = x_{m+1/2} - x_{m-1/2} \tag{2}$$

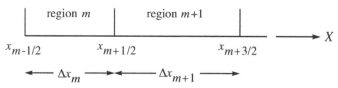

Fig. 1. Definition of the 1D domain.

and where

$$f_{m+1/2} \equiv f(x_{m+1/2}) \equiv M^{(0)}_{m+1/2} \quad \text{and} \quad M^{(j)}_{m-1/2} \equiv \frac{1}{j!}\frac{d^j f}{dx^j}\bigg|_{x_{m-1/2}}. \tag{3}$$

A Ceschino expansion is nothing but the Taylor's expansion for the derivatives $f^{(k)}(x)$ of function $f(x)$. It is written

$$M^{(k)}_{m+1/2} = \sum_{j=k}^{J}(\Delta x_m)^{j-k}\binom{j}{k}M^{(j)}_{m-1/2} + \mathcal{O}(\Delta x_m)^{J-k+1} \tag{4}$$

where the binomial coefficients are defined as

$$\binom{j}{k} \equiv \frac{j!}{(j-k)!\,k!}. \tag{5}$$

Our interpolation strategy is based on two– and three–point coupling relations obtained directly from the Ceschino polynomial expansion (4). Two points relations are used at the extremities of the domain and three–point relations are used inside. Cubic Hermite polynomials will also be introduced to perform the interpolation operation.

2.1 Two–points Ceschino coupling relations
Our relations are coupling the first N derivatives of $f(x)$, with $N = 1$ leading to a cubic interpolation strategy. We set $J = 2N$ in Eq. (4), leading to a truncation error of order $2N + 1$ if $k = 0$. We next perform a linear combination of the first N components $M^{(k)}_{m+1/2}$, introducing coefficients θ_k. The linear combination permits to maintain the order of the truncation error to $2N + 1$. We write

$$\sum_{k=0}^{N}\theta_k M^{(k)}_{m+1/2} = \sum_{k=0}^{N}\sum_{j=k}^{2N}\theta_k(\Delta x_m)^{j-k}\binom{j}{k}M^{(j)}_{m-1/2} + \mathcal{O}(\Delta x_m)^{2N+1}. \tag{6}$$

After permutation of the two summations with the corresponding indices j and k in the right-hand-side, we get

$$\sum_{k=0}^{N}\theta_k M^{(k)}_{m+1/2} = \sum_{k=0}^{N}\sum_{j=0}^{k}\theta_j(\Delta x_m)^{k-j}\binom{k}{j}M^{(k)}_{m-1/2}$$
$$+ \sum_{k=N+1}^{2N}\sum_{j=0}^{N}\theta_j(\Delta x_m)^{k-j}\binom{k}{j}M^{(k)}_{m-1/2} + \mathcal{O}(\Delta x_m)^{2N+1}. \tag{7}$$

We choose coefficients θ_j in such a way that

$$\sum_{j=0}^{N} \theta_j (\Delta x_m)^{k-j} \binom{k}{j} = 0 \; ; \; k = N+1, 2N \tag{8}$$

and we define coefficients $\bar{\theta}_k$ as

$$\bar{\theta}_k = -\sum_{j=0}^{k} \theta_j (\Delta x_m)^{k-j} \binom{k}{j} \; ; \; k = 0, N \; . \tag{9}$$

We have obtained our $(2N+1)$–th order two–points Ceschino coupling relations as

$$\sum_{k=0}^{N} \left[\bar{\theta}_k M^{(k)}_{m-1/2} + \theta_k M^{(k)}_{m+1/2} \right] = 0 \; . \tag{10}$$

where the $\mathcal{O}(\Delta x_m)^{2N+1}$ error term is not given.

We need to determine a set of $2(N+1)$ coefficients θ_k and $\bar{\theta}_k$. Equations (8) and (9) permit to determine $2N+1$ of them, leaving θ_0 to be fixed. However, all values of θ_0 leads to valid solutions, making this choice arbitrary. We have chosen $\theta_0 = 1/(\Delta x_m)^2$ in order to simplify the resulting mathematical formalism.

In the specific case of cubic Ceschino interpolation, we set $N = 1$, so that Eqs. (8) and (9) reduce to

$$2\Delta x_m \, \theta_1 = -(\Delta x_m)^2 \, \theta_0$$
$$\bar{\theta}_0 = -\theta_0$$
$$\text{and} \; \bar{\theta}_1 = -\Delta x_m \, \theta_0 - \theta_1 \tag{11}$$

so that our coefficients are

$$\bar{\theta}_0 = -\frac{1}{(\Delta x_m)^2} \; , \quad \theta_0 = \frac{1}{(\Delta x_m)^2}$$
$$\bar{\theta}_1 = -\frac{1}{2\Delta x_m} \; \text{and} \; \theta_1 = -\frac{1}{2\Delta x_m} \; . \tag{12}$$

2.2 Three–points Ceschino coupling relations

The three–points Ceschino coupling relations span two consecutive regions along the X axis, as depicted in Fig. 1. We set $J = 3N$ in Eq. (4), leading to a truncation error of order $3N + 1$ if $k = 0$. The Ceschino expansion are written

$$M^{(k)}_{m-1/2} = \sum_{j=k}^{3N} (-\Delta x_m)^{j-k} \binom{j}{k} M^{(j)}_{m+1/2} + \mathcal{O}(\Delta x_m)^{3N-k+1}$$

$$M^{(k)}_{m+3/2} = \sum_{j=k}^{3N} (\Delta x_{m+1})^{j-k} \binom{j}{k} M^{(j)}_{m+1/2} + \mathcal{O}(\Delta x_{m+1})^{3N-k+1} \tag{13}$$

where the mesh widths are equal to

$$\Delta x_m = x_{m+1/2} - x_{m-1/2} \quad \text{and} \quad \Delta x_{m+1} = x_{m+3/2} - x_{m+1/2} \; . \tag{14}$$

We next perform a linear combination of the first N components $M^{(k)}_{m-1/2}$ and $M^{(k)}_{m+3/2}$, introducing coefficients $\check{\beta}_k$ and β_k. The linear combination permits to maintain the order of the truncation error to $3N + 1$. We write

$$\sum_{k=0}^{N} \check{\beta}_k\, M^{(k)}_{m-1/2} + \beta_k\, M^{(k)}_{m+3/2}$$

$$= \sum_{k=0}^{N} \sum_{j=k}^{3N} \left[\check{\beta}_k\, (-\Delta x_m)^{j-k} + \beta_k\, (\Delta x_{m+1})^{j-k} \right] \binom{j}{k} M^{(j)}_{m+1/2} \tag{15}$$

where the truncation error is a linear combination of $\mathcal{O}(\Delta x_m)^{3N+1}$ and $\mathcal{O}(\Delta x_{m+1})^{3N+1}$. After permutation of the two summations with the corresponding indices j and k in the right-hand-side, we get

$$\sum_{k=0}^{N} \check{\beta}_k\, M^{(k)}_{m-1/2} + \beta_k\, M^{(k)}_{m+3/2}$$

$$= \sum_{k=0}^{N} \sum_{j=0}^{k} \left[\check{\beta}_j\, (-\Delta x_m)^{k-j} + \beta_j\, (\Delta x_{m+1})^{k-j} \right] \binom{k}{j} M^{(k)}_{m+1/2}$$

$$+ \sum_{k=N+1}^{3N} \sum_{j=0}^{N} \left[\check{\beta}_j\, (-\Delta x_m)^{k-j} + \beta_j\, (\Delta x_{m+1})^{k-j} \right] \binom{k}{j} M^{(k)}_{m+1/2} \cdot \tag{16}$$

We choose coefficients $\check{\beta}_j$ and β_j in such a way that

$$\sum_{j=0}^{N} \left[\check{\beta}_j\, (-\Delta x_m)^{k-j} + \beta_j\, (\Delta x_{m+1})^{k-j} \right] \binom{k}{j} = 0 \, ; \quad k = N+1, 3N \tag{17}$$

and we define coefficients $\bar{\beta}_k$ as

$$\bar{\beta}_k = - \sum_{j=0}^{k} \left[\check{\beta}_j\, (-\Delta x_m)^{k-j} + \beta_j\, (\Delta x_{m+1})^{k-j} \right] \binom{k}{j} \, ; \quad k = 0, N \, . \tag{18}$$

We have obtained our $(3N + 1)$-th order three–points Ceschino coupling relations as

$$\sum_{k=0}^{N} \left[\check{\beta}_k\, M^{(k)}_{m-1/2} + \bar{\beta}_k\, M^{(k)}_{m+1/2} + \beta_k\, M^{(k)}_{m+3/2} \right] = 0 \, . \tag{19}$$

We need to determine a set of $3(N + 1)$ coefficients $\check{\beta}_k$, $\bar{\beta}_k$ and β_k. Equations (18) and (19) permit to determine $3N + 1$ of them, leaving $\check{\beta}_0$ and β_0 to be fixed. A first set of coefficients can be obtained by setting $\check{\beta}_0 = -1/(\Delta x_m)^2$ and $\beta_0 = 1/(\Delta x_{m+1})^2$. A second independent set can be obtained by setting $\check{\beta}'_0 = 1/(\Delta x_m)^3$ and $\beta'_0 = 1/(\Delta x_{m+1})^3$. Any other consistent set is a linear combination of these two.

In the specific case of cubic Ceschino interpolation, we set $N = 1$, so that Eqs. (17) and (18) reduce to

$$-2\Delta x_m\, \check{\beta}_1 + 2\Delta x_{m+1}\, \beta_1 = -(\Delta x_m)^2\, \check{\beta}_0 - (\Delta x_{m+1})^2\, \beta_0$$
$$3(\Delta x_m)^2\, \check{\beta}_1 + 3(\Delta x_{m+1})^2\, \beta_1 = (\Delta x_m)^3\, \check{\beta}_0 - (\Delta x_{m+1})^3\, \beta_0$$
$$\bar{\beta}_0 = -(\check{\beta}_0 + \beta_0)$$
$$\text{and} \quad \bar{\beta}_1 = \Delta x_m\, \check{\beta}_0 - \Delta x_{m+1}\, \beta_0 - (\check{\beta}_1 + \beta_1) \tag{20}$$

so that our two independent sets of coefficients are

$$\check{\beta}_0 = -\frac{1}{(\Delta x_m)^2} , \quad \bar{\beta}_0 = \frac{1}{(\Delta x_m)^2} - \frac{1}{(\Delta x_{m+1})^2} , \quad \hat{\beta}_0 = \frac{1}{(\Delta x_{m+1})^2} ,$$

$$\check{\beta}_1 = -\frac{1}{3\Delta x_m} , \quad \bar{\beta}_1 = -\frac{2}{3}\left[\frac{1}{\Delta x_m} + \frac{1}{\Delta x_{m+1}}\right] , \quad \hat{\beta}_1 = -\frac{1}{3\Delta x_{m+1}} \qquad (21)$$

and

$$\check{\beta}_0 = \frac{1}{(\Delta x_m)^3} , \quad \bar{\beta}_0 = -\frac{1}{(\Delta x_m)^3} - \frac{1}{(\Delta x_{m+1})^3} , \quad \hat{\beta}_0 = \frac{1}{(\Delta x_{m+1})^3} ,$$

$$\check{\beta}_1 = \frac{1}{2(\Delta x_m)^2} , \quad \bar{\beta}_1 = \frac{1}{2}\left[\frac{1}{(\Delta x_m)^2} - \frac{1}{(\Delta x_{m+1})^2}\right] , \quad \hat{\beta}_1 = -\frac{1}{2(\Delta x_{m+1})^2} .$$

$$(22)$$

2.3 Interpolation with cubic Hermite polynomials

Knowledge of $M^{(0)}_{m+1/2}$ and the capability to easily obtain $M^{(1)}_{m+1/2}$ on each tabulated point $x_{m+1/2}$ makes possible the interpolation of function $f(x)$ at each values of the independent variable x with a cubic Hermite polynomial in x. Such polynomial guarantee that the interpolated value and first derivative of the dependent variable remains continuous in x over the complete domain. As pointed out by (Rozon et al., 1981), this continuity property of the first derivative is often required in numerical applications such as those based on perturbation theory.

The first operation consists to solve a tridiagonal linear matrix system for obtaining the unknown vector $M^{(1)} = \text{col}\{M^{(1)}_{m+1/2}; \; m = 0, M\}$ over a M–region domain, considering the known values $M^{(0)}_{m+1/2}$ of $f(x)$ at tabulation points $x_{m+1/2}$. The linear matrix system is made with the first independent set of coefficients from Eq. (21) for linking the unknowns inside the domain. We have selected the first set in order to obtain a symmetric $\mathbb{C}$ matrix with minimum powers of Δx_m as coefficients. The first and last line coefficients are obtained from Eq. (12). Using coefficients from Eq. (12) with those from Eq. (22) leads to a singular $\mathbb{C}$ matrix. This last observation gives an additional clue for selecting three-point coefficients from Eq. (21). The linear system is written

$$\mathbb{C} \, M^{(1)} = S^{(0)} \qquad (23)$$

where the symmetric tridiagonal matrix is written

$$\mathbb{C} = \begin{bmatrix} \dfrac{1}{\Delta x_1} & \dfrac{1}{\Delta x_1} & 0 & \cdots & 0 \\[2mm] \dfrac{1}{\Delta x_1} & 2\left(\dfrac{1}{\Delta x_1} + \dfrac{1}{\Delta x_2}\right) & \dfrac{1}{\Delta x_2} & \cdots & 0 \\[2mm] 0 & \dfrac{1}{\Delta x_2} & 2\left(\dfrac{1}{\Delta x_2} + \dfrac{1}{\Delta x_3}\right) & \cdots & 0 \\[2mm] \vdots & \vdots & \vdots & \ddots & \vdots \\[2mm] 0 & 0 & 0 & \cdots & \dfrac{1}{\Delta x_M} \end{bmatrix} \qquad (24)$$

and where the source term is written

$$
S^{(0)} = \begin{bmatrix}
\frac{2}{(\Delta x_1)^2}\left(M_{3/2}^{(0)} - M_{1/2}^{(0)}\right) \\
\frac{3}{(\Delta x_1)^2}\left(M_{3/2}^{(0)} - M_{1/2}^{(0)}\right) + \frac{3}{(\Delta x_2)^2}\left(M_{5/2}^{(0)} - M_{3/2}^{(0)}\right) \\
\frac{3}{(\Delta x_2)^2}\left(M_{5/2}^{(0)} - M_{3/2}^{(0)}\right) + \frac{3}{(\Delta x_3)^2}\left(M_{7/2}^{(0)} - M_{5/2}^{(0)}\right) \\
\vdots \\
\frac{2}{(\Delta x_M)^2}\left(M_{M+1/2}^{(0)} - M_{M-1/2}^{(0)}\right)
\end{bmatrix}. \tag{25}
$$

The solution of the linear system in Eq. (23) can be performed without pivoting, as matrix $\mathbb{C}$ is diagonally dominant.

We next introduce the cubic Hermite polynomials defined over a reference region $-1/2 \leq u \leq 1/2$. They are

$$
H_1(u) = 3\left(\frac{1}{2} - u\right)^2 - 2\left(\frac{1}{2} - u\right)^3
$$

$$
H_2(u) = \left(\frac{1}{2} - u\right)^2 - \left(\frac{1}{2} - u\right)^3
$$

$$
H_3(u) = 3\left(\frac{1}{2} + u\right)^2 - 2\left(\frac{1}{2} + u\right)^3
$$

$$
H_4(u) = \left(\frac{1}{2} + u\right)^2 + \left(\frac{1}{2} + u\right)^3 \tag{26}
$$

so that a function $f(u)$ defined over this domain can be expressed as

$$
f(u) \simeq f(-1/2)\,H_1(u) + f'(-1/2)\,H_2(u) + f(1/2)\,H_3(u) + f'(1/2)\,H_4(u) \tag{27}
$$

where $-1/2 \leq u \leq 1/2$.

The above relation can be generalized to the interpolation of function $f(x)$ at ξ over region m. We first perform the change of variable

$$
u = \frac{1}{\Delta x_m}\left[\xi - \frac{1}{2}\left(x_{m-1/2} + x_{m+1/2}\right)\right] \tag{28}
$$

so that

$$
\mathcal{I}\{f(x); \xi\} = M_{m-1/2}^{(0)} H_1(u) + \Delta x_m\, M_{m-1/2}^{(1)} H_2(u) + M_{m+1/2}^{(0)} H_3(u)
$$
$$
+ \Delta x_m\, M_{m+1/2}^{(1)} H_4(u) \tag{29}
$$

where $x_{m-1/2} \leq \xi \leq x_{m+1/2}$.

2.4 Introduction of interpolation factors

Interpolation factors are useful to interpolate a large number of dependent variables at a unique value ξ of the independent variable. The interpolation factors are function only of the tabulated abscissas $\{x_{m+1/2}; \ m = 0, M\}$ and on the interpolation abscissa x. Using interpolation factors $\{t_{m+1/2}(\xi); \ m = 0, M\}$, an interpolated dependent variable $\mathcal{I}\{f(x); \xi\}$ of $f(\xi)$ is obtained from

$$\mathcal{I}\{f(x); \xi\} = \sum_{m=0}^{M} t_{m+1/2}(\xi) \, f(x_{m+1/2}) \tag{30}$$

where

$$\sum_{m=0}^{M} t_{m+1/2}(\xi) = 1 \ . \tag{31}$$

Interpolation factors can be obtained if the interpolation operation is *distributive*, that is, if it can be distributed to the sum of two functions $f(x)$ and $g(h)$ according to

$$\begin{aligned}
\mathcal{I}\{f(x) + g(x); \xi\} &= \sum_{m=0}^{M} t_{m+1/2}(\xi) \left[f(x_{m+1/2}) + g(x_{m+1/2}) \right] \\
&= \mathcal{I}\{f(x); \xi\} + \mathcal{I}\{g(x); \xi\} \ .
\end{aligned} \tag{32}$$

The simplest form of interpolation factors are those corresponding to linear Lagrange interpolation. In this case, the interpolated value of $f(x)$, with $x_{m-1/2} \leq \xi \leq x_{m+1/2}$, is given by Eq. (30) with

$$t_\alpha(\xi) = \begin{cases} \frac{1}{2} - u, & \text{if } \alpha = m - 1/2 \, ; \\ \frac{1}{2} + u, & \text{if } \alpha = m + 1/2 \, ; \\ 0, & \text{otherwise.} \end{cases} \tag{33}$$

Similar interpolation factors exist for cubic Ceschino interpolation and can be obtained with the following procedure. The source term defined in Eq. (25) can be written in matrix form as

$$S^{(0)} = \mathbb{S} \, M^{(0)} \tag{34}$$

where

$$\mathbb{S} = \begin{bmatrix} -\dfrac{2}{(\Delta x_1)^2} & \dfrac{2}{(\Delta x_1)^2} & 0 & \cdots & 0 \\[2mm] -\dfrac{3}{(\Delta x_1)^2} & \dfrac{3}{(\Delta x_1)^2} - \dfrac{3}{(\Delta x_2)^2} & \dfrac{3}{(\Delta x_2)^2} & \cdots & 0 \\[2mm] 0 & -\dfrac{3}{(\Delta x_2)^2} & \dfrac{3}{(\Delta x_2)^2} - \dfrac{3}{(\Delta x_3)^2} & \cdots & 0 \\[2mm] \vdots & \vdots & \vdots & \ddots & \vdots \\[2mm] 0 & 0 & 0 & \cdots & \dfrac{2}{(\Delta x_M)^2} \end{bmatrix} . \tag{35}$$

The interpolated value of $f(\xi)$, with $x_{m-1/2} \leq \xi \leq x_{m+1/2}$, is therefore given by the relation

$$\mathcal{I}\{f(x); \xi\} = \left[H_1(\xi)^\top + H_2(\xi)^\top \, \mathbb{C}^{-1} \mathbb{S} \right] M^{(0)} \tag{36}$$

where $H_1(\xi) = \{H_{1,m+1/2}(\xi); \; m = 0, M\}$ with

$$H_{1,\alpha}(\xi) = \begin{cases} 3\left(\frac{1}{2} - u\right)^2 - 2\left(\frac{1}{2} - u\right)^3, & \text{if } \alpha = m - 1/2 \; ; \\ 3\left(\frac{1}{2} + u\right)^2 - 2\left(\frac{1}{2} + u\right)^3, & \text{if } \alpha = m + 1/2 \; ; \\ 0, & \text{otherwise} \end{cases} \tag{37}$$

and $H_2(\xi) = \{H_{2,m+1/2}(\xi); \; m = 0, M\}$ with

$$H_{2,\alpha}(\xi) = \begin{cases} \left(\frac{1}{2} - u\right)^2 - \left(\frac{1}{2} - u\right)^3, & \text{if } \alpha = m - 1/2 \; ; \\ \left(\frac{1}{2} + u\right)^2 + \left(\frac{1}{2} + u\right)^3, & \text{if } \alpha = m + 1/2 \; ; \\ 0, & \text{otherwise.} \end{cases} \tag{38}$$

The vector $T(\xi) = \{t_{m+1/2}(\xi); \; m = 0, M\}$ of interpolation factors is obtained after transposition of Eq. (36), leading to

$$\mathcal{I}\{f(x); \xi\} = M^{(0)^\top}\left[H_1(\xi) + \mathbb{S}^\top \, \mathbb{C}^{-1} H_2(\xi)\right] \tag{39}$$

so that

$$T(\xi) = H_1(\xi) + \mathbb{S}^\top \, \mathbb{C}^{-1} H_2(\xi) \; . \tag{40}$$

3. Matlab scripts and numerical examples

Two Matlab scripts are proposed in Appendices A and B as prototypes of the cubic Ceschino interpolation method. The first script, alterp() is used to obtain the terp factors corresponding to an interpolation (if lderiv=false) or to a derivation (if lderiv=true). The second script, alteri() is used to obtain the terp factors corresponding to the definite integration of $f(x)$. The following Matlab session is an example of interpolation similar to the spline Matlab tutorial.

```
x=0:10;   y=sin(x);
xx=0:.25:10;
yy=zeros(1,size(xx,2));
for i=1:size(xx,2)
   yy(i)=y*alterp(x,xx(i),false);
end
plot(x,y,'o',xx,yy)
```

Execution of the above script leads to Fig. 2. Similarly, the first derivative of $f(x) = sin(x)$ can be computed by setting $lderiv = true$, as described in the following Matlab session.

```
yy=zeros(1,size(xx,2));
for i=1:size(xx,2)
   yy(i)=y*alterp(x,xx(i),true);
end
plot(x,cos(x),'o',xx,yy)
```

Execution of the above script leads to Fig. 3. We observe that the order of the numerical derivation approximation is less than the order of the interpolation, as expected. The higher derivation errors are observed at extremities of the domain, where two-point Ceschino coupling relation are used.

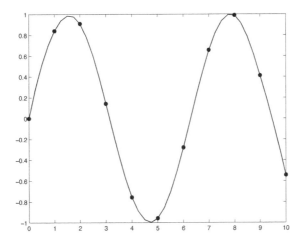

Fig. 2. Interpolation example.

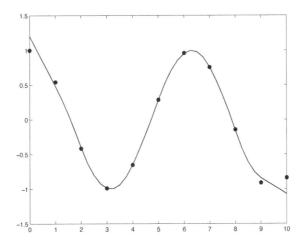

Fig. 3. Derivation example.

4. Conclusion

We have presented a straightforward numerical technique based on Ceschino polynomial expansion. Three applications of this approach permit to perform interpolation, derivation and definite integration of tabulated data. Equation (36) is efficient to interpolate few dependent variables over a large number of points ζ. Equation (39) introduces the concept of *interpolation factors* and is efficient to interpolate a large number of dependent variables over a few number of points ζ. Matlab scripts are provided as basic implementation of the Ceschino interpolating method.

The Ceschino interpolation technique is an alternative to the cubic spline approach based on different mathematical bases. In fact, the interpolating function obtained by this method is a piecewise polynomial function of degree 3 which is only a C^1 function compared to the cubic spline which is a C^2 function. It would be important to obtain error estimates to compare both approaches. However, the Ceschino interpolation technique is currently implemented in legacy applications and its behavior is already found acceptable.

Appendix A

The first Matlab script is used to compute interpolation/derivation factors (a.k.a., terp factors) using Eq. (40). The user must provide the tabulated abscissa defined as $\{x_{m+1/2}; m = 0, M\}$ and one interpolation point ξ. A logical variable, lderiv, select interpolation or derivation mode. The script returns a column vector containing the corresponding terp factors $\{t_{m+1/2}(\xi); m = 0, M\}$.

```
function terp=alterp(x,val,lderiv)
% determination of the terp interpolation/derivation factors using
% the order 4 Ceschino method with cubic Hermite polynomials.
% function terp=alterp(x,val,lderiv)
% input parameters:
% x         abscissas (row vector)
% val       abscissa of the interpolated point.
% lderiv    set to true to compute the first derivative with respect to x.
%           set to false to interpolate.
% output parameters:
% terp      interpolation factors (column vector)
% (c) 2007 Alain Hebert, Ecole Polytechnique de Montreal
   n=size(x,2) ;
   if n <= 1
      error('invalid number of points')
   end
   terp=zeros(n,1) ;
   if n == 2
      if lderiv
         terp(1)=-1.0/(x(2)-x(1)) ;
         terp(2)=1.0/(x(2)-x(1)) ;
      else
         terp(1)=(x(2)-val)/(x(2)-x(1)) ;
         terp(2)=1.0-terp(1) ;
      end
   else
      wk=zeros(3,n) ;
%----
%  interval identification.
%----
      temp1=find(val>=x(1:end-1)) ;
      temp2=find(val<=x(2:end)) ;
      if (size(temp1,2) == 0) | (size(temp2,2) == 0)
         error('unable to interpolate')
      end
      i0=temp1(end) ;
      dx=x(i0+1)-x(i0) ;
      u=(val-0.5*(x(i0)+x(i0+1)))/dx ;
```

```
      if lderiv
         h1=(-6.0*(0.5-u)+6.0*(0.5-u)^2)/dx ;
         h2=(-2.0*(0.5-u)+3.0*(0.5-u)^2)/dx ;
         h3=(6.0*(0.5+u)-6.0*(0.5+u)^2)/dx ;
         h4=(-2.0*(0.5+u)+3.0*(0.5+u)^2)/dx ;
         test=0.0 ;
      else
         h1=3.0*(0.5-u)^2-2.0*(0.5-u)^3 ;
         h2=(0.5-u)^2-(0.5-u)^3 ;
         h3=3.0*(0.5+u)^2-2.0*(0.5+u)^3 ;
         h4=-(0.5+u)^2+(0.5+u)^3 ;
         test=1.0 ;
      end
      terp(i0)=h1 ;
      terp(i0+1)=h3 ;
      wk(3,i0)=h2*dx ;
      wk(3,i0+1)=h4*dx ;
%----
%  compute the coefficient matrix.
%----
      hp=1.0/(x(2)-x(1)) ;
      wk(1,1)=hp ;
      wk(2,1)=hp ;
      for i=2:n-1
         hm=hp ;
         hp=1.0/(x(i+1)-x(i)) ;
         wk(1,i)=2.0*(hm+hp) ;
         wk(2,i)=hp ;
      end
      wk(1,n)=hp ;
      wk(2,n)=hp ;
%----
%  forward elimination.
%----
      pmx=wk(1,1) ;
      wk(3,1)=wk(3,1)/pmx ;
      for i=2:n
         gar=wk(2,i-1) ;
         wk(2,i-1)=wk(2,i-1)/pmx ;
         pmx=wk(1,i)-gar*wk(2,i-1) ;
         wk(3,i)=(wk(3,i)-gar*wk(3,i-1))/pmx ;
      end
%----
%  back substitution.
%----
      for i=n-1:-1:1
         wk(3,i)=wk(3,i)-wk(2,i)*wk(3,i+1) ;
      end
%----
%  compute the interpolation factors.
%----
      gar=zeros(1,n+2) ;
      gar(2:n+1)=wk(3,:) ;
      wk=zeros(3,n) ;
      hp2=1.0/(x(2)-x(1)) ;
```

```
   wk(2,1)=-2.0*hp2*hp2 ;
   wk(1,2)=2.0*hp2*hp2 ;
   for i=2:n-1
      hp1=hp2 ;
      hp2=1.0/(x(i+1)-x(i)) ;
      wk(3,i-1)=-3.0*hp1*hp1 ;
      wk(2,i)=3.0*hp1*hp1-3.0*hp2*hp2 ;
      wk(1,i+1)=3.0*hp2*hp2 ;
   end
   wk(3,n-1)=-2.0*hp2*hp2 ;
   wk(2,n)=2.0*hp2*hp2 ;
   for j=1:n
      terp(j)=terp(j)+gar(j:j+2)*wk(:,j) ;
      test=test-terp(j) ;
   end
   if abs(test) > 1.0e-5
      error('wrong terp factors')
   end
   terp(find(abs(terp) <= 1.0e-7))=0.0 ;
end
```

Appendix B

The second Matlab script is used to compute integration factors permitting to evaluate a definite integral. The user must provide the tabulated abscissa $\{x_{m+1/2}; \ m = 0, M\}$ and the integration limits. The script returns a column vector containing the corresponding terp factors.

```
function terp=alteri(x,val0,val1)
% determination of the terp integration factors using the order 4
% Ceschino method with cubic Hermite polynomials.
% function terp=alteri(x,val0,val1)
% input parameters:
% x       abscissas (row vector)
% val0    left integration limit.
% val1    right integration limit.
% output parameters:
% terp    integration factors (column vector)
% (c) 2007 Alain Hebert, Ecole Polytechnique de Montreal
   n=size(x,2) ;
   if n <= 1
      error('invalid number of points')
   elseif val1 <= val0
      error('invalid limits')
   elseif (val0 < x(1)) | (val1 > x(n))
      error('unable to integrate')
   end
   terp=zeros(n,1) ;
   if n == 2
      terp(1)=(x(2)-0.5*(val0+val1))*(val1-val0)/(x(2)-x(1)) ;
      terp(2)=(0.5*(val0+val1)-x(1))*(val1-val0)/(x(2)-x(1)) ;
   else
      wk=zeros(3,n) ;
%----
```

```
%  interval identification.
%----
      for i0=1:n-1
          if (val0 < x(i0+1)) & (val1 > x(i0))
             a=max(val0,x(i0)) ;
             b=min(val1,x(i0+1)) ;
             cc=0.5*(b-a) ;
             dx=x(i0+1)-x(i0) ;
             u1=(a-0.5*(x(i0)+x(i0+1)))/dx ;
             u2=(b-0.5*(x(i0)+x(i0+1)))/dx ;
             uu(1)=0.5*(-(u2-u1)/sqrt(3.0)+u1+u2) ;
             uu(2)=0.5*((u2-u1)/sqrt(3.0)+u1+u2) ;
             for js=1:2
                h1=(3.0*(0.5-uu(js))^2-2.0*(0.5-uu(js))^3)*cc ;
                h2=((0.5-uu(js))^2-(0.5-uu(js))^3)*cc ;
                h3=(3.0*(0.5+uu(js))^2-2.0*(0.5+uu(js))^3)*cc ;
                h4=(-(0.5+uu(js))^2+(0.5+uu(js))^3)*cc ;
                terp(i0)=terp(i0)+h1 ;
                terp(i0+1)=terp(i0+1)+h3 ;
                wk(3,i0)=wk(3,i0)+h2*dx ;
                wk(3,i0+1)=wk(3,i0+1)+h4*dx ;
             end
          end
      end
%----
%  compute the coefficient matrix.
%----
      hp=1.0/(x(2)-x(1)) ;
      wk(1,1)=hp ;
      wk(2,1)=hp ;
      for i=2:n-1
          hm=hp ;
          hp=1.0/(x(i+1)-x(i)) ;
          wk(1,i)=2.0*(hm+hp) ;
          wk(2,i)=hp ;
      end
      wk(1,n)=hp ;
      wk(2,n)=hp ;
%----
%  forward elimination.
%----
      pmx=wk(1,1) ;
      wk(3,1)=wk(3,1)/pmx ;
      for i=2:n
          gar=wk(2,i-1) ;
          wk(2,i-1)=wk(2,i-1)/pmx ;
          pmx=wk(1,i)-gar*wk(2,i-1) ;
          wk(3,i)=(wk(3,i)-gar*wk(3,i-1))/pmx ;
      end
%----
%  back substitution.
%----
      for i=n-1:-1:1
          wk(3,i)=wk(3,i)-wk(2,i)*wk(3,i+1) ;
      end
```

```
%----
% compute the integration factors.
%----
    test=1.0 ;
    gar=zeros(1,n+2) ;
    gar(2:n+1)=wk(3,:) ;
    wk=zeros(3,n) ;
    hp2=1.0/(x(2)-x(1)) ;
    wk(2,1)=-2.0*hp2*hp2 ;
    wk(1,2)=2.0*hp2*hp2 ;
    for i=2:n-1
       hp1=hp2 ;
       hp2=1.0/(x(i+1)-x(i)) ;
       wk(3,i-1)=-3.0*hp1*hp1 ;
       wk(2,i)=3.0*hp1*hp1-3.0*hp2*hp2 ;
       wk(1,i+1)=3.0*hp2*hp2 ;
    end
    wk(3,n-1)=-2.0*hp2*hp2 ;
    wk(2,n)=2.0*hp2*hp2 ;
    for j=1:n
       terp(j)=terp(j)+gar(j:j+2)*wk(:,j) ;
       test=test-terp(j)/(val1-val0) ;
    end
    if abs(test) > 1.0e-5
       error('wrong terp factors')
    end
    terp(find(abs(terp) <= 1.0e-7))=0.0 ;
end
```

5. References

Ceschino, F. (1956). *L'intégration approchée des équations différentielles*, Compte Rendu de l'Académie des Sciences, Paris, 243, pp. 1478 – 1479.

Hébert, A. (2009). *Applied Reactor Physics*, Presses Internationales Polytechnique, ISBN 978-2-553-01436-9, 424 p., Montréal.

MacFarlane, R. E. (1984). *TRANSX-CTR: A code for Interfacing MATXS Cross-Section Libraries to Nuclear Transport Codes for Fusion Systems Analysis*, LA-9863-MS, Los Alamos Scientific Laboratory, New Mexico.

Pageau, R. (1975). *Application des méthodes TCNR et des séries de Fourier aux Problèmes statique bi-dimensionnels en physique des réacteurs*, Master Thesis, École Polytechnique de Montréal.

Rozon, D.; Hébert, A.; McNabb, D. (1981). *The Application of Generalized Perturbation Theory and Mathematical Programming to Equilibrium Refueling Studies of a CANDU Reactor*, Nucl. Sci. Eng., 78, pp. 211 – 226.

4

Comparison of Methodologies for Analysis of Longitudinal Data Using MATLAB

João Eduardo da Silva Pereira, Janete Pereira Amador
and Angela Pellegrin Ansuj
Federal University of Santa Maria
Brazil

1. Introduction

In several areas of scientific knowledge there is a need for studying the behavior of one or more variables using data generated by repeated measurements of the same unit of observations along time or spatial region. Due to this, many experiments are constructed in which various treatments are applied on the same plot at different times, or only one treatment is applied to an experimental unit and it is made a measurement of a characteristic or a set of features in more than one occasion [Khattree & Naik, 2000]. Castro and Riboldi [Castro & Riboldi, 2005] define data collected under these kinds of experimental setups as repeated measures. More specifically, he asserts that "repeated measures is understood as the data generated by repeatedly observing a number of investigation units under different conditions of evaluation, assuming that the units of investigation are a random sample of a population of interest". In order to analyze repeated measures data it is necessary to take a care about not independency between observations. This is so because it is expected a high degree of correlation between data collected on the same observation unit over time, and there is usually more variability in the measurements between the subjects than within a given subject. A very common type of repeated measures is longitudinal data, i.e., repeated measures where the observations within units of investigation were not or can not have been randomly assigned to different conditions of evaluation, usually time or position in space.

There are basically two paths to be taken in the analysis of longitudinal data; univariate analysis, which requires as a precondition a rigid structure of covariances, or multivariate analysis, which, despite being more flexible, is less efficient in detecting significant differences than the univariate methodology.

In Advances in Longitudinal Data Analysis [Fitzmaurice et al., 2009], Fitzmaurice comments that despite the advances made in statistical methodology in the last 30 years there has been a lag between recent developments and their widespread application to substantive problems, and adds that part of the problem why the advances have been somewhat slow to move into the mainstream is due to their limited implementation in widely available standard computer software.

In this context this work proposes to develop a single and easy computational implementation to solve a great number of practical problems of analysis of longitudinal

data, through the decomposition of the sum of squares error of the polynomial models of regression.
In light of the above, not independents the computational support MatLab looks likes an ideal tool for the implementation and dissemination of this kind of statistical analysis methods, and linear models, first because its matrix structure fits perfectly well for linear models which facilitates the construction of models for univariate and multivariate analysis, and second because being a large diffusion tool of, it allows for that the models to be implemented, modified and reused in several uses in different situations by several users who have access to a MatLab community on the internet. This avoids the need for the acquisition of expensive software with black box structure.

2. Review

As far as the analysis of experiments using longitudinal data is concerned the methods traditionally used are: univariate analyis or Univariate Profile Model whereby longitudinal data is considered as if it were observations done in subdivisions of the slots, usually requiring that the variance of the response be constant in the occasions of evaluation and that the covariance between responses in different occasions be equal; multivariate analysis or Multivariate Profile Model whereby it is admitted that these variances and covariances be distinct. Despite its apparent versatility, as far as the dimension of the matrix of variances and covariances, the multivariate model becomes less attractive, because its results are hard to interpret, and its estimates are not consistent. The univariate profile model gives consistent estimates and should be used every time when its presuppositions are met. Otherwise, the multivariate profile model is a viable alternative [Castro & Riboldi, 2005; Johnson & Wichern, 1998].
Using the univariate analysis in split-plot designs, regarding time as a sub-plot may cause problems because, as it is known, this design presupposes that the covariance matrix meets the condition of sphericity which does not always happen. What is found in the literature is that repeated measures in one same experimental unit along time are in general correlated, and that these correlations are greater for closer times [Malheiros, 1999].
Xavier [Xavier, 2000] asserts that a sufficient condition for the F test of the analysis of variance of the sub-plots for the time factor and the interaction time*treatments, be valid, is that the covariance matrix has a so called composite symmetry shape. The composite symmetry occurs when the variance and covariance matrix may be expressed as:

$$\Sigma = \begin{bmatrix} (\sigma^2 + \sigma_1^2) & \sigma_1^2 & \sigma_1^2 & \sigma_1^2 \\ \sigma_1^2 & (\sigma^2 + \sigma_1^2) & \sigma_1^2 & \sigma_1^2 \\ \sigma_1^2 & \sigma_1^2 & (\sigma^2 + \sigma_1^2) & \sigma_1^2 \\ \sigma_1^2 & \sigma_1^2 & \sigma_1^2 & (\sigma^2 + \sigma_1^2) \end{bmatrix} \tag{1}$$

where:
σ^2 : is the variance of the sub-plot (within-subjects);
σ_1^2 : is the variance of the plot (among-subjects).

The composite symmetry condition implies that the random variable be equally correlated and has equal variances considering the different occasions. A more general condition of the

Σ is described by Huynh and Feldt [Huynh & Feldt, 1970]. This condition, called HUYNH-FELDT (H-F) or sphericity condition (circularity), specifies that the elements of the Σ matrix be expressed for one $\lambda > 0$, as:

$$\Sigma = \begin{bmatrix} \sigma_1^2 & \dfrac{(\sigma_1^2 + \sigma_2^2)}{2} - \lambda & \dfrac{(\sigma_1^2 + \sigma_3^2)}{2} - \lambda & \dfrac{(\sigma_1^2 + \sigma_4^2)}{2} - \lambda \\[3mm] \dfrac{(\sigma_1^2 + \sigma_2^2)}{2} - \lambda & \sigma_2^2 & \dfrac{(\sigma_2^2 + \sigma_3^2)}{2} - \lambda & \dfrac{(\sigma_2^2 + \sigma_4^2)}{2} - \lambda \\[3mm] \dfrac{(\sigma_3^2 + \sigma_1^2)}{2} - \lambda & \dfrac{(\sigma_3^2 + \sigma_2^2)}{2} - \lambda & \sigma_3^2 & \dfrac{(\sigma_3^2 + \sigma_4^2)}{2} - \lambda \\[3mm] \dfrac{(\sigma_4^2 + \sigma_1^2)}{2} - \lambda & \dfrac{(\sigma_4^2 + \sigma_2^2)}{2} - \lambda & \dfrac{(\sigma_4^2 + \sigma_3^2)}{2} - \lambda & \sigma_4^2 \end{bmatrix} \qquad (2)$$

where λ is the difference between the means of the variances and the means of the covariances.

The H-F condition is necessary and sufficient for the F test in the usual analysis of variance in split-plot in time to be valid. This condition is equivalent to specifying that the variances of the difference between pairs of errors are equal, and if the variances are all equal then the condition is equivalent to compound symmetry [Xavier, 2000].

To check the condition of circularity Mauchly [Mauchly, 1940] presents the test of sphericity. This test uses H-F condition for the covariance matrix of (t-1) normalized orthogonal contrasts for repeated measures not correlated with equal variances. Vonesh and Chinchilli [Vonesh & Chinchilli, 1997] state that the sphericity test is not very powerful for small samples and is not robust when there is violation of the normality assumption.

According to Box; Greenhouse & Geisser; and Huynh & Feldt [Box, 1954; Greenhouse & Geisser, 1959; Huynh & Feldt, 1976], although the matrix Σ may not satisfy the condition of sphericity, the central F distribution may be used, in an approximate form, if a correction in the degrees of freedom associated with the causes of variation involving the time factor is made. The degrees of freedom correction in these sources of variation is done by multiplying the original degrees by a factor ε. When Σ is uniform, the value of $\varepsilon = 1$.

According to Freitas [Freitas, 2007] the correction of the number of degrees of freedom should be made only in statistics that involve comparisons within subjects (time factor and interaction time*treatments). The statistics involving comparisons between subjects do not need corrections in the degrees of freedom because there is always an exact central F distribution.

When the pattern of the Σ matrix is not satisfied, not even close, the multivariate techniques are used since this type of solution is applicable to any Σ matrix. The only requirement of the multivariate procedure is that the Σ matrix should be common to all treatments.

Due to the essentially multivariate nature of the response vectors, in studies involving longitudinal data, the multivariate analysis technique also known as multivariate profile analysis is a natural alternative to the problem at hand [Wald, 2000]. The multivariate profile analysis is well discussed in the literature by authors such as [Lima, 1996; Morrison, 1990; Singer, 1986].

The multivariate profile analysis is one of the statistics technique used to analyze observations derived from experiments that use longitudinal data. This technique bases itself both in the number of experimental units and the sample size [Castro, 1997].

Unlike the univariate profile analysis model, the multivariate profile analysis model does not require that the variance of the repeated measures or that the correlation between pairs of repeated measures remain constant along time. Nevertheless, both models require that the variances and the correlations be homogeneous in each moment in time [Vieira, 2006].

The routine techniques for analysis of variance impose the condition of independence of observations. However, this restriction generally does not apply to longitudinal data where the observations in the same individual are usually correlated. In such case, the adequate manner for treating the observations would be the multivariate form [Vonesh & Chinchilli, 1997].

Cole & Grizzle [Cole & Grizzle, 1966] use the multivariate analysis of variance according to the Smith et al. [Smith et al., 1962] formulation and comment on its versatility in the construction of specific hypothesis testing that may be obtained as particular cases of the general linear multivariate hypothesis test procedure. They assert that such hypothesis may be tested by three alternative criterions, all of which dependent on characteristic roots of matrix functions due to the hypothesis and of the matrix due to the error: criterion of the maximum characteristic root, criterion of the product of the roots (criterion of the verosimilarity ratio) and criterion of the sum of the roots. The authors illustrate the application of the multivariate analysis of variance and demonstrate that the information requested from these experiments may be formulated in terms of the following null hypotheses:

i.   there are no principal effects of "measured conditions" (occasions);
ii.   there are no effects of treatments;
iii. there is no interaction of treatment and occasions.

The multivariate analysis of variance is a powerful instrument to analyze longitudinal data but if the uniformity hypothesis of the variance and covariance matrix is not rejected the univariate analysis should be employed. Nonetheless, if the variance and covariance matrix of repeated measures has the serial correlation structure one should use an analysis method that takes into account the structure of this matrix in order that one might have an increment in the testing power. In this way the multivariate analysis of variance becomes the most convenient one if not the only appropriate one among the available procedures [Cole & Grizzle, 1966; Smith et al., 1962].

Lima [Lima, 1996] asserts that the multivariate profile analysis possesses as its main advantage the fact that is allows for the adoption of a very general model to represent the structure of covariances admitting that the variances of responses in each time and the covariances of responses between distinct times be different.

In studying longitudinal data investigation methods, Greenhouse & Geisser [Greenhouse & Geisser, 1959] observed that the ratios between the mean squares obtained in the analysis of variance for the mixed univariate model will only have exact distribution of probability F if the observations in time be normally distributed with equal variances and be mutually independent or equally correlated. Because these presuppositions are strict, the authors prefer considering the observations in time as a vector of samples of a normal multivariate distribution with an arbitrary variance and covariance matrix. Being so, the multivariate perspective presented by Morrison [Morrison, 1990] allows for the adoption of a general model to represent the covariance structure of the observations. In this case, the covariance

matrix is known as being non structured where all variances and covariances might be different and, as pointed out by Andreoni [Andreoni, 1989], it is only applicable when:
- there be no theoretical or empirical basis to establish any pattern for this matrix;
- there be no need to extrapolate the model beyond the occasions of the considered observations.

The quantity of parameters associated with the non structured matrix that need to be estimated is proportional to the number of conditions of evaluation. In situations where the number is large, when the number of experimental units is small in relation to the number of evaluation events or when there is the presence of many incomplete observations the efficiency of the estimators might be affected. In some cases it may be impossible to estimate the parameters of this covariance matrix [Wald, 2000].

Meredith & Stehman [Meredith & Stehman, 1991] state that the disadvantage of the multivariate analysis is the lack of power to estimate the parameters of the covariance matrix in case when t (number of measurement events or times) is large and n is small.

Stuker [Stuker, 1986] comments on the restriction of the multivariate analysis of covariance in which the number of experimental units minus the number of treatments should be greater than the number of observations taken in each experimental unit otherwise the required matrix due to error for these tests is singular.

Timm [Timm, 1980] claims that the restrictions to the application of the multivariate profile analysis occur due to the need for complete individual response profiles and to the low power of these hypothesis tests due to excessive parametering. On the other hand, except for these restrictions, the majority of the cases in longitudinal data studies, the analysis procedure of multivariate analysis of variance is the most convenient if not the only appropriate one among the available techniques.

3. Materials and methods

3.1 Data

In order to conduct the study it was created a data matrix with the following structure: $\underline{Y} = y_{ijk}$, where y_{ijk} is the observation j belonged the period i of the treatment k. To simulate growth curves composed of two treatments, seven observations over time and five repetitions, each observation of Y matrix was defined as $y_{ijk} = f_i + \varepsilon_{ijr}$ with a fixed part f_i, with i = 1,2, and where $f_1 = 46 + 88X - 57X^2$ and $f_2 = 42 + 88X + 53X^2$ and a variable portion ε_{ijk} randomly generated with normal distribution with zero mean and variance proportional to $E(f_i)$ in which the variation coefficient remains constant in 0,05, under these conditions is imposed on the model f_1 a linear growth higher than compared to the f_2 model and both with the same regression model.

3.1.1 Data base structure

To analyze the longitudinal data, the data base was structured in the following way; the first column refers to the independent variable $X = [x_i]$ or to periods with i = 1...p, the second column the response variable $Y = [y_{ijk}]$, in which y_{ijk}, refers to the observation referring to the repetition j of the period i of treatment k, with j = 1...r ., and the third column refers to the control variable $F = [f_k]$ or treatments, with j = 1...t .

$$\text{File.txt} = \begin{bmatrix} 1 & y_{111} & 1 \\ \cdot & y_{121} & \cdot \\ \cdot & \cdot & \cdot \\ \cdot & \cdot & \cdot \\ p & y_{prt} & t \end{bmatrix} \tag{3}$$

The following Matlab commands upload and dimension the file in addition to determining the index of the column of each variable.

M=load('-ascii', 'file.txt');
[n,c]=size(M);
a=input('column of the independent variable X =');
b=input('column of the dependent variable Y =');
aa=input('initial column of the control variable curve =');
nc=input('number of curves to be compared =');
npc=input('number of points per curve =');

3.2 Data analysis

Once the data base is correctly structured the first step is to adjust the best polynomial model that explains the variation of Y in function of the X periods. Towards this, the parameters of the polynomial of adjustment will be estimated by the matrix expression below.

$$\hat{Y} = BX \tag{4}$$

$$\beta = [bo \quad b_1 \quad .... \quad b_g] \tag{5}$$

in which g is a degree of the polynomial

$$X = [1 \quad x_i \quad x_i^2 . \quad . \quad . \quad x_i^g] \tag{6}$$

$$\hat{\beta} = (X'X)^{-1}(X'Y) \tag{7}$$

To determine what is the best degree of the polynomial for the data under analysis it was used a scatterplot. The following commands prepare the data for visualization.

x=M(:,a:(b-1));
Y=M(:,b:(aa-1));
Trat=M(:,aa);
M=[x Y Trat];
[tmp,idx]=sort(M(:,aa));
M=M(idx,:),
set(plot(x,Y,'o'))

From the scatterplot, choose the degree of polynomial to be adjusted.

g=input('choose the degree of polynomial Degree =');

The following procedures were used to estimate $\hat{\beta}$

[n,r]=size(M);
X=ones(n,npc);

```
y1=ones(n,1);
for i=2:npc
X(:,i)=M(:,a).*y1;
y1=X(:,i);
end
X=X(:,1:(d+1));
BT=(inv((X'*X)))*(X'*(M(:,b:aa-1)));
```

To test the hypothesis: $H_0 : \beta = 0$ against $H_1 : \beta \neq 0$, the F test is employed.

$$F = \frac{QMr}{QM\varepsilon} \tag{8}$$

that have the Snedecor F distribution with (g-1) and (n-g) degrees of freedom.

$$QMr = \frac{1}{(g-1)}\beta(X'Y) - n\bar{Y}^2 \tag{9}$$

$$QM\varepsilon = \frac{1}{(n-g)}[(Y'Y) - \beta(X'Y)] = \frac{1}{(n-g)}(Y - \hat{Y})'(Y - \hat{Y}) \tag{10}$$

And to measure the degree of explanation of the variability of Y according to the polynomial model it is used the coefficient of determination.

$$R^2 = \frac{SQr}{SQT} \tag{11}$$

$$SQr = \beta(X'Y) - n\bar{Y}^2 \tag{12}$$

$$SQT = (Y'Y) - n\bar{Y}^2 \tag{13}$$

And to measure the degree of explanation of the Y variability in function of the polynomial model it is employed the determination coefficient.

$$R^2 = \frac{SQr}{SQT} \tag{14}$$

in which

$$SQr = \beta(X'Y) - n\bar{Y}^2 \tag{15}$$

and

$$SQT = (Y'Y) - n\bar{Y}^2 \tag{16}$$

After the adjustment of the polynomial model for the data set, the next step is to adjust the same model for each of the k treatments separately, so

$$\hat{Y}_k = (X'X)^{-1}(X'Y_k) \tag{17}$$

Where

$$\hat{b}_k = (X'X)^{-1}(X'Yk) \tag{18}$$

The test for comparing the curves is based on the decomposition of SQε in one part explained by the variation between the curves and the other by the variation within the curves.

$$SQ\varepsilon = \sum_{k=1}^{t} (\hat{Y} - \hat{Y}k)'(\hat{Y} - \hat{Y}k) + \sum_{k=1}^{t} (\hat{Y}k - Y_k)'(\hat{Y}k - Yk) \tag{19}$$

in which $\sum_{K=1}^{t} (\hat{Y} - \hat{Y}k)'(\hat{Y} - \hat{Y}k)$ is the variation explained by the treatments, and $\sum_{K=1}^{t} (\hat{Y}k - Y_k)'(\hat{Y}k - Yk)$ is the variation within each treatment.

$$\text{And the} \quad F = \frac{\sum\limits_{k=1}^{t} ((\hat{Y} - \hat{Y}k)'(\hat{Y} - Yk))(n - t)(p - 1)}{\sum\limits_{K=1}^{t} ((\hat{Y} - Yk)'(\hat{Y} - Yk))(p - 1)(t - 1)} \tag{20}$$

has a Snedecor F distribution with $(p - 1)(t - 1)$ and $(n - t)(p - 1)$ degrees of freedom.

$$\text{And the reason} \quad F = \frac{\sum\limits_{k=1}^{t} ((\hat{Y} - \hat{Y}k)'(\hat{Y} - Yk))(n - t)(p - 1)}{\sum\limits_{K=1}^{t} ((\hat{Y} - Yk)'(\hat{Y} - Yk))(p - 1)(t - 1)} \tag{21}$$

Has a Snedecor F distribution with $(p - 1)(t - 1)$ and $(n - t)(p - 1)$ degrees of freedom.

The following commands calculate the regression parameters for the individual curves.

```
[c,r]=size(M1);
Yobs(:,i)=M1(:,b)
X=ones(c,npc);
y1=ones(c,1);
for j=2:npc
X(:,j)=M1(:,a).*y1;
y1=X(:,j);
end
Y=M1(:,b);
X=X(:,1:(d+1));
B(:,i)=(inv((X'*X)))*(X'*Y);
Y1est(:,i)=X*BT;
end
```

The following commands print the graph with the curves estimated.

```
Yest=X*B;
y=[Y1est Yest];
x=X(:,b);
plot(x,y)
```

The following commands execute analysis of variance.

```
[n,c]=size(M)
 SQmodelo=sum(sum((Y1est-Yest).*(Y1est-Yest)))
SQerro=sum(sum((Yest-Yobs).*(Yest-Yobs)))
SQtotal=sum(sum((Y1est-Yobs).*(Y1est-Yobs)))
glmodelo=(npc-1)*(nc-1)
gltotal=(n-nc)
glerro=gltotal-glmode
R=(SQmodelo/SQtotal)
F=(SQmodelo/glmodelo)/(SQerro/glerro)
p=fpdf(F,glmodelo,glerro)
```

The following commands format the ANOVA Table printout.

```
Table=zeros(3,5);
Table(:,1)=[ RSS SSE TSS]';
Table(:,2)=[df1 df2 df3]';
Table(:,3)=[ RSS/df1 SSE/df2 Inf ]';
Table(:,4)=[ F Inf Inf ]';
Table(:,5)=[ p Inf Inf ]';
colheads = ['Source     ';'     SS ';'     df ';...
       '    MS  ';'    F ';'   Prob>F '];
  atab = num2cell(Table);
for i=1:size(atab,1)
  for j=1:size(atab,2)
    if (isinf(atab{i,j}))
      atab{i,j} = [];
    end
  end
end
if (nargout > 1)
  anovatab = atab
end
```

The following commands prepare the file for the multivariate analysis.

```
M=[X Yobs];
nt=M(:,2);
  x=nt(1);
  n=1;
  idx=1;
  for i=2:length(nt)
    if nt(i)==x(idx)
      n(idx)=n(idx)+1;
    else
```

```
        idx=idx+1;
        x(idx)=nt(i);
        n(idx)=1;
    end
n=cumsum(n);
    B=ones(d+1,nc);
    for i=1:length(n)
        idx=find(M(:,aa)==M(n(i),aa));
M2=M(idx,:);
    end
```

For the multivariate analysis it was employed a new structure of the data file.

File2.txt= $[x_{jk} \quad y_{1jk} \quad \cdot \quad \cdot \quad \cdot \quad y_{pjk}]$

File2.txt=[X Y]

In which, the first column has the values for the j repetitions for each of the k treatments, each one of the following i columns contains the values of Y for the j repetitions of the k treatments. As seen in the structure below.

$$
\text{File2.txt} = \begin{bmatrix}
x_{11} & y_{111} & \cdot & \cdot & \cdot & \cdot & \cdot & y_{711} \\
x_{21} & y_{121} & \cdot & \cdot & \cdot & \cdot & \cdot & y_{721} \\
x_{31} & y_{131} & \cdot & \cdot & \cdot & \cdot & \cdot & y_{731} \\
x_{41} & y_{141} & \cdot & \cdot & \cdot & \cdot & \cdot & y_{741} \\
x_{51} & y_{151} & \cdot & \cdot & \cdot & \cdot & \cdot & y_{751} \\
x_{12} & y_{112} & \cdot & \cdot & \cdot & \cdot & \cdot & y_{712} \\
x_{22} & y_{122} & \cdot & \cdot & \cdot & \cdot & \cdot & y_{722} \\
x_{32} & y_{132} & \cdot & \cdot & \cdot & \cdot & \cdot & y_{732} \\
x_{42} & y_{142} & \cdot & \cdot & \cdot & \cdot & \cdot & y_{742} \\
x_{52} & y_{152} & \cdot & \cdot & \cdot & \cdot & \cdot & y_{752}
\end{bmatrix}
\tag{22}
$$

The following commands change the structure of the file.

```
        M=Mtemp;
    [n,c]=size(M);
    nt=M(:,1);
    z=nt(1);
    n=1;
    idx=1;
    for i=2:length(nt);
        if nt(i)==z(idx)
            n(idx)=n(idx)+1;
        else
            idx=idx+1;
            z(idx)=nt(i);
            n(idx)=1;
        end
```

```
    end
    n=cumsum(n);
    for i=1:npc
        idx=find(M(:,a)==M(n(i),a));
        M1=M(idx,:);
        trat=M1(:,aa);
        M1=M1(:,b);
        Ymult(:,i)=M1;
    end
    Y=[trat Ymult];
```

For the multivariate data analysis the employed procedure was proposed by Johnson and Wishern [Johnson and Wishern, 1998] in which the standardized variable employed for the comparison of the curves is

$$\Lambda = \frac{|W|}{|W_p|} \tag{23}$$

in which $W = (X'\beta - X'\beta T)' * (X'\beta - X'\beta T)$ (24)

$$\beta = \begin{bmatrix} b_{10} & b_{20} \\ b_{11} & b_{21} \\ b_{12} & b_{22} \end{bmatrix} = \begin{bmatrix} b_{dk} \end{bmatrix} \tag{25}$$

where $\begin{bmatrix} b_{dk} \end{bmatrix}$ is the polynomial coefficient of d order of the k treatment.

$$\beta = (X'S^{-1}X)^{-1}(X'S^{-1}\bar{Y}) \tag{26}$$

$$S = \frac{1}{(rt)}(Y - \bar{Y})'(Y - \bar{Y}) \tag{27}$$

$$W_p = (Y - X'\beta T)' * (Y - X'\beta T) \tag{28}$$

$$\beta T = (X'S_p^{-1}X)^{-1}(X'S_p^{-1}\bar{Y}) \tag{29}$$

$$S_p = \frac{1}{(n-t)}\sum_{K=1}^{t}(n_k - 1)S_k^2 \tag{30}$$

Where $S_k^2 = matrix.of.cov\,ariance.of.the.treatment.k$

In order to test if there is a difference between curves the standardized variable is employed

$$\chi^2 = -\left(N - \frac{1}{2}(p - d - t)\right)\ln\Lambda \tag{31}$$

has a chi square distribution with (p-q-1) degrees of freedom.
The following commands run the multivariate analysis.

```
x=x';
[n,c]=size(Y);
M=Y
temp=M(:,b:c);
Y1obs=temp';
V=cov(temp);
S=inv(V);
temp=(sum(temp))./n;
Y=temp;
[n,c]=size(V);
   X=ones(n,c);
   y1=ones(n,1);
   for i=2:c
      X(:,i)=x.*y1;
      y1=X(:,i);
   end
   d=input('choose the polynomial degree =');
   X=X(:,1:(d+1));
   BT=(inv(X'*S*X))*(X'*S*Y');
   Y1est=X*BT;
   plot(x,Y1est)
   [n,c]=size(Y1obs);
   temp=ones(n,c);
   for i=1:c
      temp(:,i)=Y1est;
   end
   Y1est=temp;
   Temp=Y1obs-Y1est;
   W=Temp*Temp';
```

The following commands run the analysis of individual curves.

```
   nt=M(:,a);
   z=nt(a);
  n=1;
   idx=1;
   for i=2:length(nt)
      if nt(i)==z(idx)
         n(idx)=n(idx)+1;
      else
         idx=idx+1;
         z(idx)=nt(i);
         n(idx)=1;
      end
   end
   k=n;
   n=cumsum(n);
```

```
B=zeros(d+1,length(n));
v=zeros(length(W));
sp=zeros(length(S));
for i=1:length(n)
    idx=find(M(:,a)==M(n(i),a));
    M1=M(idx,:);
    [r,c]=size(M1);
    temp=M1(:,b:c);
    Yobs=temp';
    V=cov(temp);
    V=(k(i)-1)*V;
    temp=(sum(temp))./r;
    Y(i,:)=temp;
    temp=(V+v)/(n(i)-2);
    v=temp;
    S=inv(v);
    B=(inv(X'*S*X))*(X'*S*Y');
end
Temp=zeros(npc);
 for i=1:length(n)
    idx=find(M(:,1)==M(n(i),1));
    M1=M(idx,:);
    [r,c]=size(M1);
    temp=M1(:,b:c);
    Yobs=temp';
    temp=zeros(npc,r);
    Yest=X*B(:,z(i));
    for j=1:5
       temp(:,j)=Yest;
    end
    temp=((Yobs-temp)*(Yobs-temp)');
    Temp=temp+Temp;
    Wp=Temp;
end
    Wilks=((det(Wp))/(det(W)))
    Qsquare=-(N-0.5*(npc-nc-2+d))*log(Wilks)
    df=(npc-nc-1)*d
    chi2pdf(Qsquare,df)
```

4. Results

The following parameters must be furnished when running the program:
independent variable column X   =1
dependent variable column Y =2
initial column of the control variable curve =3
number of curves to be compared =2
number of points per curve =7

The following graph is generated in order to choose the degree of the polynomial to be adjusted.

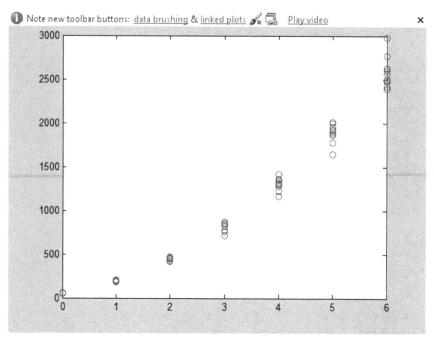

Fig. 1. Scatterplot of the data.

A second degree polynomial was chosen to model the data according to the scatterplot above.

The estimated coefficients for the second order polynomial were:

$$\hat{Y}_T = 48.464 + 81965X + 56.806X^2 \ ]$$

with (P<0000,1)

$$R^2 = 0.3405$$

The analysis of variance of the complete polynomial model is presented in table 1.

Causes of variation	DF	SS	SQ	F	P
Polynomial	2	5.2799E+007	2.6384E+007	3.8235E+003	1.2054E-072
Error	68	4.6924E+005	6.9006E+003		
Total	69	5.3238E+007			

Table 1. ANOVA for polynomial model

The output of the program has the following format
anovatab1 =

[5.2769e+007] [2] [2.6384e+007] [3.8235e+003] [1.2054e-072]
[4.6924e+005] [68] [6.9006e+003]   []   []
[5.3238e+007] [69]   []   []   []

After the choice of the polynomial model and its test of significance, the same model was applied on each one of the treatments separately, the results are as follows:

$$\hat{Y}_1 = 50.31 + 89.10X + 57.10X^2$$

$$\hat{Y}_2 = 46.90 + 76.82X + 56.55X^2$$

$$R^2 = 0.3405$$

The analysis of variance for decomposition of error was employed to test the difference between the curves and is presented in table 2.

Causes of variation	DF	SS	SQ	F	P
Polynomial	6	1.5976E+005	2.6626E+004	5.4202	2.52652E-004
Error	63	3.0948E+005	4.912E+003		
Total	69	4.6924E+005			

Table 2. Analysis of variance to compare the curves.

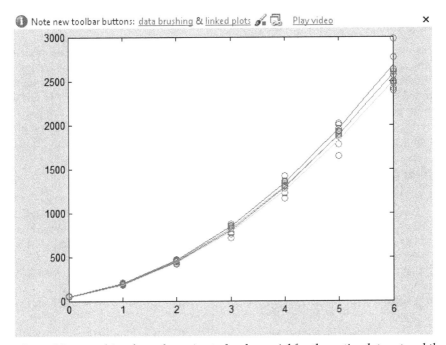

Fig. 2. Central line resulting from the estimated polynomial for the entire data set and the external lines, one for each treatment.

The output of the program has the following format:
B =   50.3069   46.9023
       89.0928   76.8230
       57.0744   56.5484
After the choice of the polynomial model and its test of significance, the same model was applied on each one of the treatments separately, the results are as follows:
anovatab =
  [1.5976e+005]   [6]   [2.6626e+004]   [5.4202]   [2.5262e-004]
  [3.0948e+005]   [63]   [4.9124e+003]   []   []
  [4.6924e+005]   [69]   []   []   []
The graph below presents a central line resulting from the estimated polynomial for the whole data set and the external lines are one for each treatment.
For the multivariate test it was calculated the standardized variable

$$\chi^2 = -\left(N - \frac{1}{2}(p - d - t)\right)\ln \Lambda = 192.0591 \text{ with } (P<0{,}001).$$

The program outputs were as follows.
Wilks =   0.0581
Chi square =   192.0591
df =   8
ans =   1.4552e-037

5. Conclusion

Given its matrix structure, Matlab presented itself as an efficient tool for linear models. The programs and the methodology presented were efficient to the comparing of polynomial growth curves. The modular sequence in which the programs were developed allows the user to implement new routines as well as new methodology proposals for the solution of the proposed problem. The solutions presented for the problem of comparison of polynomial growth curves may be used in part or in conjunction for the solution of other linear models problems.

6. References

Andrade, D. F. & Singer, J. M. (1986). Análise de dados longitudinais. *Proceedings of VII Simpósio Nacional de Probabilidade e Estatística*, pp. 19-26, Campinas, SP, Brazil, 1986.

Andreoni, S. (1989). Modelos de efeitos aleatórios para a análise de dados longitudinais não balanceados em relação ao tempo. Dissertation (MS. in Statistics) Institute of Mathematics, São Paulo University, São Paulo, Brazil, 1989.

Box, G. E. P. (1954). Some Theorems on Quadratic Forms Applied in the Study of Analysis of Variance Problems, I. Effect of Inequality of Variance in the One-Way Classification. *Annals of Mathematical Statistics*, Vol.25, No. 2, 1954, DOI: 10.1214, pp. 290-302.

Castro, S. M. J. (1997). A metodologia de análise de dados longitudinais. Thesis (BS. in Statistics), Federal University of Rio Grande do Sul, Porto Alegre, Brazil.

Castro, S. M. J. & Riboldi, J. (2005). A construção do modelo em dados longitudinais: escolha dos efeitos fixos e aleatórios, modelagem das estruturas de covariância. *Proceedings of the Annual Meeting of the Brazilian Region of the International Biometrics Society, and of the Simpósio de Estatística Aplicada a Experimentação Agronômica*, pp. 157-158, Londrina, Paraná, Brazil, 2005.

Cole, J. W. L. & Grizzle, J. E. (1966). Applications of Multivariate Analysis of Variance to Repeated Measurements Experiments. *Biometrics*, Vol. 22, 1966, ISSN 0006341x, pp. 810 – 828.

Fitzmaurice, G. et al. Ed(s).). (2009). *Longitudinal Data Analysis*. Chapman & Hall/CRC Taylor & Francis Group, ISBN 978-1-58488-658-7, Boca Raton, Florida.

Freitas, G. E. (2007). Análise de dados longitudinais em experimentos com cana-de-açúcar. Dissertation (MS. in Agronomics), Escola Superior de Agricultura "Luis de Queiroz", São Paulo University, Piracicaba, Brazil, 2007.

Greenhouse, S. W. & Geisser, S. (1959). On methods in the analysis of profile data. *Psychometrika*, Vol.24, No. 2, June 1959, DOI: 10.1007, pp.95-112.

Huynh, H. & Feldt, L.S. (1970) Condition under which mean square ratios in repeated measurements designs have exact F-distributions. *J. Am. Stat. Assoc.*, Vol.72, 1970, ISSN 0162-1459, pp.320-340.

Huynh, H. & Feldt, L. S. (1976). Estimation of the box correction for degrees of freedom from sample data in randomized block and split-plot designs. *J. Educational and Behavioral Statistics*, Vol.1, No.1, March 1976, DOI: 10.3102/10769986001001069, pp.69-82.

Johnson, R. A. & Wichern, D. W. (1998). *Applied multivariate statistical analysis*, 4 ed. Prentice Hall, ISBN 0-13-834194-x, Upper Saddle River, New Jersey.

Khattree, R. & Naik, D. N. (2000). Multivariate data reduction and discrimination with SAS software. SAS Institute Inc., ISBN 1-58025-696-1, Cary, North Carolina, USA.

Lima, C. G. (1996). Análise de dados longitudinais provenientes de experimento em blocos casualizados. Dissertation (PhD in Agronomics), Escola Superior de Agricultura "Luiz de Queiroz", São Paulo University, Piracicaba, Brazil, 1996.

Malheiros, E.B. (1999). Precisão da análise de dados longitudinais, com diferentes estruturas para a matriz de variâncias e covariância, quando se utiliza o esquema em parcelas subdivididas. *Revista de Matemática e Estatística UNESP*, Vol.17, 1999, ISSN 0102-0811, pp.263-273.

Mauchly, J. W. (1940). Significance test for sphericity of a normal n-variate distribution. *An. Math. Stat.*, Vol.11, No. 2, June 1940,ISSN 00034851, pp.204-209.

Meredith, M.P.; Stehman, S.V. (1991). Repeated measures experiments in forestry: focus on analysis of response curves. *Canadian Journal of Forest Research*, Vol.21, 1991, ISSN 0045-5067, pp.957-965.

Smith, H. R. et al. (1962). Multivariate Analysis of Variance. (MANOVA). *Biometrics*, Vol.2, 1962, ISSN 0006-341X, pp. 61 – 67.

Morrison, D. F. (1990). *Multivariate Statistical Methods*. 3 ed, McGraw-Hill, ISBN 0-07-043187-6, Singapore.

Stuker, H. (1986). Análise multivariada para dados onde a característica observada é subdividida em K classes. Dissertation (MS in Agronomics), Escola Superior de Agricultura "Luiz de Queiroz", São Paulo University, Piracicaba, 1986.

Timm, N.H. (1980). Multivariate analysis of variance of repeated measurements. In: *Handbook of Statistics Analysis of Variance*, Vol. 1, P. R. Krishnaiah (Ed), pp.41-87, North-Holland, ISBN:0444853359, New York.

Vieira, F. T. P. A. (2006). Uma Abordagem Multivariada em Experimento Silvipastoril com Leucaena leucocephala (Lam.) de Wit. no Agreste de Pernambuco. Dissertation (MS. in Biometrics), Rural Federal University of Pernambuco, Pernambuco, Brazil, 2006.

Vonesh, F. E. & Chinchilli, V.M. (1997). *Linear and nonlinear models for the analysis of repeated measurements.* Marcel Dekker, ISBN 0-8247-8248-8, New York.

Wald, V. B. (2000). A metodologia de modelos mistos não lineares aplicados à análise de dados longitudinais em plantas forrageiras. Dissertation (MS in Zootechnique), Federal University of Rio Grande do Sul, Brazil, 2000.

Xavier, L. H. (2000). Modelos univariado e multivariado para análise de medidas repetidas e verificação da acurácia do modelo univariado por meio de simulação. Dissertation (MS in Statistics and Agronomics experimentation), Escola Superior de Agricultura "Luiz de Queiroz", São Paulo University, Piracicaba, Brazil, 2000.

5

Decomposition Approach for Inverse Matrix Calculation

Krasimira Stoilova and Todor Stoilov
Institute of Information and Communication Technologies
Academy of Sciences
Bulgaria

1. Introduction

Frequently, numerical algorithms are based on sequentially solution of linear set of equation $Ax=b$, applying small influences of few components of matrix A, which changes to a new one A^*. Thus, new equation set is defined, with new matrix A^*, which has to be solved for the current numerical iteration. Instead of solving the new equation set, it is beneficial to evaluate a new inverse matrix A^{*-1}, having the evaluations for the previous inverse matrix A^{-1}. Many control algorithms, on-line decision making and optimization problems reside on the prompt evaluation of the inverse matrix A^{-1}, stated as a quadratic nonsingular, e.g. $A.A^{-1}=A^{-1}.A=I$, where I is identity matrix. Currently, for the evaluation of the inverse matrix A^{-1} three general types of A factorization are applied: LU factorization, QR – decomposition and SVD-decomposition to singular values of A.

LU – factorization. It results after the application of Gauss elimination to linear set of equations $Ax=b$ to obtain a good computational form of A (Fausett, 1999). The factorization of A is obtained by multiplication of two triangular matrices, upper U and lower L triangular, related to the initial one by $LU=A$, or

$$\begin{vmatrix} l_{11} & 0 & 0 \\ l_{21} & l_{22} & 0 \\ l_{31} & l_{32} & l_{33} \end{vmatrix} \cdot \begin{vmatrix} u_{11} & u_{12} & u_{13} \\ 0 & u_{22} & u_{23} \\ 0 & 0 & u_{33} \end{vmatrix} = \begin{vmatrix} a_{11} & a_{12} & a_{13} \\ a_{21} & a_{22} & a_{23} \\ a_{31} & a_{32} & a_{33} \end{vmatrix}.$$

The LU factorization can be applied for the solution of linear set of equations to evaluate the inverse matrix of A: A^{-1}. The evaluation of A^{-1} is performed on two steps, for given LU factorization of A, $A=LU$ (L,U - given):

First: the matrix equation $LY=I$ is solved. The first column of matrix Y is found from the linear equation system $LY(:,1)=\begin{vmatrix} 1 & 0 & ... & 0 \end{vmatrix}^T$. The next columns of Y are calculated by solving this linear equation set with the next columns of matrix I. The solution of this set of equations is found by sequential substitution from top to down, because the matrix L is a lower triangular and there is no need to find the inverse L^{-1}.

Second: Using the solution matrix Y^* a new linear matrix equation system is solved $U.X=Y^*$. Because U is upper triangular, each column of X is calculated with the corresponding column of Y^* by substitutions from bottom to top. Thus, no inverse matrix U^{-1} is calculated, which speeds up the calculations.

The solution $X=A^{-1}$ is the inverse matrix of the initial one A. Thus, the inverse matrix A^{-1} is found by LU factorization of A and twice solution of triangular linear matrix equation systems, applying substitution technique.

QR decomposition The QR decomposition of matrix A is defined by the equality $A=Q.R$, where R is upper triangular matrix and Q is orthogonal one, $Q^{-1}=Q^T$. Both matrices Q and R are real ones. As the inverse A^{-1} is needed, $A^{-1}=R^{-1}.Q^{-1}$. Following the orthogonal features of Q, it is necessary to evaluate only R^{-1}, which can be done from the linear matrix system $R.Y=I$. Because R is upper triangular matrix, the columns of the inverse matrix $Y=R^{-1}$ can be evaluated with corresponding columns of the identity matrix I by merely substitutions from bottom to down. Hence, the inverse matrix A^{-1} is found by QR factorization of A, sequential evaluation of R^{-1} by substitutions in linear upper triangular matrix system and finally by multiplication of R^{-1} and Q^T.

SVD – decomposition to singular values This decomposition is very powerful, because it allows to be solved system equations when A is singular, and the inverse A^{-1} does not exist in explicit way (Flannery, 1997). The SVD decomposition, applied to a rectangular MxN matrix A, represents the last like factorization of three matrices:

$$A=U.W.V^T,$$

where U is MxN orthogonal matrix, W is NxN diagonal matrix with nonnegative components (singular values) and V^T is a transpose NxN orthogonal matrix V or

$$U^TU=V^TV=I_{NxN}.$$

The SVD decomposition can always be performed, nevertheless of the singularity of the initial matrix A. If A is a square NxN matrix, hence all the matrices U, V and W are square with the same dimensions. Their inverse ones are easy to find because U and V are orthogonal and their inverses are equal to the transpose ones. W is a diagonal matrix and the corresponding inverse is also diagonal with components $1/w_j$, $j=1,N$. Hence, if matrix A is decomposed by SVD factorization, $A=U.W.V^T$, then the inverse one is $A^{-1}=V.[diag1/w_j].U^T$. The problem of the evaluation of the inverse A^{-1} appears if a singular value w_j exists, which tends to zero value. Hence, if matrix A is a singular one, the SVD decomposition easily estimates this case.

Hence, the peculiarities of LU, QR and SVD factorizations determine the computational efficiency of the evaluations for finding the inverse matrix A^{-1}. Particularly, the simplest method, from evaluation point of view, is LU factorization followed by QR decomposition and SVD factorization. All these methods do not use peculiarities, if matrix A^* slightly differs from the initial matrix A. The inverse of A^* has to be evaluated starting with its factorization and sequentially solution of linear matrix equation systems. Hence, it is worth to find methods for evaluation of the inverse of A^*, which differs from A in few components and A^{-1} is available. The new matrix A^* can contain several modified components a_{ij}. Hence, the utilization of components from the inverse A^{-1} for the evaluation of the new inverse matrix A^{*-1} can speed up considerably the numerical calculations in different control algorithms and decreases the evaluation efforts. Relations for utilization of components of A^{-1} for evaluation of a corresponding inverse of a modified matrix A^{*-1} are derived in (Strassen, 1969). The components of the inverse matrix can be evaluated analytically.

Finding the inverse matrix is related with a lot of calculations. Instead of direct finding an inverse matrix, it is worth to find analytical relations where lower dimensions inverse matrices components are available. Here analytical relations for inverse matrix calculation are derived and the corresponding MATLAB codes are illustrated.

2. Analytical relations among the components of inverse matrix

Initial optimization problem is given in the form

$$\min_x \left\{ \frac{1}{2} \begin{vmatrix} x_1^T & x_2^T \end{vmatrix} \begin{vmatrix} Q_1 & 0 \\ 0 & Q_2 \end{vmatrix} \begin{vmatrix} x_1 \\ x_2 \end{vmatrix} + \begin{vmatrix} R_1^T & R_2^T \end{vmatrix} \begin{vmatrix} x_1 \\ x_2 \end{vmatrix} \right\} \tag{1}$$

$$a_1 x_1 + a_2 x_2 = d$$
$$b_1 x_1 \quad\quad = C_1$$
$$\quad\quad b_2 x_2 = C_2$$

where the matrices dimensions are: $x_1 |_{n_1 x 1}$; $Q_1 |_{n_1 x n_1}$; $R_1 |_{n_1 x 1}$; $a_1 |_{m_0 x n_1}$; $d |_{m_0 x 1}$

$x_2 |_{n_2 x 1}$; $Q_2 |_{n_2 x n_2}$; $R_2 |_{n_2 x 1}$; $a_2 |_{m_0 x n_2}$; $b_1 |_{m_1 x n_1}$; $C_1 |_{m_1 x 1}$; $b_2 |_{m_2 x n_2}$; $C_2 |_{m_2 x 1}$;

$$Q = \begin{vmatrix} Q_1 & 0 \\ 0 & Q_2 \end{vmatrix} ; R = \begin{vmatrix} R_1 \\ R_2 \end{vmatrix}$$

Peculiarity of problem (1) is that the connected condition $a_1 x_1 + a_2 x_2 = d$ distributes a common resource d while the subsystems work with own resources C_1 and C_2. For simplicity of the writing it can be put

$$A_1 |_{(m_0 + m_1 + m_2) x n_1} = \begin{vmatrix} a_1 & {}_{m_0 x n_1} \\ b_1 & {}_{m_1 x n_1} \\ 0 & {}_{m_2 x n_1} \end{vmatrix} ; A_2 |_{(m_0 + m_1 + m_2) x n_2} = \begin{vmatrix} a_2 & {}_{m_0 x n_2} \\ 0 & {}_{m_1 x n_2} \\ b_2 & {}_{m_2 x n_2} \end{vmatrix} ;$$

$$D = \begin{vmatrix} d \\ C_1 \\ C_2 \end{vmatrix}_{(m_0 + m_1 + m_2) x 1} ; A = \begin{vmatrix} A_1 & A_2 \end{vmatrix} |_{(m_0 + m_1 + m_2) x (n_1 x n_2)} . \tag{2}$$

2.1 Decomposition of the initial problem by goal coordination

The initial problem (1) can be solved by two manners using hierarchical approach according to the hierarchical multilevel systems (Mesarovich et al, 1973; Stoilov & Stoilova, 1999): by goal coordination and by predictive one. Taking into account the substitutions

$$Q = \begin{vmatrix} Q_1 & 0 \\ 0 & Q_2 \end{vmatrix} ; R = \begin{vmatrix} R_1 \\ R_2 \end{vmatrix} ; A = \begin{vmatrix} A_1 & A_2 \end{vmatrix} ; x = \begin{vmatrix} x_1 \\ x_2 \end{vmatrix} , \tag{3}$$

the solution of (1) can be found in analytical form (Stoilova, 2010) :

$$x^{opt} = -Q^{-1}\left[R - A^T(AQ^{-1}A^T)^{-1}(AQ^{-1}R + D)\right] \tag{4}$$

or

$$x_1^{opt} = -Q_1^{-1}R_1 + Q_1^{-1}A_1^T\left(A_1Q_1^{-1}A_1^T + A_2Q_2^{-1}A_2^T\right)^{-1}\left(A_1Q_1^{-1}R_1 + A_2Q_2^{-1}R_2 + D\right) \tag{5}$$

$$x_2^{opt} = -Q_2^{-1}R_2 + Q_2^{-1}A_2^T\left(A_1Q_1^{-1}A_1^T + A_2Q_2^{-1}A_2^T\right)^{-1}\left(A_1Q_1^{-1}R_1 + A_2Q_2^{-1}R_2 + D\right).$$

It is necessary to be known the matrices $A_1, A_2, Q_1, Q_2, R_1, R_2$ for evaluating the solutions (5)
Determination of $AQ^{-1}A^T$
Applying (3) it is obtained

$$AQ^{-1}A^T = \begin{vmatrix} A_1 & A_2 \end{vmatrix}\begin{vmatrix} Q_1^{-1} & 0 \\ 0 & Q_2^{-1} \end{vmatrix}\begin{vmatrix} A_1^T \\ A_2^T \end{vmatrix} = A_1Q_1^{-1}A_1^T + A_2Q_2^{-1}A_2^T. \tag{6}$$

Using (2) it follows

$$A_1Q_1^{-1}A_1^T = \begin{vmatrix} a_1Q_1^{-1}a_1^T{}_{m_0 x m_0} & a_1Q_1^{-1}b_1^T{}_{m_0 x m_1} & 0_{m_0 x m_2} \\ b_1Q_1^{-1}a_1^T{}_{m_1 x m_0} & b_1Q_1^{-1}b_1^T{}_{m_1 x m_1} & 0_{m_1 x m_2} \\ 0_{m_2 x m_0} & 0_{m_2 x m_1} & 0_{m_2 x m_2} \end{vmatrix}, \tag{7}$$

$$A_2Q_2^{-1}A_2^T = \begin{vmatrix} a_2Q_2^{-1}a_2^T{}_{m_0 x m_0} & 0_{m_0 x m_1} & a_2Q_2^{-1}b_2^T{}_{m_0 x m_2} \\ 0_{m_1 x m_0} & 0_{m_1 x m_1} & 0_{m_1 x m_2} \\ b_2Q_2^{-1}a_2^T{}_{m_2 x m_0} & 0_{m_2 x m_1} & b_2Q_2^{-1}b_2^T{}_{m_2 x m_2} \end{vmatrix}. \tag{8}$$

After substitution of (7) and (8) in (6) $AQ^{-1}A^T$ and $(AQ^{-1}A^T)^{-1}$ can be determined

$$AQ^{-1}A^T = A_1Q_1^{-1}A_1^T + A_2Q_2^{-1}A_2^T = \begin{vmatrix} a_1Q_1^{-1}a_1^T + a_2Q_2^{-1}a_2^T{}_{m_0 x m_0} & a_1Q_1^{-1}b_1^T{}_{m_0 x m_1} & a_2Q_2^{-1}b_2^T{}_{m_0 x m_2} \\ b_1Q_1^{-1}a_1^T{}_{m_1 x m_0} & b_1Q_1^{-1}b_1^T{}_{m_1 x m_1} & 0_{m_1 x m_2} \\ b_2Q_2^{-1}a_2^T{}_{m_2 x m_0} & 0_{m_2 x m_1} & b_2Q_2^{-1}b_2^T{}_{m_2 x m_2} \end{vmatrix} \tag{9}$$

$$(AQ^{-1}A^T)^{-1} = (A_1Q_1^{-1}A_1^T + A_2Q_2^{-1}A_2^T)^{-1} =$$

$$= \begin{vmatrix} a_1Q_1^{-1}a_1^T + a_2Q_2^{-1}a_2^T{}_{m_0 x m_0} & a_1Q_1^{-1}b_1^T{}_{m_0 x m_1} & a_2Q_2^{-1}b_2^T{}_{m_0 x m_2} \\ b_1Q_1^{-1}a_1^T{}_{m_1 x m_0} & b_1Q_1^{-1}b_1^T{}_{m_1 x m_1} & 0_{m_1 x m_2} \\ b_2Q_2^{-1}a_2^T{}_{m_2 x m_0} & 0_{m_2 x m_1} & b_2Q_2^{-1}b_2^T{}_{m_2 x m_2} \end{vmatrix}^{-1}. \tag{10}$$

The manner of definition of matrix $AQ^{-1}A^T$ shows that it is a symmetric one.

Determination of $AQ^{-1}R + D$

Using (2) and (3) it follows

$$AQ^{-1}R + D = \begin{vmatrix} a_1 Q_1^{-1} R_1 + a_2 Q_2^{-1} R_2 + d \\ b_1 Q_1^{-1} R_1 + C_1 \\ b_2 Q_2^{-1} R_2 + C_2 \end{vmatrix} \tag{11}$$

Determination of $(AQ^{-1}A^T)^{-1}(AQ^{-1}R + D)$

Using (10) and (11), it is obtained

$$(AQ^{-1}A^T)^{-1}(AQ^{-1}R + D) = \begin{vmatrix} a_1 Q_1^{-1} a_1^T + a_2 Q_2^{-1} a_2^T {}_{m_0 x m_0} & a_1 Q_1^{-1} b_1^T {}_{m_0 x m_1} & a_2 Q_2^{-1} b_2^T {}_{m_0 x m_2} \\ b_1 Q_1^{-1} a_1^T {}_{m_1 x m_0} & b_1 Q_1^{-1} b_1^T {}_{m_1 x m_1} & 0_{m_1 x m_2} \\ b_2 Q_2^{-1} a_2^T {}_{m_2 x m_0} & 0_{m_2 x m_1} & b_2 Q_2^{-1} b_2^T {}_{m_2 x m_2} \end{vmatrix}^{-1} \begin{vmatrix} a_1 Q_1^{-1} R_1 + a_2 Q_2^{-1} R_2 + d \\ b_1 Q_1^{-1} R_1 + C_1 \\ b_2 Q_2^{-1} R_2 + C_2 \end{vmatrix}$$

$$(AQ^{-1}A^T)^{-1}(AQ^{-1}R + D) = \begin{vmatrix} \alpha_{11 m_0 x m_0} & \alpha_{12 m_0 x m_1} & \alpha_{13 m_0 x m_2} \\ \alpha_{21 m_1 x m_0} & \alpha_{22 m_1 x m_1} & \alpha_{23 m_1 x m_2} \\ \alpha_{31 m_2 x m_0} & \alpha_{32 m_2 x m_1} & \alpha_{33 m_2 x m_2} \end{vmatrix} \begin{vmatrix} a_1 Q_1^{-1} R_1 + a_2 Q_2^{-1} R_2 + d \\ b_1 Q_1^{-1} R_1 + C_1 \\ b_2 Q_2^{-1} R_2 + C_2 \end{vmatrix}$$

where

$$(AQ^{-1}A^T)^{-1} = \alpha = \begin{vmatrix} \alpha_{11} & \alpha_{12} & \alpha_{13} \\ \alpha_{21} & \alpha_{22} & \alpha_{23} \\ \alpha_{31} & \alpha_{32} & \alpha_{33} \end{vmatrix}_{(m_0 + m_1 + m_2) x (m_0 + m_1 + m_2)} \tag{12}$$

Taking into account the structure of matrix $(AQ^{-1}A^T)^{-1}$, then $\alpha_{23} = 0$, $\alpha_{32} = 0$. The manner of definition of the inverce matrix α shows that it is a symmetric one. Consequently, the term $(AQ^{-1}A^T)^{-1}(AQ^{-1}R + D)$ is

$$(AQ^{-1}A^T)^{-1}(AQ^{-1}R + D) = \begin{vmatrix} \alpha_{11}(a_1 Q_1^{-1} R_1 + a_2 Q_2^{-1} R_2 + d) + \alpha_{12}(b_1 Q_1^{-1} R_1 + C_1) + \alpha_{13}(b_2 Q_2^{-1} R_2 + C_2) {}_{m_0 x 1} \\ \alpha_{21}(a_1 Q_1^{-1} R_1 + a_2 Q_2^{-1} R_2 + d) + \alpha_{22}(b_1 Q_1^{-1} R_1 + C_1) + \underbrace{\alpha_{23}(b_2 Q_2^{-1} R_2 + C_2)}_{0} {}_{m_1 x 1} \\ \alpha_{31}(a_1 Q_1^{-1} R_1 + a_2 Q_2^{-1} R_2 + d) + \underbrace{\alpha_{32}(b_1 Q_1^{-1} R_1 + C_1)}_{0} + \alpha_{33}(b_2 Q_2^{-1} R_2 + C_2) {}_{m_2 x 1} \end{vmatrix} \tag{13}$$

Determination of $A^T(AQ^{-1}A^T)^{-1}(AQ^{-1}R + D)$

After a substitution of (2) in (13) it follows

$$\begin{vmatrix} a_1^T \big|_{n_1 x m_0} & b_1^T \big|_{m_1 x m_0} & 0_{n_1 x m_2} \\ a_2^T \big|_{n_2 x m_0} & 0_{n_2 x m_1} & b_2^T \big|_{n_2 x m_2} \end{vmatrix} (AQ^{-1}A^T)^{-1}(AQ^{-1}R+D) =$$

$$= \begin{vmatrix} a_1^T & b_1^T \end{vmatrix} \begin{vmatrix} \underbrace{\alpha_{11}}_{m_0 x m_0} \\ \underbrace{\alpha_{21}}_{m_1 x m_0} \end{vmatrix} \underbrace{(a_1 Q_1^{-1}R_1 + a_2 Q_2^{-1}R_2 + d)}_{m_0 x 1} + \begin{vmatrix} a_1^T & b_1^T \end{vmatrix} \begin{vmatrix} \underbrace{\alpha_{12}}_{m_0 x m_1} \\ \underbrace{\alpha_{22}}_{m_1 x m_1} \end{vmatrix} \underbrace{(b_1 Q_1^{-1}R_1 + C_1)}_{m_1 x 1} + \begin{vmatrix} a_1^T & b_1^T \end{vmatrix} \begin{vmatrix} \underbrace{\alpha_{13}}_{m_0 x m_2} \\ 0 \\ \underbrace{}_{m_1 x m_2} \end{vmatrix} \underbrace{(b_2 Q_2^{-1}R_2 + C_2)}_{m_2 x 1}$$

$$\begin{vmatrix} a_2^T & b_2^T \end{vmatrix} \begin{vmatrix} \underbrace{\alpha_{11}}_{m_0 x m_0} \\ \underbrace{\alpha_{31}}_{m_2 x m_0} \end{vmatrix} \underbrace{(a_1 Q_1^{-1}R_1 + a_2 Q_2^{-1}R_2 + d)}_{m_0 x 1} + \begin{vmatrix} a_2^T & b_2^T \end{vmatrix} \begin{vmatrix} \underbrace{\alpha_{12}}_{m_0 x m_1} \\ 0 \\ \underbrace{}_{m_2 x m_1} \end{vmatrix} \underbrace{(b_1 Q_1^{-1}R_1 + C_1)}_{m_1 x 1} + \begin{vmatrix} a_2^T & b_2^T \end{vmatrix} \begin{vmatrix} \underbrace{\alpha_{13}}_{m_0 x m_2} \\ \underbrace{\alpha_{33}}_{m_2 x m_2} \end{vmatrix} \underbrace{(b_2 Q_2^{-1}R_2 + C_2)}_{m_2 x 1}$$

Consequently, the term $A^T(AQ^{-1}A^T)^{-1}(AQ^{-1}R+D)$ becomes

$$A^T(AQ^{-1}A^T)^{-1}(AQ^{-1}R+D) = \begin{bmatrix} \begin{vmatrix} a_1^T & b_1^T \end{vmatrix} \begin{vmatrix} \alpha_{11} & \alpha_{12} & \alpha_{13} \\ \alpha_{21} & \alpha_{22} & 0 \end{vmatrix} \begin{vmatrix} a_1 Q_1^{-1}R_1 + a_2 Q_2^{-1}R_2 + d \\ b_1 Q_1^{-1}R_1 + C_1 \\ b_2 Q_2^{-1}R_2 + C_2 \end{vmatrix} \\ \begin{vmatrix} a_2^T & b_2^T \end{vmatrix} \begin{vmatrix} \alpha_{11} & \alpha_{12} & \alpha_{13} \\ \alpha_{31} & 0 & \alpha_{33} \end{vmatrix} \begin{vmatrix} a_1 Q_1^{-1}R_1 + a_2 Q_2^{-1}R_2 + d \\ b_1 Q_1^{-1}R_1 + C_1 \\ b_2 Q_2^{-1}R_2 + C_2 \end{vmatrix} \end{bmatrix} \quad (14)$$

After putting (3) and (14) in (5) the analytical solutions of the initial problem (1) are

$$x_1^{opt} = -Q_1^{-1}R_1 + Q_1^{-1} \begin{bmatrix} \begin{vmatrix} a_1^T & b_1^T \end{vmatrix} \begin{vmatrix} \alpha_{11} & \alpha_{12} & \alpha_{13} \\ \alpha_{21} & \alpha_{22} & 0 \end{vmatrix} \begin{vmatrix} a_1 Q_1^{-1}R_1 + a_2 Q_2^{-1}R_2 + d \\ b_1 Q_1^{-1}R_1 + C_1 \\ b_2 Q_2^{-1}R_2 + C_2 \end{vmatrix} \end{bmatrix} \quad (15)$$

$$x_2^{opt} = -Q_2^{-1}R_2 + Q_2^{-1} \begin{bmatrix} \begin{vmatrix} a_2^T & b_2^T \end{vmatrix} \begin{vmatrix} \alpha_{11} & \alpha_{12} & \alpha_{13} \\ \alpha_{31} & 0 & \alpha_{33} \end{vmatrix} \begin{vmatrix} a_1 Q_1^{-1}R_1 + a_2 Q_2^{-1}R_2 + d \\ b_1 Q_1^{-1}R_1 + C_1 \\ b_2 Q_2^{-1}R_2 + C_2 \end{vmatrix} \end{bmatrix}$$

Analytical relations (15) are a result of applying a goal coordination for solving the initial problem (1). They are useful only if the components α_{ij} of the inverse matrix (12) are known. However, if α_{ij} are not known (the usual case) relations (15) can not be applied.

2.2 Decomposition of the initial problem by predictive coordination
According to the hierarchical approach, the subsystems work independently. The idea of the predictive coordination is that the coordinator influences to each subsystem by independent impacts instead of common impact in goal coordination. For the initial problem (1)

decomposition by goal coordination can not be fully accomplished because of the connected relation $a_1 x_1 + a_2 x_2 = d$. Applying predictive coordination, the connected restriction can be decomposed to:

$$a_1 x_1 = y_1 \; ; a_2 x_2 = y_2 \tag{16}$$

observing the condition for resource limitation

$$y_1 + y_2 = d \tag{17}$$

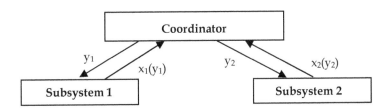

Fig. 1. Hierarchical approach for solving (1)

Applying (16), the initial optimization problem (1) is decomposed to two optimization subproblems with lower dimensions than the initial one:

$$\min\left\{\frac{1}{2} x_1^T Q_1 x_1 + R_1^T x_1\right\} \quad \min\left\{\frac{1}{2} x_2^T Q_2 x_2 + R_2^T x_2\right\} \tag{18}$$

$$\underbrace{a_1}_{m_0 x n_1} \; \underbrace{x_1}_{} = \underbrace{y_1}_{m_0 x 1} \quad \underbrace{a_2}_{m_0 x n_2} \; \underbrace{x_2}_{} = \underbrace{y_2}_{m_0 x 1}$$

$$\underbrace{b_1}_{m_1 x n_1} \; \underbrace{x_1}_{} = \underbrace{C_1}_{m_1 x 1} \; ; \; \underbrace{b_2}_{m_2 x n_2} \; \underbrace{x_2}_{} = \underbrace{C_2}_{m_2 x 1}$$

where

$$A_1\big|_{(m_0+m_1+m_2)x n_1} = \begin{vmatrix} a_1 \\ b_1 \\ 0 \end{vmatrix} \begin{matrix} m_0 x n_1 \\ m_1 x n_1 \\ m_2 x n_1 \end{matrix} \; ; A_2\big|_{(m_0+m_1+m_2)x n_2} = \begin{vmatrix} a_2 \\ 0 \\ b_2 \end{vmatrix} \begin{matrix} m_0 x n_2 \\ m_1 x n_2 \\ m_2 x n_2 \end{matrix} \; = \; y_1 = \begin{vmatrix} d_1 \\ C_1 \\ 0 \end{vmatrix} \begin{matrix} m_0 x 1 \\ m_1 x 1 \\ m_2 x 1 \end{matrix} \; = \; y_2 = \begin{vmatrix} d_2 \\ 0 \\ C_2 \end{vmatrix} \begin{matrix} m_0 x 1 \\ m_1 x 1 \\ m_2 x 1 \end{matrix}$$

and it can be realized

$$\overset{=}{y_1} + \overset{=}{y_2} = D \text{ or } y_1 + y_2 = d \; .$$

The analytical solution of the first subproblem (18), according to (4), is

$$x_1^{opt} = -Q_1^{-1}\left[R_1 - A_1^T (A_1 Q_1^{-1} A_1^T)^{-1} (A_1 Q_1^{-1} R_1 + D) \right].$$

The analysis of matrix A_1 shows that it has zero rows. Respectively, the square matrix

$$A_1 Q_1^{-1} A_1^T = \begin{vmatrix} a_1 \\ b_1 \\ 0 \end{vmatrix}_{(m+l_1+l_2) \times n_1} \quad Q_1|_{n_1 x n_1} \begin{vmatrix} a_1^T & b_1^T & 0 \end{vmatrix}_{n_1 x (m+l_1+l_2)} = \begin{vmatrix} a_1 Q_1^{-1} a_1^T & a_1 Q_1^{-1} b_1^T & 0 \\ b_1 Q_1^{-1} a_1^T & b_1 Q_1^{-1} b_1^T & 0 \\ 0 & 0 & 0 \end{vmatrix}$$

has zero rows and columns, which means that the inverse matrix $(AQ^{-1}A^T)^{-1}$ does not exist. However, in the solution of problem (1) takes part a sum of the matrices $(A_i Q_i^{-1} A_i^T)^{-1}$, so that the sum matrix $(AQ^{-1}A^T)^{-1}$ has a full rank. This matrix has a high dimension and for it can not be used the specific structure $A_i Q_i^{-1} A_i^T$. To use the less rank of matrices $A_i Q_i^{-1} A_i^T$, the definition of subproblems (18) has to be done by rejecting the zero rows in matrices A_1 and A_2.
Respectively, the subproblems are obtained of the initial problem (1) by additional modification of the admissible areas, determined by the matrices A_1 and A_2 instead of direct decomposition. In that manner the modified subproblems will present only the corresponding meaning components as follows:

$$A_1 = \begin{vmatrix} a_1 \\ b_1 \\ 0 \end{vmatrix} \Rightarrow \bar{A}_1 = \begin{vmatrix} a_1 \\ b_1 \end{vmatrix}; A_2 = \begin{vmatrix} a_2 \\ 0 \\ b_2 \end{vmatrix} \Rightarrow \bar{A}_2 = \begin{vmatrix} a_2 \\ b_2 \end{vmatrix}; y_1 = \begin{vmatrix} y_1 \\ C_1 \\ 0 \end{vmatrix} \Rightarrow \bar{y}_1 = \begin{vmatrix} y_1 \\ C_1 \end{vmatrix}; y_2 = \begin{vmatrix} y_2 \\ 0 \\ C_2 \end{vmatrix} \Rightarrow \bar{y}_2 = \begin{vmatrix} y_2 \\ C_2 \end{vmatrix}.$$

The modified subproblems (19) have lower dimension in comparison with (18), obtained by direct decomposition

$$\min\left\{\frac{1}{2}x_1^T Q_1 x_1 + R_1^T x_1\right\}; \min\left\{\frac{1}{2}x_2^T Q_2 x_2 + R_2^T x_2\right\} \tag{19}$$

$$\bar{A}_1 x_1 = \bar{y}_1 ; \bar{A}_2 x_2 = \bar{y}_2$$

$$\bar{A}_1 = \begin{vmatrix} a_1 \\ b_1 \end{vmatrix}_{(m_0+m_1) x n_1} ; \bar{A}_2 = \begin{vmatrix} a_2 \\ b_2 \end{vmatrix}_{(m_0+m_2) x n_2}$$

$$\bar{y}_1 = \begin{vmatrix} y_1 \\ C_1 \end{vmatrix}_{(m_0+m_1) x 1} ; \bar{y}_2 = \begin{vmatrix} y_2 \\ C_2 \end{vmatrix}_{(m_0+m_2) x 1}.$$

The solutions of (18), obtained in analytical forms using (4), are

$$x_i^{opt} = -Q_i^{-1}\left[R_i - \bar{A}_i^T (\bar{A}_i Q_i^{-1} \bar{A}_i^T)^{-1}(\bar{A}_i Q_i^{-1} R_i + \bar{y}_i)\right] \quad i = 1,2.$$

After substitution of matrices $\bar{A}_i$ with the corresponding matrix components, it follows

$$x_1(y_1) = -Q_1^{-1}\left[R_1 - \begin{vmatrix} a_1^T & b_1^T \end{vmatrix}\begin{vmatrix} a_1 Q_1^{-1} a_1^T & a_1 Q_1^{-1} b_1^T \\ b_1 Q_1^{-1} b_1^T & b_1 Q_1^{-1} a_1^T \end{vmatrix}^{-1}\begin{vmatrix} a_1 Q_1^{-1} R_1 + y_1 \\ b_1 Q_1^{-1} R_1 + C_1 \end{vmatrix}\right].$$

It is put

$$
\begin{vmatrix}
\underbrace{a_1 Q_1^{-1} a_1^T}_{m_0 x m_0} & \underbrace{a_1 Q_1^{-1} b_1^T}_{m_0 x m_1} \\
\underbrace{b_1 Q_1^{-1} a_1^T}_{m_1 x m_0} & \underbrace{b_1 Q_1^{-1} b_1^T}_{m_1 x m_1}
\end{vmatrix}^{-1} = \beta =
\begin{vmatrix}
\underbrace{\beta_{11}}_{m_0 x m_0} & \underbrace{\beta_{12}}_{m_0 x m_1} \\
\underbrace{\beta_{21}}_{m_1 x m_0} & \underbrace{\beta_{22}}_{m_1 x m_1}
\end{vmatrix} .
\tag{20}
$$

where the matrix β is a symmetric one by definition. Consequently, $x_1(y_1)$ can be developed to:

$$
x_1(y_1) = -Q_1^{-1} R_1 + Q_1^{-1} \left[\begin{vmatrix} a_1^T & b_1^T \end{vmatrix} \begin{vmatrix} \beta_{11} & \beta_{12} \\ \beta_{21} & \beta_{22} \end{vmatrix} \begin{vmatrix} a_1 Q_1^{-1} R_1 + y_1 \\ b_1 Q_1^{-1} R_1 + C_1 \end{vmatrix} \right].
\tag{21}
$$

Analogically, $x_2(y_2)$ is

$$
x_2(y_2) = -Q_2^{-1} R_2 + Q_2^{-1} \left[\begin{vmatrix} a_2^T & b_2^T \end{vmatrix} \begin{vmatrix} \gamma_{11} & \gamma_{12} \\ \gamma_{21} & \gamma_{22} \end{vmatrix} \begin{vmatrix} a_2 Q_2^{-1} R_2 + y_2 \\ a_2 Q_2^{-1} R_2 + C_2 \end{vmatrix} \right].
\tag{22}
$$

where matrix γ is a symmetric one by definition, $\gamma_{12} = \gamma_{21}^T$

$$
\gamma =
\begin{vmatrix}
\underbrace{\gamma_{11}}_{m_0 x m_0} & \underbrace{\gamma_{12}}_{m_0 x m_2} \\
\underbrace{\gamma_{21}}_{m_2 x m_0} & \underbrace{\gamma_{22}}_{m_2 x m_2}
\end{vmatrix} =
\begin{vmatrix}
\underbrace{a_2 Q_2^{-1} a_2^T}_{m_0 x m_0} & \underbrace{a_2 Q_2^{-1} b_2^T}_{m_0 x m_2} \\
\underbrace{b_2 Q_1^{-1} a_2^T}_{m_2 x m_0} & \underbrace{b_2 Q_2^{-1} b_2^T}_{m_2 x m_2}
\end{vmatrix}^{-1} .
$$

If the optimal resources y_1^{opt}, y_2^{opt} are known, after their substitution in (21)-(22), the solution of the initial problem (1) can be obtained

$$
x_1^{opt} = x_1(y_1^{opt}), \qquad x_2^{opt} = x_2(y_2^{opt}) .
$$

The determination of the optimal resources y_1^{opt}, y_2^{opt} is done by solution of the coordination problem.

2.2.1 Determination of the coordination problem
After substitution of relations $x_1(y_1)$ and $x_2(y_2)$ in the initial problem (1) and taking into account the resource constraint (17), the coordination problem becomes

$$
\min_{y \in S_y} w(y) = \min \left\{ \frac{1}{2} x_1^T(y_1) Q_1 x_1(y_1) + R_1^T x_1(y_1) + \frac{1}{2} x_2^T(y_2) Q_2 x_2(y_2) + R_2^T x_2(y_2) \right\}
$$

$$
S_y \equiv y_1 + y_2 = d ,
$$

or

$$\min\{w(y) = w_1(y_1) + w_2(y_2)\} \tag{23}$$

$$y_1 + y_2 = d$$

where

$$w_i(y_i) = \frac{1}{2} x_i^T(y_i) Q_i x_i(y_i) + R_i^T x_i(y_i), \quad i = 1, 2.$$

As $x_i(y_i)$ is inexplicit function, it can be approximated in Mac-Laurin series at point $y_i = 0$

$$x_1(y_1)_{n_1 x 1} = x_{10 n_1 x 1} + X_{1 n_1 x m_0} y_{1 m_0 x 1} \tag{24}$$

where

$$x_{i0}^1 = -Q_1^{-1} R_1 + Q_1^{-1} \begin{vmatrix} a_1^T & b_1^T \end{vmatrix} \begin{Vmatrix} \beta_{11} & \beta_{12} \\ \beta_{21} & \beta_{22} \end{Vmatrix} \begin{vmatrix} a_1 Q_1^{-1} R_1 \\ b_1 Q_1^{-1} R_1 + C_1 \end{vmatrix} \tag{25}$$

$$X_{1 n_1 x m_0} = Q_1^{-1}{}_{n_1 x n_1} \begin{vmatrix} a_1^T & b_1^T \\ \underbrace{}_{n_1 x m_0} & \underbrace{}_{n_1 x m_1} \end{vmatrix} \begin{Vmatrix} \beta_{11 m_0 x m_0} \\ \beta_{21 m_1 x m_0} \end{Vmatrix} \tag{26}$$

where x_{10} is solution of subproblem (19) having zero resource, $y_1 = 0$.
Analogically, for the second subproblem is valid:

$$x_2(y_2)_{n_2 x 1} = x_{20 n_2 x 1} + X_{2 n_2 x m_0} y_{2 m_0 x 1} \tag{27}$$

where

$$x_{20} = -Q_2^{-1} R_2 + Q_2^{-1} \begin{vmatrix} a_2^T & b_2^T \end{vmatrix} \begin{Vmatrix} \gamma_{11} & \gamma_{12} \\ \gamma_{21} & \gamma_{22} \end{Vmatrix} \begin{vmatrix} a_2 Q_2^{-1} R_2 \\ b_2 Q_2^{-1} R_2 + C_2 \end{vmatrix} \tag{28}$$

$$X_{2 n_2 x m_0} = Q_2^{-1}{}_{n_2 x n_2} \begin{vmatrix} a_2^T & b_2^T \\ \underbrace{}_{n_2 x m_0} & \underbrace{}_{n_2 x m_2} \end{vmatrix} \begin{Vmatrix} \gamma_{11 m_0 x m_0} \\ \gamma_{21 m_2 x m_0} \end{Vmatrix} \tag{29}$$

After substitution of (24) in $w_1(y_1)$ of (23), it follows:

$$w_1(y_1) = \frac{1}{2}(x_{10}^T + y_1^T X_1^T) Q_1 (x_{10} + X_1 y_1) + R_1^T (x_{10} + X_1 y_1) =$$

$$= \frac{1}{2} x_{10}^T Q_1 x_{10} + \frac{1}{2} x_{10}^T Q_1 X_1 y_1 + \frac{1}{2} y_1^T X_1^T Q_1 x_{10} + \frac{1}{2} y_1^T X_1^T Q_1 X_1 y_1 + R_1^T x_{10} + R_1^T X_1 y_1$$

The components $x_{10}^T Q_1 X_1 y_1$ and $y_1^T X_1^T Q_1 x_{10}$ are equal, as they are transposed of corresponding equal relations. Consequently, the coordination problem becomes

$$w_1(y_1) \equiv \frac{1}{2} y_1^T X_1^T Q_1 X_1 y_1 + y_1^T X_1^T Q_1 x_{10} + y_1^T X_1^T R_1 \tag{30}$$

or

$$w_1(y_1) \equiv \frac{1}{2} y_1^T q_1 y_1 + y_1^T r_1$$

where

$$q_1 = X_1^T Q_1 X_1 \; ; r_1 = X_1^T Q_1 x_{10} + X_1^T R_1$$

Analogically, for the second subproblem, it follows:

$$w_2(y_2) \equiv \frac{1}{2} y_2^T X_2^T Q_2 X_2 y_2 + y_2^T X_2^T Q_2 x_{20} + y_2^T X_2^T R_2 \tag{31}$$

or

$$w_2(y_2) \equiv \frac{1}{2} y_2^T q_2 y_2 + y_2^T r_2$$

where

$$q_2 = X_2^T Q_2 X_2 \; ; r_2 = X_2^T Q_2 x_{20} + X_2^T R_2 .$$

Functions $w_i(y_i)$ has to be presented in terms of the initial problem (1) by the following transformations.

Development of q_1

Relation q_1 is presented like

$$q_1 = X_1^T Q_1 X_1 = \begin{vmatrix} \beta_{11}^T & \beta_{21}^T \end{vmatrix} \begin{vmatrix} a_1 \\ b_1 \end{vmatrix} Q_1^{-1} \underbrace{Q_1 Q_1^{-1}}_{I} \begin{vmatrix} a_1^T & b_1^T \end{vmatrix} \begin{vmatrix} \beta_{11} \\ \beta_{21} \end{vmatrix} = \begin{vmatrix} \beta_{11}^T & \beta_{21}^T \end{vmatrix} \begin{vmatrix} a_1 \\ b_1 \end{vmatrix} Q_1^{-1} \begin{vmatrix} a_1^T & b_1^T \end{vmatrix} \begin{vmatrix} \beta_{11} \\ \beta_{21} \end{vmatrix}$$

or

$$q_1 = \begin{vmatrix} \beta_{11}^T & \beta_{21}^T \end{vmatrix} \begin{vmatrix} a_1 Q_1^{-1} a_1^T & a_1 Q_1^{-1} b_1^T \\ b_1 Q_1^{-1} a_1^T & b_1 Q_1^{-1} b_1^T \end{vmatrix} \begin{vmatrix} \beta_{11} \\ \beta_{21} \end{vmatrix} = \begin{vmatrix} \beta_{11}^T & \beta_{21}^T \end{vmatrix} \begin{vmatrix} a_1 Q_1^{-1} a_1^T \beta_{11} + a_1 Q_1^{-1} b_1^T \beta_{21} \\ b_1 Q_1^{-1} a_1^T \beta_{11} + b_1 Q_1^{-1} b_1^T \beta_{21} \end{vmatrix} . \tag{32}$$

According to the manner of definition of matrix β from (20) the following matrix equality is performed

$$\begin{vmatrix} \underset{m_0 x m_0}{a_1 Q_1^{-1} a_1^T} & \underset{m_0 x m_1}{a_1 Q_1^{-1} b_1^T} \\ \underset{m_1 x m_0}{b_1 Q_1^{-1} a_1^T} & \underset{m_1 x m_1}{b_1 Q_1^{-1} b_1^T} \end{vmatrix} \begin{vmatrix} \underset{m_0 x m_0}{\beta_{11}} & \underset{m_0 x m_1}{\beta_{12}} \\ \underset{m_1 x m_0}{\beta_{21}} & \underset{m_1 x m_1}{\beta_{22}} \end{vmatrix}^{-1} = \begin{vmatrix} \underset{m_0 x m_0}{I} & \underset{m_0 x m_1}{0} \\ \underset{m_1 x m_0}{0} & \underset{m_1 x m_1}{I} \end{vmatrix} \tag{33}$$

i.e. an unit matrix is obtained. Consequently, the following equations are performed

$$a_1 Q_1^{-1} a_1^T \beta_{11} + a_1 Q_1^{-1} b_1^T \beta_{21} = I_{m_0 x m_0} \tag{34}$$

$$b_1 Q_1^{-1} a_1^T \beta_{11} + b_1 Q_1^{-1} b_1^T \beta_{21} = 0_{m_1 x m_0} \,.$$

After substitution of (34) in (32) it is obtained

$$q_1 = \left| \underset{m_0 x m_0}{\beta_{11}^T} \quad \underset{m_0 x m_1}{\beta_{21}^T} \right| \left| \begin{array}{c} \underset{m_0 x m_0}{I} \\ 0 \\ \underset{m_1 x m_0}{} \end{array} \right| = \underset{m_0 x m_0}{\beta_{11}}$$

as β_{11} is a symmetric and square or

$$q_1 = \beta_{11} \,. \tag{35}$$

Analogically,

$$q_2 = \gamma_{11} \tag{36}$$

Development of r_i.
In a similar way the relations of r_i are developed to the expressions

$$r_1 = X_1^T (Q_1 x_{10} + R_1) = \left| \beta_{11}^T \quad \beta_{21}^T \right| \left| \begin{array}{c} a_1 Q_1^{-1} R_1 \\ b_1 Q_1^{-1} R_1 + C_1 \end{array} \right| \tag{37}$$

$$r_2 = X_2^T (Q_2 x_{20} + R_2) = \left| \gamma_{11}^T \quad \gamma_{21}^T \right| \left| \begin{array}{c} a_2 Q_2^{-1} R_2 \\ b_2 Q_2^{-1} R_2 + C_2 \end{array} \right| \,.$$

The coordination problem becomes

$$\min \left\{ w_1(y_1) + w_2(y_2) = \frac{1}{2} y_1^T q_1 y_1 + r_1^T y_1 + \frac{1}{2} y_2^T q_2 y_2 + r_2^T y_2 \right\} \tag{38}$$

$$y_1 + y_2 = d \quad \Rightarrow \quad \left| \underset{m_0 x m_0}{I} \quad \underset{m_0 x m_0}{I} \right|_{m_0 x 2 m_0} ; y = \left| \begin{array}{c} y_1 \\ y_2 \end{array} \right| ; \quad q = \left| \begin{array}{cc} q_1 & 0 \\ 0 & q_2 \end{array} \right| \quad r = \left| \begin{array}{c} r_1 \\ r_2 \end{array} \right| ;$$

The coordination problem (38) is a linear-quadratic one and its solution can be found in an analytical form according to (4) or

$$y^{opt} = -q^{-1} \left[r - A_I^T (A_I q^{-1} A_I^T)^{-1} (A_I q^{-1} r + d) \right] \,. \tag{39}$$

Relation (39) is developed additionally to the form

$$y_1^{opt} = -q_1^{-1} r_1 + q_1^{-1} (q_1^{-1} + q_2^{-1})^{-1} (q_1^{-1} r_1 + q_2^{-1} r_2 + d) \tag{40}$$

$$y_2^{opt} = -q_2^{-1} r_2 + q_2^{-1} (q_1^{-1} + q_2^{-1})^{-1} (q_1^{-1} r_1 + q_2^{-1} r_2 + d) \,.$$

2.2.2 Presenting the resources y_i^{opt} in terms of the initial problem

It is necessary the values of y_i^{opt} to be presented by the matrices and vectors of the initial problem a_i, b_i, Q_i, R_i, C_i, β, γ, $i=1,2$. According to (35) and (36), it is performed

$$q_1 = \beta_{11} \qquad \Rightarrow \qquad q_1^{-1} = \beta_{11}^{-1} \tag{41}$$

$$q_2 = \gamma_{11} \qquad \Rightarrow \qquad q_2^{-1} = \gamma_{11}^{-1}.$$

After additional transformations it follows

$$y_1^{opt} = \beta_{11}^{-1} \begin{vmatrix} \beta_{11}^T & \beta_{21}^T \end{vmatrix} \begin{vmatrix} a_1 Q_1^{-1} R_1 \\ b_1 Q_1^{-1} R_1 + C_1 \end{vmatrix} + \beta_{11}^{-1}(\beta_{11}^{-1} + \gamma_{11}^{-1})^{-1} \left[\beta_{11}^{-1} \begin{vmatrix} \beta_{11}^T & \beta_{21}^T \end{vmatrix} \begin{vmatrix} a_1 Q_1^{-1} R_1 \\ b_1 Q_1^{-1} R_1 + C_1 \end{vmatrix} + \gamma_{11}^{-1} \begin{vmatrix} \gamma_{11}^T & \gamma_{21}^T \end{vmatrix} \begin{vmatrix} a_2 Q_2^{-1} R_2 \\ b_2 Q_2^{-1} R_2 + C_2 \end{vmatrix} + d \right] \tag{42}$$

$$y_2^{opt} = \gamma_{11}^{-1} \begin{vmatrix} \gamma_{11}^T & \gamma_{21}^T \end{vmatrix} \begin{vmatrix} a_2 Q_2^{-1} R_2 \\ b_2 Q_2^{-1} R_2 + C_2 \end{vmatrix} + \gamma_{11}^{-1}(\gamma_{11}^{-1} + \beta_{11}^{-1})^{-1} \left[\beta_{11}^{-1} \begin{vmatrix} \beta_{11}^T & \beta_{21}^T \end{vmatrix} \begin{vmatrix} a_1 Q_1^{-1} R_1 \\ b_1 Q_1^{-1} R_1 + C_1 \end{vmatrix} + \gamma_{11}^{-1} \begin{vmatrix} \gamma_{11}^T & \gamma_{21}^T \end{vmatrix} \begin{vmatrix} a_2 Q_2^{-1} R_2 \\ b_2 Q_2^{-1} R_2 + C_2 \end{vmatrix} + d \right].$$

After substitution of optimal resources y_i^{opt}, $i=1,2$ from (42) in the expressions of $x_1(y_1)$ from (21) and $x_2(y_2)$ from (22) the analytical relations $x_1(y_1^{opt})$ and $x_2(y_2^{opt})$, which are solutions of the initial problem (1) are obtained. To get the explicit analytical form of relations $x_i(y_i^{opt})$, (42) is substituted in (21) and (22) and after transformations follows

$$x_1(y_1^{opt}) = -Q_1^{-1} R_1 + Q_1^{-1} \begin{vmatrix} a_1^T & b_1^T \end{vmatrix} \begin{vmatrix} (\beta_{11}^{-1} + \gamma_{11}^{-1})^{-1} & (\beta_{11}^{-1} + \gamma_{11}^{-1})^{-1}\beta_{11}^{-1}\beta_{21}^T & (\beta_{11}^{-1} + \gamma_{11}^{-1})^{-1}\gamma_{11}^{-1}\gamma_{21}^T \\ \beta_{21}\beta_{11}^{-1}(\beta_{11}^{-1} + \gamma_{11}^{-1})^{-1} & \beta_{21}\beta_{11}^{-1}(\beta_{11}^{-1} + \gamma_{11}^{-1})^{-1}\beta_{11}^{-1}\beta_{21}^T + & \beta_{21}\beta_{11}^{-1}(\beta_{11}^{-1} + \gamma_{11}^{-1})^{-1}\gamma_{11}^{-1}\gamma_{21}^T \\ & +\beta_{22} - \beta_{21}\beta_{11}^{-1}\beta_{21}^T \end{vmatrix} \tag{43}$$

$$* \begin{vmatrix} a_1 Q_1^{-1} R_1 + a_2 Q_2^{-1} R_2 + d \\ b_1 Q_1^{-1} R_1 + C_1 \\ b_2 Q_2^{-1} R_2 + C_2 \end{vmatrix}$$

$$x_2(y_2^{opt}) = -Q_2^{-1} R_2 + Q_2^{-1} \begin{vmatrix} a_2^T & b_2^T \end{vmatrix} \begin{vmatrix} (\beta_{11}^{-1} + \gamma_{11}^{-1})^{-1} & (\beta_{11}^{-1} + \gamma_{11}^{-1})^{-1}\beta_{11}^{-1}\beta_{21}^T & (\beta_{11}^{-1} + \gamma_{11}^{-1})^{-1}\gamma_{11}^{-1}\gamma_{21}^T \\ \gamma_{21}\gamma_{11}^{-1}(\beta_{11}^{-1} + \gamma_{11}^{-1})^{-1} & \gamma_{21}\gamma_{11}^{-1}(\beta_{11}^{-1} + \gamma_{11}^{-1})^{-1}\beta_{11}^{-1}\beta_{21}^T & \gamma_{21}\gamma_{11}^{-1}(\beta_{11}^{-1} + \gamma_{11}^{-1})^{-1}\gamma_{11}^{-1}\gamma_{21}^T + \\ & & +\gamma_{22} - \gamma_{21}\gamma_{11}^{-1}\gamma_{21}^T \end{vmatrix} *$$

$$\begin{vmatrix} a_1 Q_1^{-1} R_1 + a_2 Q_2^{-1} R_2 + d \\ b_1 Q_1^{-1} R_1 + C_1 \\ b_2 Q_2^{-1} R_2 + C_2 \end{vmatrix}. \tag{44}$$

The obtained results in (43) and (44) $x_i(y_i^{opt})$, $i = 1,2$ are after applying the predictive coordination for solving the initial problem (1). The solutions x_i^{opt}, $i = 1,2$ from (15) are obtained by applying goal coordination to the same initial problem. As the solutions $x_i(y_i^{opt})$, $i = 1,2$ and x_i^{opt}, $i = 1,2$ are equal, after equalization of (15) with (43) and (44) relations among the components of the inverse matrix α and the components of the inverse β and γ are obtained. According to (15) and (43), it follows:

$$\alpha_{11} = (\beta_{11}^{-1} + \gamma_{11}^{-1})^{-1} \ ; \ \alpha_{12} = (\beta_{11}^{-1} + \gamma_{11}^{-1})^{-1} \beta_{11}^{-1} \beta_{21}^{T} \ ; \ \alpha_{13} = (\beta_{11}^{-1} + \gamma_{11}^{-1})^{-1} \gamma_{11}^{-1} \gamma_{21}^{T}$$

$$\alpha_{21} = \beta_{21} \beta_{11}^{-1} (\beta_{11}^{-1} + \gamma_{11}^{-1})^{-1} \ ; \ \alpha_{22} = \beta_{21} \beta_{11}^{-1} (\beta_{11}^{-1} + \gamma_{11}^{-1})^{-1} \beta_{11}^{-1} \beta_{21}^{T} + \beta_{22} - \beta_{21} \beta_{11}^{-1} \beta_{21}^{T} \ ;$$

$$\alpha_{23} = \beta_{21} \beta_{11}^{-1} (\beta_{11}^{-1} + \gamma_{11}^{-1})^{-1} \gamma_{11}^{-1} \gamma_{21}^{T} \tag{45}$$

$$\alpha_{31} = \gamma_{21} \gamma_{11}^{-1} (\beta_{11}^{-1} + \gamma_{11}^{-1})^{-1} \ ; \ \alpha_{32} = \gamma_{21} \gamma_{11}^{-1} (\beta_{11}^{-1} + \gamma_{11}^{-1})^{-1} \beta_{11}^{-1} \beta_{21}^{T} \ ;$$

$$\alpha_{33} = \gamma_{21} \gamma_{11}^{-1} (\beta_{11}^{-1} + \gamma_{11}^{-1})^{-1} \gamma_{11}^{-1} \gamma_{21}^{T} + \gamma_{22} - \gamma_{21} \gamma_{11}^{-1} \gamma_{21}^{T} \ .$$

Consequently, after applying the both coordination strategies towards the same initial problem (1) analytical relations (15) and respectively (43) and (44) are obtained. This allows to be received analytical relations among the components of the inverse matrices α, β and γ, which were not able to be determined directly because by definition:

$$\alpha = \begin{vmatrix} a_1 Q_1^{-1} a_1^T + a_2 Q_2^{-1} a_2^T & a_1 Q_1^{-1} b_1^T & a_2 Q_2^{-1} b_2^T \\ b_1 Q_1^{-1} a_1^T & b_1 Q_1^{-1} b_1^T & 0 \\ b_2 Q_2^{-1} a_2^T & 0 & b_2 Q_2^{-1} b_2^T \end{vmatrix}^{-1} \ ;$$

$$\beta = \begin{vmatrix} a_1 Q_1^{-1} a_1^T & a_1 Q_1^{-1} b_1^T \\ b_1 Q_1^{-1} a_1^T & b_1 Q_1^{-1} b_1^T \end{vmatrix}^{-1} \quad \gamma = \begin{vmatrix} a_2 Q_2^{-1} a_2^T & a_2 Q_2^{-1} b_2^T \\ b_2 Q_2^{-1} a_2^T & b_2 Q_2^{-1} b_2^T \end{vmatrix}^{-1} \ .$$

Consequently, using (45) the components of the inverse matrix α can be determined when β and γ are given. This allows the matrix α to be determined by fewer calculations in comparison with its direct inverse transformation because the inverse matrices β and γ have less dimensions. Relations (45) can be applied for calculation of the components α_{ij} of the inverse matrix α (with large dimension) by finding the inverse matrices β and γ (with fewer dimensions). The computational efficiency for evaluating the inverse matrix with high dimension using relations (45) is preferable in comparison with its direct calculation (Stoilova & Stoilov, 2007).

3. Predictive coordination for block-diagonal problem of quadratic programming with three and more subsystems

Analytical relations for predictive coordination strategy for the case when the subsystems in the bi-level hierarchy are more than two are developed. The case of bi-level hierarchical system with three subsystems is considered, figure 2

The initial optimization problem, solved by the hierarchical system is stated as

$$\min \frac{1}{2} \begin{vmatrix} x_1^T & x_2^T & x_3^T \end{vmatrix} \begin{vmatrix} Q_1 & 0 & 0 \\ 0 & Q_2 & 0 \\ 0 & 0 & Q_3 \end{vmatrix} \begin{vmatrix} x_1 \\ x_2 \\ x_3 \end{vmatrix} + \begin{vmatrix} R_1^T & R_2^T & R_3^T \end{vmatrix} \begin{vmatrix} x_1 \\ x_2 \\ x_3 \end{vmatrix} \tag{46}$$

$$a_1 x_{1m_0 x n_1} + a_2 x_{2m_0 x n_2} + a_3 x_{3m_0 x n_3} = d \qquad (47)$$

$$b_1 x_{1m_1 x n_1} \qquad\qquad = C_1$$
$$b_2 x_{2m_2 x n_2} \qquad\qquad = C_2$$
$$b_3 x_{3m_3 x n_3} \quad = C_3$$

where the dimensions of the vectors and matrices are appropriately defined

$$x_{1n_1 x 1} ; x_{2n_2 x 1} ; x_{3n_3 x 1} ; R_{1n_1 x 1} ; R_{2n_2 x 1} ; R_{3n_3 x 1} ;$$
$$a_{1m_0 x n_1} ; a_{2m_0 x n_2} ; a_{3m_0 x n_3} ; d_{m_0 x 1} ;$$
$$b_{1m_1 x n_1} ; b_{2m_2 x n_2} ; b_{3m_3 x n_3} ; C_{1m_1 x 1} ; C_{2m_2 x 1} ; C_{3m_3 x 1} ;$$

$$C = \begin{vmatrix} d \\ C_1 \\ C_2 \\ C_3 \end{vmatrix}_{(m_0+m_1+m_2+m_3)x(n_1+n_2+n_3)} ; \quad Q = \begin{vmatrix} Q_1 & 0 & 0 \\ 0 & Q_2 & 0 \\ 0 & 0 & Q_3 \end{vmatrix} ; \quad R = \begin{vmatrix} R_1 \\ R_2 \\ R_3 \end{vmatrix} ;$$

$$A = \begin{vmatrix} a_1 & a_2 & a_3 \\ b_1 & 0 & 0 \\ 0 & b_2 & 0 \\ 0 & 0 & b_3 \end{vmatrix}_{(m_0+m_1+m_2+m_3)x(n_1+n_2+n_3)}.$$

The peculiarity of problem (46), which formalizes the management of hierarchical system with three subsystems, concerns the existence of local resources C_1, C_2, C_3, which are used by each subsystem. According to the coupling constraint (47) additional resources d are allocated among the subsystems. Problem (46) can be presented in a general form, using the substitutions

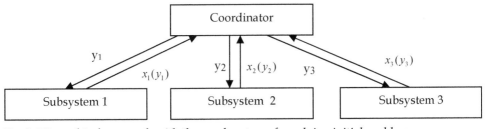

Fig. 2. Hierarchical approach with three subsystems for solving initial problem

$$A_1 \Big|_{(m_0+m_1+m_2+m_3)x n_1} = \begin{vmatrix} a_1 & {\scriptstyle m_0 x n_1} \\ b_1 & {\scriptstyle m_1 x n_1} \\ 0 & {\scriptstyle m_2 x n_1} \\ 0 & {\scriptstyle m_3 x n_1} \end{vmatrix} ; \quad A_3 \Big|_{(m_0+m_1+m_2+m_3)x n_3} = \begin{vmatrix} a_3 & {\scriptstyle m_0 x n_3} \\ 0 & {\scriptstyle m_1 x n_3} \\ 0 & {\scriptstyle m_2 x n_3} \\ b_3 & {\scriptstyle m_3 x n_3} \end{vmatrix} ; \quad D = \begin{vmatrix} d \\ C_1 \\ C_2 \\ C_3 \end{vmatrix}_{(m_0+m_1+m_2+m_3)x 1} \qquad (48)$$

$$A = \left| A_1 \quad A_2 \quad A_3 \right|_{(m_0 + m_1 + m_2 + m_3) \times (n_1 + n_2 + n_3)}.$$

Analogically to the previous case with two subsystems, analytical relations for determining the inverse matrix components by matrices with fewer dimensions are obtained

$$\alpha_{11} = (\beta_{11}^{-1} + \gamma_{11}^{-1} + \delta_{11}^{-1})^{-1}; \quad \alpha_{12} = (\beta_{11}^{-1} + \gamma_{11}^{-1} + \delta_{11}^{-1})^{-1} \beta_{11}^{-1} \beta_{21}^{T} \tag{49}$$

$$\alpha_{13} = (\beta_{11}^{-1} + \gamma_{11}^{-1} + \delta_{11}^{-1})^{-1} \gamma_{11}^{-1} \gamma_{21}^{T}; \quad \alpha_{14} = (\beta_{11}^{-1} + \gamma_{11}^{-1} + \delta_{11}^{-1})^{-1} \delta_{11}^{-1} \delta_{21}^{T}$$

$$\alpha_{21} = \beta_{21} \beta_{11}^{-1} (\beta_{11}^{-1} + \gamma_{11}^{-1} + \delta_{11}^{-1})^{-1}; \quad \alpha_{22} = \beta_{21} \beta_{11}^{-1} (\beta_{11}^{-1} + \gamma_{11}^{-1} + \delta_{11}^{-1})^{-1} \beta_{11}^{-1} \beta_{21}^{T} + \beta_{22} - \beta_{21} \beta_{11}^{-1} \beta_{21}^{T}$$

$$\alpha_{23} = \beta_{21} \beta_{11}^{-1} (\beta_{11}^{-1} + \gamma_{11}^{-1} + \delta_{11}^{-1})^{-1} \gamma_{11}^{-1} \gamma_{21}^{T}; \quad \alpha_{24} = \beta_{21} \beta_{11}^{-1} (\beta_{11}^{-1} + \gamma_{11}^{-1} + \delta_{11}^{-1})^{-1} \delta_{11}^{-1} \delta_{21}^{T}$$

$$\alpha_{31} = \gamma_{21} \gamma_{11}^{-1} (\beta_{11}^{-1} + \gamma_{11}^{-1} + \delta_{11}^{-1})^{-1}; \quad \alpha_{32} = \gamma_{21} \gamma_{11}^{-1} (\beta_{11}^{-1} + \gamma_{11}^{-1} + \delta_{11}^{-1})^{-1} \beta_{11}^{-1} \beta_{21}^{T}$$

$$\alpha_{33} = \gamma_{21} \gamma_{11}^{-1} (\beta_{11}^{-1} + \gamma_{11}^{-1} + \delta_{11}^{-1})^{-1} \gamma_{11}^{-1} \gamma_{21}^{T} + \gamma_{22} - \gamma_{21} \gamma_{11}^{-1} \gamma_{21}^{T}; \quad \alpha_{34} = \gamma_{21} \gamma_{11}^{-1} (\beta_{11}^{-1} + \gamma_{11}^{-1} + \delta_{11}^{-1})^{-1} \delta_{11}^{-1} \delta_{21}^{T}$$

$$\alpha_{41} = \delta_{21} \delta_{11}^{-1} (\beta_{11}^{-1} + \gamma_{11}^{-1} + \delta_{11}^{-1})^{-1}; \quad \alpha_{42} = \delta_{21} \delta_{11}^{-1} (\beta_{11}^{-1} + \gamma_{11}^{-1} + \delta_{11}^{-1})^{-1} \beta_{11}^{-1} \beta_{21}^{T}$$

$$\alpha_{43} = \delta_{21} \delta_{11}^{-1} (\beta_{11}^{-1} + \gamma_{11}^{-1} + \delta_{11}^{-1})^{-1} \gamma_{11}^{-1} \gamma_{21}^{T}; \quad \alpha_{44} = \delta_{21} \delta_{11}^{-1} (\beta_{11}^{-1} + \gamma_{11}^{-1} + \delta_{11}^{-1})^{-1} \delta_{11}^{-1} \delta_{21}^{T} + \delta_{22} - \delta_{21} \delta_{11}^{-1} \delta_{21}^{T}.$$

The initial problem can be solved by four or more subsystems. The relations between the components of the matrix $\alpha = (\alpha_{ij})$ and the matrices with lower sizes $\beta, \gamma, \dots \omega$ are given below

$$\left|
\begin{array}{cccc}
\alpha_{11} = & \alpha_{12} = & \alpha_{13} = & \alpha_{1j} = \\
(\beta_{11}^{-1} + \dots + \omega_{11}^{-1})^{-1} & (\beta_{11}^{-1} + \dots + \omega_{11}^{-1})^{-1} \beta_{11}^{-1} \beta_{21}^{T} & (\beta_{11}^{-1} + \dots + \omega_{11}^{-1})^{-1} \gamma_{11}^{-1} \gamma_{21}^{T} \quad \dots & (\beta_{11}^{-1} + \dots + \omega_{11}^{-1})^{-1} * \\
& & & * \omega_{11}^{-1} \omega_{21}^{T} \\[4pt]
\alpha_{21} = & \alpha_{22} = & \alpha_{23} = & \alpha_{2j} = \\
\beta_{21} \beta_{11}^{-1} (\beta_{11}^{-1} + \dots + \omega_{11}^{-1})^{-1} & \beta_{21} \beta_{11}^{-1} (\beta_{11}^{-1} + \dots + \omega_{11}^{-1})^{-1} * & \beta_{21} \beta_{11}^{-1} (\beta_{11}^{-1} + \dots + \omega_{11}^{-1})^{-1} * & \beta_{21} \beta_{11}^{-1} (\beta_{11}^{-1} + \dots + \omega_{11}^{-1})^{-1} * \\
& * \beta_{11}^{-1} \beta_{21}^{T} + \beta_{22} - \beta_{21} \beta_{11}^{-1} \beta_{21}^{T} & * \gamma_{11}^{-1} \gamma_{21}^{T} \quad \dots & * \omega_{11}^{-1} \omega_{21}^{T} \\[4pt]
\alpha_{31} = & \alpha_{32} = & \alpha_{33} = & \alpha_{3j} = \\
\gamma_{21} \gamma_{11}^{-1} (\beta_{11}^{-1} + \dots + \omega_{11}^{-1})^{-1} & \gamma_{21} \gamma_{11}^{-1} (\beta_{11}^{-1} + \dots + \omega_{11}^{-1})^{-1} * & \gamma_{21} \gamma_{11}^{-1} (\beta_{11}^{-1} + \dots + \omega_{11}^{-1})^{-1} * & \gamma_{21} \gamma_{11}^{-1} (\beta_{11}^{-1} + \dots + \omega_{11}^{-1})^{-1} * \\
& * \beta_{11}^{-1} \beta_{21}^{T} & * \gamma_{11}^{-1} \gamma_{21}^{T} + \gamma_{22} - \gamma_{21} \gamma_{11}^{-1} \gamma_{21}^{T} \quad \dots & * \omega_{11}^{-1} \omega_{21}^{T} \\[4pt]
\vdots & & & \\[4pt]
\alpha_{i1} = & \alpha_{i2} = & \alpha_{i3} = & \alpha_{ij} = \\
\omega_{21} \omega_{11}^{-1} (\beta_{11}^{-1} + \dots + \omega_{11}^{-1})^{-1} & \omega_{21} \omega_{11}^{-1} (\beta_{11}^{-1} + \dots + \omega_{11}^{-1})^{-1} * & \omega_{21} \omega_{11}^{-1} (\beta_{11}^{-1} + \dots + \omega_{11}^{-1})^{-1} * & \omega_{21} \omega_{11}^{-1} (\beta_{11}^{-1} + \dots + \omega_{11}^{-1})^{-1} * \\
& * \beta_{11}^{-1} \beta_{21}^{T} & * \gamma_{11}^{-1} \gamma_{21}^{T} \quad \dots & \omega_{11}^{-1} \omega_{21}^{T} + \omega_{22} - \omega_{21} \omega_{11}^{-1} \omega_{21}^{T}
\end{array}
\right| \tag{50}$$

4. Assessment of the calculation efficiency of the analytical results for determination of inverse matrix components

For simplicity of working the notations for right matrices with lower dimensions are introduced. In the case of 2 subsystems, the matrices c and d are the corresponding right matrices of the inverse matrices β and γ. By definition having in mind (46) c and d are symmetric ones

$$c = \begin{vmatrix} \underset{m_0 x m_0}{c_{11}} & \underset{m_0 x m_1}{c_{12}} \\ \underset{m_1 x m_0}{c_{21}} & \underset{m_1 x m_1}{c_{22}} \end{vmatrix} = \begin{vmatrix} \underset{m_0 x m_0}{\underbrace{a_1 Q_1^{-1} a_1^T}} & \underset{m_0 x m_1}{\underbrace{a_1 Q_1^{-1} b_1^T}} \\ \underset{m_1 x m_0}{\underbrace{b_1 Q_1^{-1} a_1^T}} & \underset{m_1 x m_1}{\underbrace{b_1 Q_1^{-1} b_1^T}} \end{vmatrix} ; \quad \beta = \begin{vmatrix} \beta_{11} & \beta_{12} \\ \beta_{21} & \beta_{22} \end{vmatrix} = c^{-1}$$

$$d = \begin{vmatrix} \underset{m_0 x m_0}{d_{11}} & \underset{m_0 x m_2}{d_{12}} \\ \underset{m_2 x m_0}{d_{21}} & \underset{m_2 x m_2}{d_{22}} \end{vmatrix} = \begin{vmatrix} \underset{m_0 x m_0}{\underbrace{a_2 Q_2^{-1} a_2^T}} & \underset{m_0 x m_2}{\underbrace{a_2 Q_2^{-1} b_2^T}} \\ \underset{m_2 x m_0}{\underbrace{b_2 Q_1^{-1} a_2^T}} & \underset{m_2 x m_2}{\underbrace{b_2 Q_2^{-1} b_2^T}} \end{vmatrix} \quad \gamma = \begin{vmatrix} \gamma_{11} & \gamma_{12} \\ \gamma_{21} & \gamma_{22} \end{vmatrix} = d^{-1}.$$

Analogically, for 3 subsystems the right matrix is e and the corresponding inverse matrix is δ $(e - \delta)$; for 4 subsystems - $(f - \varphi)$.

An *example* for computational efficiency of the proposed relations (45) /2 subsystems is given below with a symmetric matrix AL with dimension from 17×17 to 26×26 which varies according to variation of dimension m_1 from 2 to 11, while m_0 is 4 and m_2 is 11. Matrix AL is in the form

$$AL = \begin{array}{c|c|c} m_0=4 & m_1=2 \div 11 & m_2=11 \\ \hline c_{11}+d_{11} & c_{12} & d_{12} \\ \hline c_{21} & c_{22} & 0 \\ \hline d_{21} & 0 & d_{22} \end{array}$$

The MATLAB's codes are given below:

```
%example of inversion of AL  (dimension 26x26) when m₁=11

c₁₁=[1 2 3 1;  2 3 2 2;  3 2 4 2;   1 2 2 1];

c₁₂=[ -2   1   0  -1   2   4    0  -1  -3   2   2;    -5   0   2   1   4   6   -5
7   1   9   1;    0   7   2   1   3  -8   9   1   0   2   3;    4   2  -1   0   2   -1
2   1   3   1   1];

c₂₁=c₁₂';

c₂₂=[ 1    2    1   -3    1    0    1    5    2    8    2;
      2    3   -4    1    0    2    9    8    5    1   -3;
      1   -4    1   -1    1    5   -6    2    1    3    1;
     -3    1   -1    4    3    2    1    0   -1   -2    2;
            1    0    1    3    2    1    1    5   -3    3   -1;
      0    2    5    2    1    4    2    1    0    1    1;
      1    9   -6    1    1    2    6    3    1    0    2;
      5    8    2    0    5    1    3    5   -2    7    0;
            2    5    1   -1   -3    0    1   -2    3    1    1;
```

```
    8   1   3  -2   3   1   0   7   1   4   2;
    2  -3   1   2  -1   1   2   0   1   2   4];


c=[c11 c12; c21 c22];
d11=[3  0   0 -2;      0 -6   2   0;      0   2 -2 -1;      -2   0 -1   2];

d12=[1  0   2   1   3  -4   2   0   1  -3   1 ;
     3 -1   0   2  -2  -1   0   1   1   0   2 ;
     3  0   1   0   5   3   7   1   2  -2   0;
     2  2   0   1   3   2   1   0   1  -1   1];

d21=d12';

d22=[ 1   3   7   2   2   1   1   0  -2  -1   1;
      3   2   1   1   1  -1  -2  -3   0   1   0 ;
      7   1   5   2   4   2   3  -1  -3  -2   1 ;
      2   1   2   1   2   3   0   1  -2  -4   2;
      2   1   4   2   1  -1   3   7  -1   2   0;
      1  -1   2   3  -1   0   2   1   4   1   2;
      1  -2   3   0   3   2   2   1  -3  -1   1;
      0  -3  -1   1   7   1   1   0   1   2   1;
     -2   0  -3  -2  -1   4  -3   1  -2   0   2;
     -1   1  -2  -4   2   1  -1   2   0   1   1;
      1   0   1   2   0   2   1   1   2   1   5];

d=[d11 d12; d21 d22];

%definition of AL

mm=size(c12);
m0=mm(1);              %m0=4
m1=mm(2);              %m1=11
mm=size(d12);
m2=mm(2);              %m2=11
m10=zeros(m1,m2);
m20=m10';

al=[c11+d11   c12   d12; c21   c22   m10;   d21   m20   d22];

flops(0);
alpha1=inv(al);        %direct inversion  of AL
fl_al=flops            %flops for direct matrix inversion

%matrix inversion by hierarchical approach
flops(0);

beta=inv(c);
gama=inv(d);
invbeta11=inv(beta(1:m0,1:m0));
invgama11=inv(gama(1:m0,1:m0));
invbeta11beta21T=invbeta11*beta(m0+1:m0+m1,1:m0)';
invgama11gama21T=invgama11*gama(m0+1:m0+m2,1:m0)';
```

```
ff=flops
flops(0);
alpha11=inv(invbeta11+invgama11);
alpha12=alpha11*invbeta11beta21T;
alpha13=alpha11*invgama11*gama(m0+1:m0+m2,1:m0)';

alpha21=alpha12';
alpha22=invbeta11beta21T'*alpha12+beta(m0+1:m0+m1,m0+1:m0+m1)-
beta(m0+1:m0+m1,1:m0)*invbeta11beta21T;
alpha23=invbeta11beta21T'*alpha13;

alpha31=alpha13';
alpha32=alpha23';
alpha33=invgama11gama21T'*alpha13+gama(m0+1:m0+m2,m0+1:m0+m2)-
gama(m0+1:m0+m2,1:m0)*invgama11gama21T;

alpha=[alpha11 alpha12 alpha13; alpha21 alpha22 alpha23; alpha31
alpha32 alpha33];

fl_nic=flops
fl_full=ff+fl_nic            %flops using noniterative coordination


al2=inv(alpha);             %verification
```

This code has been used for two types of calculations:
1. Direct calculation of α - inversion of matrix AL by built-in MATLAB function INV. The amount of calculations is presented as a dashed red line in Figure 3.
2. Evaluation of α applying relations (45). The amount of calculation is presented as a solid blue line in Figure 3.

The comparison of the both manners of calculations shows that the analytical relations are preferable when the matrix dimension increases. From experimental considerations it is preferable to hold the relation $3m_0 < m_1 + m_2$, which gives boundaries for the decomposition of the initial matrix AL. For the initial case of $m_0=4$ $m_1=2$ $m_2=11$ these values are near to equality of the above relation and that is why the decomposition approach does not lead to satisfactory result.

Second example A 29×29 symmetric block-diagonal matrix denoted by AL is considered. It has to be inversed to the matrix α by two manners: direct MATLAB's inversion and using relations (45) and (50). This matrix will be calculated by hierarchical approach and decomposition with 2, 3, and 4 subsystems.

Case 1. The right matrix AL can be inversed to α by the above analytical relations applying 4 subsystems where AL is presented by the matrices c, d, e and f in the manner:

	m_0	m_1	m_2	m_3	m_4
	$c_{11}+d_{11}+e_{11}+f_{11}$	c_{12}	d_{12}	e_{12}	f_{12}
	c_{21}	c_{22}	0	0	0
$AL =$	d_{21}	0	d_{22}	0	0
	e_{21}	0	0	e_{22}	0
	f_{21}	0	0	0	f_{22}

$AL=$

$m_0=3$			$m_1=6$						$m_2=6$						$m_3=7$							$m_4=7$						
5	1	-3	-1	2	4	-1	2	1	-4	1	0	1	-3	2	0	2	1	1	-2	0	-3	1	0	3	6	-1	1	4
1	4	5	-3	1	0	5	4	-1	-2	-1	0	-2	1	4	2	4	0	-5	7	1	-4	3	2	1	-1	4	-1	-2
-3	5	-4	3	2	1	0	3	2	-2	1	0	1	-1	-2	1	-2	1	3	1	0	1	4	1	3	2	4	1	-2
-1	-3	3	3	-4	1	0	2	1	0	0	0	0	0	0	0	0	0	0	0	0	0	0	0	0	0	0	0	0
2	1	2	-4	1	-1	1	5	-1	0	0	0	0	0	0	0	0	0	0	0	0	0	0	0	0	0	0	0	0
4	0	1	1	-1	7	3	2	3	0	0	0	0	0	0	0	0	0	0	0	0	0	0	0	0	0	0	0	0
-1	5	0	0	1	3	9	1	2	0	0	0	0	0	0	0	0	0	0	0	0	0	0	0	0	0	0	0	0
2	4	3	2	5	2	1	8	-1	0	0	0	0	0	0	0	0	0	0	0	0	0	0	0	0	0	0	0	0
1	-1	2	1	-1	3	2	-1	2	0	0	0	0	0	0	0	0	0	0	0	0	0	0	0	0	0	0	0	0
-4	-2	-2	0	0	0	0	0	0	1	-1	-2	-1	-1	1	0	0	0	0	0	0	0	0	0	0	0	0	0	0
1	-1	1	0	0	0	0	0	0	-1	-2	3	0	1	2	0	0	0	0	0	0	0	0	0	0	0	0	0	0
0	0	0	0	0	0	0	0	0	-2	3	-1	1	-2	4	0	0	0	0	0	0	0	0	0	0	0	0	0	0
1	-2	1	0	0	0	0	0	0	-1	0	1	-2	-4	2	0	0	0	0	0	0	0	0	0	0	0	0	0	0
-3	1	1	0	0	0	0	0	0	-1	1	-2	-4	1	3	0	0	0	0	0	0	0	0	0	0	0	0	0	0
2	4	-2	0	0	0	0	0	0	1	2	4	2	3	2	0	0	0	0	0	0	0	0	0	0	0	0	0	0
0	2	1	0	0	0	0	0	0	0	0	0	0	0	0	2	1	5	1	1	-2	1	0	0	0	0	0	0	0
2	4	-2	0	0	0	0	0	0	0	0	0	0	0	0	1	3	2	4	1	3	2	0	0	0	0	0	0	0
1	0	1	0	0	0	0	0	0	0	0	0	0	0	0	5	2	3	2	1	-1	1	0	0	0	0	0	0	0
1	-5	3	0	0	0	0	0	0	0	0	0	0	0	0	1	4	2	5	-1	3	-2	0	0	0	0	0	0	0
-2	7	1	0	0	0	0	0	0	0	0	0	0	0	0	1	1	1	-1	6	1	-1	0	0	0	0	0	0	0
0	1	0	0	0	0	0	0	0	0	0	0	0	0	0	-2	3	-1	3	1	2	1	0	0	0	0	0	0	0
-3	-4	1	0	0	0	0	0	0	0	0	0	0	0	0	1	2	1	-2	-1	1	3	0	0	0	0	0	0	0
1	3	4	0	0	0	0	0	0	0	0	0	0	0	0	0	0	0	0	0	0	0	1	-1	3	1	2	1	4
0	2	1	0	0	0	0	0	0	0	0	0	0	0	0	0	0	0	0	0	0	0	-1	2	1	3	-2	1	0
3	1	3	0	0	0	0	0	0	0	0	0	0	0	0	0	0	0	0	0	0	0	3	1	1	-2	-1	-2	1
6	-1	2	0	0	0	0	0	0	0	0	0	0	0	0	0	0	0	0	0	0	0	1	3	-2	1	-3	1	-2
-1	4	4	0	0	0	0	0	0	0	0	0	0	0	0	0	0	0	0	0	0	0	2	-2	-1	-3	2	1	-1
1	-1	1	0	0	0	0	0	0	0	0	0	0	0	0	0	0	0	0	0	0	0	1	1	-2	1	1	3	1
4	-2	-2	0	0	0	0	0	0	0	0	0	0	0	0	0	0	0	0	0	0	0	4	0	1	-2	-1	1	1

$c=$

$m_0=3$			$m_1=6$					
2	-1	2	-1	2	4	-1	2	1
-1	1	2	-3	1	0	5	4	-1
2	2	3	3	2	1	0	3	2
-1	-3	3	3	-4	1	0	2	1
2	1	2	-4	1	-1	1	5	-1
4	0	1	1	-1	7	3	2	3
-1	5	0	0	1	3	9	1	2
2	4	3	2	5	2	1	8	-1
1	-1	2	1	-1	3	2	-1	2

$d=$

$m_0=3$			$m_2=6$					
-1	-1	-1	-4	1	0	1	-3	2
-1	2	0	-2	-1	0	-2	1	4
-1	0	-2	-2	1	0	1	-1	-2
-4	-2	-2	1	-1	-2	-1	-1	1
1	-1	1	-1	-2	3	0	1	2
0	0	0	-2	3	-1	1	-2	4
1	-2	1	-1	0	1	-2	-4	2
-3	1	1	-1	1	-2	-4	1	3
2	4	-2	1	2	4	2	3	2

(51)

$$
e = \begin{array}{c c}
\begin{array}{cc} m_0=3 & \end{array} & \begin{array}{c} m_3=7 \end{array}\\
\left|\begin{array}{ccc|ccccccc}
3 & 0 & -2 & 0 & 2 & 1 & 1 & -2 & 0 & -3\\
0 & -4 & 2 & 2 & 4 & 0 & -5 & 7 & 1 & -4\\
-2 & 2 & 1 & 1 & -2 & 1 & 3 & 1 & 0 & 1\\
\hline
0 & 2 & 1 & 2 & 1 & 5 & 1 & 1 & -2 & 1\\
2 & 4 & -2 & 1 & 3 & 2 & 4 & 1 & 3 & 2\\
1 & 0 & 1 & 5 & 2 & 3 & 2 & 1 & -1 & 1\\
1 & -5 & 3 & 1 & 4 & 2 & 5 & -1 & 3 & -2\\
-2 & 7 & 1 & 1 & 1 & 1 & -1 & 6 & 1 & -1\\
0 & 1 & 0 & -2 & 3 & -1 & 3 & 1 & 2 & 1\\
-3 & -4 & 1 & 1 & 2 & 1 & -2 & -1 & 1 & 3
\end{array}\right|
\end{array}
$$

$$
f = \begin{array}{c c}
\begin{array}{cc} m_0=3 & \end{array} & \begin{array}{c} m_4=7 \end{array}\\
\left|\begin{array}{ccc|ccccccc}
1 & 3 & -2 & 1 & 0 & 3 & 6 & -1 & 1 & 4\\
3 & 5 & 1 & 3 & 2 & 1 & -1 & 4 & -1 & -2\\
-2 & 1 & -4 & 4 & 1 & 3 & 2 & 4 & 1 & -2\\
\hline
1 & 3 & 4 & 1 & -1 & 3 & 1 & 2 & 1 & 4\\
0 & 2 & 1 & -1 & 2 & 1 & 3 & -2 & 1 & 0\\
3 & 1 & 3 & 3 & 1 & 1 & -2 & -1 & -2 & 1\\
6 & -1 & 2 & 1 & 3 & -2 & 1 & -3 & 1 & -2\\
-1 & 4 & 4 & 2 & -2 & -1 & -3 & 2 & 1 & -1\\
1 & -1 & 1 & 1 & 1 & -2 & 1 & 1 & 3 & 1\\
4 & -2 & -2 & 4 & 0 & 1 & -2 & -1 & 1 & 1
\end{array}\right|
\end{array}
$$

Here is assessed the efficiency of usage of relations (50) for finding the inverse matrix α when the matrices with fewer dimensions c, d, e and f are given. The assessment is done by measurement of "flops" in MATLAB environment. A part of the MATLAB's codes which performs relations (50) for inverse matrix calculations and assess the computational performance are given below

```
al=[c11+d11+e11    c12    d12    e12 ;    c21    c22    m10    m30;    d21
m20    d22    m40;    e21    m50    m60    e22];
flops(0);
alpha1=inv(al);
fl_al=flops
flops(0);
beta=inv(c);
gama=inv(d);
delta=inv(e);
invbeta11=inv(beta(1:m0,1:m0));
invgama11=inv(gama(1:m0,1:m0));
invdelta11=inv(delta(1:m0,1:m0));
invbeta11beta21T=invbeta11*beta(m0+1:m0+m1,1:m0)';
invgama11gama21T=invgama11*gama(m0+1:m0+m2,1:m0)';
invdelta11delta21T=invdelta11*delta(m0+1:m0+m3,1:m0)';
ff=flops
flops(0);
alpha11=inv(invbeta11+invgama11+invdelta11);
alpha12=alpha11*invbeta11beta21T;
alpha13=alpha11*invgama11*gama(m0+1:m0+m2,1:m0)';
alpha14=alpha11*invdelta11delta21T;
alpha21=alpha12';
alpha22=invbeta11beta21T'*alpha12+beta(m0+1:m0+m1,m0+1:m0+m1)-
beta(m0+1:m0+m1,1:m0)*invbeta11beta21T;
alpha23=invbeta11beta21T'*alpha13;
alpha24=alpha21*invdelta11delta21T;
alpha31=gama(m0+1:m0+m2,1:m0)*invgama11*alpha11;
alpha32=alpha31*invbeta11beta21T;
alpha33=invgama11gama21T'*alpha13+gama(m0+1:m0+m2,m0+1:m0+m2)-
gama(m0+1:m0+m2,1:m0)*invgama11gama21T;
alpha34=alpha31*invdelta11delta21T;
```

```
alpha41=delta(m0+1:m0+m3,1:m0)*invdelta11*alpha11;
alpha42=alpha41*invbeta11beta21T;
alpha43=alpha41*invgama11gama21T;
alpha44=alpha41*invdelta11delta21T+delta(m0+1:m0+m3,m0+1:m0+m3)-
delta(m0+1:m0+m3,1:m0)*invdelta11delta21T;
alpha=[alpha11    alpha12    alpha13    alpha14;
alpha21    alpha22    alpha23    alpha24;
alpha31    alpha32    alpha33    alpha34;
alpha41    alpha42    alpha43    alpha44];
fl_nic=flops;
fl_full=ff+fl_nic
al2=inv(alpha);%verification
```

For direct inversion of AL the flops are 50220 and for using (50) - 16329, figure 4.

Case 2. The same matrix AL is given however α is determined by a different manner - by 3 subsystems:

$$AL = \begin{vmatrix} c_{11}+d_{11}+e_{11} & c_{12} & d_{12} & e_{12} \\ c_{21} & c_{22} & 0 & 0 \\ d_{21} & 0 & d_{22} & 0 \\ e_{21} & 0 & 0 & e_{22} \end{vmatrix}$$

where c and d are the same as in (51) , however the right matrix e is different. It utilizes the previous matrices e and f:

$$e = \begin{array}{|ccccccccccccccccc|}
\multicolumn{3}{l}{m_0=3} & & & & & & & \multicolumn{3}{l}{m_3=14} & & & & & \\
4 & 3 & -4 & 0 & 2 & 1 & 1 & -2 & 0 & -3 & 1 & 0 & 3 & 6 & -1 & 1 & 4 \\
3 & 1 & 3 & 2 & 4 & 0 & -5 & 7 & 1 & -4 & 3 & 2 & 1 & -1 & 4 & -1 & -2 \\
-4 & 3 & -5 & 1 & -2 & 1 & 3 & 1 & 0 & 1 & 4 & 1 & 3 & 2 & 4 & 1 & -2 \\
0 & 2 & 1 & 2 & 1 & 5 & 1 & 1 & -2 & 1 & 0 & 0 & 0 & 0 & 0 & 0 & 0 \\
2 & 4 & -2 & 1 & 3 & 2 & 4 & 1 & 3 & 2 & 0 & 0 & 0 & 0 & 0 & 0 & 0 \\
1 & 0 & 1 & 5 & 2 & 3 & 2 & 1 & -1 & 1 & 0 & 0 & 0 & 0 & 0 & 0 & 0 \\
1 & -5 & 3 & 1 & 4 & 2 & 5 & -1 & 3 & -2 & 0 & 0 & 0 & 0 & 0 & 0 & 0 \\
-2 & 7 & 1 & 1 & 1 & 1 & -1 & 6 & 1 & -1 & 0 & 0 & 0 & 0 & 0 & 0 & 0 \\
0 & 1 & 0 & -2 & 3 & -1 & 3 & 1 & 2 & 1 & 0 & 0 & 0 & 0 & 0 & 0 & 0 \\
-3 & -4 & 1 & 1 & 2 & 1 & -2 & -1 & 1 & 3 & 0 & 0 & 0 & 0 & 0 & 0 & 0 \\
1 & 3 & 4 & 0 & 0 & 0 & 0 & 0 & 0 & 0 & 1 & -1 & 3 & 1 & 2 & 1 & 4 \\
0 & 2 & 1 & 0 & 0 & 0 & 0 & 0 & 0 & 0 & -1 & 2 & 1 & 3 & -2 & 1 & 0 \\
3 & 1 & 3 & 0 & 0 & 0 & 0 & 0 & 0 & 0 & 3 & 1 & 1 & -2 & -1 & -2 & 1 \\
6 & -1 & 2 & 0 & 0 & 0 & 0 & 0 & 0 & 0 & 1 & 3 & -2 & 1 & -3 & 1 & -2 \\
-1 & 4 & 4 & 0 & 0 & 0 & 0 & 0 & 0 & 0 & 2 & -2 & -1 & -3 & 2 & 1 & -1 \\
1 & -1 & 1 & 0 & 0 & 0 & 0 & 0 & 0 & 0 & 1 & 1 & -2 & 1 & 1 & 3 & 1 \\
4 & -2 & -2 & 0 & 0 & 0 & 0 & 0 & 0 & 0 & 4 & 0 & 1 & -2 & -1 & 1 & 1 \\
\end{array}$$

The calculations in flops for direct inversing of AL are 50220 and using (49) - 23082, figure 4

Case 3. The inverse matrix α is determined by 2 subsystems and AL is in the form

$$AL \qquad \begin{vmatrix} c_{11}+d_{11} & c_{12} & d_{12} \\ c_{21} & c_{22} & 0 \\ d_{21} & 0 & d_{22} \end{vmatrix}$$

where c is the same as in (51) but the right matrix d covers d, e and f from *Case* 1 or d and e from *Case* 2.

The calculations for direct inversing AL are 50232 flops and for using (45) are 37271, figure 4

The results of the experiments of the second example show that if the number of the subsystems increases, the computational efficiency increases because the matrices' dimensions decrease. This is in harmony with the multilevel hierarchical idea for decomposition of the initial problem leading to better efficiency of the system's functionality.

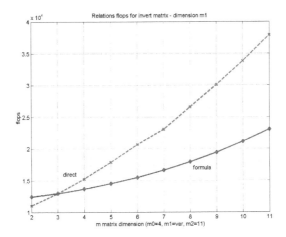

Fig. 3. Relation flops- m_1 matrix dimension

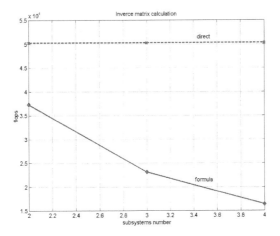

Fig. 4. Relation flops-subsystems number

5. Conclusion

The inverse matrix evaluations are decomposed to a set of operations, which does not consist of calculations of inverse high order matrix. Such decomposition benefits the inverse calculations when the initial large scale matrix is composed of low order matrices, which inverses are calculated with less computational efforts. The decomposition approach benefits the case when an initial matrix is known with its inverse, but few modifications of its components change it and new inverse has to be calculated. The decomposition approach for the inverse calculations is assessed and increase of the computational efficiency is illustrated. The MATLAB implementation of the presented sequence of calculations (49)−(50) is easy to perform because it results in consequent matrix sum and multiplications, and low order inverse matrix evaluations.

6. References

Fausett, L.(1999). *Applied numerical analysis*. Prentice Hall, NY, 596 p.

Flannery, B.(1997) *Numerical recipes in C. The art of Scientific Computing*. Cambridge University press, William Press, Second edition, 965p.

Mesarovich, M., D. Mako I. Takahara (1973) *Theory of Hierarchical Multilevel Systems*, Moscow, Mir (in Russian)

Stoilov T., K. Stoilova (1999). *Noniterative coordination in multilevel systems*. Kluwer Academic Publisher, ISBN 0-7923-5879-1, Dordrecht /Boston/London.

Stoilova, K. (2010). *Noniterative predictive coordination*. Professor M. Drinov Academic Publisher, ISBN 978-954-322-268-1, Sofia (in Bulgarian)

Stoilova K., T. Stoilov (2007) Computational efficiency of inverse matrix evaluations. Proceedings of International Conference Computer Systems and Technologies "CompSysTech 2007", ISBN 978-954-9641-50-9, Russe, Bulgaria, pp.IIIA.2-1 – IIIA.2-6.

Strassen V., (1969). Numerische Mathematik, vol.13, pp.354-356.

6

Educational Simulator for Particle Swarm Optimization and Economic Dispatch Applications

Woo Nam Lee and Jong Bae Park
Konkuk University
Korea

1. Introduction

Optimization problems are widely encountered in various fields in science and technology. Sometimes such problems can be very complex due to the actual and practical nature of the objective function or the model constraints. Most of power system optimization problems have complex and nonlinear characteristics with heavy equality and inequality constraints. Recently, as an alternative to the conventional mathematical approaches, the heuristic optimization techniques such as genetic algorithms (GAs), Tabu search, simulated annealing, and particle swarm optimization (PSO) are considered as realistic and powerful solution schemes to obtain the global or quasi-global optimums (K. Y. Lee et al., 2002).

In 1995, Eberhart and Kennedy suggested a PSO based on the analogy of swarm of bird and school of fish (J. Kennedy et al., 1995). The PSO mimics the behavior of individuals in a swarm to maximize the survival of the species. In PSO, each individual makes his decision using his own experience together with other individuals' experiences (H. Yoshida et al., 2000). The algorithm, which is based on a metaphor of social interaction, searches a space by adjusting the trajectories of moving points in a multidimensional space. The individual particles are drawn stochastically toward the present velocity of each individual, their own previous best performance, and the best previous performance of their neighbours (M. Clerc et al., 2002).

The practical economic dispatch (ED) problems with valve-point and multi-fuel effects are represented as a non-smooth optimization problem with equality and inequality constraints, and this makes the problem of finding the global optimum difficult. Over the past few decades, in order to solve this problem, many salient methods have been proposed such as a hierarchical numerical method (C. E. Lin et al., 1984), dynamic programming (A. J. Wood et al., 1984), evolutionary programming (Y. M. Park et al., 1998; H. T. Yang et al., 1996; N. Sinba et al., 2003), Tabu search (W. M. Lin et al., 2002), neural network approaches (J. H. Park et al., 1993; K. Y. Lee et al., 1998), differential evolution (L. S. Coelho et al., 2006), particle swarm optimization (J. B. Park et al., 2005; T. A. A. Victoire et al., 2004; T. A. A. Victoire et al., 2005), and genetic algorithm (D. C. Walters et al., 1993).

This chapter would introduce an educational simulator for the PSO algorithm. The purpose of this simulator is to provide the undergraduate students with a simple and useable tool for gaining an intuitive feel for PSO algorithm, mathematical optimization problems, and power system optimization problems. To aid the understanding of PSO, the simulator has been developed under the user-friendly graphic user interface (GUI) environment using MATLAB. In this simulator, instructors and students can set parameters related to the performance of PSO and can observe the impact of the parameters to the solution quality. This simulator also displays the movements of each particle and convergence process of a group. In addition, the simulator can consider other mathematical or power system optimization problems with simple additional MATLAB coding.

2. Overview of particle swarm optimization

Kennedy and Eberhart (J. Kennedy et al., 1995) developed a PSO algorithm based on the behavior of individuals of a swarm. Its roots are in zoologist's modeling of the movement of individuals (e.g., fishes, birds, or insects) within a group. It has been noticed that members within a group seem to share information among them, a fact that leads to increased efficiency of the group (J. Kennedy et al., 2001). The PSO algorithm searches in parallel using a group of individuals similar to other AI-based heuristic optimization techniques.

In a physical n-dimensional search space, the position and velocity of individual i are represented as the vectors $X_i = (x_{i1}, \cdots, x_{in})$ and $V_i = (v_{i1}, \cdots v_{in})$ in the PSO algorithm. Let $Pbest_i = \left(x_{i1}^{Pbest}, \cdots, x_{in}^{Pbest}\right)$ and $Gbest = \left(x_1^{Gbest}, \cdots, x_n^{Gbest}\right)$ be the best position of individual i and its neighbors' best position so far, respectively. The modified velocity and position of each individual can be calculated using the current velocity and the distance from $Pbest_i$ to $Gbest$ as follows:

$$V_i^{k+1} = \omega V_i^k + c_1 rand_1 \times (Pbest_i^k - X_i^k)$$
$$+ c_2 rand_2 \times (Gbest^k - X_i^k) \tag{1}$$

$$X_i^{k+1} = X_i^k + V_i^{k+1} \tag{2}$$

where,

V_i^k velocity of individual i at iteration k,

ω weight parameter,

c_1, c_2 acceleration coefficients,

$rand_1, rand_2$ random numbers between 0 and 1,

X_i^k position of individual i at iteration k,

$Pbest_i^k$ best position of individual i until iteration k,

$Gbest^k$ best position of the group until iteration k.

The constants c_1 and c_2 represent the weighting of the stochastic acceleration terms that pull each particle toward the Pbest and Gbest positions. Suitable selection of inertia weight provides a balance between global and local explorations, thus requiring less iteration on average to find a sufficiently optimal solution. In general, the inertia weight ω has a linearly decreasing dynamic parameter framework descending from ω_{max} to ω_{min} as follows (K. Y. Lee et al., 2002; H. Yoshida et al., 2000; J. B. Park et al., 2005).

$$\omega = \omega_{max} - \frac{\omega_{max} - \omega_{min}}{Iter_{max}} \times Iter \tag{3}$$

Were, $Iter_{max}$ is maximum iteration number and $Iter$ is current iteration number.

3. Structure of educational PSO simulator

3.1 Purpose and motivation of simulator

As a result of the rapid advances in computer hardware and software, computer-based power system educational tools have grown from very simple implementations, providing the user with little more than a stream of numerical output, to very detailed representations of the power system with an extensive GUI. Overbye, et al. had developed a user-friendly simulation program, PowerWorld Simulator, for teaching power system operation and control (T. J. Overbye et al., 2003). They applied visualization to power system information to draw user's attention and effectively display the simulation results. Through these works, they expected that animation, contouring, data aggregation and virtual environments would be quite useful techniques that are able to provide efficient learning experience to users. Also they presented experimental results associated with human factors aspects of using this visualization (D. A. Wiegmann et al., 2005; D. A. Wiegmann et al., 2006; N. Sinba et al., 2003).

Therefore, like other previous simulators, the motivation for the development of this simulator is to provide the students with a simple and useable tool for gaining an intuitive feel for the PSO algorithm, mathematical and power system optimization problems.

3.2 Functions of simulator

The basic objectives of this simulator were to make it easy to use and to provide effective visualization capability suitable for presentations as well as individual studies. This educational simulator was developed by MATLAB 2009b. MATLAB is a scientific computing language developed by The Mathworks, Inc. that is run in an interpreter mode on a wide variety of operating systems. It is extremely powerful, simple to use, and can be found in most research and engineering environments.

The structure and data flow of the developed PSO simulator is shown in Fig. 1. The simulator consists of 3-parts, that is, i) user setting of optimization function as well as parameters, ii) output result, and iii) visualized output variations, as shown in Figs. 2, 3, and 4, respectively. Since the main interaction between user and the simulator is performed through the GUI, it presents novice users with the information they need, and provides easy access for advanced users to additional detailed information. Thus, the GUI is instrumental in allowing users to gain an intuitive feel of the PSO algorithm, rather than just learning how to use this simulator.

In this simulator, parameters (i.e., maximum number of the iteration, maximum and minimum number of inertia weight, acceleration factors c_1 and c_2, and number of particles) that have the influence of PSO performance can be directly inputted by users. In addition,

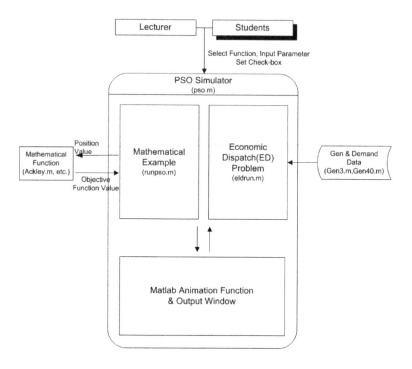

Fig. 1. Structure of the developed PSO simulator

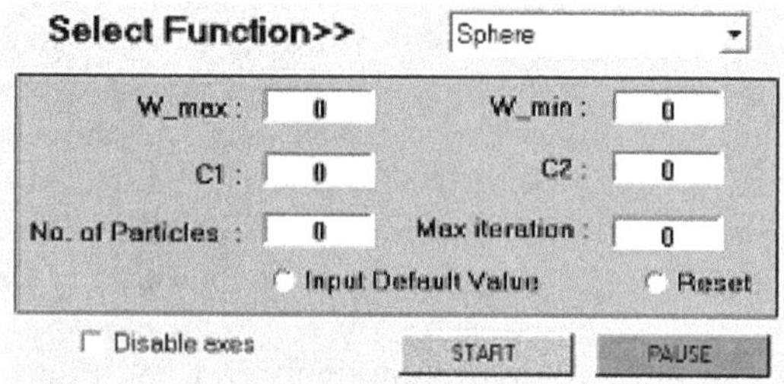

Fig. 2. A window for user setting

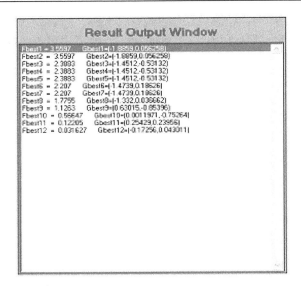

Fig. 3. Output result window

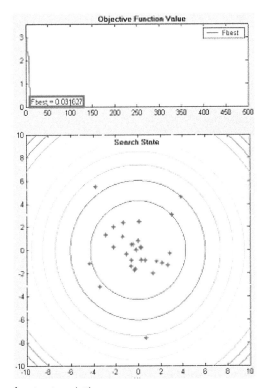

Fig. 4. Viewing parts of output variation

"Input Default Value" check-box was added for users who don't know the proper parameter values of the PSO. If the users push the "START" button finally, then the users can observe the evolution process of the particles on contours of the objective function (in case of a mathematical example) or the output histogram of each generator through MATLAB animation functions and check the changes of the values of the objective function and control variables at each iteration. The "Disable axes" check-box is used when the users want to show only the values of the final result fast. When the check-box is checked, only the final results (i.e., the value of the objective function and control variables) are expressed in the "Result Output Window". At any point in time in the simulation, the user can pause or restart the simulation by pushing the "PAUSE" button. As shown in Figs. 5 and 6, user can observe movements of each particle as well as the trend of the value of the objective function.

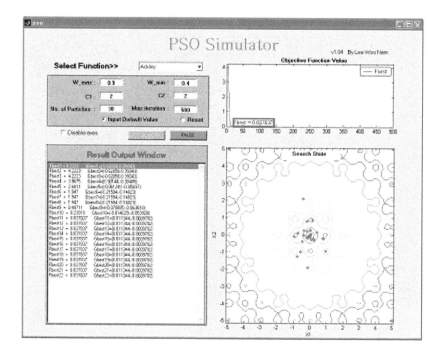

Fig. 5. Simulation for a mathematical example

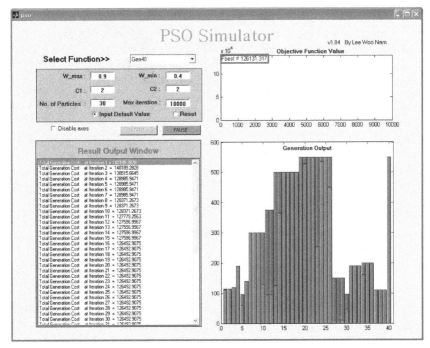

Fig. 6. Simulation for an economic dispatch problem.

4. Economic dispatch(ED) problem

4.1 Basic ED problem formulation

The ED problem is one of the basic optimization problems for the students who meet the power system engineering. The objective is to find the optimal combination of power generations that minimizes the total generation cost while satisfying an equality constraint and a set of inequality constraints. The most simplified cost function can be represented in a quadratic form as following (A. J. Wood et al., 1984):

$$C = \sum_{j \in J} F_j(P_j) \tag{4}$$

$$F_j(P_j) = a_j + b_j P_j + c_j P_j^2 \tag{5}$$

where,
C total generation cost;
F_j cost function of generator j;
a_j, b_j, c_j cost coefficients of generator j;
P_j electrical output of generator j;

J set for all generators.

While minimizing the total generation cost, the total generated power should be the same as the total load demand plus the total line loss. However, the transmission loss is not considered in this paper for simplicity. In addition, the generation output of each generator should be laid between minimum and maximum limits as follows:

$$P_{j\min} \le P_j \le P_{j\max} \tag{6}$$

where $P_{j\min}$ and $P_{j\max}$ are the minimum and maximum output of generator j, respectively.

4.2 Valve-point effects

The generating units with multi-valve steam turbines exhibit a greater variation in the fuel-cost functions. Since the valve point results in ripples, a cost function contains high order nonlinearities (H. T. Yang et al., 1996; N. Sinba et al., 2003; D. C. Walters et al. 1993). Therefore, the cost function (5) should be replaced by the following to consider the valve-point effects:

$$F_j(P_j) = a_j + b_j P_j + c_j P_j^2 + \left| e_j \times \sin(f_j \times (P_{j\min} - P_j)) \right| \tag{7}$$

where e_j and f_j are the cost coefficients of generator j reflecting valve-point effects.

Here, the sinusoidal functions are added to the quadratic cost functions.

5. Case studies

This simulator can choose and run five different mathematical examples and two different ED problems: (i) The Sphere function, (ii) The Rosenbrock (or banana-valley) function, (iii) Ackley's function, (iv) The generalized Rastrigin function, (v) The generalized Griewank function, (vi) 3-unit system with valve-point effects, and (vii) 40-unit system with valve-point effects. In the case of each mathematical example (functions (i)-(v)), two input variables (i.e., 2-dimensional space) have been set in order to show the movement of particles on contour. For the case study, 30 independent trials are conducted to observe the variation during the evolutionary processes and compare the solution quality and convergence characteristics.

To successfully implement the PSO, some parameters must be assigned in advance. The population size NP is set to 30. Since the performance of PSO depends on its parameters such as inertia weight ω and two acceleration coefficients (i.e., c_1 and c_2), it is very important to determine the suitable values of parameters. The inertia weight is varied from 0.9 (i.e., $\omega_{\max}$) to 0.4 (i.e., $\omega_{\min}$), as these values are accepted as typical for solving wide varieties of problems. Two acceleration coefficients are determined through the experiments for each problem so as to find the optimal combination.

5.1 Mathematical examples

For development of user's understanding of the PSO algorithm, five non-linear mathematical examples are used here. In each case, the maximum number of iterations (i.e., $iter_{\max}$) was set to 500. The acceleration coefficients (i.e., c_1 and c_2) was equally set to 2.0

from the experimental results for each case using the typical PSO algorithm. And all of the global minimum value of each function is known as 0. The global minimum value was successfully verified by the simulator.

5.1.1 The sphere function
The function and the initial position range of input variables (i.e., x_i) are as follows:

$$f_0(x) = \sum_{i=1}^{n} x_i^2$$ (8)

$$-5.12 \leq x_i \leq 5.12$$

Initial and final stages of the optimization process for the Sphere function are shown in Fig. 7.

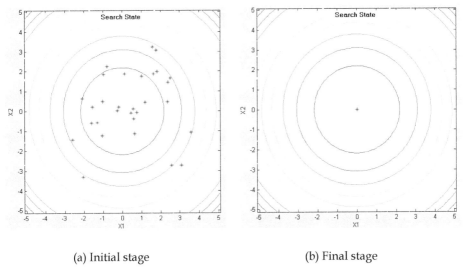

(a) Initial stage   (b) Final stage

Fig. 7. Optimization process for the sphere function.

5.1.2 The rosenbrock (or banana-valley) function
The function and the initial position range of input variables (i.e., x_i) are as follows:

$$f_1(x) = \sum_{i=1}^{n/2} (100(x_{2i} - x_{2i-1}^2)^2 + (1 - x_{2i-1})^2)$$ (9)

$$-2.048 \leq x_i \leq 2.048$$

Initial and final stages of the optimization process for the Rosenbrock function are shown in Fig. 8.

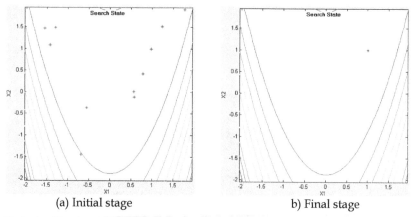

(a) Initial stage   b) Final stage

Fig. 8. Optimization process for the Rosenbrock function.

5.1.3 The ackley's function

The function and the initial position range of input variables (i.e., x_i) is as follows:

$$f_2(x) = -20\exp\left(-0.2\sqrt{\frac{1}{n}\sum_{i=1}^{n}x_i^2}\right) - \exp\left(\frac{1}{n}\sum_{i=1}^{n}\cos(2\pi x_i)\right) + 20 + e \qquad (10)$$

$$-30 \le x_i \le 30$$

Initial and final stages of the optimization process for the Ackley's function are shown in Fig. 9.

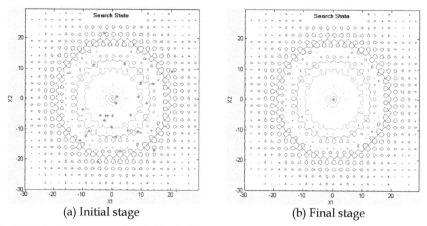

(a) Initial stage   (b) Final stage

Fig. 9. Optimization process for Ackley's function.

5.1.4 The generalized rastrigin function

The function and the initial position range of input variables (i.e., x_i) is as follows:

$$f_3(x) = \sum_{i=1}^{n}(x_i^2 - 10\cos(2\pi x_i) + 10) \tag{11}$$

$$-5.12 \le x_i \le 5.12$$

Initial and final stages of the optimization process for the generalized Rastrigin function are shown in Fig. 10.

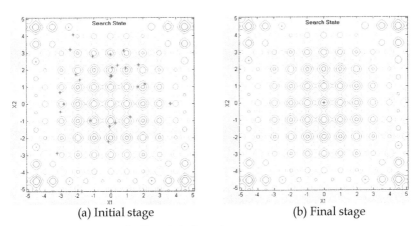

(a) Initial stage   (b) Final stage

Fig. 10. Optimization process for Rastrigin function.

5.1.5 The generalized griewank function

The function and the initial position range of input variables (i.e., x_i) is as follows:

$$f_4(x) = \frac{1}{4000}\sum_{i=1}^{n} x_i^2 - \prod_{i=1}^{n}\cos\left(\frac{x_i}{\sqrt{i}}\right) + 1 \tag{12}$$

$$-200 \le x_i \le 200$$

Initial and final stages of the optimization process for the generalized Griewank function are shown in Fig. 11.

Table 1 shows the average values of objective functions and two input variables for each function achieved by the PSO simulator.

Function Name	Objective Function Value	x_1	x_2
Sphere	0	0	0
Rosenbrock	0	1	1
Ackley	-8.8818e-16	-2.9595e-16	1.6273e-16
Rastrigin	0	9.7733e-10	-7.9493e-10
Griewank	0	100	100

Table 1. Results for Each Test Function

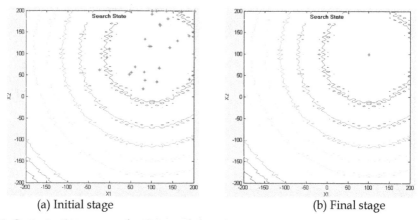

(a) Initial stage   (b) Final stage

Fig. 11. Optimization process for Griewank function.

5.2 Economic dispatch(ED) problems with valve-point effects

This simulator also offers examples to solve ED problem for two different power systems: a 3-unit system with valve-point effects, and a 40-unit system with valve-point effects. The total demands of the 3-unit and the 40-unit systems are set to 850MW and 10,500MW, respectively. All the system data and related constraints of the test systems are given in (N. Sinba et al., 2003). Because these systems have more than 3 input variables, the simulator shows a histogram for the generation output instead of the contour and particles. Since the global minimum for the total generation cost is unknown in the case of the 40-unit system, the maximum number of iterations (i.e., $iter_{max}$) is set to 10,000 in order to sufficiently search for the minimum value.

Table 2 shows the minimum, mean, maximum, and standard deviation for the 3-unit system obtained from the simulator. The generation outputs and the corresponding costs of the best solution for 3-unit system are described in Table 3.

Case	Minimum Cost ($)	Average Cost ($)	Maximum Cost ($)	Standard Deviation
3-Unit System	8234.0717	8234.0717	8234.0717	0

* Global value of the 3-unit system was known as 8234.0717.T

Table 2. Convergence Results for 3-Unit System

Unit	Generation	Cost
1	300.2669	3087.5099
2	400.0000	3767.1246
3	149.7331	1379.4372
TP/TC	850.0000	8234.0717

*TP: total power [MW], TC: total generation cost [$]

Table 3. Generation Output of Each Generator and The Corresponding Cost in 3-Unit System

In order to find the optimal combination of parameters (i.e., ω_{max}, ω_{min}, c_1, and c_2 B), six cases are considered as given in Table 4. The parameters are determined through the experiments for 40-unit system using the simulator. In Table 4, the effects of parameters are illustrated

Cases	ω_{max}	ω_{min}	c1,c2	Minimum Cost ($)	Average Cost ($)	Maximum Cost ($)	Standard Deviation
1	1.0	0.5	1	121755.49	122221.90	122624.07	156.97
2	0.9	0.4	1	121761.40	122343.32	123087.16	303.62
3	0.8	0.3	1	121949.15	122842.59	124363.11	602.06
4	1.0	0.5	2	121865.23	122285.12	122658.29	175.19
5	0.9	0.4	2	121768.69	122140.32	122608.27	187.74
6	0.8	0.3	2	121757.09	122158.00	122615.71	212.36

Table 4. Influence of Acceleration Coefficients for 40-Unit System

The result screens for 3-unit and 40-unit system are shown in Figs. 12 and 13, respectively. Each histogram expresses the result of generation output for each generator.

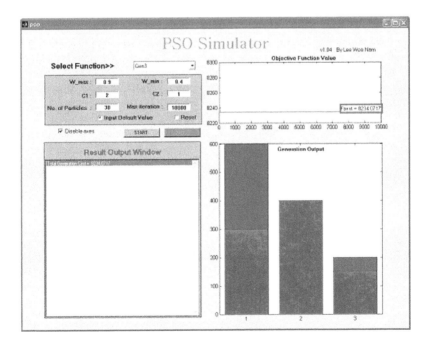

Fig. 12. Result screen for the 3-units system.

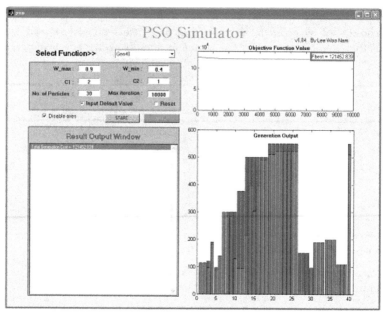

Fig. 13. Result screen for the 40-units system.

6. Conclusion

This chapter presents an educational simulator for particle swarm optimization (PSO) and application for solving mathematical test functions as well as ED problems with non-smooth cost functions. Using this simulator, instructors and students can select the test functions for simulation and set the parameters that have an influence on the PSO performance. Through visualization process of each particle and variation of the value of objective function, the simulator is particularly effective in providing users with an intuitive feel for the PSO algorithm. This simulator is expected to be an useful tool for students who study electrical engineering and optimization techniques.

7. Appendix 1: pso.m

```
function varargout = pso(varargin)
gui_Singleton = 1;
gui_State = struct('gui_Name',        mfilename, ...
    'gui_Singleton',  gui_Singleton, ...
    'gui_OpeningFcn', @pso_OpeningFcn, ...
    'gui_OutputFcn',  @pso_OutputFcn, ...
    'gui_LayoutFcn',  [] , ...
    'gui_Callback',   []);
if nargin & isstr(varargin{1})
    gui_State.gui_Callback = str2func(varargin{1});
end
if nargout
    [varargout{1:nargout}] = gui_mainfcn(gui_State, varargin{:});
else
```

```
    gui_mainfcn(gui_State, varargin{:});
end
function pso_OpeningFcn(hObject, eventdata, handles, varargin)
handles.output = hObject;
guidata(hObject, handles);
function varargout = pso_OutputFcn(hObject, eventdata, handles)
varargout{1} = handles.output;
function select_func_CreateFcn(hObject, eventdata, handles)
if ispc
    set(hObject,'BackgroundColor','white');
else
    set(hObject,'BackgroundColor',get(0,'defaultUicontrolBackgroundColor'));
end
function select_func_Callback(hObject, eventdata, handles)
function default_value_Callback(hObject, eventdata, handles)
set(handles.default_value, 'Value', 1);
set(handles.reset, 'Value', 0);
set(handles.wmax, 'String', 0.9);
set(handles.wmin, 'String', 0.4);
set(handles.X_max, 'String', 5.12);
set(handles.X_min, 'String', -5.12);
set(handles.c1, 'String', 2);
set(handles.c2, 'String', 2);
set(handles.N, 'String', 30);
set(handles.itmax, 'String', 500);
function reset_Callback(hObject, eventdata, handles)
set(handles.default_value, 'Value', 0);
set(handles.reset, 'Value', 1);
set(handles.wmax, 'String', 0);
set(handles.wmin, 'String', 0);
set(handles.X_max, 'String', 0);
set(handles.X_min, 'String', 0);
set(handles.c1, 'String', 0);
set(handles.c2, 'String', 0);
set(handles.N, 'String', 0);
set(handles.itmax, 'String', 0);
function wmax_CreateFcn(hObject, eventdata, handles)
if ispc
    set(hObject,'BackgroundColor','white');
else
set(hObject,'BackgroundColor',get(0,'defaultUicontrolBackgroundColor'));
end
function wmax_Callback(hObject, eventdata, handles)
wmax = str2double(get(hObject,'String'));
if isnan(wmax)
    set(hObject, 'String', 0);
    errordlg('Input must be a number','Error');
end
pso_para = getappdata(gcbf, 'metricdata');
pso_para.wmax = wmax;
setappdata(gcbf, 'metricdata', pso_para);
function wmin_CreateFcn(hObject, eventdata, handles)
if ispc
    set(hObject,'BackgroundColor','white');
else
set(hObject,'BackgroundColor',get(0,'defaultUicontrolBackgroundColor'));
end
```

```
function wmin_Callback(hObject, eventdata, handles)
wmin = str2double(get(hObject,'String'));
if isnan(wmin)
    set(hObject, 'String', 0);
    errordlg('Input must be a number','Error');
end
pso_para = getappdata(gcbf, 'metricdata');
pso_para.wmin = wmin;
setappdata(gcbf, 'metricdata', pso_para);
function c1_CreateFcn(hObject, eventdata, handles)
if ispc
    set(hObject,'BackgroundColor','white');
else
set(hObject,'BackgroundColor',get(0,'defaultUicontrolBackgroundColor'));
end
function c1_Callback(hObject, eventdata, handles)
c1 = str2double(get(hObject,'String'));
if isnan(c1)
    set(hObject, 'String', 0);
    errordlg('Input must be a number','Error');
end
pso_para = getappdata(gcbf, 'metricdata');
pso_para.c1 = c1;
setappdata(gcbf, 'metricdata', pso_para);
function c2_CreateFcn(hObject, eventdata, handles)
if ispc
    set(hObject,'BackgroundColor','white');
else
set(hObject,'BackgroundColor',get(0,'defaultUicontrolBackgroundColor'));
end
function c2_Callback(hObject, eventdata, handles)
c2 = str2double(get(hObject,'String'));
if isnan(c2)
    set(hObject, 'String', 0);
    errordlg('Input must be a number','Error');
end
pso_para = getappdata(gcbf, 'metricdata');
pso_para.c2 = c2;
setappdata(gcbf, 'metricdata', pso_para);
function N_CreateFcn(hObject, eventdata, handles)
if ispc
    set(hObject,'BackgroundColor','white');
else
set(hObject,'BackgroundColor',get(0,'defaultUicontrolBackgroundColor'));
end
function N_Callback(hObject, eventdata, handles)
N = str2double(get(hObject,'String'));
if isnan(N)
    set(hObject, 'String', 0);
    errordlg('Input must be a number','Error');
end
pso_para = getappdata(gcbf, 'metricdata');
pso_para.N = N;
setappdata(gcbf, 'metricdata', pso_para);
function itmax_CreateFcn(hObject, eventdata, handles)
if ispc
    set(hObject,'BackgroundColor','white');
```

```matlab
else
set(hObject,'BackgroundColor',get(0,'defaultUicontrolBackgroundColor'));
end
function itmax_Callback(hObject, eventdata, handles)
itmax = str2double(get(hObject,'String'));
if isnan(itmax)
    set(hObject, 'String', 0);
    errordlg('Input must be a number','Error');
end
function start_Callback(hObject, eventdata, handles)
if get(handles.select_func,'value')>=7
    eldrun
else
    runpso
end
function Result_window_CreateFcn(hObject, eventdata, handles)
if ispc
    set(hObject,'BackgroundColor','white');
else
set(hObject,'BackgroundColor',get(0,'defaultUicontrolBackgroundColor'));
end
function Result_window_Callback(hObject, eventdata, handles)
function pause_Callback(hObject, eventdata, handles)
if isequal(get(handles.pause,'String'),'PAUSE')
    set(handles.start,'Enable','on');
    set(handles.pause,'String','RESUME');
    uiwait;
else
    set(handles.start,'Enable','off');
    set(handles.pause,'String','PAUSE');
    uiresume;
end
function disable_Callback(hObject, eventdata, handles)
function close_Callback(hObject, eventdata, handles)
delete(get(0,'CurrentFigure'));
function X_max_Callback(hObject, eventdata, handles)
X_max = str2double(get(hObject,'String'));
if isnan(X_max)
    set(hObject, 'String', 0);
    errordlg('Input must be a number','Error');
end
pso_para = getappdata(gcbf, 'metricdata');
pso_para.X_max = X_max;
setappdata(gcbf, 'metricdata', pso_para);
function X_max_CreateFcn(hObject, eventdata, handles)
if ispc
    set(hObject,'BackgroundColor','white');
else
set(hObject,'BackgroundColor',get(0,'defaultUicontrolBackgroundColor'));
end
function X_min_Callback(hObject, eventdata, handles)
X_min = str2double(get(hObject,'String'));
if isnan(X_min)
    set(hObject, 'String', 0);
    errordlg('Input must be a number','Error');
end
pso_para = getappdata(gcbf, 'metricdata');
```

```
pso_para.X_min = X_min;
setappdata(gcbf, 'metricdata', pso_para);
function X_min_CreateFcn(hObject, eventdata, handles)
if ispc
    set(hObject,'BackgroundColor','white');
else
set(hObject,'BackgroundColor',get(0,'defaultUicontrolBackgroundColor'));
end
```

8. Appendix 2: runpso.m

```
cla;
set(handles.start,'Enable','off');
set(handles.pause,'String','PAUSE','Enable','on');
set(handles.text14,'String','Search State ');
functnames = get(handles.select_func,'String');
functname = functnames{get(handles.select_func,'Value')};
wmax = str2double(get(handles.wmax, 'String'));
wmin = str2double(get(handles.wmin, 'String'));
X_max = str2double(get(handles.X_max, 'String'));
X_min = str2double(get(handles.X_min, 'String'));
c1 = str2double(get(handles.c1, 'String'));
c2 = str2double(get(handles.c2, 'String'));
N = str2double(get(handles.N, 'String'));
itmax = str2double(get(handles.itmax, 'String'));
pso_para = getappdata(gcbf, 'metricdata');
pso_para.wmax = wmax;
pso_para.wmin = wmin;
pso_para.X_max = X_max;
pso_para.X_min = X_min;
pso_para.c1 = c1;
pso_para.c2 = c2;
pso_para.N = N;
pso_para.itmax = itmax;
setappdata(gcbf, 'metricdata', pso_para);
D=2; % Dimension
% Weight Parameter
for iter=1:pso_para.itmax
    W(iter)= pso_para.wmax-((pso_para.wmax-
pso_para.wmin)/pso_para.itmax)*iter;
end
%Initialization of positions of agents
% agents are initialized between -5.12,+5.12 randomly
a= X_min;  %min
b= X_max;  %max
x=a+(b-a)*rand(pso_para.N,D,1);
%Initialization of velocities of agents
%Between -5.12 , +5.12, (which can also be started from zero)
m=X_min;
n=X_max;
V=m+(n-m)*rand(pso_para.N,D,1);
%Function to be minimized.
```

```
F = feval(functname,x(:,:,1));
% Saving address and value; C:Value of E, I: The Number of Particle
[C,I]=min(abs(F(:,1,1)));  B(1,1,1)=C;
XX(1,1,1)=I;
gbest(1,:,1)=x(I,:,1);
%Matrix composed of gbest vector
for p=1:pso_para.N
    for r=1:D
        G(p,r,1)=gbest(1,r,1);
    end
end
Fbest(1,1,1) = feval(functname,G(1,:,1));
pbest=x;
% Calculating Velocity
V(:,:,2) = W(1) * V(:,:,1) + pso_para.c1*rand*(pbest(:,:,1)-
x(:,:,1)) + pso_para.c2*rand*(G(:,:,1)-x(:,:,1));
x(:,:,2)=x(:,:,1) + V(:,:,2);
for i=1:pso_para.N
    for j=1:D
        if x(i,j,2)<a
            x(i,j,2)=a;
        else
            if x(i,j,2)>b
                x(i,j,2)=b;
            else
            end
        end
    end
end
Fb(1,1,1) = feval(functname,gbest(1,:,1));
if get(handles.disable,'Value')==0
    %%%%%%%%%%%%%%%%%%%%%%%%% Contour Plot %%%%%%%%%%%%%%%%%%%%%%%%%%%
    axes(handles.axes2);
    axis([a b a b])
    con_m=a:0.1:b;
    con_n=con_m;
    [con_m,con_n]=meshgrid(con_m,con_n);
    for q=1:length(con_m(1,:))
        for z=1:length(con_n(1,:))
            r(q,z)= feval(functname,[con_m(q,z),con_n(q,z)]);
        end
    end
    r_save=r;
    [c,h]=contour(con_m,con_n,r_save,10);
    xlabel('X1')
    ylabel('X2')
    title('Search State')
    %%%%%%%%%%%%%%%%%%%%%%%%%%%%%%%%%%%%%%%%%%%%%%%%%%%%%%%%%%%%%%%%
end

for j=2:pso_para.itmax
```

```matlab
% Calculation of new positions
F(:,1,j) = feval(functname,x(:,:,j));
[C,I]=min(abs(F(:,1,j)));
B(1,1,j)=C;
for i=1:D
    gbest(1,i,j)=x(I,i,j);
end
Fb(1,1,j) = feval(functname,gbest(1,:,j));
[C,I]=min(Fb(1,1,:));
if Fb(1,1,j)<=C
    for k=1:D
        gbest(1,k,j)=gbest(1,k,j);
    end
else
    for m=1:D
        gbest(1,m,j)=gbest(1,m,I);
    end
end
%Matrix composed of gbest vector
for p=1:pso_para.N
    for r=1:D
        G(p,r,j)=gbest(1,r,j);
    end
end
Fbest(1,1,j) = feval(functname,G(1,:,j));
for i=1:pso_para.N;
    [C,I]=min(F(i,1,:));
    if  F(i,1,j)<=C
        pbest(i,:,j)=x(i,:,j);
    else
        pbest(i,:,j)=x(i,:,I);
    end
end
V(:,:,j+1)= W(j)*V(:,:,j) + pso_para.c1*rand*(pbest(:,:,j)-
x(:,:,j)) + pso_para.c2*rand*(G(:,:,j)-x(:,:,j));
x(:,:,j+1)=x(:,:,j)+V(:,:,j+1);
for k=1:pso_para.N
    for m=1:D
        if x(k,m,j+1)<a
            x(k,m,j+1)=a;
        else
            if x(k,m,j+1)>b
                x(k,m,j+1)=b;
            else
            end
        end
    end
end
if get(handles.disable,'Value')==0
    set(gcf,'Doublebuffer','on');
```

```
%%%%%%%% Display to the ListBox%%%%%%%%
        ResultStr(1) = [{['Fbest','1',' ','=',' ',
num2str(Fbest(1,1,1)),'
','Gbest','1','=','(',num2str(gbest(1,1,1)),',',num2str(gbest(1,2,1)
),')']}];
        ResultStr(j) = [{['Fbest',num2str(j),' ','=',' ',
num2str(Fbest(1,1,end)),'
','Gbest',num2str(j),'=','(',num2str(gbest(1,1,end)),',',num2str(gbe
st(1,2,end)),')']}];
        set(handles.Result_window, 'String', ResultStr);
        %%%%%%%% end of Display %%%%%%%%%%%%%%%%%%%

        %%%%%%%%%%%%%%%%% AXE-1 %%%%%%%%%%%%%%%%%%%
        axes(handles.axes1);
        cla;
        set(gca,'xlim',[0 pso_para.itmax],'ylim',[0 Fbest(1,1,1)]),
        plot(Fbest(:),'r-')
        if j<=pso_para.itmax/2
            text(j,Fbest(1,1,end),['Fbest = ',
num2str(Fbest(1,1,end))],'HorizontalAlignment','Left','VerticalAlign
ment','bottom','EdgeColor','blue','LineWidth',3);
        else
            text(j,Fbest(1,1,end),['Fbest = ',
num2str(Fbest(1,1,end))],'HorizontalAlignment','Right','VerticalAlig
nment','bottom','EdgeColor','blue','LineWidth',3);
        end
        legend('Fbest');
        hold on
        %%%%%%%%%%%%%%%%%%%%%%%%%%%%%%%%%%%%%%%%%%%%

        %%%%%%%%%%%%%%%%% AXE-2 %%%%%%%%%%%%%%%%%%%
        axes(handles.axes2);
        axis([a b a b])
        [c,h]=contour(con_m,con_n,r_save,10);
        hold on
        plot(pbest(:,1,j),pbest(:,2,j),'r*')
        xlabel('X1')
        ylabel('X2')
        drawnow
        hold off
        %%%%%%%%%%%%%%%%%%%%%%%%%%%%%%%%%%%%%%%%%%%%
    end
end
if get(handles.disable,'Value')==1
    ResultStr = [{['Fbest ','=',' ', num2str(Fbest(1,1,end)),'
','Gbest','=','(',num2str(gbest(1,1,end)),',',num2str(gbest(1,2,end)
),')']}];
    set(handles.Result_window, 'String', ResultStr);
end
set(handles.start,'Enable','on');
set(handles.pause,'String','PAUSE','Enable','off');
```

9. Appendix 3: eldrun.m

```
cla;
set(handles.start,'Enable','off');
set(handles.pause,'String','PAUSE','Enable','on');
set(handles.text14,'String','Generation Output');
functnames = get(handles.select_func,'String');
functname = functnames{get(handles.select_func,'Value')};
wmax = str2double(get(handles.wmax, 'String'));
wmin = str2double(get(handles.wmin, 'String'));
c1 = str2double(get(handles.c1, 'String'));
c2 = str2double(get(handles.c2, 'String'));
N = str2double(get(handles.N, 'String'));
itmax = str2double(get(handles.itmax, 'String'));
pso_para = getappdata(gcbf, 'metricdata');
pso_para.wmax = wmax;
pso_para.wmin = wmin;
pso_para.c1 = c1;
pso_para.c2 = c2;
pso_para.N = N;
pso_para.itmax = itmax;
setappdata(gcbf, 'metricdata', pso_para);

[Gen,Demand]=feval(functname);

%Initialization of PSO parameters
D=size(Gen,1); % Dimension (Number of Generator)
CR = 0.5;
for iter=1:pso_para.itmax
    W(iter)= pso_para.wmax-((pso_para.wmax-
pso_para.wmin)/pso_para.itmax)*iter;
end
%Initialization of positions of agents
%agents are initialized between P_min,P_max randomly
for i=1:D
    P_min(i) = Gen(i,6);      % P_min
    P_max(i) = Gen(i,7);      % P_max
end
% Constraints handling
for i=1:pso_para.N
    yes=1;
    while yes==1
        p=randperm(D);

        for n=1:D-1
            g = p(n);
            x(i,g) = P_min(g) +  (P_max(g)-P_min(g)) * rand;
            A(n) = x(i,g);
        end
        SUM=0;
        for f=1:D-1
```

```
            SUM = SUM + A(f);
        end
        A(D) = Demand - SUM;
        g=p(D);
        if A(D) < P_min(g)
            A(D) = P_min(g);
            ok=0;
        else
            if A(D) > P_max(g)
                A(D) = P_max(g);
                ok=0;
            else
                ok=1;
                yes=0;
            end
        end

        L=1;
        while ok==0
            A(L) = Demand -(sum(A(:))-A(L));
            if A(L) < P_min(p(L))
                A(L) = P_min(p(L));
                ok=0;
                L = L+1;
                if L==D+1
                    ok=1;
                    yes=1;
                else
                end
            else
                if A(L) > P_max(p(L))
                    A(L) = P_max(p(L));
                    ok=0;
                    L= L+1;
                    if L==D+1
                        ok=1;
                        yes =1;
                    else
                    end
                else
                    ok=1;
                    yes=0;
                end
            end
        end
    end
    for k=1:D
        x(i,p(k))=A(k);
    end
end
%Initialization of velocities of agents
```

```matlab
%Between V_min , V_max, (which can also be started from zero)
for i=1:pso_para.N
    for j=1:D
        m(j) = Gen(j,6) - x(i,j);   %V_min
        n(j) = Gen(j,7) - x(i,j);   %V_max
        V(i,j) = m(j) + (n(j)-m(j)) * rand;
    end
end
% End of Initialization
% Function to be minimized.
for i=1:pso_para.N;
    for j=1:D;
        Cost(i,j) = Gen(j,1) + Gen(j,2)*x(i,j) + Gen(j,3)*x(i,j).^2
+ abs(Gen(j,4)*sin(Gen(j,5)*(Gen(j,6)-x(i,j))));
    end
    F(i,1) = sum(Cost(i,:));   % Total Cost
end
pbest=x;
[C,I]=min(abs(F(:,1)));
B(1,1)=C;
XX(1,1)=I;
gbest(1,:)=x(I,:);
Gen_sum(1,1) = sum(gbest(1,:));
%Matrix composed of gbest vector
for j=1:D;
    Cost_Best(1,j) =
Gen(j,1)+Gen(j,2)*gbest(1,j)+Gen(j,3)*gbest(1,j).^2
+abs(Gen(j,4)*sin(Gen(j,5)*(Gen(j,6)-gbest(1,j))));
end
Fbest(1,1) = sum(Cost_Best(1,:));   % Total Cost
% Constraints handling
for i=1:pso_para.N
    yes=1;
    while yes==1
        p=randperm(D);
        for n=1:D-1
            g = p(n);
            V(i,g) = W(1) * V(i,g) + c1*rand*(pbest(i,g)-x(i,g)) +
c2*rand*(gbest(1,g)-x(i,g));
            x(i,g)=x(i,g) + V(i,g);
            if rand<=CR
                x_adj(i,g) = x(i,g);
            else
                x_adj(i,g) = pbest(i,g);
            end
            A(n) = x_adj(i,g);
            if A(n) < P_min(g)
                A(n) = P_min(g);
            else
                if A(n) > P_max(g)
                    A(n) = P_max(g);
```

```
            else
            end
        end
end
SUM=0;
for u=1:D-1
    SUM = SUM + A(u);
end
A(D) = Demand - SUM;

g=p(D);
if A(D) < P_min(g)
    A(D) = P_min(g);
    ok=0;
else
    if A(D) > P_max(g)
        A(D) = P_max(g);
        ok=0;
    else
        ok=1;
    end
    yes=0;
end

L=1;
while ok==0
    A(L) = Demand -(sum(A(:))-A(L));
    if A(L) < P_min(p(L))
        A(L) = P_min(p(L));
        ok=0;
        L = L+1;
        if L==D+1
            ok=1;
            yes=1;
        else
        end
    else
        if A(L) > P_max(p(L))
            A(L) = P_max(p(L));
            ok=0;
            L= L+1;
            if L==D+1
                ok=1;
                yes =1;
            else
            end
        else
            ok=1;
        end

        yes=0;
```

```
                    end
                end
            end
        for k=1:D
            x_adj(i,p(k))=A(k);
        end
    end

    for j=2:pso_para.itmax
        % Calculation of new positions
        for i=1:pso_para.N
            for k=1:D
                Cost(i,k) =
Gen(k,1)+Gen(k,2)*x_adj(i,k)+Gen(k,3)*x_adj(i,k).^2
+abs(Gen(k,4)*sin(Gen(k,5)*(Gen(k,6)-x_adj(i,k))));
            end
            F(i,j) = sum(Cost(i,:)); % Total Cost
        end

        for i=1:pso_para.N
            [C,I]=min(F(i,:));
            if  F(i,j)<=C
                pbest(i,:)=x_adj(i,:);
            else
            end
        end
        for i=1:pso_para.N
            for k=1:D
                Cost_pbest(i,k) =
Gen(k,1)+Gen(k,2)*pbest(i,k)+Gen(k,3)*pbest(i,k).^2
+abs(Gen(k,4)*sin(Gen(k,5)*(Gen(k,6)-pbest(i,k))));
            end
            F_pbest(i,1) = sum(Cost_pbest(i,:)); % Total Cost
        end
        [C,I]=min(F_pbest(:,1));
        for k=1:D
            gbest(1,k)=pbest(I,k);
        end
        Gen_sum(j,1) = sum(gbest(1,:));
        Fbest(j,1) = C;
        % Constraints handling
        for i=1:pso_para.N
            yes=1;
            while yes==1
                p=randperm(D);
                for n=1:D-1
                    g = p(n);
                    V(i,g) = W(j) * V(i,g) + c1*rand*(pbest(i,g)-x(i,g))
+ c2*rand*(gbest(1,g)-x(i,g));
                    x(i,g) = x(i,g) + V(i,g);
                    if rand<=CR
```

```
            x_adj(i,g) = x(i,g);
      else
            x_adj(i,g) = pbest(i,g);
      end
      A(n) = x_adj(i,g);
      if A(n) < P_min(g)
            A(n) = P_min(g);
      else
            if A(n) > P_max(g)
                A(n) = P_max(g);
            else
            end
      end
end
SUM=0;
for f=1:D-1
      SUM = SUM + A(f);
end
A(D) = Demand - SUM;

g=p(D);
if A(D) < P_min(g)
      A(D) = P_min(g);
      ok=0;
else
      if A(D) > P_max(g)
            A(D) = P_max(g);
            ok=0;
      else
            ok=1;
            yes=0;
      end

end
L=1;
while ok==0
      A(L) = Demand -(sum(A(:))-A(L));
      if A(L) < P_min(p(L))
            A(L) = P_min(p(L));
            ok=0;
            L = L+1;
            if L==D+1
                ok=1;
                yes=1;
            else
            end
      else
            if A(L) > P_max(p(L))
                A(L) = P_max(p(L));
                ok=0;
                L= L+1;
```

```
                    if L==D+1
                        ok=1;
                        yes=1;
                    else
                    end
                else
                    ok=1;
                    yes=0;
                end
            end
        end
    end
    for k=1:D
        x_adj(i,p(k))=A(k);
    end
end

if get(handles.disable,'Value')==0
    set(gcf,'Doublebuffer','on');
    %%%%%%%%% Display to the ListBox%%%%%%%%%%%
    ResultStr(1) = [{['Total Generation Cost    at Iteration
','1',' ','=',' ', num2str(Fbest(1,1))]}];
    ResultStr(j) = [{['Total Generation Cost    at Iteration
',num2str(j),'  ','=',' ', num2str(Fbest(end,1))]}];
    set(handles.Result_window, 'String', ResultStr);
    %%%%%%%%% end of Display %%%%%%%%%%%%%%%%%%%

    %%%%%%%%%%%%%%%%%%% AXE-1  %%%%%%%%%%%%%%%%%%
    axes(handles.axes1);
    cla;
    set(gca,'xlim',[0 pso_para.itmax],'ylim',[0 Fbest(1,1)]),
    plot(Fbest(:),'r-')
    if j<=pso_para.itmax/2
        text(j,Fbest(end,1),['Fbest = ',
num2str(Fbest(end,1))],'HorizontalAlignment','Left','VerticalAlignme
nt','bottom','EdgeColor','blue','LineWidth',3);
    else
        text(j,Fbest(end,1),['Fbest = ',
num2str(Fbest(end,1))],'HorizontalAlignment','Right','VerticalAlignm
ent','bottom','EdgeColor','blue','LineWidth',3);
    end
    legend('Fbest');
    hold on
    %%%%%%%%%%%%%%%%%%%%%%%%%%%%%%%%%%%%%%%%%%%%%%%%%%

    %%%%%%%%%%%%%%%%%%% AXE-2  %%%%%%%%%%%%%%%%%%
    axes(handles.axes2);
    axis([0 D+1 0 max(Gen(:,7))+50])
    bar(Gen(:,7),'r')
    hold on
    bar(gbest,'w')
```

```
        drawnow
        %%%%%%%%%%%%%%%%%%%%%%%%%%%%%%%%%%%%%%%%%%%%%%%%%%
    else
    end
end
if get(handles.disable,'Value')==1
    cla;
    ResultStr = [{['Total Generation Cost ','=',' ',
num2str(Fbest(end,1))]}];

    set(handles.Result_window, 'String', ResultStr);
end
%%%%%%%%%%%%%%%%%%%%    AXE-2   %%%%%%%%%%%%%%%%%%%
axes(handles.axes2);
axis([0 D+1 0 max(Gen(:,7))+50])
bar(Gen(:,7),'r')
hold on
bar(gbest(end,:),'w')
drawnow
%%%%%%%%%%%%%%%%%%%%%%%%%%%%%%%%%%%%%%%%%%%%%%%%%%%%%%%%%
set(handles.start,'Enable','on');
set(handles.pause,'String','PAUSE','Enable','off');
```

10. References

A. J. Wood and B. F. Wollenbergy (1984). Power Genration, Operation, and Control, *New York: Wiley*.

C. E. Lin and G. L. Viviani (1984). Hierarchical economic dispatch for piecewise quadratic cost functions, *IEEE Trans. Power App. System*, vol. PAS-103, no. 6, pp. 1170-1175.

D. A. Wiegmann, G. R. Essenberg, T. J. Overbye, and Y. Sun (2005). Human Factor Aspects of Power System Flow Animation, *IEEE Trans. Power Syst.*, vol. 20, no. 3, pp. 1233-1240.

D. A. Wiegmann, T. J. Overbye, S. M. Hoppe, G. R. Essenberg, and Y. Sun (2006). Human Factors Aspects of Three-Dimensional Visualization of Power System Information, *IEEE Power Eng. Soci. Genral Meeting*, pp. 7.

D. C. Walters and G. B. Sheble (1993). Genetic algorithm solution of economic dispatch with the valve point loading, *IEEE Trans. Power Syst.*, vol. 8, pp. 1325-1332.

H. T. Yang, P. C. Yang, and C. L. Huang (1996). Evolutionary programming based economic dispatch for units with nonsmooth fuel cost functions, *IEEE Trans. Power Syst.*, vol. 11, no. 1, pp. 112-118.

H. Yoshida, K. Kawata, Y. Fukuyama, S. Takayama, and Y. Nakanishi (2000). A particle swarm optimization for reactive power and voltage control considering voltage security assessment, *IEEE Trans. Power System*, vol. 15, pp. 1232-1239.

J. B. Park, K. S. Lee, J. R. Shin, and K. Y. Lee (2005). A particle swarm optimization for economic dispatch with nonsmooth cost functions, *IEEE Trans. Power Syst.*, vol. 20, no. 1, pp. 34-42.

J. H. Park, Y. S. Kim, I. K. Eom, and K. Y. Lee (1993). Economic load dispatch for piecewise quadratic cost function using Hopfield neural network, *IEEE Trans. Power Syst.*, vol. 8, pp. 1030-1038.

J. Kennedy and R. Eberhart (1995). Particle swarm optimization, *Proc. IEE Int. Conf. Neural Networks (ICNN'95)*, vol. IV, Perth, Australia, pp.1942-1948.

J. Kennedy and R. C. Eberhart (2001). Swarm Intelligence. *San Francisco, CA: Morgan Kaufmann.*

K. Y. Lee, A. Sode-Yome, and J. H. Park (1998). Adaptive Hopfield neural network for economic load dispatch, *IEEE Trans. Power Syst.*, vol. 13, pp. 519-526.

K. Y. Lee and M. A. El-Sharkawi, Eds. (2002). Modern Heuristic Optimization Techniques with Applications to Power Systems: *IEEE Power Engineering Society (02TP160)*.

L. S. Coelho and V. C. Mariani (2006). Combining of chaotic differential evolution and quadratic programming for economic dispatch optimization with valve-point effect, *IEEE Trans. Power Syst.*, vol. 21, No. 2.

M. Clerc and J. Kennedy (2002). The particle swarm-expolsion, stability, and convergence in a multidimensional complex space, *IEEE Trans. Evol. Comput.*, vol. 6, no. 1, pp. 58-73.

N. Sinha, R. Chakrabarti, and P. K. Chattopadhyay (2003). Evolutionary programming techniques for economic load dispatch, *IEEE Trans. on Evolutionary Computations*, Vol. 7, No. 1, pp. 83-94.

T. A. A. Victoire and A. E. Jeyakumar (2004). Hybrid PSO-SQP for economic dispatch with valve-point effect, *Electric Power Syst. Research*, vol. 71, pp. 51-59.

T. A. A. Victoire and A. E. Jeyakumar (2005). Reserve constrained dynamic dispatch of units with valve-point effects, *IEEE Trans. Power Syst.*, vol. 20, No. 3, pp. 1273-1282.

T. J. Overbye, D. A. Wiegmann, A. M. Rich, and Y. Sun (2003). Human Factor Aspects of Power System Voltage Contour Visualizations, *IEEE Trans. Power Syst.*, vol. 18, no. 1, pp. 76-82.

W. M. Lin, F. S. Cheng, and M. T. Tasy (2002). An improved Tabu search for economic dispatch with multiple minima, *IEEE Trans. Power Syst.*, vol. 17, pp. 108-112.

Y. M. Park, J. R. Won, and J. B. Park (1998). A new approach to economic load dispatch based on improved evolutionary programming, *Eng. Intell. Syst. Elect. Eng. Commun.*, vol. 6, no. 2, pp. 103-110.

Part 2

Database Development

7

The Impact of the Data Archiving File Format on Scientific Computing and Performance of Image Processing Algorithms in MATLAB Using Large HDF5 and XML Multimodal and Hyperspectral Data Sets

Kelly Bennett[1] and James Robertson[2]

[1]*U.S. Army Research Laboratory, Sensors and Electron Devices Directorate, Adelphi, MD*
[2]*Clearhaven Technologies LLC, Severna Park, MD*
U.S.A

1. Introduction

Scientists require the ability to effortlessly share and process data collected and stored on a variety of computer platforms in specialized data storage formats. Experiments often generate large amounts of raw and corrected data and metadata, which describes and characterizes the raw data. Scientific teams and groups develop many formats and tools for internal use for specialized users with particular references and backgrounds. Researchers need a solution for querying, accessing, and analyzing large data sets of heterogeneous data, and demand high interoperability between data and various applications (Shasharina et al., 2007; Shishedjiev et al., 2010).

Debate continues regarding which data format provides the greatest transparency and produces the most reliable data exchange. Currently, Extensible Markup Language (XML) and Hierarchical Data Format 5 (HDF5) formats are two solutions for sharing data. XML is a simple, platform-independent, flexible markup meta-language that provides a format for storing structured data, and is a primary format for data exchange across the Internet (McGrath, 2003). XML data files use Document Type Definitions (DTDs) and XML Schemas to define the data structures and definitions, including data formatting, attributes, and descriptive information about the data. A number of applications exist that use XML-based storage implementations for applications, including radiation and spectral measurements, simulation data of magnetic fields in human tissues, and describing and accessing fusion and plasma physics simulations (Shasharina et al., 2007; Shishedjiev et al., 2010).

HDF5 is a data model, library, and file format for storing and managing data. HDF5 is portable and extensible, allowing applications to evolve in their use of HDF5 (HDF Group). HDF5 files provide the capability for self-documenting storage of scientific data in that the HDF5 data model provides structures that allow the file format to contain data about the file structure and descriptive information about the data contained in the file (Barkstrom, 2001). Similar to XML, numerous applications using the HDF5 storage format exist, such as fusion and plasma physics, astronomy, medicine and bio-imaging (Shasharina et al., 2007; Dougherty et al., 2009).

In this chapter, we will use hyperspectral images stored in XML and HDF5 format to compare the relative performance of the file format using computationally intensive signal and image processing algorithms running in MATLAB on Windows® 64-bit and Linux 64-bit workstations. Hyperspectral imaging refers to the multidimensional character of the spectral data set, where the acquisition of images takes place over many contiguous spectral bands throughout the visible and infrared (IR) regions (Goetz et al., 1985). Sensor fusion and advanced image processing techniques are now possible using the information from these different bands that allow applications in aerospace, defense, medicine, and other fields of study.

To assist researchers in exchanging the data needed to develop, test, and optimize the techniques, selecting the best file format for computing environments (such as MATLAB) requires additional analysis. Such analysis includes analyzing the relative performance of the file format, including scalability, with respect to various computational tools, computer architectures, and operating systems (Bennett & Robertson, 2010). In this chapter we provide insights into the challenges researchers face with a growing set of data, along with expectations for performance guidelines on workstations for processing large HDF5 and XML hyperspectral image data. Additionally, in this chapter, we provide specific results comparing data load, process, and memory usage for the differing data formats, along with detailed discussions and implications for researchers.

2. Analysis of HDF5 and XML Formats

The goals of this analysis are to:
1. Determine strengths and weaknesses of using HDF5 and XML formats for typical processing techniques associated with large hyperspectral images;
2. Compare and analyze processing times on Windows and Linux 64-bit workstations for HDF5 and XML hyperspectral images; and
3. Identify areas that require additional research to help improve efficiencies associated with processing large HDF5 and XML files, such as hyperspectral images.

3. Methodology for Analysis of HDF5 and XML Formats

To address the analysis goals a set of 100 files containing multimodal hyperspectral images, ranging in size from 57 MB to 191 MB, stored in HDF5 format provided the input for the creation of HDF5 and XML dataset files as part of a preprocessing step for further analysis. The created HDF5 and XML dataset files provided the input to a series of analysis techniques typically associated with image and signal processing. Two different workstations running 64-bit Windows and Linux operating systems are used. The workstations are equipped with MATLAB (scientific programming language). Table 1 displays the descriptions of each of the workstations.

The hyperspectral images were originally stored in HDF5 format and included several different types of metadata in the form of HDF5 Groups and Datasets. Metadata in a typical HDF5 file includes ground truth, frequency bandwidths, raw image data, TIFF (Tagged

---

® Registered trademark of Microsoft Corporation.

Image File Format)-formatted images, collection information, and other ancillary information, allowing researchers to understand the images and their collection parameters.

Descriptor	Windows 64-bit	Linux 64-bit
Operating System	Windows 7 home premium	Red Hat Enterprise Linux 5
CPU	Intel i7 920 @2.67 GHz	2 processor, quad core Xeon 2.0 GHz
Memory	6 GB	16 GB
MATLAB version	7.11.0 (R2010b)	7.11.0 (R2010b)

Table 1. Research Equipment Descriptions.

Each original HDF5 file went through a number of preprocessing steps to remove the metadata in preparation for analysis. For analysis purposes, we needed to remove the metadata from the original HDF5 files and create new HDF5 and XML formatted files consisting of only raw sensor data prior to performing image processing. These steps included loading the original HDF5 file structures, searching through the HDF5 groups to find the raw image data, saving the new HDF5 file, creating and populating an XML document node, and saving the XML file. Figure 1 shows the overall steps in processing the original HDF5 file, along with some critical MATLAB code associated with each of those steps.

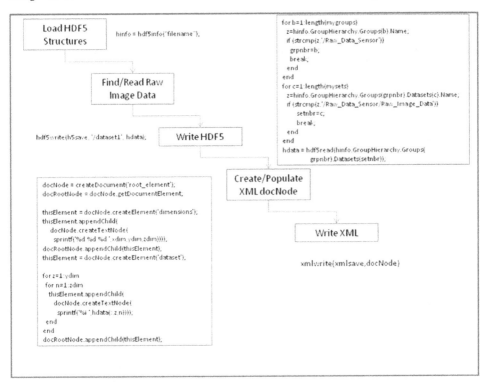

Fig. 1. Original HDF5 File Preprocessing Overview for the creation of HDF5 and XML Dataset Files.

After creating the HDF5 and XML files for the raw sensor data, each file was loaded into MATLAB, converted to an array as needed, and run through a number of image processing steps. XML stores the array data as a large ASCII character string, which requires converting the character array into a numeric array before beginning any processing. Unfortunately, the arrays were too large to use MATLAB's str2num() function, so a novel custom method was developed to read each character and convert it into numbers before writing the numbers into a MATLAB array.

Technique	Description	Example MATLAB Call
Image Adjustment	Maps the values in intensity to new values such that 1% of data saturates at low and high intensities of the original image.	im2= imadjust(im);
Histogram	Calculates a histogram where the variable bin specifies the number of bins used in the histogram.	[COUNTS,X] = imhist(im2,bin);
Descriptive Statistics	Computes the mean and standard deviations of the image values.	imagemean=mean2(im2); imagestd=std2(im2);
Median Noise Filter	Performs a median filtering of the image using a 3-by-3 neighborhood.	J=medfilt2(im2);
Weiner Noise Filter	Performs a filtering of the image using pixel-wise adaptive Wiener filtering, using neighborhoods of size fx-by-fy to estimate the local image mean and standard deviation	K = wiener2(im2,[fx fy]);
Sobel Edge Detection	Sobel method finds edges using the Sobel approximation to the derivative. It returns edges at those points where the gradient is maximum	BW1 = edge(im2,'sobel');
Canny Edge Detection	The Canny method finds edges by looking for local maxima of the gradient. The derivative of a Gaussian filter provides the approach for calculating the gradient.	BW2 = edge(im2,'canny');
FFT 2D Threshold Feature Detection	FFT approach to template matching and feature detection.	z= im2(minx:maxx,miny:maxy); C = real(ifft2(fft2(im2) .* fft2(rot90(z,2),dims(1),dims(2)))); t=max(C(:)) - .05*max(C(:));

Table 2. Image Processing Technique Descriptions.

Once stored as numeric arrays, the processing for the XML and the HDF5 files were the same and these processing steps include image adjustment, histogram calculation, and descriptive statistics, filtering to remove noise, edge detection and 2-D FFT threshold feature detection. Each of these image-processing techniques includes possible techniques users may invoke when processing hyperspectral images. Table 2 provides a brief description of each of these techniques and an example call within MATLAB. In Table 2, "im" represents the original image and 'im2' represents a processed image of 'im'. Each row in Table 2 shows various processing operations performed on 'im' or 'im2'. Figure 2 shows the flow of the image processing techniques.

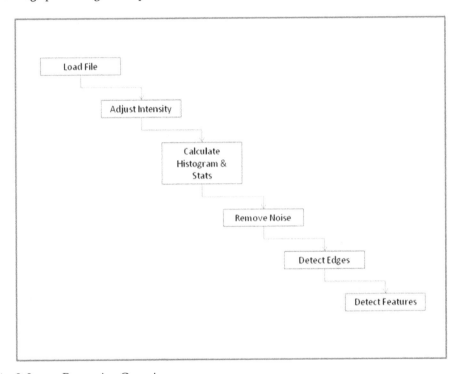

Fig. 2. Image Processing Overview.

Some of the metrics used for assessing the performance of each file format are calculation of load times, process times, and memory usage statistics for each file format and machine. These metrics reveal the computational performance of processing large archived data files in MATLAB using typical image processing algorithms. MATLAB's tic and toc methods were convenient to measure elapsed times associated with each processing step. Hyperspectral images consist of multiple segments representing different spectral bands or narrow frequency bands, with data collected for each image segment and averaged for reporting purposes. For example, an image with 62 segments would generate data for each of the 62 segments and the mean of those values, with the results described in the Results section of this paper. A typical sequence of elapsed time measurement would occur as shown in Figure 3. In the Figure 3 example, all files ("i") and segments ("j") perform the timing process for the image adjustment algorithm.

```
% Adjust the image for better display
tic;
im2= imadjust(im);
adjustIM(i,j)=toc;
```

Fig. 3. Elapsed Time Measurement Example Code.

After loading each created dataset file, both in HDF5 and XML, measuring the memory will determine the average memory usage. For the Windows environment, MATLAB's memory functions perform the process of determining the physical memory available at that point in time. For the Linux environment, system calls to the Linux memory functions determine the physical memory available after loading the file. MATLAB does not provide a Linux memory function at this time. Figure 4 shows a typical Windows memory call.

```
% Measure Windows Memory
[USERVIEW, SYSTEMVIEW] = memory;
pmem(i,j)=SYSTEMVIEW.PhysicalMemory.Available;
```

Fig. 4. Windows Memory Measurement Example Code.

Test	Description	Performance Factors
LU	Perform LU of a full matrix	Floating-point, regular memory access
FFT	Perform FFT of a full vector	Floating-point, irregular memory access
ODE	Solve van der Pol equation with ODE45	Data structures and MATLAB function files
Sparse	Solve a symmetric sparse linear system	Mixed integer and floating-point
2-D	Plot Bernstein polynomial graph	2-D line drawing graphics
3-D	Display animated L-shape membrane logo	3-D animated OpenGL graphics

Table 3. MATLAB's Benchmark Descriptions.

Prior to running the algorithms, each computer system performed baseline benchmarks. MATLAB has a convenient built-in benchmark named "bench" that executes six different MATLAB tasks and compares the execution speed with the speed of several other computers. Table 3 shows the six different tasks.

The LU test performs a matrix factorization, which expresses a matrix as the product of two triangular matrices. One of the matrices is a permutation of a lower triangular matrix and the other an upper triangular matrix. The fast Fourier transform (FFT) test performs the discrete Fourier transform computed using an FFT algorithm. The ordinary differential equation (ODE) test solves equations using the ODE45 solver. The Sparse test converts a matrix to sparse form by removing any zero elements. Finally, the 2-D and 3-D measure 2-D and 3-D graphics performance, including software or hardware support for OpenGL (Open Graphics Library).

The benchmark results in a speed comparison between the current machine and industry-available machines.

4. Data analysis

Data analysis included calculating descriptive statistics on each test to include mean, standard deviation, variance, minimum and maximum values, and t-test analysis; to determine relationships and differences in performance measurements comparing XML and HDF5 formats for both computer systems. The t-test is one of the most commonly used statistics to determine whether two datasets are significantly different from one another (Gay & Airasian, 2003). The t-test determines if the observed variation between the two datasets is sufficiently larger than a difference expected purely by chance. For this research, the significance level (α) was set at 0.05. This value is commonly accepted and is the default value for many statistical packages that include the t-test (Gay & Airasian, 2003; SAS Institute, 2003; MathWorks, 2011).

For each processing, memory, or loading algorithm, the descriptive statistics for each hyperspectral image create relevant data for a final analysis. The information obtained from averaging across each segment of the multiple segmented images creates the analytical data products used in the results.

In addition to the descriptive statistics for each process, graphical plots illustrate the load times, process times, and memory usage as a function of file size for each data type and test environment. These plots provide an ability to identify differences between the XML and HDF5 data types and possible processing bottlenecks and limitations.

5. Results and Implications

Scientists and researchers need a reliable format for exchanging large datasets for use in computational environments (such as MATLAB). MATLAB has many advantages over conventional languages (such as FORTRAN, and C++) for scientific data analysis, such as ease of use, platform independence, device-independent plotting, graphical user interface, and the MATLAB compiler (Chapman, 2008). Previous results have shown HDF5 format provided faster load and process times than XML formats, and loads large amounts of data without running into memory issues (Bennett & Robertson, 2010). This research supports these findings.

This section provides results and discussion of this current research. After the baseline benchmarks provide results for each machine, the analysis will show example images and descriptive statistics for each image-processing algorithm, along with tables, plots, and discussion comparing HDF5 and XML formats for each task.

Table 4 shows the average of 10 MATLAB bench time results for each of the machines for the LU, FFT, ODE, Sparse, 2D, and 3D tests. For most tests, the Windows 64-bit machine performed better (as indicated by smaller execution times) than the Linux 64-bit machine. One exception to this was the 2D graphics, where the Linux 64-bit machine was slightly faster than the Windows machine. Based on these results, the Windows 64-bit machine should perform slightly faster for the subsequent image processing tasks.

Machine	LU	FFT	ODE	Sparse	2D	3D
Windows 64-bit	0.0389	0.0511	0.1353	0.1789	0.4409	0.7531
Linux 64-bit	0.0872	0.1221	0.2267	0.3137	0.3301	0.8154

Table 4. MATLAB's Bench Results.

Figure 5 shows a typical image used in this analysis. This image represents one specific frequency range (spectral band) for a 460 x 256 image after adjusting of the intensity for display.

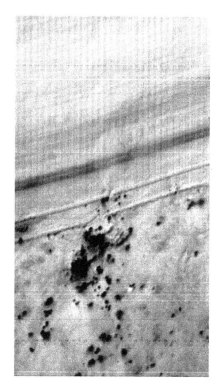

Fig. 5. Example 460 x 256 Image.

A quad chart (Figure 6) displays processed images showing some of the techniques. The first image in Figure 6 is an image in the upper-left corner representing the image adjusted for intensity. The image in the upper-right corner represents the image after the Weiner noise filter is applied. Next, the image in the lower-left corner represents the image after the Canny edge detection is applied. Lastly, the image in the lower-right corner represents the FFT threshold results.

Recall from Figure 1, preparing the images for processing requires several steps. The first step was to load the HDF5 structures, followed by finding and loading the HDF5 raw image data, saving the HDF5 raw image data, populating the XML docNode, and saving the XML raw image data.

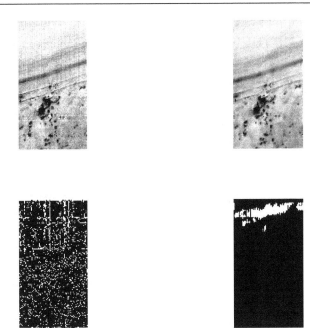

Fig. 6. Quad Image Example 460 by 256 Image.

A total of 100 original HDF5 files, ranging from 57 to 191 MB in size, provide the input for the creation of the HDF5 and XML dataset files. Table 5 displays the original HDF5 file size statistics for this research. The original HDF5 files contained ground truth, collection information, processed data, and spectral content, in addition to the raw image data. The computed image processing statistics use only the raw image data extracted from the HDF5 files and saved to HDF5 and XML formats.

Descriptor	Value (MB)
Mean	116.7304
Minimum	56.9807
Maximum	191.7729
Standard Deviation	28.5472
Variance	814.9406

Table 5. Original HDF5 File Size Descriptions.

The average times associated with each of these steps are shown in Table 6 for the Windows 64-bit and Table 7 for Linux 64-bit machine. The column labeled **"Total (s)"** represents the sum of each of the processing steps for the respective machines. For the current configuration of the Windows 64-bit machine, the mean preparation time per file was just over 9 s, with preparation times ranging between almost 7 and approximately 16.5 s. For the current configuration of the Linux 64-bit machine, the mean preparation time per file was almost 11 s, with times ranging between almost 9 and approximately 19.5 s.

Statistic	Load (s)	Read (s)	HDF5 Save (s)	docNode (s)	XML Save (s)	Total (s)
Mean	0.3313	0.3665	0.0996	7.129	1.1577	9.0841
Minimum	0.0261	0.0097	0.0168	6.0196	0.9191	6.9913
Maximum	1.1602	0.7236	0.5047	12.2276	1.9504	16.567
Standard Deviation	0.2269	0.1384	0.1275	1.8607	0.301	
Variance	0.0515	0.0192	0.0163	3.4623	0.0906	

Table 6. Windows 64-bit HDF5 Data Average Preparation Times.

Statistic	Load (s)	Read (s)	HDF5 Save (s)	docNode (s)	XML Save (s)	Total (s)
Mean	0.043	0.0226	0.0653	9.5711	1.0478	10.75
Minimum	0.0076	0.0107	0.044	8.146	0.7723	8.9806
Maximum	0.3131	0.1311	0.1404	16.775	2.1607	19.52
Standard Deviation	0.0382	0.0171	0.0245	2.6023	0.3637	
Variance	0.0015	0.0003	0.0006	6.7721	0.1322	

Table 7. Linux 64-bit HDF5 Data Average Preparation Times.

Table 8 shows the average free physical memory for each system during the preprocessing steps. Free physical memory can vary throughout a run based on system processing during the run and the amount of memory allocated to MATLAB for processing the run. For all runs during this research, the MATLAB Java heap memory was set to its maximum possible value to avoid any potential out-of-memory issues. In MATLAB version 2010b, selecting File, then Preferences, then General, and then Java Heap Memory, and then using the scroll bar to set its maximum setting changes the memory. The maximum setting for the Windows 64-bit machine was 1533 MB, while the maximum setting for the Linux 64-bit machine was 4011 MB. One trade-off with the Java heap memory being larger in Linux is that less physical memory is available for the run. However, increasing the Java heap memory does allow for larger possible Java objects, which is useful when dealing with large image arrays.

Statistic	Windows 64-bit (GB)	Linux 64-bit (GB)
Mean	2.7223	0.2374
Minimum	2.5234	0.0791
Maximum	2.9228	1.8715
Standard Deviation	0.0738	0.3696
Variance	0.0054	0.1366

Table 8. Free Physical Memory during HDF5 Preparation Steps.

After the preparation steps are complete, saving the raw image data to HDF5 and XML files is the next step. The new raw image files in HDF5 and XML contain only the image

dimension information and the raw image pixel values. Table 9 provides the file statistics of
the raw image data in both HDF5 and XML format. In all cases, the XML files are larger
compared to the HDF5 files. In most cases, the resulting XML file is between 2.5 and 3 three
times as large as the similar HDF5 file. This finding is consistent with other published
results (Bennett & Robertson, 2010).

Statistic	HDF5 Raw Image Size (MB)	XML Raw Image Size (MB)
Mean	17.8374	49.3223
Minimum	13.9301	41.0791
Maximum	30.1252	86.0207
Standard Deviation	6.6819	13.7911
Variance	44.6480	190.1954

Table 9. HDF5 and XML Raw Image File Size Statistics.

After saving the raw image data to HDF5 and XML files, each file was loaded and processed
according to the steps shown previously in Figure 2. These steps include loading the file,
adjusting the image, calculating image statistics, removing noise, detecting edges, and
detecting features. Algorithms include two different noise removal algorithms (Median and
Weiner Filtering) and two different edge detection algorithms (Sobel and Canny). All of
these algorithms, unmodified for this research effort, are available within the MATLAB
Image Processing toolbox.
Table 10 shows the statistical results of the execution times for each of these image-
processing algorithms for HDF5 and XML formats for the Windows 64-bit. Table 11 shows
the results for the Linux 64-bit machine.

	HDF5					XML				
Process	Mean	Min	Max	Std	Var	Mean	Min	Max	Std	Var
Load (s)	0.0258	0.0013	0.0530	0.0072	0.0001	0.7309	0.6117	1.3135	0.2059	0.0424
Adjust (s)	0.0162	0.0058	0.0778	0.0235	0.0006	0.0419	0.0055	0.2366	0.0828	0.0069
Histogram (s)	0.0128	0.0013	0.0730	0.0262	0.0007	0.0225	0.0022	0.1256	0.0447	0.0020
Mean2 (s)	0.0005	0.0001	0.0026	0.0008	0.0000	0.0007	0.0001	0.0037	0.0013	0.0000
STD2 (s)	0.0124	0.0009	0.0735	0.0261	0.0007	0.0089	0.0005	0.0489	0.0179	0.0003
Median (s)	0.0057	0.0021	0.0273	0.0081	0.0001	0.0822	0.0097	0.4280	0.1545	0.0239
Weiner (s)	0.1111	0.0098	0.6541	0.2309	0.0533	0.1307	0.0088	0.7117	0.2597	0.0674
Sobel (s)	0.0663	0.0069	0.3890	0.1347	0.0181	0.0661	0.0051	0.3542	0.1288	0.0166
Canny (s)	0.7276	0.0673	4.1964	1.4975	2.2425	0.5622	0.0532	2.9744	1.0781	1.1622
FFT Feature (s)	0.1222	0.0124	0.6884	0.2398	0.0575	0.1461	0.0122	0.7627	0.2759	0.0761
Total (s)	1.1006	0.1079	6.2351			1.7922	0.7090	6.9594		

Table 10. Windows 64-bit HDF5 and XML Image Processing Execution Times.

On both the Windows and Linux machines, the total execution times for the HDF5 files were significantly less than the total execution times for the XML files. Comparing the results for the mean execution time for the Windows machine, HDF5 demonstrates excellent performance (~1.1 s) compared to XML (~1.8 s). The execution times for the windows machine ranged between ~0.1 and ~6.2 s for the HDF5 files, compared to ~0.7 - ~6.9 s for the XML files. Similarly, comparing the results for the mean execution time for the Linux machine, HDF5 demonstrates excellent performance (~1.5 s) compared to XML (~3.1 s). The execution times for the Linux machine ranged between ~0.15 and ~9.2 s for the HDF5 files, compared to ~1.3 - ~12.3 s for the XML files.

The total execution time difference for both the Windows and Linux machines is primarily due to the "load" process. Loading XML files requires far more execution time due to the larger file sizes of the created XML data files (~3 times larger file size when storing the raw data in XML format).

Additional loading difficulties with XML files include:

1. Slowness of the serialization process of converting Unicode XML into binary memory storage (McGrath, 2003).

2. MATLAB loading algorithm ('xmlread' method) uses the Document Object Model (DOM) to load XML files. DOM is memory and resource intensive, and can consume as much as 10 times the computer memory as the size of the actual XML data file (Wang et al., 2007).

3. In general, and of particular concern for users performing 32-bit processing, processing speeds associated with XML loading can be greatly diminished as virtual memory becomes insufficient compared with the size of the XML file as the computer starts to run out of memory.

Process	HDF5					XML				
	Mean	Min	Max	Std	Var	Mean	Min	Max	Std	Var
Load (s)	0.0199	0.0021	0.0509	0.0095	0.0001	1.3520	1.2015	2.0415	0.2444	0.0597
Adjust (s)	0.0250	0.0087	0.1276	0.0371	0.0014	0.0757	0.0095	0.4293	0.1503	0.0226
Histogram (s)	0.0160	0.0017	0.0914	0.0326	0.0011	0.0290	0.0028	0.1697	0.0598	0.0036
Mean2 (s)	0.0007	0.0003	0.0036	0.0010	0.0000	0.0020	0.0004	0.0106	0.0036	0.0000
STD2 (s)	0.0216	0.0019	0.1309	0.0447	0.002	0.0136	0.0012	0.0806	0.0285	0.0008
Median (s)	0.0631	0.0074	0.3595	0.1265	0.0160	0.1135	0.0127	0.6524	0.2291	0.0525
Weiner (s)	0.1564	0.0179	0.8985	0.3137	0.0984	0.1615	0.0140	0.9496	0.3351	0.1123
Sobel (s)	0.0699	0.0090	0.4486	0.1385	0.0192	0.1221	0.0095	0.7272	0.2573	0.0662
Canny (s)	0.8779	0.0746	5.1806	1.8290	3.3453	0.9195	0.0667	5.4927	1.9447	3.7817
FFT Feature (s)	0.2810	0.0229	1.8790	0.5845	0.3416	0.2960	0.0235	1.7437	0.6157	0.3791
Total (s)	1.5315	0.1465	9.1706			3.0850	1.3417	12.2973		

Table 11. Linux 64-bit HDF5 and XML Image Processing Execution Times.

Some other results worth mentioning confirm the expected relative calculation times between differing noise filters and edge detection methods. As expected, the Weiner Filter (using adaptive techniques) took more time than the Median Filter. In addition, the more complex Canny edge detection algorithm took more time than the Sobel edge detection algorithm.

The load times were larger for the XML files compared to the HDF5 files. This difference is most likely due to the larger XML file size. Figure 7 visually displays the load times for the XML and HDF5 files for the Linux 64-bit machine. Figure 8 shows a similar result for the Windows 64-bit machine.

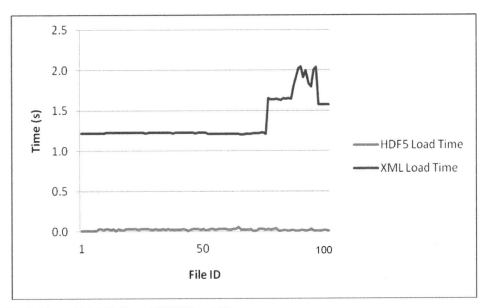

Fig. 7. Linux 64-bit XML and HDF5 Load Times.

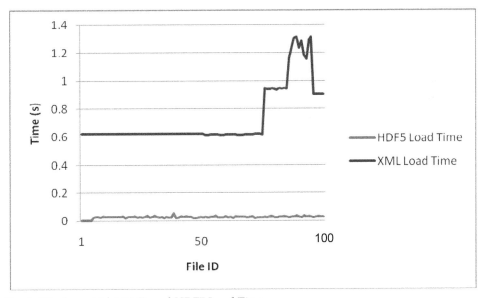

Fig. 8. Windows 64-bit XML and HDF5 Load Times.

Corresponding increases in XML file size contribute to the large jumps observed in the XML load times around file ID 75 and 90 (Figures 7 and 8). Similar arguments made earlier in the chapter (slowness of serialization of converting Unicode to binary storage and resource intensive DOM loading methods) offer explanation of the larger loading process times compared to the more efficient loading of HDF5 binary files.

HDF5 load times do not significantly vary depending on file size. Efficient methods of loading HDF5 binary data files, combined with excellent memory usage and use of computing resources, into the MATLAB workspace, demonstrate the superior benefit of archiving data in HDF5 versus XML. HDF5 provides seamless integration of data into MATLAB without performance degradation (especially for large data sets) and is the 'de facto' standard for MATLAB data files containing workspaces over 2 GB in size (Mather & Rogers, 2007).

The load times (Figures 7 and 8) for both HDF5 and XML show similar behavior on both the Windows and Linux machines. The cross platform behavior demonstrates the file size dependency for XML loading performance, and the lack of file size dependency for HDF5 loading performance. As expected from the benchmark testing results, the XML loading performance on the Windows machine is slightly faster than the Linux.

An additional processing step is required to prepare the large raw data for processing. In XML files, the raw image data is stored as ASCII characters with whitespace separators. As the image gets larger, converting from the ASCII character data to a MATLAB array can take considerable time. MATLAB has a num2str() function that works very nice for small arrays, but this function would not work for these large character arrays. A novel process allows the reading of each character, one at a time, parse on spaces, and then load into the array, resulting in a tremendous savings (as much as two orders of magnitude) in processing time. C or other software development languages may provide other more efficient methods to reduce this processing restriction. However, preparing the XML data for processing is a very important process step. Additional new research and software tools may simplify and expedite the process.

T-test analysis on the total image processing times confirmed that there was a significant difference between the HDF5 and XML file processing times not attributable to random chance. Specifically, HDF5 files took less processing time than XML files on the Windows 64-bit machine ($t(198) = 2.27$, $\rho = .0014$) and the Linux 64-bit machine ($t(198) = 3.25$, $\rho = .0244$). The $t(198)$, or t-value, represents the difference of the mean values for total processing times for HDF5 and XML, respectively, divided by the standard error of the two means. The 198 represents the degrees of freedom, or sample size minus 2 for an unpaired t-test, which is appropriate for the independent groups in this analysis. The important value (ρ) represents the probability of the difference (t-value) being due to chance is .0014 for the Windows 64-bit machine, and .0244 for the Linux 64-bit machine. Setting the significance level to .05 indicates that in both cases, the difference in processing times between HDF5 and XML is not by chance. These results suggest a significant difference between the total process times for HDF5 and XML files for both machines. Further t-test analysis on the individual components contributing to the total process time indicated significant differences in execution times for load, adjust, and mean calculations for the Linux 64-bit machine and load, adjust, and median noise filter for the Windows 64-bit machine. It seems reasonable the load times would be different between the XML and HDF5 formats. To provide insight into the differences between the XML and HDF5 formats for the image adjust, median noise filter, and image mean calculations, requires additional research and analysis, since these routines should provide similar results because the data format should not impact the results for these processes.

Table 12 displays the t-test results for each of the components, resulting in significant differences between the XML and HDF5 files. The t-test results for each of the other components shows no significant difference between XML and HDF files.

Test	Windows 64-bit	Linux 64-bit
Load	$t(198) = 34.39$, $\rho < .0001$	$t(198) = 54.73$, $\rho < .0001$
Image Adjust	$t(198) = 2.99$, $\rho = .0031$	$t(198) = 3.29$, $\rho = .0012$
Image Mean	$t(198) = 1.55$, $\rho = .122$ (Not significant)	$t(198) = 3.35$, $\rho = .0009$
Median Filter	$t(198) = 4.97$, $\rho < .0001$	$t(198) = 1.93$, $\rho = .050$ (Not significant)

Table 12. T-test Process Time Components Results.

Figures 9 and 10 graphically depict these findings by displaying the total processing time for the HDF5 and XML files for the Linux 64-bit and Windows 64-bit test systems. In both cases, the XML process times were significantly greater than the HDF5 process times.

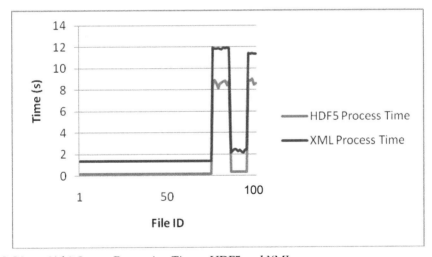

Fig. 9. Linux 64-bit Image Processing Times- HDF5 and XML.

For each file format and test machine, the amount of calculated free physical memory usage during the image processing stage shows definite differences between the file formats. Table 13 shows the descriptive statistics of these data. Similar to the preprocessing step, setting the maximum Java heap memory to maximum for each run results in no out-of-memory errors. For both machines, the XML files required more physical memory than the HDF5 files, as indicated by less free physical memory in Table 13. This result is consistent with XML loading requiring relatively large amounts of memory compared to the XML file size (Wang et al., 2007).

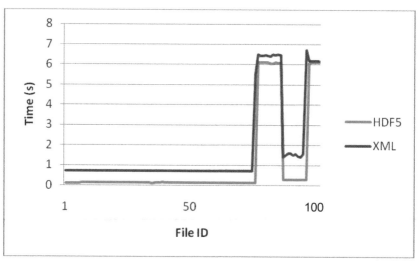

Fig. 10. Windows 64-bit Image Processing Times- HDF5 and XML.

Statistic	Windows 64-bit (GB)		Linux 64-bit (GB)	
	HDF5	XML	HDF5	XML
Mean	3.6608	3.2726	13.6388	11.0808
Minimum	3.5995	3.0064	11.9786	11.0215
Maximum	3.6874	3.7858	14.4033	11.1872
Standard Deviation	0.0194	0.4446	0.6277	0.0924
Variance	0.0004	0.1976	0.394	0.0085

Table 13. Free Physical Memory during Image Processing Steps.

6. Ethics of data sharing

There is a large, complex set of concerns when openly sharing data — especially electronic data over the Internet. From a scientific viewpoint of discovery, open sharing of scientific data allows many researchers and scientists the ability to form a common understanding of data, which is essential for furthering science. However, there are many ethical concerns in the process of sharing data, particularly over the Web. For example, a given medical study group collects sensitive, personal medical information as part of a medical case study using public government funds. All of the data is stored (archived) on a government computer system. Many years later, another researcher wants to use the data for another study, which could help save the lives of many people. Should the second researcher be able to use the archived data for a purpose other than the intent of the original study? Many arguments come into discussion in this situation. The right to use data paid for with publically collected funds seems reasonable; however, what about the right of human participants to privacy? What happens if a data release into the public domain harms any of the participants? Such harm may take the form of job loss or denial of life insurance, etc. The ethics of sharing data is complex and the ethical dilemma of sharing data is an area of study requiring much thought and discussion.

Many of the ethical concerns stem from a balance of beneficial results from sharing data versus ethical concerns researchers have in such sharing. Ethical data sharing and management involves reconciliation of diverse conflicting values (Sieber, 2005). Among these concerns are the sharing of data for the benefit of society and science, while protecting the interest of human participants in data collections (Mauthner & Perry, 2010). For many years, researchers took the position of protecting the interests of the human participants in such data; however, with the advent of sharing data across the Web, the interest of human participants is certainly less sure and threatens the overall fabric of the trust-based relationship that exists between researcher and participant. A definite loss of data control can exist when sharing data across the Web, possibility resulting in the loss of privacy and protection of human participants (Mauthner & Perry, 2010).

Another ethical concern is the rights of those who collect data and receive no recognition by those who download the data through public Web interfaces for use in their research. The process of collecting high quality data requires much time, effort, and expense; moreover, many of the individuals who collect data (data producers) are in a positional or career situation where they are vulnerable to receiving little recognition for their data collection efforts by indiscriminate availability of data over the Web. Such individuals are not nearly as protected as data users, such as algorithm designers, who can protect their interests through intellectual property rights (Mauthner & Perry, 2010).

Along with recognition of the data as a contribution deserving recognition, intellectual property rights assigning ownership and rightful claims to the data are another ethical concern. Reductions or even elimination of researcher's data rights occurs when funding agencies require a researcher to share data, especially over the Web, allowing anyone to access the information. Certain government agencies are always balancing the public's right to information collected with public funds, and the right to protect both the researcher's intellectual property and the test participant's privacy rights.

Archiving and disseminating data over the Web creates a "data as commodity" mindset, where the ethical concerns of both the researcher and human participant become lost in the impersonal downloading of archived data (Mauthner & Perry, 2010). When sharing data, regardless of the methods, confidentially of human participants is important at all times. Data providers must take great care in judging the sensitivity of the data and may find it necessary to restrict access based on ethical, legal, or security justifications, even in the case of publicly funded data collections. Further safeguards in data dissemination include restricting others (end users) of disseminating data as a third party; thus, requiring an end user to go to the original source to acquire the data (MIT Libraries, 2011).

The ethics of data sharing is clearly more complex today than before the advent of the Internet. However, many general guiding principles apply to all data sharing situations. As a core group of guiding principles, every data collector and provider has a duty to:

1. Protect the confidentially of human participants in data collections (UK Data Archive, 2011).
2. Avoid providing sensitive information of human test participants, which may endanger data test participants (UK Data Archive, 2011).
3. Consult with the test participants on making data publically available and be sensitive to their wishes (UK Data Archive, 2011).
4. Inform the test participants on the use of the data, and the methods, procedures, and intentions of archiving and disseminating the data, prior to using them as test participants (UK Data Archive, 2011).

5. Make data available to the public, which doesn't violate ethical, legal, or security principles (UK Data Archive, 2011).

7. Conclusions

This research processed 100 large hyperspectral images in both HDF5 and XML formats on Windows 64-bit and Linux 64-bit machines. A number of image processing steps available within MATLAB, including intensity adjustment, histogram calculation, statistical analysis, noise removal, edge detection and feature extraction, provided the algorithms to fulfill the goals of the research:

1. Determine strengths and weaknesses of using HDF5 and XML formats for typical processing techniques associated with large hyperspectral images.
2. Compare and analyze processing times on Windows and Linux 64-bit machines for HDF5 and XML hyperspectral images.
3. Identify areas that require additional research to help improve efficiencies associated with processing large HDF5 and XML hyperspectral images.

The research identified a number of strengths and weaknesses. First, the overall image processing results show reduced processing times for images stored in HDF5 compared to XML format. The main contribution to this difference is the large load time and the preprocessing step required to convert an ASCII XML character string to a numeric array in MATLAB. The relative size of the files is the main factor in the difference in load speed with the XML files being almost three times as large as the HDF5 files. A larger file will always take more time to load using any application.

The preprocessing required to convert an ASCII XML character string to a numeric array was very time-consuming and a potential huge process bottleneck. The processing of large XML files requires additional tools and approaches with an easier out-of-the-box solution, making XML processing more practical. In addition to the processing time differences, HDF5 requires less physical memory and, hence, allows larger objects to be loaded without out-of-memory errors. HDF5 data files are much smaller (~3 times) than the corresponding XML versions of same data files. Binary files in general are far more efficient in storing numerical data than XML files using Unicode. As discussed earlier, XML loading of data can consume as much as 10 times the amount of computer memory as the size of the actual XML file (Wang et al., 2007), and conversion of Unicode to binary storage is memory intensive requiring much more physical memory and resources than the loading of HDF5 files of similar data (McGrath, 2003). MATLAB can process very large arrays, but it will run out of memory quickly when processing very large XML files. On another test machine that was running MATLAB with only 760 MB Java heap memory, several of the larger XML datasets would not load. HDF5 files on any machine even when experimenting with HDF5 files as large as 800MB did not experience any problems. Clearly, for machines with less memory available and smaller processing capability, HDF5 files are preferred. Defining upper limit processing for both HDF5 and XML files requires additional research and analysis. The upper limit appears to have relationships to processing speed, physical memory, and other constraints. Exploring these limits as a function of different environmental parameters requires recommended future research.

The archiving and processing of large image data requires the use of HDF5, until additional tools and processes are in place that allow for the quick and efficient processing of XML files using computational tools such as MATLAB.

There are many important ethical considerations when sharing data, especially over the Web. Additional considerations to protect the privacy and interests of human participants in data collections require additional guidance when sharing data in a completely public forum where the researcher (and organization) has no control over how the data is used. There will always exist a balance between sharing data for scientific discovery and advancement, and ethical concerns and requirements.

8. References

Barkstrom, B., "Ada 95 Bindings for the NCSA Hierarchical Data Format", proceedings of the 2001 annual ACM SIGAda International Conference on ADA (2001).

Bennett, K., Robertson, J., "The Impact of the Data Archiving Format on the Sharing of Scientific Data for Use in Popular Computational Environments", Proc. SPIE 7687, Orlando Florida (April 2010).

Chapman, S.J., "MATLAB Programming for Engineers; 4th edition; Thomson publishing, Ontario, Canada, 2008.

Dougherty, M., Folk, M., Zadok, E., Bernstein, H., Bernstein, F., Eliceiri, K., Benger, W., Best, C., "Unifying Biological Image Formats with HDF5", communications of the ACM (CACM), 52(10): p. 42-47 (2009).

Gay, L.R. Airasian, P. Educational Research. Prentice Hall, Columbus, Ohio, 2003.

Goetz, A.F.H., Vane, G., Solomon, E., Rock, B.N., "Imaging Spectrometry for Earth Remote Sensing", *Science*, Vol. 228, p. 1147-1153 (1985).

Mather, J., Rogers, A., "HDF5 in MATLAB", Presentation at the HDF5 and HDF-EOS Workshop X, Raytheon System Corporation, Upper Marlboro, MD (November 2007).

MATLAB User's Guide, "Statistical Toolbox, Ttest2", http://www.mathworks.com/help/toolbox/stats/ (April, 2011).

Mauthner, M., Perry, O., "Ethical Issues in Digital Data Archiving and Sharing", eResearch Ethics, http://eresearch-ethics.org (October 2010).

McGrath, R., "XML and Scientific File Formats," Report generated by National Center for Supercomputing Applications, University of Illinois, Urbana-Champaign, in support of work under a Cooperative Agreement with NASA under NASA grant NAG 5-2040 and NAG NCCS-599 (August 2003).

MIT Libraries, "Data Management and Publishing: Ethical and Legal Issues", http://libraries.mit.edu (November 2011).

SAS/STAT User's Guide, "T-Test Procedure", http://support.sas.com/documentation (April, 2011).

Shasharina, S., Li, C., Nanbor, W., Pundaleeka, R., Wade-Stein, D., "Distributed Technologies for Remote Access of HDF Data", proceedings of the 16th IEEE International Workshop on Enabling Technologies: Infrastructure for Collaborative Enterprises (2007).

Shishedjiev, B., Goranova M., Georgieva, J., "XML-based Language for Specific Scientific Data Description",proceedings of the 2010 Fifth International Conference on Internet and Web Applications and Services (2010).

Sieber, J., "Ethics of Sharing Scientific and Technological Data: A Heuristic for Coping with Complexity & Uncertainty", Data Science Journal, Vol 4, p. 165 (December 2005).

UK   Data   Archive,   "Create   and   Manage   Data   -   Consent   and   Ethics:
       Ethical/Legal/Overview", http://www.data-archive.ac.uk (2011).
Wang, F., Li, J., Homayounfar, "A Space Efficient XLM DOM Parser", Data and Knowledge
       Engineering,Volume 60, Issue 1, p. 185-207 (2007).

8

A Cluster-Based Method for Evaluation of Truck's Weighing Control Stations

Abbas Mahmoudabadi[1] and Arezoo Abolghasem[2]
*[1]PhD Candidate, Technical and Engineering Faculty, Payam-e-Noor
University & General Director of Traffic Safety Department,
Road Maintenance and Transportation Organization, Tehran
[2]Transportation Engineer, Road Maintenance and Transportation Organization, Tehran
Iran*

1. Introduction

Effective and safe road network is essential to economic growth and social welfare (Islamic Republic of Iran Majlis, 2005). More than 550 million tons of goods are transported by road network in Islamic Republic of Iran, which is a large amount of total cargo transportation's rate (RMTO, 2009). Overloading of vehicles increases safety risk and pavement damages (Planning and Management Organization, 1996), so to improve road safety and restrain pavement damages, legislation based on maximum allowable axle and total load is applied for heavy vehicles, which are passing on the roads (Mohammadi, 1999). Law enforcement control is done by weighing control equipments, which have been installed near the arterial roads, and to evaluate law enforcement, clustering method can be used as an effective technique.

Clustering method is used to classify data and decision making in transportation studies. Some researchers (Ahmed and Kanhere, 2007) used clustering method for public transport modeling in order to improve situation and possibility of changing decision in public transportation. They showed that using a step forward algorithm for clustering the nodes in finding routes problems while using clustering method, improves effectiveness of algorithm.

Clustering has been used to classify accident types (Depaire et al. 2008). They used a model based on clustering data, which divide accident data to 7 homogenous groups and finally analyzed injuries in each group .Comparing results based on divided groups and total data analysis showed that classifying data could be used for safety issues researchers with more accuracy.

(Fielding et. al 1985) used clustering method for analyzing transit systems equipments, considering vehicle's size, average speed, urban transportation situation, and bus specified routes, and have classified transit situation to 12 categories. Difference of characteristics for all categories was identified using variance analysis, detached group and tree decision-making method. Grouping data were made by seven main transit efficiency factors and finally some suggestion for each group was supposed to productivity evaluation.

In this paper after a brief review on methods of controlling cargo transportation and existing regulation in rural roads network, an evaluation method of trucks weighing control is presented using clustering analysis method. For evaluation and comparing results, available data on trucks weighing control, which have been collected by local authorities in all over the country, have been analyzed based on clustering and finally weighing stations have been categorized in different groups.

2. Goods transportation controlling on road network

Overloading vehicles are important from two sides of decreasing transportation safety and fateful damages on roads surface and infrastructures. Overloaded vehicles in addition to damage road surface, because of Pre-designing of braking system particularly at slides and curves, endanger other vehicles. Increasing goods' transportation will lead to economical growth from one side of the view, and the other side will increase maintenance costs and safety risks. Studies show that the most important factor of roads destruction is heavy vehicle's axle load. Based on researches the damage on roads surface is related to the vehicle axle load by a non-linear acceleration rate mostly in a polynomial equation of forth degree. Because of limited budget in roads maintenance activities, it is essential to apply over loaded vehicles limitation rules effectively. In spite of heavy maintenance costs, do not repairing road surfaces leads to destroy vehicles and decreasing traffic speed, so pavement management is very important issue because of overloading vehicles passage .

At the present, the method of trucks weighing control in Iran is using weighing control equipments including static, dynamic, and portable scales at weighing stations (and Weigh in Motion System in 6 points). Maximum permitted axle load for different types of heavy vehicles, which has been identified by laws, is under the control of weighing stations.

3. Proposed method

According to importance of controlling overloaded vehicles, performance evaluation of weighing control is inevitable. Identifying effective parameters on weighing control, data standardizing and ranking weighing stations have done in this paper in the sequence process using a well-known method of statistical process of clustering.

3.1 Clustering method

Clustering method is a statistical method that divides observation data according to their similarity to homogenous and detached groups (Sharma, 1996). In this method, similarity criterion is firstly identified. The number of groups would be analyzed and recognized. Observation data in each group are similar to each other based on similarity criterion and each group is different from the other groups. It is possible to consider more than one variable simultaneously as similarity criterion in clustering method. However, there are some different methods of identifying similarity criterions, but the common method for defining similarity is known as equation number 1 while the similarity of itk and jtk observed data of k_{th} variable is defined by P2ij.

$$P^2{}_{ij} = \sum_{k=1}^{p} (x_{ik} \; x_{jk})^2 \qquad (1)$$

Clustering is a hierarchically process means that the nearest observations are merged continuously to make larger groups. This process will be continued until number of groups is reached to the proposed number of desired clusters. Merging observations is done by different methods such as Centroid, Farthest- Neighbour, Nearest- Neighbour, Average

Linkage, and Ward method usually chosen by analysts based on acceptable frequency. Based on experience, experts' view and comparing results of clustering Ward method is used to merge data in this research.

3.2 Data normalization

Because of existing the effective parameters in decision-making techniques, if there are different dimensions, for variables normalization or standardizing methods are used to assimilate (Sharma, 1996). If data can be fitted by a normal distribution function, normalization method is used. In addition, there are different methods of output and input data normalization, which the most regular methods convert data to, numbers between 0 to 1 and -1 to 1. Equations (2) and (3) converts data to zero to 1 numbers and are used for data more than zero.

$$X_{new} = \frac{X_{old}}{X_{max}} \tag{2}$$

$$X_{new} = \frac{X_{old} - X_{min}}{X_{max} - X_{min}} \tag{3}$$

If it is necessary to convert data in the range of -1 to 1, equation (4) is used:

$$\begin{cases} X_{new} = \dfrac{X_{old}}{X_{max}} & \forall\, X_{old} \geq 0 \\[2mm] X_{new} = \dfrac{X_{old}}{X_{min}} & \forall\, X_{old} \leq 0 \end{cases} \tag{4}$$

In order to standardize data assuming distribution function is normal, equation (5) is used which X_{old} is preliminary amount of factor and X_{new} is standardized form:

$$X_{new} = \frac{X_{old} - \overline{X}}{\sqrt{\displaystyle\sum_{i=1}^{n} \frac{(X_i - \overline{X})^2}{n-1}}} \tag{5}$$

3.3 Data gathering

To evaluate truck's weighing control performance, number of registered overloaded vehicles, amount of detected overload, the type of scale, average heavy vehicle's daily traffic, and number of overloaded vehicles with more than 5 tons overload are collected from all over the country in 6 mount period to use defined below parameters:

- Number of registered overloaded vehicles of six months period
- Detected amount of overloading of six months period
- Proportion of registered overloaded vehicles of six months period to the same period in last year
- Proportion of detected amount of overloading of six months period to the same period in last year
- Average heavy vehicles daily traffic of six months period

- The fraction of number of overloaded vehicles with more than 5 ton overload to total registered overloaded vehicles of six months period

Tables 1 and 2 show maximum, minimum, average, and standard deviation of collected data before and after standardizing data respectively. As it is observed, to homogenize data, standardization is used because of having a normal distribution function.

Row	Parameter's Name	Experimental Data			
		Max	Min	Average	Standard Deviation
1	Number of registered overloaded vehicles	1754	2	193	255
2	Detected amount of overloading(ton)	4014	2	519	655
3	Proportion of detected overloaded vehicles of six months period to the same period in last year	615	-96	88	143
4	Amount of detected overloading proportion of six months period to the same period in last year	718	-94	89	162
5	Average daily heavy vehicles traffic	41059	103	3887	6493
6	Number of more than 5 ton overloaded vehicles to number of total overload proportion	0.35	0	0.07	0.09

Table 1. Parameters, experimental data

Row	Parameter's Name	Standardized Data			
		Max	Min	Average	Standard Deviation
1	Number of detected overloaded vehicles	6.12	-0.75	0	1
2	Detected amount of overloading(ton)	5.37	-0.79	0	1
3	Proportion of detected overloaded vehicles of six months period to the same period in last year	3.69	-1.29	0	1
4	Amount of detected overloading proportion of six months period to the same period in last year	3.89	-1.13	0	1
5	Average daily heavy vehicles traffic	5.72	-0.58	0	1
6	Number of more than 5 ton overloaded vehicles to number of total overload proportion	3.16	-0.87	0	1

Table 2. Parameters, standardized data

3.4 Setting number of clusters

The number of clusters is specified in two ways. In the first method, analysts specify number of clusters when the number of clusters needs to be applied to other decision-making process, for example using clustering method to fuzzy modeling. Second method of specifying number of clusters, is minimizing Within-Group Sum of Squares (Sharma, 1996) while the sum of total deviation is calculated and number of clusters is identified in such a way that inter clusters sum of squares, which is named missed sum of squares, would be minimized. Also proportional sum of deviation squares as Between-Group Sum of Squares is used as a criterion to specifying number of clusters.

Since the number of clusters in this research work is not too important, second method which is more scientific has been used and the number of clusters is specified in such a way that minimizes Within-Group, deviation. Table 3 shows total deviation, Within-Group and Between-Group deviation and proportion of Within-Group to total deviation which is decision making parameter.

According to table (3), if it is proposed that 85 percent of deviation is reserved, number of clusters would be 16, and if it is proposed to reserve 90 percent of deviation, number of clusters would be 22. As it is shown at table (3) rest of deviations after 22 would change slowly means increasing the number of clusters doesn't have significant rule in decision process.

Figure (1) shows changes in total deviation, Within-Group and Between-Group deviation based on the number of clusters. As it has been shown in this figure, difference between Total deviation and Between-Group deviation would be decreased after 16, since 16 covers 85 percent of deviations, so in this research 16 number of clusters has been considered to evaluate weighing stations performance in controlling goods transported by heavy vehicles.

Row	Number of Clusters	Deviation From Average Sum of Square Errors			
		Total	Within Groups	Between Groups	Proportion of Between Groups to Total
1	4	750	352	398	53
2	6	750	236	514	69
3	8	750	183	567	76
4	10	750	156	594	79
5	12	750	145	605	81
6	14	750	122	628	84
7	16	750	113	637	85
8	18	750	102	648	86
9	20	750	81	669	89
10	22	750	77	673	90
11	24	750	68	682	91
12	26	750	63	687	92
13	28	750	61	689	92
14	30	750	55	695	93

Table 3. Deviation from average sum of square errors

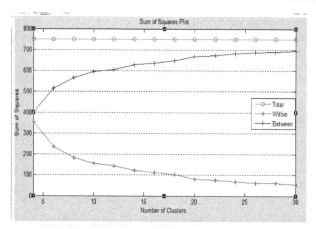

Fig. 1. Plot of square errors (Within, Between and Total)

4. How to use MATLAB software

There is a command in MATLAB software, which has ability to cluster observations based on many parameters. As shown in tables 1 and 2, there are six parameters for clustering. Clusterdata is a well-known command in order to cluster data. There is a matrix 126×6 contains data used in this research work. If matrix named as X figure 2 shows the format of data.

Code	X(:,1)	X(:,2)	X(:,3)	X(:,4)	X(:,5)	X(:,6)
5707	0.011113	-0.0353	-0.64109	-0.81193	-0.46864	-0.86858
5704	0.819076	0.992241	-0.65484	-0.90436	-0.36345	-0.86858
...	...	...	...	...	...	...
5108	0.611202	1.519068	-0.08919	-0.82648	0.333153	0.958812
5106	-0.68703	-0.72033	0.783371	1.209399	0.448663	-0.86858

Fig. 2. Matrix contains data with six parameters

When command "clusterdata" is typed, results, are generated and are shown in a matrix contain two columns. The first column corresponds the row of observation and the second corresponds assigned cluster. For example if the first row of result matrix contains, 1 and 15, it means that station coded as 5707 in the first row of matrix X, belong to the 14th cluster.

The other command in MATLAB is kmeans, which is used to calculate the distance between observation and centre of the cluster. There is a output variable of SUMD in kmeans command to set distances and within group sum of square errors will be calculated by sum of the square distances of variable SUMD. Between sum of square errors will be calculated by total sum of square errors minus within sum of square errors while total sum of square errors is calculated as below (Sharma, 1996):

$$\text{Total sum of square errors} = (126-1) \times 6 = 750$$

When 126 is the number of observations and 6 is the number of standardized parameters.

5. Results

Considering the number of clusters by 16 and Ward Method to merging data, using clustering method of well-known software of MATLAB version R2008a, weighing station grades considering six identified variables are presented as table 4.

Class	Station's code	Number of stations
1	1126, 3603	2
2	3607, 3601	2
3	4507, 4102, 8708, 2109	4
4	1106	1
5	1125, 1104, 5408, 8701	4
6	5409, 8705, 8706, 3202, 2110, 9101	6
7	5108, 5107, 5109, 9703, 9702	5
8	1190, 1112, 3609, 3606, 3602, 7504	6
9	1108, 3608, 3604	3
10	9748, 4502, 8709, 3203, 3303, 7702, 2107	7
11	5102, 1122, 7503, 5401, 5406, 1403, 4110, 2104, 5703, 5704	11
12	5106, 1116, 4508, 4553, 4506, 4106, 41014, 4108, 4106, 4104, 6108, 6107, 2116, 2106, 9104, 9105	14
13	2105, 6401, 5402, 5403, 5404, 9701, 9506, 9502, 2111, 2105	10
14	5104, 1103, 1114, 7502, 4503, 4501, 4504, 1405, 4117, 6110, 6105, 8702, 7701, 2108, 2101, 5701, 5702, 5707	19
15	6402, 6404, 6403, 5407, 6106, 6102, 6101, 8704, 3201, 3301, 7706, 9505, 9501, 2103, 2102, 9103, 9102	17
16	3610, 7505, 6405, 4114, 4111, 4122, 4109, 4105, 4112, 4101, 6108, 6103, 7704, 9503, 5706	15

Table 4. Results (Clusters contain the number of stations)

6. Conclusion and future research

In this research, number of detected overloaded vehicles, amount of overload, scale's type, average heavy vehicle's daily traffic, and number of overloaded vehicles with more than 5 ton overload are collected from all over the country in a six month period and using standardization method are homogenized. By using minimum deviation method of Average within-Groups, number of clusters is calculated and considering Ward method for merging data, and using clustering method, the performance of weighing stations have been classified in 16 groups. Results show that this method is appropriate to use evaluation of weighing control performance in weighing stations.

Future studies, recommended using ranking method by similarity factors for traffic laws enforcement control, and any other important factors such as vehicles speed, overtaking, and left diversion control. Ranking enforcement stations and at a wider view ranking provinces could provide a comprehensive and precise image for mangers about enforcement stations performance.

7. References

Ahmed, S.; Kanhere, S.S, (Oct 2007), "Cluster-based Forwarding in Delay Tolerant Public Transport, Networks", 32nd IEEE Conference, Pages 625-634.

Bolghari, M., (2010, 1389 local calender), "Driving laws and regulations", Second version, Department of transportation, Tehran municipality, 2010.

Depaire, B., Wets, G., Vanhoof, K., (July 2008), "Traffic accident segmentation by means of latent class clustering", Accident Analysis and Preventation, Vol, 40, Issue 4, Pages 1257-1266.

Fielding, G.J., Brenner, M.E., Faust, K., (May 1985), "Typology for Bus Transit", Transportation Research, Part A, Vol 40, Issue 4, Pages 1257-1266.

Islamic Republic of Iran Majlis, (2005, 1384 local calender) "Forth five-year developing plan of Islamic republic of Iran", available on www.majlis.ir

Mohammadi Asa, A., (1999, 1378 local calender), "Laws and regulations in road transport", Road maintenance and transportation organization.

Planning and management organization, (1996, 1375 local calender) "Road pavement and asphalt manual", Vol. 234.

Road Maintenance and Transportation Organization, (2009, 1388 local calender) "Annual survey of road transport in Iran", available on www.rmto.ir

Subhash Sharma, (1996), "Applied Multivariable Techniques", University of South Carolina, USA.

9

Energy Management in Buildings Using MATLAB

Shahram Javadi
Islamic AZAD University, Central Tehran Branch
Iran

1. Introduction

MATLAB is an applicable software in various aspects of engineering such as Electrical engineering and its different sub majors. There are a lot of examples and demos on these majors, although there is a few text or example on MATLAB application in energy management. In this text, I have provided a general application of energy management in buildings using MATLAB software.

Considering limit source of fuel energy, we need to use energy and resources carefully and it is an economical and ecological challenge as well as being one which is important for survival and which can only be mastered by highly qualified engineers. A significant percentage of the energy used nationally is consumed in buildings, which means there are considerable potential for savings and a corresponding need for responsible behavior.The building sector worldwide uses up to 40% of primary energy requirements and also a considerable amount of overall water requirements.

Building Energy Management Systems (BEMS), aims to improve environment within the building and may control temperature, carbon dioxide levels. BEMS is not sufficient enough due to human interference. Human is a dynamic part of the building; therefore he/she should be taken into account in the control strategy. Latest trends in designing Intelligent Building Energy management Systems (IBEMS) integrate a Man Machine Interface that could store the human's preferences and adapt the control strategy accordingly.

BEMS have been developed after the Energy crisis in the late 70's combined with the fast development of computers science. The aims of these systems are to monitor and control the environmental parameters of the buildings and at the same time to minimize the energy consumption and cost. Since then, BEMS have become commercial tools and are implemented in a wide range of applications, especially in large office buildings; thus useful experience is available regarding their benefits and drawbacks.

Systems linked to a BMS typically represent 40% of a building's energy usage; if lighting is included, this number approaches 70%.

Some Benefits of BMS are:

- Building tenant/occupants
- Good control of internal comfort conditions
- Possibility of individual room control
- Increased staff productivity

- Effective monitoring and targeting of energy consumption
- Improved plant reliability and life
- Effective response to HVAC-related complaints
- Save time and money during the maintenance

BEMS is used to create a central computer controlled method which has three basic functions: controlling, monitoring and optimizing. It comprises:

- Power systems
- Illumination system
- Electric power control system
- Heating, Ventilation and Air-conditioning HVAC System
- Security and observation system
- Magnetic card and access system
- Fire alarm system
- Lifts, elevators etc.
- Plumbing system
- Burglar alarms
- Other engineering systems
- Trace Heating

BEMS uses a control strategy with the following objectives:

i.   To obtain a flexible system for operator to maintain thermal, visual, security, illumination and air quality in a building.
ii. To reduce the energy consumption for all loads in a building.
iii. To provide a monitoring/controlling system in a building.

The above objectives are achieved by the use of a fuzzy controller at each zone level of the building, supervised by a suitable cost function. The detailed description of the control strategy has been described in next parts.

2. Fuzzy systems

Fuzzy logic originally is identified and set forth by Lotfi A. Zadeh is a form of multi-valued logic derived from fuzzy set theory to deal with reasoning that is fluid or approximate rather than fixed and exact. In contrast with "crisp logic", where binary sets have two-valued logic, fuzzy logic variables may have a truth value that ranges in degree between 0 and 1. Put more simply, fuzzy logic is a superset of conventional (boolean) logic that has been extended to handle the concept of partial truth, where the truth value may range between completely true and completely false. Furthermore, when linguistic variables are used, these degrees may be managed by specific functions. As the complexity of a system increases, it becomes more difficult and eventually impossible to make a precise statement about its behavior, eventually arriving at a point of complexity where the fuzzy logic method born in humans is the only way to get at the problem.

Fuzzy logic is used in system control and analysis design, because it shortens the time for engineering development and sometimes, in the case of highly complex systems, is the only way to solve the problem.

A fuzzy controller consists of the following major components depicted in figure 1:

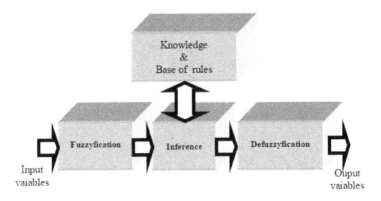

Fig. 1. Fuzzy system diagram

3. Considered systems for energy management

3.1 Illumination system

Lighting or illumination is the deliberate application of light to achieve some aesthetic or practical effect. Lighting includes use of both artificial light sources such as lamps and natural illumination of interiors from daylight. Daylighting (through windows, skylights, etc.) is often used as the main source of light during daytime in buildings given its high quality and low cost. Artificial lighting represents a major component of energy consumption, accounting for a significant part of all energy consumed worldwide. Artificial lighting is most commonly provided today by electric lights, but gas lighting, candles, or oil lamps were used in the past, and still are used in certain situations. Proper lighting can enhance task performance or aesthetics, while there can be energy wastage and adverse health effects of poorly designed lighting. Indoor lighting is a form of fixture or furnishing, and a key part of interior design. Lighting can also be an intrinsic component of landscaping

Providing daylight in a building does not by itself lead to energy efficiency. Even a well day building may have a high level of lighting energy use if the lighting controls are inappropriate. However, improved control in building management and automation system through research and development will definitely help to improve energy savings in buildings. This part presents the development of an automated fuzzy lighting/dimming control system. The schematic diagram of the system is shown in Fig. 1. Fuzzy logic is an innovative technology that allows the description of desired system behavior using everyday spoken language Fuzzy logic can be derived into three stages which are: Fuzzification, Fuzzy Inference and Defuzzification. In a typical application, all three stages must be employed.

3.1.1. Indoor natural lighting

What we have to do is solve an equation of the type

$$E = \frac{\Phi_{rec}}{A}$$

Where E is the illumination level required at the work surface and A is the total area of the plane where the work is done. The factor Φ_{rec} is the flux of light received on the working surface.

The average indoor illuminance E_{in} (lx) is calculated (DHW Li and JC Lam, 2000, "*Measurements of solar radiation and illuminance on vertical surfaces and daylighting implications*") using the equation:

$$E_{in} = \frac{A_w \tau E_v}{A_{in}(1-\rho)} \tag{1}$$

where
A_w (m2) the window surface
τ (-) the light transmittance of the window glazing
E_v (lx) the vertical illuminance on the window
A_{in} (m2) the total area of all indoor surfaces
ρ (-) the area weighted mean reflectance of all indoor surfaces.

The vertical illuminance on the window Ev (lx) is given by the following equation

$$E_v = k_G G_v \tag{2}$$

with
k_G (lm.W-1) the luminous efficacy of global solar radiation
G_v (W.m-2) the global solar radiation on the window surface

The luminous efficacy of global solar radiation (M. Perraudeau, 1994, "*Estimation of illuminances from solar radiation data*") can be calculated by the following relation

$$k_G = \frac{D_h}{G_h} k_D + \left(1 - \frac{D_h}{G_h}\right) k_s \tag{3}$$

with
D_h (W.m-2) the diffuse horizontal solar radiation
G_h (W.m-2) the global horizontal solar radiation
k_D (lm.W-1) the luminous efficacy of diffuse solar radiation
k_S (lm.W-1) the luminous efficacy of beam solar radiation.

The luminous efficacy of diffuse solar radiation is calculated (P. Littlefair, 1993, S. Ashton and H. Porter, "*Luminous efficacy algorithms*",) using the equation:

$$k_D = 144 - 29C \tag{4}$$

$$1 - C = 0.55NI - 1.22NI^2 + 1.68NI^3 \tag{5}$$

$$NI = \frac{1 - \dfrac{D_h}{G_h}}{1 - 0.12037\sin^{-0.82}(\theta_z)} \tag{6}$$

with θ_z (deg) the solar zenith angle.

Finally, the luminous efficacy of the beam solar radiation can be calculated (S. Aydinli and J. Krochmann, 1983, *"Data on daylight and solar radiation: Guide on Daylight"*) using the relation

$$k_S = 17.72 + 4.4585\ \theta z - 8.7563 \times 10\text{-}2\ (\theta z)2 + 7.3948 \times 10\text{-}4$$
$$(\theta z)3 - 2.167 \times 10\text{-}6\ (\theta z)4 - 8.4132 \times 10\text{-}10\ (\theta z)5 \tag{7}$$

3.1.2 Artificial lighting

The Equation below is used to calculate the average artificial light intensity inside the buildings:

$$E_{AL} = \frac{u^{\cdot}_{AL} \cdot N \cdot (P \cdot V \cdot n)}{2\pi \cdot (H - h)^2} \tag{8}$$

Where:

$u^{\cdot}_{AL}$: The actuating signal of the artificial light controller, ranging from 0-1. This signal is driven by the artificial lighting fuzzy controller. The same signal is also fed into the building model (Archimed.bui) to drive the actuator for the artificial lights. If $u^{\cdot}_{AL} = 0$ means that all lights are off. If $u^{\cdot}_{AL} = 1$ means that all lights are on at full power.

3.1.3 Fuzzy controller for lighting

All lighting control systems are based on one of the following strategies:

* Occupancy sensing, in which lights are turned on and off or dimmed according to occupancy;
* Scheduling, in which lights are turned off according to a schedule;
* Tuning, in which power to electric lights is reduced to meet current user needs;
* Daylight harvesting (daylighting control), in which electric lights are dimmed or turned off in response to the presence of daylight;
* Demand response, in which power to electric lights is reduced in response to utility curtailment signals or to reduce peak power charges at a facility;
* Adaptive compensation, in which light levels are lowered at night to take advantage of the fact that people need and prefer less light at night than they do during the day.

Daylight is a dynamic source of lighting and the variations in daylight can be quite large depending on season, location or latitude, and cloudiness. Different skylight levels can be found under the same sunlight conditions, and, even when the sky pattern remains the same, the range of solar illuminances may increase as a result of a momentary turbidity filter or scattering of particles over the sun. In consequence, any prediction system has to be flexible to allow for the multivariate changes that characterize the combination of sunlight and skylight.

The proposed daylighting fuzzy control uses two sensing devices (an occupancy/motion sensor and a photosensor), continuously electronic dimming ballasts for every luminaries aiming the control of the electric lighting output, and a fuzzy controller.

A proposed algorithm is assigned to control the illumination:

if *illuminance is between 500 and 550 lux and motion sensor is ON* **then** *all lamps is full powered*

else *use the fuzzy controller for lighting control*

The input linguistic variables of the fuzzy controller are the level of the illuminance measured by the photosensor (A) while the output variable is the level of the DC control signal sent to electronic ballasts in the control zone (μ_1). The fuzzy membership functions of Input/Output variables are shown in figures 2 and 3:

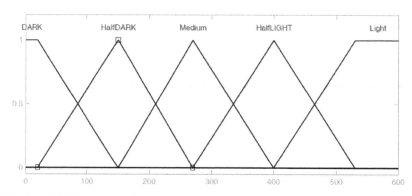

Fig. 2. Membership Function of Input A

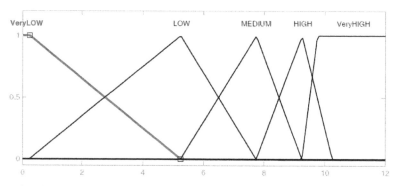

Fig. 3. Membership Function of Output (DC Voltage Level)

A rule-based fuzzy controller is evaluated for this system as follow:
1.   If A is DARK then DC-Output-Level is VERY-HIGH
2.   If A is HALF-DARK then DC-Output-Level is HIGH
3.   If A is MEDIUM then DC-Output-Level is MEDIUM
4.   If A is HALF-LIGHT then DC-Output-Level is LOW
5.   If A is LIGHT then DC-Output-Level is VERY-LOW

Control surface of this system is shown in figure 4. As it is seen, the controller is very smooth action and it causes the ballast has a long life with a low harmonic feed into the grid.

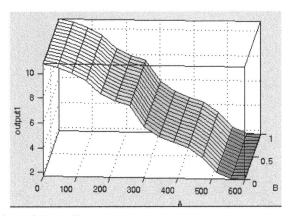

Fig. 4. Control Surface of Controller

3.2 HVAC system

In this part the role of fuzzy modeling in heating, ventilating and air conditioning (HVAC) and control models is presented. HVAC design professionals are required to evaluate numerous design alternatives and properly justify their final conceptual selection through modeling. This trend, coupled with the knowledge of experienced designers, increasing complexity of the systems, unwillingness to commit additional funds to the design phase itself, can only be satisfied by approaching the conceptual design process in more scientific, comprehensive and rational manner as against the current empirical and often adhoc approach. Fuzzy logic offers a promising solution to this conceptual design through fuzzy modeling. Numerous fuzzy logic studies are available in the non- mechanical engineering field and allied areas such as diagnostics, energy consumption analysis, maintenance, operation and its control. Relatively little exists in using fuzzy logic based systems for mechanical engineering and very little for HVAC conceptual design and control. Temperature and relative humidity are essential factors in meeting physiological requirements.

To identify the FLC's variables, various (control or explicit) parameters may be considered depending on the HVAC system, sensors and actuators such as:

- Room Temperature as a thermal comfort index
- Relative Humidity
- Difference between supply and room temperatures
- Indoor Air Quality (CO_2 concentration)
- Outdoor Temperature
- HVAC system actuators (valve positions, operating modes, fan speeds, etc.)

As man is more sensitive to temperature than to humidity, most of the comforts air-conditioning systems are designed to provide relatively accurate temperature control and relative humidity.

Two parameters T (Temperature) and H (Humidity) are controlled by Fuzzy controller system in order to regulate the room temperature and humidity to their desired values, T_{ref} and H_{ref} (Zheng Xiaoqing, 2002 , "*Self-Tuning Fuzzy Controller for Air-Conditioning Systems*"). The block diagram of the air-conditioning control system is a simple closed loop system as shown in figure 5.

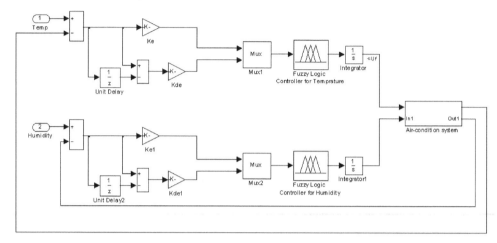

Fig. 5. Block diagram of the air-conditioning control system

As it is seen, two independent fuzzy controllers are assigned to control Temperature and Humidity parameters. Error signal and its derivation are fed to each fuzzy controller. The output of fuzzy controllers is assigned as inputs of air conditioner system. The output of system is feedback to controller to make a closed-loop controller.

The control strategy used can be expressed by the following linguistic rules:

If **room temperature** *is higher than the set point, then increase the* **supply air fan speed**.

If **room humidity** *is higher than the set point, then increase the* **chilled water valve opening.**

Seven linguistic variables are chosen for each of Temperature and Humidity error and also their derivations as follow:

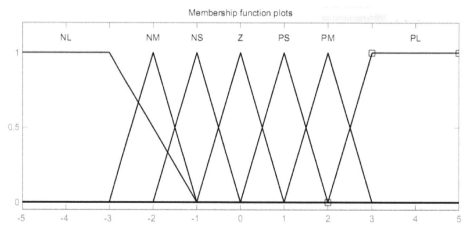

Fig. 6. Membership functions of inputs

Also seven linguistic variables are chosen for **supply air fan speed** and **chilled water valve opening** as its outputs. It is show in figure 7.

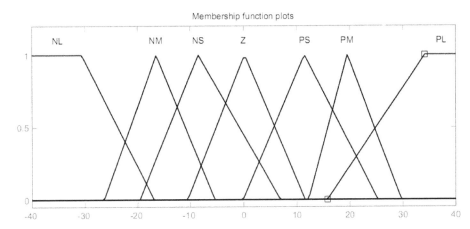

Fig. 7. Membership functions of outputs

Rule base of this controller is defined as table 1:

	NL	NM	NS	Z	PS	PM	PL
NL	PL	PL	PM	PM	PS	PS	NS
NM	PL	PL	PM	PS	PS	NS	NS
NS	PM	PS	PS	PS	NS	NS	NM
Z	PM	PM	PS	Z	NS	NM	NM
PS	PM	PS	PS	NS	NS	NM	NM
PM	PS	PS	NS	NS	NM	NL	NL
PL	PS	NS	NS	NM	NM	NL	NL

Table 1. Rules of Fuzzy HVAC

For example:

> If the **room temperature error** *is NL and its* **rate of change** *is NL, then* **supply air fan speed** *is PL*

or

> If the **room humidity error** *is NL and its* **rate of change** *is NL, then* **chilled water valve opening** *is PL*

In this case we have 49 rules to have smooth control surface for HVAC control.

3.3 Elevator system

With the advancement of intelligent computerized buildings in recent years, there have been strong demands for intelligent elevator control with more sophistication and diverse functions. The design criteria of an intelligent elevator control system would include optimizing the movement of a group of elevators with respect to time, energy, load, etc. In this paper, a new elevator group supervisory control system based on the ordinal structure fuzzy logic algorithm is proposed. The system determines the optimum car to answer a hall call using the knowledge and experiential rules of experts. Software has been developed to simulate the traffic flow of three elevator cars in a 15-floor building. The software simulates the movements of the cars as found in practical elevator systems. It can be verified through simulation that the new system can bring about considerable improvements in the average waiting time, riding time, etc. in comparison with conventional methods.

In a conventional elevator system, the task of controlling a large number of elevators is numerically evaluated by calculating a specified fixed-evaluation function. It has been realized that knowledge and experiential rules of experts can be incorporated in the elevator system to improve performance. However, such expert knowledge is fragmentary and fuzzy which are difficult to organize. Furthermore, the choice of "good" rules and evaluation functions are too complicated in many cases. It is difficult to adequately incorporate such knowledge into products using conventional software and hardware technology.

In order to overcome such problems as described above, a new elevator control system using fuzzy logic algorithm is proposed based on the ordinal structure theory. This system determines the optimum car within a group of elevators to answer a hall call using the knowledge and experiential rules of experts. Instead of using the simple up and down hall call buttons, destination oriented keypads at each floor is used. This system requires the passengers to enter their desired floors on the keypad before they enter the car. The system then assigns the passenger the respective optimal car to take through information displayed on dot matrix displays near the keypad. This new elevator supervisory control system has several objectives which can meet users' satisfaction. It can improve not only the average waiting time, but also the riding time, load, energy and so on. This paper discusses the design and operations of the proposed fuzzy logic elevator control system.

In order to achieve good traffic performance, the elevator fuzzy control system uses six kinds of parameters as the control inputs and one parameter for the output. These parameters represent the criteria or objectives to be optimized in this elevator system which are as follows:

- Waiting Time: Total time an elevator needed to travel from its current position to the new hall call.
- Riding Time: Total time a passenger spent in the elevator until he reached as his destination.
- Loading: Number of passengers in an elevator.
- Travelling Distance: Distance between elevator position and new hall call in terms of number of floors.
- Hall call Area Weight: The area weight of the elevator which goes to the floor where a new hall call is generated.
- Destination Area Weight: The area weight of the elevator which goes to the floor where the destination of the new hall call is generated.
- Priority: Output of the fuzzy controller, where the elevator with highest value will be assigned.

As can be observed, it is difficult to configure six kinds of parameters at a time using the conventional fuzzy reasoning method. Thus, the ordinal structure model of fuzzy reasoning is used. With this model, all the fuzzy inference rules are described in one dimensional space for each input and output. The membership function of the inputs and output variables are shown in Figures 9 and 10.

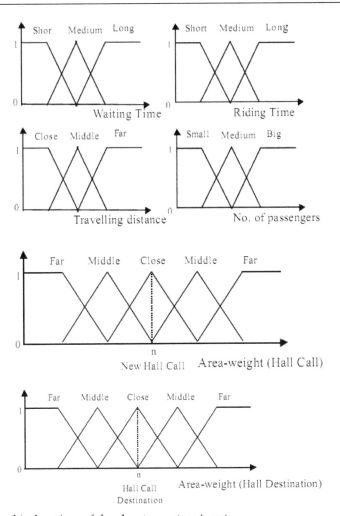

Fig. 8. Membership functions of the elevator system inputs.

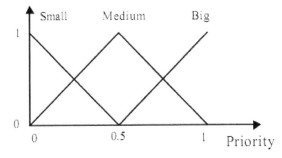

Fig. 9. The membership function of the output of the elevator system.

The proposed fuzzy inference rules are shown in Table 2:

Rule No.	Inference Rules
R1	If waiting time is *Short* then priority is *Big*.
R2	If waiting time is *Medium* then priority is *Medium*
R3	If waiting time is *Long* then priority is *Small*.
R4	If riding time is *Short* then priority is *Big*.
R5	If riding time is *Medium* then priority is *Medium*.
R6	If loading is *Long* then priority is *Small*
R7	If loading is *Small* then priority is *Big*
R8	If loading is *Medium* then priority is *Medium*
R9	If loading is *Big* then priority is *Small*
R10	If travelling distance is *Close* then priority is *Big*
R11	If travelling distance is *Middle* then priority is *Medium*
R12	If travelling distance is *Far* then priority is *Small*.
R13	If hall call area weight is *Close* then priority is *Big*.
R14	If hall call area weight is *Middle* then priority is *Medium*
R15	If hall call area weight is *Far* then priority is *Small*.
R16	If destination area weight is *Close* then priority is *Big*.
R17	If destination area weight is *Middle* then priority is *Medium*.
R18	If destination area weight is *Far* then priority is *Small*.

Table 2. A total of 18 fuzzy inference rules

4. Conclusion

In this chapter one of the applications of MATLAB is introduced in order to apply energy management in buildings. Three major systems were considered and a fuzzy controller was developed for each of them. It can be open a new vision to the students to learn MATLAB more applicable and more efficient.

5. References

A. Guillemin and N. Morel, 2001, *"An innovative lighting controller integrated in a self-adaptive building control system"*, Energy and Buildings, vol. 33, no. 5, pp. 477–87.

DHW Li and JC Lam, 2000, *"Measurements of solar radiation and illuminance on vertical surfaces and daylighting implications"*, Renewable Energy, vol. 20, pp. 389-404

M. Perraudeau, 1994, *"Estimation of illuminances from solar radiation data"*, Joule 2 DAYLIGHT II Program: Availability of Daylight – Design of a European Daylighting Atlas, CSTB Nantes.

P. Littlefair, 1993, S. Ashton and H. Porter, *"Luminous efficacy algorithms"*, Joule 1 Program – Dynamic characteristics of daylight data and daylighting design in Buildings, Final Report, CEC Brussels.

S. Aydinli and J. Krochmann, 1983, *"Data on daylight and solar radiation: Guide on Daylight"*, Draft for CIE TC 4.2.

Zheng Xiaoqing, 2002 , *"Self-Tuning Fuzzy Controller for Air-Conditioning Systems"*, M.Sc. Thesis

Part 3

Control Applications

10

Synchronous Generator Advanced Control Strategies Simulation

Damir Sumina, Neven Bulić, Marija Mirošević and Mato Mišković
University of Zagreb/Faculty of Electrical Engineering and Computing,
University of Rijeka, Faculty of Engineering,
University of Dubrovnik/Department of Electrical Engineering and Computing
Croatia

1. Introduction

During the last two decades, a number of research studies on the design of the excitation controller of synchronous generator have been successfully carried out in order to improve the damping characteristics of a power system over a wide range of operating points and to enhance the dynamic stability of power systems (Kundur, 1994; Noroozi et.al., 2008; Shahgholian, 2010). When load is changing, the operation point of a power system is varied; especially when there is a large disturbance, such as a three-phase short circuit fault condition, there are considerable changes in the operating conditions of the power system. Therefore, it is impossible to obtain optimal operating conditions through a fixed excitation controller. In (Ghandra et.al., 2008; Hsu & Liu, 1987), self-tuning controllers are introduced for improving the damping characteristics of a power system over a wide range of operating conditions. Fuzzy logic controllers (FLCs) constitute knowledge-based systems that include fuzzy rules and fuzzy membership functions to incorporate human knowledge into their knowledge base. Applications in the excitation controller design using the fuzzy set theory have been proposed in (Karnavas & Papadopoulos, 2002; Hiyama et. al., 2006; Hassan et. al., 2001). Most knowledge-based systems rely upon algorithms that are inappropriate to implement and require extensive computational time. Artificial neural networks (ANNs) and their combination with fuzzy logic for excitation control have also been proposed, (Karnavas & Pantos, 2008; Salem et. al., 2000a, Salem et. al., 2000b). A simple structure with only one neuron for voltage control is studied in (Malik et. al., 2002; Salem et. al., 2003). The synergetic control theory (Jiang, 2009) and other nonlinear control techniques, (Akbari & Amooshahi, 2009; Cao et.al., 2004), are also used in the excitation control.

One of the disadvantages of artificial intelligence methods and nonlinear control techniques is the complexity of algorithms required for implementation in a digital control system. For testing of these methods is much more convenient and easier to use software package Matlab Simulink. So, this chapter presents and compares two methods for the excitation control of a synchronous generator which are simulated in Matlab Simulink and compared with conventional control structure. The first method is based on the neural network (NN) which uses the back-propagation (BP) algorithm to update weights on-line. In addition to the function of voltage control the proposed NN has the function of stabilizing generator oscillations. The second method proposes a fuzzy logic controller (FLC) for voltage control and the stabilization of generator oscillations. The proposed control algorithms with neural networks and a fuzzy controller are tested on a simulation model of synchronous generator weakly connected through transmissions lines to an AC network. The simulations are carried out by step changes in voltage reference.

2. Simulation models

Simulation models of synchronous generator and different control structures are made in Matlab Simulink. The generator is connected over transformer and transmission lines to the AC network (Fig. 1).

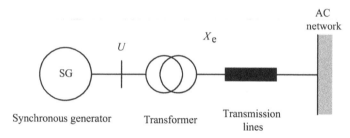

Fig. 1. Synchronous generator connected to AC network

2.1 Simulation model of a synchronous generator

Mathematical model of synchronous generator is represented in dq axis form. Based on that it is necessary to perform transformation from abc coordinate system to dq coordinate system. Assumption is that voltages are symmetrical in all phases and there is only one harmonic of magnetic flux in air gap. Equations are represented in per-unit system and time is absolute.

The synchronous generator under consideration is assumed to have three armature windings, one field winding, and damper windings. One damper winding is located along the direct axis (D) and another is located along the quadrature axis (Q). Accordingly, the basis for the mathematical model of the synchronous generator is a system of voltage equations of the generator in the rotating dq coordinate system, where u, i, r, x and Ψ denote voltage, current, resistance, reactance and flux, respectively (Kundur, 1994):

$$-u_d = r \cdot i_d + \frac{1}{\omega_s} \cdot \frac{d\Psi_d}{dt} + \omega \cdot \Psi_q \tag{1}$$

$$-u_q = r \cdot i_q + \frac{1}{\omega_s} \cdot \frac{d\Psi_q}{dt} - \omega \cdot \Psi_d \tag{2}$$

$$u_f = r_f \cdot i_f + \frac{1}{\omega_s} \cdot \frac{d\Psi_f}{dt} \tag{3}$$

$$0 = r_D \cdot i_D + \frac{1}{\omega_s} \cdot \frac{d\Psi_D}{dt} \tag{4}$$

$$0 = r_Q \cdot i_Q + \frac{1}{\omega_s} \cdot \frac{d\Psi_Q}{dt} \tag{5}$$

The equations defining the relations between fluxes and currents are:

$$\Psi_d = x_d \cdot i_d + x_{ad} \cdot i_f + x_{dD} \cdot i_D \tag{6}$$

$$\Psi_q = x_q \cdot i_q + x_{qQ} \cdot i_Q \tag{7}$$

$$\Psi_f = x_{ad} \cdot i_d + x_f \cdot i_f + x_{fD} \cdot i_D \tag{8}$$

$$\Psi_D = x_{dD} \cdot i_d + x_{fD} \cdot i_f + x_D \cdot i_D \tag{9}$$

$$\Psi_Q = x_{qQ} \cdot i_q + x_Q \cdot i_Q \tag{10}$$

The motion equations are defined as follows:

$$\frac{d\delta}{dt} = (\omega - 1) \cdot \omega_s \tag{11}$$

$$\frac{d\omega}{dt} = \frac{1}{2H} \cdot (T_m - T_e) \tag{12}$$

where δ is angular position of the rotor, ω is angular velocity of the rotor, ω_s is synchronous speed, H is inertia constant, T_m is mechanical torque, and T_e is electromagnetic torque. The electromagnetic torque of the generator T_e is determined by equation:

$$T_e = \Psi_q \cdot i_d - \Psi_d \cdot i_q \tag{13}$$

Connection between the synchronous generator and AC network is determined by the following equations:

$$u_d = i_d \cdot r_e + \frac{x_e}{\omega_s} \cdot \frac{di_d}{dt} + \omega \cdot x_e \cdot i_q + u_{sd} \tag{14}$$

$$u_q = i_q \cdot r_e + \frac{x_e}{\omega_s} \cdot \frac{di_q}{dt} - \omega \cdot x_e \cdot i_d + u_{sq} \tag{15}$$

$$u_{sd} = U_m \cdot (-\sin \delta) \tag{16}$$

$$u_{sq} = U_m \cdot \cos \delta \tag{17}$$

transformer and transmission line resistance, x_e is transformer and transmission line reactance, and U_m is AC network voltage. Synchronous generator nominal data and simulation model parameters are given in Table 1.

Terminal voltage	400 V
Phase current	120 A
Power	83 kVA
Frequency	50 Hz
Speed	600 r/min
Power factor	0,8
Excitation voltage	100 V
Excitation current	11.8 A
d-axis synchronous reactance X_d	0.8 p.u.
q-axis synchronous reactance X_q	0.51 p.u.
Inertia constant H	1.3
d-axis transient open-circuit time constant $T_{do'}$	0.55 s
d-axis transient reactance X_d'	0.35 p.u.
d-axis subtransient reactance X_d''	0.15 p.u.
q-axis subtransient reactance X_q''	0.15 p.u.
Short-circuit time constant T_d''	0.054 s
Short-circuit time constant T_q''	0.054 s
Transformer and transmission line resistance r_e	0.05 p.u.
Transformer and transmission line reactance x_e	0.35 p.u.

Table 1. Synchronous generator nominal data and simulation model parameters

2.2 Conventional control structure

Conventional control structure (CCS) for the voltage control of a synchronous generator is shown in Fig. 3. The structure contains a proportional excitation current controller and, subordinate to it, a voltage controller. Simulation model of conventional control structure is shown in Fig. 4.

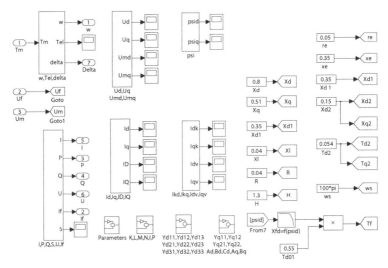

Fig. 2. Simulation model of synchronous generator

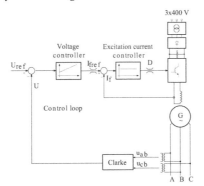

Fig. 3. Conventional control structure

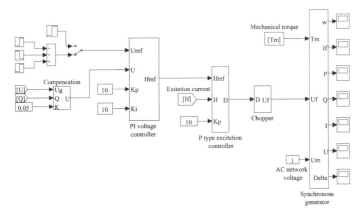

Fig. 4. Simulation model of conventional control structure

For supplying the generator excitation current, an AC/DC converter is simulated. The AC/DC converter includes a three-phase bridge rectifier, a DC link with a detection of DC voltage, a braking resistor, and a DC chopper (Fig. 5).

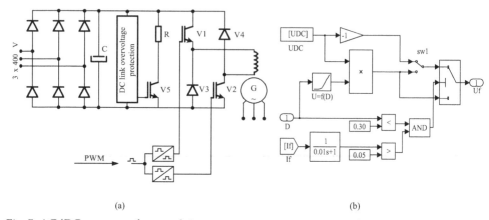

(a)   (b)

Fig. 5. AC/DC converter for supplying generator excitation current (a) and simulation model (b)

2.3 Neural network based control

The structure of the proposed NN is shown in Fig. 6. The NN has three inputs, six neurons in the hidden layer and one neuron in the output layer. The inputs in this NN are the voltage reference U_{ref}, the terminal voltage U and the previous output from the NN $y(t-1)$. Bringing the previous output to the NN input is a characteristic of dynamic neural networks. The function tansig is used as an activation function for the neurons in the hidden layer and for the neuron in the output layer.

The graphical representation of the tansig function and its derivation is shown in Fig. 7. The numerical representation of the tansig function and its derivation are given as follows (Haykin, 1994):

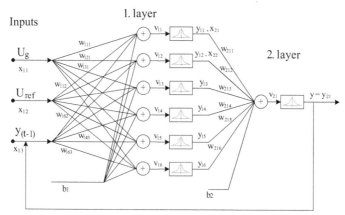

Fig. 6. Structure of the proposed neural network

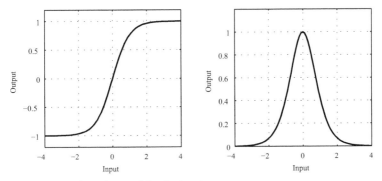

Fig. 7. Tansig activation function and its derivation

$$\psi(v) = \frac{1}{1 + e^{-cv}} - 1 \tag{18}$$

$$\psi'(v) = c\frac{4e^{-2cv}}{(1 + e^{-2cv})^2} = c \cdot (1 - \psi^2) \tag{19}$$

The NN uses a simple procedure to update weights on-line and there is no need for any off-line training. Also, there is no need for an identifier and/or a reference model. The NN is trained directly in an on-line mode from the inputs and outputs of the generator and there is no need to determine the states of the system. The NN uses a sampled value of the machine quantities to compute the error using a modified error function. This error is back-propagated through the NN to update its weights using the algorithm shown in Fig. 8. When the weights are adjusted, the output of the neural network is calculated.

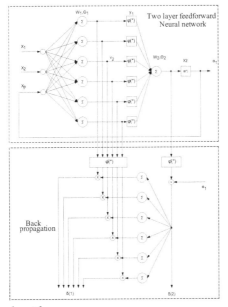

Fig. 8. Back-propagation algorithm

Training of the NN with the BP algorithm is described in (Haykin, 1994). Inputs and outputs of one neuron in the NN can be determined as follows:

$$y_{ki} = \psi\left(\sum_k w_{kij} \cdot x_{kj} + b_1\right) \tag{20}$$

The BP algorithm is an iterative gradient algorithm designed to minimize the mean square error between the actual output and the NN desired output. This is a recursive algorithm starting at the output neuron and working back to the hidden layer adjusting the weights according to the following equations:

$$w_{kij}(t+1) = w_{kij}(t) + \Delta w_{kij}(t) \tag{21}$$

$$\Delta w_{ji}(n) = \eta \cdot \delta_j(n) \cdot y_i(n) \tag{22}$$

$$\delta_j(n) = e_j(n) \cdot \phi'_j(v_j(n)) \tag{23}$$

The error function commonly used in the BP algorithm can be expressed as:

$$\Im = \frac{1}{2}(t_{ki} - y_{ki})^2 \tag{24}$$

If the neuron is in the output layer, the error function is:

$$\frac{\partial \Im}{\partial y_{ki}} = t_{ki} - y_{ki} \tag{25}$$

If the neuron is in the hidden layer, the error function is recursively calculated as (Haykin, 1994):

$$\frac{\partial \Im}{\partial y_{ki}} = \sum_{p=1}^{n(k+1)} \frac{\partial \Im}{\partial y_{k+1,p}} \cdot \psi'_{k+1,p} \cdot w_{k+1,1,i} \tag{26}$$

If the NN is used for the excitation control of a synchronous generator, it is required that we not only change the weights based only on the error between the output and the desired output but also based on the change of the error as follows:

$$\frac{\partial \Im}{\partial y_{ki}} = (t_{ki} - y_{ki}) - \frac{dy_{ki}}{dt} \tag{27}$$

In this way, the modified error function speeds up the BP algorithm and gives faster convergence. Further, the algorithm becomes appropriate for the on-line learning implementation. The error function for the NN used for voltage control is expressed as:

$$\frac{\partial \Im}{\partial y_{ki}} = K(U_{ref} - U) - k_1 \frac{dU}{dt} \tag{28}$$

In order to perform the power system stabilization, the active power deviation ΔP and the derivation of active power dP/dt are to be imported in the modified error function. The complete modified error function for the excitation control of a synchronous generator is given as follows:

$$\frac{\partial \mathfrak{I}}{\partial y_{ki}} = \left[K(U_{ref} - U) - k_1 \frac{dU}{dt} \right] - \left[k_3 (\Delta P) + k_2 \frac{dP}{dt} \right] \tag{29}$$

The modified error function is divided into two parts. The first part is used for voltage control and the second part for power system stabilization. Parameters K, k_1, k_2 and k_3 are given in Table 2. Simulation model of NN control structure is shown in Fig. 9.

K	2.5
k_1	0.3
k_2	0.6
k_3	0.25

Table 2. Parameters of neural network

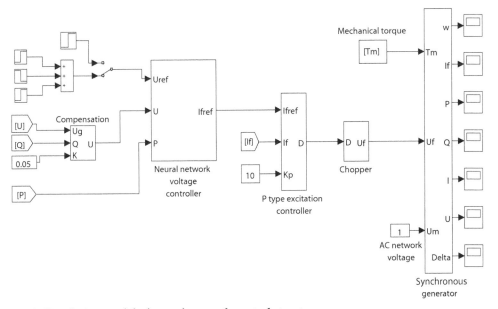

Fig. 9. Simulation model of neural network control structure

Neural network based controller is realized as S-function in Matlab and is called in every simulation step.

2.4 Fuzzy logic controller

The detailed structure of the proposed fuzzy logic controller (FLC) is shown in Fig. 10. The FLC has two control loops. The first one is the voltage control loop with the function of voltage control and the second one is the damping control loop with the function of a power system stabilizer. A fuzzy polar control scheme is applied to these two control loops.

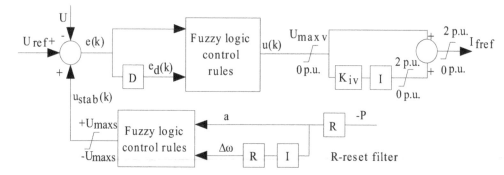

Fig. 10. Structure of the fuzzy logic stabilizing controller

The PD information of the voltage error signal e (k) is utilized to get the voltage state and to determine the reference I_{fref} for the proportional excitation current controller. To eliminate the voltage error, an integral part of the controller with parameter K_{iv} must be added to the output of the controller. The damping control signal u_{stab} is derived from the generator active power P. The signal a is a measure of generator acceleration and the signal $\Delta\omega$ is a measure of generator speed deviation. The signals a and $\Delta\omega$ are derived from the generator active power through filters and the integrator. The damping control signal u_{stab} is added to the input of the voltage control loop.

The fuzzy logic control scheme is applied to the voltage and stabilization control loop (Hiyama et. al., 1996). The generator operating point in the phase plane is given by p(k) for the corresponding control loop (Fig. 11a):

$$p(k) = (X(k), A_s \cdot Y(k)) \qquad (30)$$

where X(k) is e(k) and Y(k) is e_d(k) for the voltage control loop, and X(k) is $\Delta\omega$(k) and Y(k) is a(k) for the stabilization control loop. Parameter A_s is the adjustable scaling factor for Y(k). Polar information, representing the generator operating point, is determined by the radius D(k) and the phase angle Θ(k):

$$D(k) = \sqrt{X(k)^2 + (A_s \cdot Y(k))^2} \qquad (31)$$

$$\Theta(k) = arctg(\frac{A_s \cdot Y(k)}{X(k)}) \qquad (32)$$

The phase plane is divided into sectors A and B defined by using two angle membership functions $N(\Theta(k))$ and $P(\Theta(k))$ (Fig. 11b).

The principles of the fuzzy control scheme and the selection of the membership functions are described in (Hiyama et. al., 1996). By using the membership functions $N(\Theta(k))$ and $P(\Theta(k))$ the output control signals u(k) and u_{stab}(k) for each control loop are given as follows:

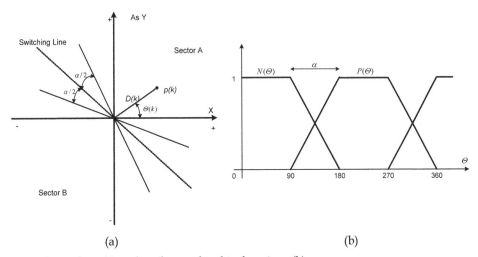

Fig. 11. Phase plane (a) and angle membership functions (b)

$$u(k) = \frac{N(\Theta(k)) - P(\Theta(k))}{N(\Theta(k)) + P(\Theta(k))} \cdot G(k) \cdot U_{maxv} \tag{33}$$

$$u_{stab}(k) = \frac{N(\Theta(k)) - P(\Theta(k))}{N(\Theta(k)) + P(\Theta(k))} \cdot G(k) \cdot U_{maxs} \tag{34}$$

The radius membership function $G(k)$ is given by:

$$G(k) = D(k) / D_r \text{ for } D(k) \leq D_r$$

$$G(k) = 1 \text{ for } D(k) > D_r (35)$$

Simulation models of the voltage control loop, stabilization control loop and fuzzy logic control structure are presented on the Figs. 12, 13, and 14, respectively. Parameters A_s, D_r and α for the voltage control loop and the damping control loop are given in Tables 3 and 4.

A_s	0.1
D_r	1
K_{iv}	10
U_{maxv}	2 p.u.
α	90°

Table 3. FLC parameters for voltage control loop

A_s	0.01
D_r	0.01
U_{maxs}	0.1 p.u.
α	90°

Table 4. FLC parameters for damping control loop

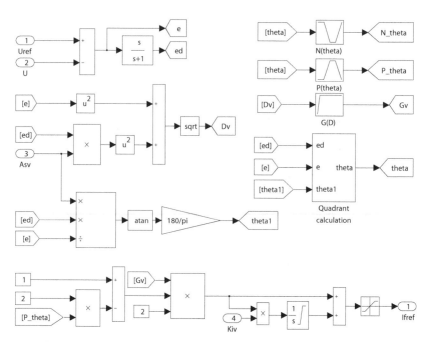

Fig. 12. Simulation model of voltage control loop

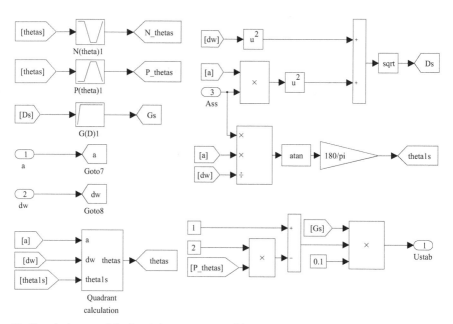

Fig. 13. Simulation model of stabilization control loop

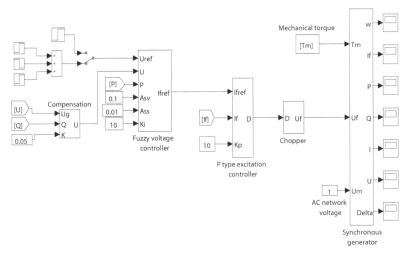

Fig. 14. Simulation model of fuzzy logic control structure

3. Simulation results

In order to verify the performance of the proposed control structures several simulations were carried out. In these experiments, voltage reference is changed in 0.1 s from 1 p.u. to 0.9 p.u. or 1.1 p.u. and in 1 s back to 1 p.u. at a constant generator active power.

For the quality analysis of the active power oscillations two numerical criteria are used: the integral of absolute error (IAE) and the integral of absolute error derivative (IAED). If the response is better, the amount of criteria is smaller.

Fig. 15 presents active power responses for step changes in voltage reference from 1 p.u. to 0.9 p.u. and back to 1 p.u. at an active power of 0.5 p.u. The numerical criteria of the responses in Fig. 15 are given in Table 5.

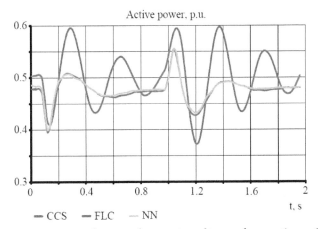

Fig. 15. Active power responses for step changes in voltage reference 1 p.u.-0.9 p.u.-1 p.u. at an active power of 0.5 p.u.

	IAE	IAED
CCS	0.389	0.279
FLC	0.255	0.097
NN	0.235	0.090

Table 5. Numerical criteria for step changes in voltage reference 1 p.u.-0.9 p.u.-1 p.u. at an active power of 0.5 p.u.

Fig. 16 shows active power responses for step changes in voltage reference from 1 p.u. to 1.1 p.u. and back to 1 p.u. at an active power of 0.5 p.u. The numerical criteria of the responses in Fig. 16 are given in Table 6.

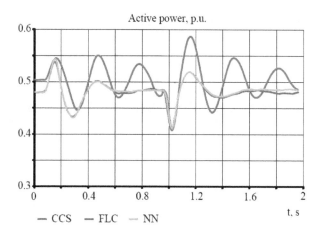

Fig. 16. Active power responses for step changes in voltage reference 1 p.u.-1.1 p.u.-1 p.u. at an active power of 0.5 p.u.

	IAE	IAED
CCS	0.264	0.196
FLC	0.202	0.092
NN	0.192	0.091

Table 6. Numerical criteria for step changes in voltage reference 1 p.u.-1.1 p.u.-1 p.u. at an active power of 0.5 p.u.

Fig. 17 presents active power responses for step changes in voltage reference from 1 p.u. to 0.9 p.u. and back to 1 p.u. at an active power of 0.8 p.u. The numerical criteria of the responses in Fig. 17 are given in Table 7.

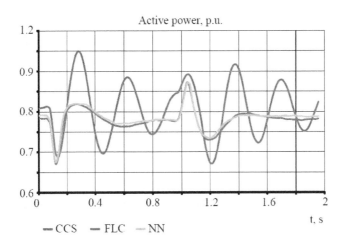

Fig. 17. Active power responses for step changes in voltage reference 1 p.u.-0.9 p.u.-1 p.u. at an active power of 0.8 p.u.

	IAE	IAED
CCS	0.52	0.373
FLC	0.248	0.114
NN	0.219	0.106

Table 7. Numerical criteria for step changes in voltage reference 1 p.u.-0.9 p.u.-1 p.u. at an active power of 0.8 p.u.

Fig. 18 shows active power responses for step changes in voltage reference from 1 p.u. to 1.1 p.u. and back to 1 p.u. at an active power of 0.8 p.u. The numerical criteria of the responses in Fig. 18 are given in Table 8.

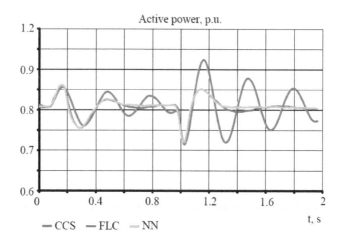

Fig. 18. Active power responses for step changes in voltage reference 1 p.u.-1.1 p.u.-1 p.u. at an active power of 0.8 p.u.

	IAE	IAED
CCS	0.312	0.234
FLC	0.130	0.097
NN	0.119	0.090

Table 8. Numerical criteria for step changes in voltage reference 1 p.u.-1.1 p.u.-1 p.u. at an active power of 0.8 p.u.

Based on the numerical criteria it can be concluded that the neural network-based controller with stabilization effect in the criteria function has two to three percent better damping of oscillations than the fuzzy logic controller.

4. Conclusion

Three different structures for the excitation control of a synchronous generator were simulated in Matlab Simulink: the first structure is a conventional control structure which includes a PI voltage controller, while the second structure includes a fuzzy logic controller, and the third structure includes a neural network-based voltage controller. Performances of the proposed algorithms were tested for step changes in voltage reference in the excitation system of a synchronous generator, which was connected to an AC network through a transformer and a transmission line.

For the performance analysis of the proposed control structures two numerical criteria were used: the integral of absolute error and the integral of absolute error derivative. In the comparison with the PI voltage controller neural network-based controller and the fuzzy logic controller show a significant damping of oscillations. It is important to emphasize that the stabilizer was not used in the conventional control structure, which would definitely reduce the difference between the conventional and the proposed control structures.

The simulation results show justification for the use of the advanced control structure based on neural networks and fuzzy logic in the excitation control system of a synchronous generator. Also, using the software package Matlab Simulink allows users to easily test the proposed algorithms.

5. References

Akbari, S., & Karim Amooshahi, M. (2009). Power System Stabilizer Design Using Evolutionary Algorithms, *International Review of Electrical Engineering*, 4, 5, (October 2009), pp. 925-931.

Cao, Y., Jiang, L., Cheng, S., Chen, D., Malik, O.P., & Hope, G.S. (1994). A nonlinear variable structure stabilizer for power system stability, *IEEE Transactions on Energy Conversion*, 9, 3, (1994), pp. 489-495.

Ghandra, A., Malik, & O. P., Hope, G.S. (1988). A self-tuning controller for the control of multi-machine power systems, *IEEE Trans. On Power Syst.*, 3, 3, (August 1988), pp. 1065-1071.

Hassan, M.A., Malik, O.P., & Hope, G.S. (1991). A Fuzzy Logic Based Stabilizer for a Synchronous Machine, *IEEE Trans. Energy Conversion*, 6, 3, (1991), pp. 407-413.

Haykin, S. (1994). *Neural Networks: A Comprehensive Foundation*, IEEE Press

Hiyama T., Oniki S., & Nagashima H. (1996). Evaluation of advanced fuzzy logic PSS on analog network simulator and actual installation on hydro generators, *IEEE Trans. on Energy Conversion*, 11, 1, (1996), pp. 125-131.

Hsu, Y.Y., & Liou, K.L. (1987). Design of self-tuning PID power system stabilizers for synchronous generators, *IEEE Trans. on Energy Conversion*, 2, 3, (1987), pp. 343-348.

Jiang, Z. (2009). Design of a nonlinear power system stabilizer using synergetic control theory, *Electric Power Systems Research*, 79, 6, (2009), pp. 855-862.

Karnavas, Y.L., & Pantos, S. (2008). Performance evaluation of neural networks for μC based excitation control of a synchronous generator, *Proceedings of 18th International Conference on Electrical Machines ICEM 2008*, Portugal, September 2008.

Karnavas, Y.L., & Papadopoulos, D. P. (2002). AGC for autonomous power system using combined intelligent techniques, *Electric Power Systems Research*, 62, 3, (July 2002), pp. 225-239.

Kundur, P. (1994). *Power System Stability and Control*, McGraw-Hill

Malik, O.P., Salem, M.M., Zaki, A.M., Mahgoub, O.A., & Abu El-Zahab, E. (2002). Experimental studies with simple neuro-controller based excitation controller, *IEE Proceedings Generation, Transmission and Distribution*, 149, 1, (2002), pp. 108-113.

Noroozi, N., Khaki, B., & Seifi, A. (2008). Chaotic Oscillations Damping in Power System by Finite Time Control, *International Review of Electrical Engineering*, 3, 6, (December 2008), pp. 1032-1038.

Salem, M.M., Malik, O.P., Zaki, A.M., Mahgoub, O.A., & Abu El-Zahab, E. (2003). Simple neuro-controller with modified error function for a synchronous generator, *Electrical Power and Energy Systems*, 25, (2003), pp. 759-771.

Salem, M.M., Zaki, A.M., Mahgoub, O.A., Abu El-Zahab, E., & Malik, O.P. (2000a). Studies on Multi-Machine Power System With a Neural Network Based Excitation Controller, *Proceedings of Power Engineering Society Summer Meeting*, 2000.

Salem, M.M., Zaki, A.M., Mahgoub, O.A., Abu El-Zahab, E., & Malik, O.P. (2000b). Experimental Veification of Generating Unit Excitation Neuro-Controller, *Proceedings of* IEEE Power Engineering Society Winter Meeting, 2000.

Shahgholian, G. (2010). Development of State Space Model and Control of the STATCOM for Improvement of Damping in a Single-Machine Infinite-Bus, *International Review of Electrical Engineering*, 5, 1, (February 2010), pp. 1367-1375.

11

MATLAB: A Systems Tool for Design of Fuzzy LMI Controller in DC-DC Converters

Carlos Andrés Torres-Pinzón and Ramon Leyva
Department of Electronic, Electrical, and Automatic Control Engineering
Rovira i Virgili University
Tarragona, Spain

1. Introduction

DC-DC switching converters are devices usually used to adapt primary energy sources to the load requirements (Erickson & Macksimovic, 2001). These devices produce a regulated output voltage despite changes in the feed voltage or in the load current. There are three basic topologies of dc-dc converters, namely the buck, the boost and the buck-boost converter. The buck converter is used to reduce output voltage, while the boost converter increase the output voltage. In the buck-boost converter, the output voltage can be maintained either higher or lower than the source but in the opposite polarity. These basic converters consist of two reactive elements; namely, an inductor and a capacitor, besides a transistor and a diode to perform the commutation, the size of reactive elements are chosen to guarantee a low level of ripple and hence an averaged dynamical model behavior is a good approximation of the switched behavior.

In order to maintain a regulated output and to have a damped enough response some control loops are added to command the converter. The signal which drives the transistor used to be a squared, constant-period and high frequency signal.

The design of the control loops is commonly based on linearized dynamic models around equilibrium point of the converter (Erickson & Macksimovic, 2001). Nevertheless, commonly the averaged dynamical models of these plants are nonlinear and their linearization is non minimum phase. Therefore, using linear controllers can only ensures stability and dynamic performances around equilibrium point, and hence, instabilities or bad performances may appear when large signal perturbations occur. This fact has prompted several authors to apply nonlinear control methods to regulate switching converters.

Some of the first researches on nonlinear controller design for dc-dc converters can be found in the studies of (Sanders & Verghese, 1992) and (Kawasaki et al., 1995). These authors propose non-linear strategies based on Lyapunov functions, which allows the converter to ensure stability over a wide range of operating conditions. More recent studies are those of (Leyva et al., 2006) and (He & Luo, 2006) which derive robust non-linear controller for large-signal stability in dc-dc converters and present efficient implementations.

Furthermore, robust control approaches have been applied in dc-dc converters which take into account nonlinearities and uncertainties (Olalla et al., 2009; 2010).

Another promising nonlinear technique for controlling power converters is the model-based fuzzy control technique. The model-based fuzzy approaches begin by constructing the corresponding (T-S) Takagi—Sugeno fuzzy model representation of the nonlinear system (Tanaka & Wang, 2001). This T-S fuzzy representation is described by fuzzy rules IF-THEN which represent local linear input-output relations of the nonlinear plant. Once fuzzy rules are obtained with linear submodels, the control design is based on the technique known as Parallel Distributed Compensator (PDC), where each control rule is designed from the corresponding rule of the T-S fuzzy model (Korba et al., 2003). The stability analysis is carried out using Lyapunov functions on the closed-loop system. The Lyapunov functions are formulated into linear matrix inequalities (LMIs). This approach is fundamentally different from heuristics based fuzzy control (Tanaka & Wang, 2001) where the rules are based on heuristic knowledge. A model-based fuzzy control for dc-dc converters have been described in (Kuang et al., 2006), where the authors show a fuzzy law for the buck and ZVT buck converters. Other authors who applied this technique in dc-dc converters are (Lan & Tan, 2009)

Nowadays, thanks to the powerful computational tools and optimization techniques, many robust and fuzzy control designs based on LMIs can be readily solved. Matlab is a powerful tool in this process. The LMI Toolbox of Matlab is an efficient software tool based on interior point methods (Gahinet et al., 1995), which it can be used to numerically solve many LMI control problems that otherwise could not be solved since they have not an analytical solution. The main advantage of the LMI formulations is the ability to combine various design constraints and objectives in a numerically tractable manner.

This chapter presents a synthesis of LMI fuzzy controllers for dc-dc converters. The chapter describes in detail a compact control design methodology which takes into account constraints such as: control effort and the decay rate of state variables. The chapter is organized as follows: First, in section 2, we review the dynamics of a buck and a boost converter. In section 3, we introduce the T-S fuzzy representation of dc-dc converters, with their corresponding uncertainties. Aspects of the LMI fuzzy control design are explained in section 4. In section 5, we present two design examples to illustrate the advantages of the procedure. The first example shows the LMI controller of a buck converter, while in the second, we obtain an LMI Fuzzy controller for a boost converter working at different operating point. Both examples have been simulated with Matlab and the results are in perfect agreement with the design specification. Finally, we summarize the main ideas in section 6.

2. Modeling of DC-DC converters. A dynamical review

This section presents basic PWM converters and their state-space models which are used in the following sections. Specifically, the section describes the dynamic behavior of buck and boost converters.

2.1 Model of PWM buck converters

Fig.1 shows a dc-dc step-down (buck) converter, this power electronic stage reduces and regulates the output voltage from a primary voltage source.

The converter switch alternates periodically between two positions. Fig. 2 shows the circuits corresponding to on and off during intervals T_{on} and T_{off}, respectively. These positions are driven by the binary signal u whose values are $u = 1$ during T_{on} and $u = 0$ during T_{off}. The voltage reduction of this converter in steady state corresponds to the ratio T_{on}/T_s. We model the converter dynamics at each position by using the Kirchhoff laws. Its dynamic expressions

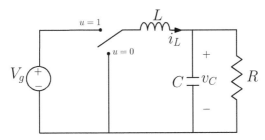

Fig. 1. Schematic circuit of a buck converter

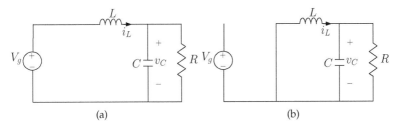

(a) (b)

Fig. 2. Equivalent circuit during T_{on} (a) and T_{off} (b).

in state-space at each position correspond to

$$\dot{x}(t) = A_{on}x(t) + B_{u_{on}} \quad during \ T_{on}$$
$$\dot{x}(t) = A_{off}x(t) + B_{u_{off}} \quad during \ T_{off} \tag{1}$$

being

$$A_{on} = A_{off} = \begin{bmatrix} 0 & -\frac{1}{L} \\ \frac{1}{C} & -\frac{1}{RC} \end{bmatrix} \quad B_{u_{on}} = \begin{bmatrix} \frac{V_g}{L} \\ 0 \end{bmatrix} \quad B_{u_{off}} = \begin{bmatrix} 0 \\ 0 \end{bmatrix} \tag{2}$$

and

$$x(t) = \begin{bmatrix} i_L(t) & v_C(t) \end{bmatrix}^T$$

where V_g is the feed voltage or primary source and v_C is the output voltage. R models the load, while L and C stand for inductance and capacitance values, respectively. The state vector $x(t)$ consists of the inductor current $i_L(t)$ and the capacitor voltage $v_C(t)$. A_{on} and $B_{u_{on}}$ are the transition matrix and input vector, respectively, during T_{on} and A_{off} and $B_{u_{off}}$ are the transition matrix and input vector during T_{off}.

The binary signal u turn on and off the switch which is controlled by means of a pulse width modulator (PWM), whose switching period T_s is equals to the sum of T_{on} and T_{off}. The PWM duty cycle is noted as d.

The expressions (1) and (2) can be written compactly in terms of the binary signal u as follows

$$\dot{x}(t) = A_{off}x(t) + B_{off} + \left(A_{on} - A_{off} \right) xu + \left(B_{on} - B_{off} \right) u \tag{3}$$

The converter operates in continuous conduction mode (CCM) when the inductor current i_L is ever greater than zero. We assume this operation mode then the switched model (3) can be approximated using state-space averaging method (Middlebrook & Cuk, 1976), replacing the binary signal u by its respective duty cycle d and the state variables by their averaged values during the switching period. The result of this averaging process can be written as

$$\dot{\bar{x}}(t) = A_{off}\bar{x}(t) + B_{off} + \left(A_{on} - A_{off}\right)\bar{x}d + \left(B_{on} - B_{off}\right)d \tag{4}$$

Thus, the averaged state vector $\bar{x}$ corresponds to $\bar{x} = \left(\bar{i}_L, \bar{v}_C\right)^T$; where $\bar{i}_L$ and $\bar{v}_C$ are the averaged values of inductor current and capacitor voltage during a switching period.

Usually the bilinear model (4) is linearized around equilibrium point by considering that the system variables consist of two components:

$$\begin{aligned}\bar{x}(t) &= X + \hat{x}(t) \\ d(t) &= D + \hat{d}(t)\end{aligned} \tag{5}$$

where X and D represent the equilibrium values and $\hat{x}$ and $\hat{d}$ are the perturbed values of the state and duty cycle. Therefore, equation (4) can be written as follows

$$\dot{\hat{x}} = \left[A_{off} + \left(A_{on} - A_{off}\right)D\right]\hat{x} + \left[\left(B_{on} - B_{off}\right) + \left(A_{on} - A_{off}\right)X\right]\hat{d} \tag{6}$$

The equilibrium state in the buck converter corresponds to

$$X = \begin{bmatrix} \frac{V_g D}{R} \\ V_g D \end{bmatrix} \tag{7}$$

Taking into account (2), we can model the buck converter as

$$\dot{\hat{x}}(t) = \begin{bmatrix} 0 & -\frac{1}{L} \\ \frac{1}{C} & -\frac{1}{RC} \end{bmatrix}\hat{x}(t) + \begin{bmatrix} \frac{V_g}{L} \\ 0 \end{bmatrix}\hat{d}(t) \tag{8}$$

The model can be augmented to ensure zero steady-state error of v_C by introducing a new state variable x_3 corresponding to

$$x_3(t) = \int \left(v_C(t) - V_{ref}\right) dt \tag{9}$$

where V_{ref} is the voltage reference.

Thus, the augmented model can be written as

$$\dot{\hat{x}}(t) = A\hat{x}(t) + B_u\hat{d}(t) \tag{10}$$

where

$$A = \begin{bmatrix} 0 & -\frac{1}{L} & 0 \\ \frac{1}{C} & -\frac{1}{RC} & 0 \\ 0 & 1 & 0 \end{bmatrix} \quad B_u = \begin{bmatrix} \frac{V_g}{L} \\ 0 \\ 0 \end{bmatrix} \tag{11}$$

In the next subsection, we develop the same procedure for the boost converter.

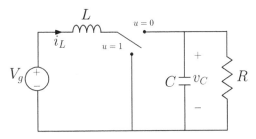

Fig. 3. Schematic circuit of a boost converter

2.2 Model of PWM boost converters

The Fig.3 shows the well-known boost converter (Erickson & Macksimovic, 2001), which is capable of regulating a dc output voltage when it is higher than the dc feed voltage.

The dynamic behavior of boost converter during T_{on} and T_{off} shown in the Fig. 4 can be written as

$$A_{on} = \begin{bmatrix} 0 & 0 \\ 0 & -\frac{1}{RC} \end{bmatrix} \quad A_{off} = \begin{bmatrix} 0 & -\frac{1}{L} \\ \frac{1}{C} & -\frac{1}{RC} \end{bmatrix} \quad B_{u_{on}} = B_{u_{off}} = \begin{bmatrix} \frac{V_g}{L} \\ 0 \end{bmatrix} \tag{12}$$

$$x(t) = \begin{bmatrix} i_L(t) & v_C(t) \end{bmatrix}^T$$

where $x(t)$ is the state-space vector composed of i_L, which represents the inductor current, and v_C, which represents the capacitor voltage. These variables are measurable and available for feedback purposes.

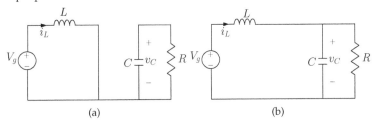

(a)   (b)

Fig. 4. Equivalent circuit of boost converter for T_{on} (a) and T_{off} (b).

Therefore, according to (12), the equilibrium state in the boost converter corresponds to

$$X = \begin{bmatrix} \frac{V_g}{RD'^2} \\ \frac{V_g}{D'} \end{bmatrix} \tag{13}$$

where $D' = 1 - D$ is the complementary steady-state duty-cycle.

Since $A_{on} \neq A_{off}$, the average model of the boost converter is bilinear, which can be written as:

$$\dot{\hat{x}} = A\hat{x} + B_u(\hat{x})\hat{d} \tag{14}$$

being

$$A = \begin{bmatrix} 0 & -\frac{D'}{L} & 0 \\ \frac{D'}{C} & -\frac{1}{RC} \\ 0 & 1 & 0 \end{bmatrix} \quad B_u(\hat{x}) = \begin{bmatrix} \frac{V_g}{D'L} + \frac{\dot{v}_C(t)}{L} \\ -\frac{V_g}{(D'^2R)C} - \frac{\hat{i}_L(t)}{C} \\ 0 \end{bmatrix} \tag{15}$$

In next section, we describes the T-S fuzzy modeling method for the DC-DC converters.

3. Takagi-Sugeno fuzzy representation of DC-DC converters

There exist several approaches to fuzzy representation of dynamic systems, between them the most common are the Mamdani fuzzy representation (Driankov et al., 1993) and the T-S fuzzy representation (Tanaka & Wang, 2001). In the first representation, it is assumed that there is no model of the plant, while the second representation is always based on a dynamical model of the plant.

This T-S representation describes the dynamic system by means of an interpolation of linear submodels. The performance requirements of a linear model may be expressed by means of LMI.

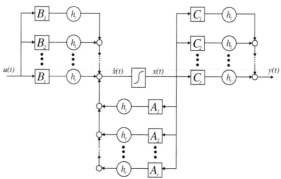

Fig. 5. Final structure of the Takagi-Sugeno fuzzy model

Figure 5 shows the model of the nonlinear plant as a group of linear models, which locally represent the relationship input-output system (Takagi & Sugeno, 1985), described of the form:

$$R_i : If \ \delta_1 \ is \ M_{i1} \ and \ldots and \ \delta_j \ is \ M_{ji} \ then$$

$$\dot{x}_i(t) = A_i x(t) + B_i u(t) \ i = 1, 2, \ldots r \tag{16}$$

Where r is the number of submodels, A_i is the system matrix of the i-th linear submodel, B_i is the input matrix, $x(t)$ is the global state-space vector, $u(t)$ is the input vector, M_{ji} are fuzzy sets, and δ_j is the scheduling vector (Korba et al., 2003).

Fuzzy sets M_{ji} have associated membership functions $\eta's$ which characterize the degree of membership (Takagi & Sugeno, 1985). The nonlinearities of the plant will determine the variables of the scheduling vector δ_i used in the antecedent, i.e., a correct election of scheduling variables will capture all the nonlinearities of the plant, in the case of the dc-dc converters the scheduling variables are function of the state variables $\delta(t) = \delta(x(t))$ (Korba et al., 2003; Tanaka & Wang, 2001). The entire fuzzy model of the plant corresponds to a fuzzy weighting of the locally valid linear submodel associated to each implications R_i (Korba et al., 2003), i.e.,

$$\dot{x}(t) = \frac{\sum_{i=1}^{r} w_i(\delta(t)) \left[A_i x(t) + B_i u(t) \right]}{\sum_{i=1}^{r} w_i(\delta(t))} \tag{17}$$

Weights $w_i(\delta(t))$ are zero or positive time-variant values and the sum of all the weights is positive.

$$\sum_{i=1}^{r} w_i(\delta(t)) > 0, \quad w_i(\delta(t)) \geq 0 \quad \forall \quad i = 1, 2, \ldots, r$$

We use the next normalized weight function $h_i(\delta(t))$ replacing $w_i(\delta(t))$,

$$h_i(\delta(t)) = \frac{w_i(\delta(t))}{\sum_{i=1}^{r} w_i(\delta(t))}$$

that fulfill with

$$0 \leq h_i(\delta(t)) \leq 1, \quad \sum_{i=1}^{r} h_i(\delta(t)) = 1 \tag{18}$$

Therefore the fuzzy model (17) can be rewritten as

$$\dot{x}(t) = \sum_{i=1}^{r} h_i(\delta(t)) \left[A_i x(t) + B_i u(t) \right] \tag{19}$$

The T-S fuzzy model of the buck converter is expressed by only one rule given that it is linear. The T-S fuzzy models of other topologies require several rules given that their dynamic behaviour is bilinear. The boost converter case is shown in the next subsection.

3.1 Takagi-Sugeno model of a boost converter
We propose the next boost converter fuzzy model consisting of the following four rules.

- R_1:

$$\text{If } \hat{i}_L \text{ is } i_{small} \text{ and } \hat{v}_C \text{ is } v_{small} \text{ then}$$
$$\dot{\hat{x}}_1(t) = A_1 \hat{x}(t) + B_1 \hat{d}(t) \tag{20}$$

- R_2:

$$\text{If } \hat{i}_L \text{ is } i_{big} \text{ and } \hat{v}_C \text{ is } v_{small} \text{ then}$$
$$\dot{\hat{x}}_2(t) = A_2 \hat{x}(t) + B_2 \hat{d}(t) \tag{21}$$

- R_3:

$$\text{If } \hat{i}_L \text{ is } i_{small} \text{ and } \hat{v}_C \text{ is } v_{big} \text{ then}$$
$$\dot{\hat{x}}_3(t) = A_3 \hat{x}(t) + B_3 \hat{d}(t) \tag{22}$$

- R_4:

$$\text{If } \hat{i}_L \text{ is } i_{big} \text{ and } \hat{v}_C \text{ is } v_{big} \text{ then}$$
$$\dot{\hat{x}}_4(t) = A_4 \hat{x}(t) + B_4 \hat{d}(t) \tag{23}$$

where

$$A_1 = A_2 = A_3 = A_4 = A = \begin{bmatrix} 0 & -\frac{D'}{L} & 0 \\ \frac{D'}{C} & -\frac{1}{RC} \\ 0 & 1 & 0 \end{bmatrix}$$

$$B_1 = \begin{bmatrix} \frac{V_g}{D'L} + \frac{v_{min}}{L} \\ -\frac{V_g}{(D'^2R)C} - \frac{i_{min}}{C} \\ 0 \end{bmatrix} \quad B_2 = \begin{bmatrix} \frac{V_g}{D'L} + \frac{v_{min}}{L} \\ -\frac{V_g}{(D'^2R)C} - \frac{i_{max}}{C} \\ 0 \end{bmatrix}$$

$$B_3 = \begin{bmatrix} \frac{V_g}{D'L} + \frac{v_{max}}{L} \\ -\frac{V_g}{(D'^2R)C} - \frac{i_{min}}{C} \\ 0 \end{bmatrix} \quad B_4 = \begin{bmatrix} \frac{V_g}{D'L} + \frac{v_{max}}{L} \\ -\frac{V_g}{(D'^2R)C} - \frac{i_{max}}{C} \\ 0 \end{bmatrix}$$

$$(24)$$

being the membership function of the fuzzy sets i_{small}, i_{big}, v_{small} and v_{big} the following ones,

$$\eta_{i_{small}}(\hat{i}_L) = \frac{i_{max} - \hat{i}_L}{i_{max} - i_{min}} \quad \eta_{i_{big}}(\hat{i}_L) = 1 - \eta_{i_{small}}(\hat{i}_L)$$

$$\eta_{v_{small}}(\hat{v}_C) = \frac{v_{max} - \hat{v}_C}{v_{max} - v_{min}} \quad \eta_{v_{big}}(\hat{v}_C) = 1 - \eta_{v_{small}}(\hat{v}_C)$$

$$(25)$$

Note that (20) correspond to the dynamic behavior around (i_{min}, v_{min}) values, and (21)-(23) describe the local behavior around the other interval bounds. Thus, the normalized weight functions are

$$\begin{array}{ll} h_1(\hat{i}_L, \hat{v}_C) = \eta_{i_{small}} \cdot \eta_{v_{small}} & h_3(\hat{i}_L, \hat{v}_C) = \eta_{i_{small}} \cdot \eta_{v_{big}} \\ h_2(\hat{i}_L, \hat{v}_C) = \eta_{i_{big}} \cdot \eta_{v_{small}} & h_4(\hat{i}_L, \hat{v}_C) = \eta_{i_{big}} \cdot \eta_{v_{big}} \end{array}$$

$$(26)$$

therefore the entire fuzzy converter model corresponds to

$$\dot{\hat{x}}(t) = \sum_{i=1}^{r} h_i\left(\hat{i}_L, \hat{v}_C\right)\left(A_i\hat{x}(t) + B_i\hat{d}(t)\right)$$

$$(27)$$

since $\sum_{i=0}^{r} h_i = 1$ and $A_i = A$ then

$$\dot{\hat{x}}(t) = A\hat{x}(t) + \left(\sum_{i=1}^{r} h_i(\hat{i}_L, \hat{v}_C)B_i\right)\hat{d}(t)$$

$$(28)$$

and it is worth to remark that (28) corresponds with the bilinear model (14) inside the polytope region $\left[\hat{i}_{min}, \hat{i}_{max}\right] \times \left[\hat{v}_{min}, \hat{v}_{max}\right]$. This operating space is depicted in Fig. (6).

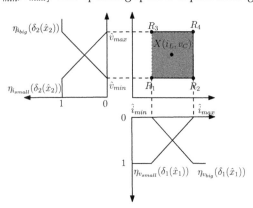

Fig. 6. *T-S* Fuzzy representation of the boost converter consisting of the 4 rules

The approach shown here can be easily adapted for the buck-boost converter, such as shown in (Torres-Pinzón & Leyva, 2009).

In next section, we explain a control strategy where the law consist of a normalized weight sum of linear feedback gains at each interval limit, which takes into account constraints such as: control effort and the decay rate of state variables.

4. LMI performance requeriments

This section presents the concept and basic procedure of the parallel distributed compensation (PDC) technique and the definitions and LMI constraints used in the synthesis of control. First, we introduce the basic concept of Lyapunov-based stability. Then, we discuss on stability concepts for fuzzy systems in form of LMI. These concepts will be applied in Section 5 to find a LMI fuzzy controller for the buck and boost converters. It can be observed that since the buck converter dynamics is linear, we obtain a linear control law for this converter that is a fuzzy controller with only one rule.

4.1 Quadratic stability conditions

Given the linear dynamic system

$$\dot{x}(t) = Ax(t) \tag{29}$$

the existence of a quadratic function of the form

$$V\left(x(t)\right) = x(t)^T \mathbf{P} x(t) \tag{30}$$

that satisfies $\dot{V}\left(x(t)\right) < 0$, is a necessary and sufficient condition to ensure that the system is asymptotically stable, i.e., all trajectories converge to zero. Where $\mathbf{P}$ is a symmetric positive definite matrix $\in \mathbb{R}^{n \times n}$. Since the expression $\dot{V}\left(x(t)\right) < 0$ has form quadratic, this condition is referred as quadratic stability, and it can be rewritten as follows

$$\dot{V}\left(x(t)\right) = x(t)^T \left(A^T \mathbf{P} + \mathbf{P}A\right) x(t) \tag{31}$$

Thus, the system is asymptotically stable if and only if there exist a symmetric matrix $\mathbf{P}$ such that

$$A^T \mathbf{P} + \mathbf{P}A < 0 \tag{32}$$

The main interest of the quadratic stability condition is that by means of a convex envelope and numerically simple test, it is possible to conclude about the overall stability of a dynamics system.

For an in-deep explanation on quadratic stability see (Boyd et al., 1994).

Based on the results (32), the following subsection present some basic results on the stability of fuzzy control systems.

4.2 Performance constraints

In this subsection, we review in detail the Parallel Distributed Compensation (PDC) technique (Tanaka & Wang, 2001). In such fuzzy technique, each control rule is associated with the corresponding rule of the fuzzy model, thus the controller rules are as follows,

$$R_i : \textbf{If } \delta_1 \text{ is } M_{i1} \text{ and} \dots \text{and } \delta_j \text{ is } M_{ji} \textbf{ Then}$$

$$u(t) = -\mathbf{F}_i x(t) \ i = 1, \dots, r \tag{33}$$

where F_i are lineal feedback gain vectors associate with each rule. And the overall fuzzy controller is represented as

$$u(t) = -\frac{\sum_{i=1}^{r} w_i F_i x(t)}{\sum_{i=1}^{r} w_i} = -\sum_{i=1}^{r} h_i F_i x(t) \tag{34}$$

Substituting the control law (34) in the fuzzy model (19), the closed loop system dynamics is given by

$$\dot{x}(t) = \sum_{i=1}^{r} \sum_{j=1}^{r} h_i h_j \left(A_i - B_i F_j\right) x(t) \tag{35}$$

In order to select the suitable feedback gain vectors F_i, we impose Lyapunov stability constraints and performance constraints on decay rate and control effort in form of LMIs. Therefore, the sufficient conditions for the stability of the open-loop fuzzy system (19) and closed-loop one (35) are obtained using quadratic stability condition of the equation (32). These conditions, derived from (Tanaka & Wang, 2001), it can be expressed by means of the next propositions.

Proposition 4.1. *The equilibrium of the continuous fuzzy system* (19) *with* $u(t) = 0$ *is asymptotically stable if there exists a common positive definite matrix* P *such that*

$$A_i^T P + P A_i < 0, \; i=1,\dots,r \\ P > 0 \tag{36}$$

that is, a common P has to exist for all subsystems

where A_i are system matrices of the linear submodels defined in the previous section.

Proposition 4.2. *The equilibrium of the continuous fuzzy control system described by* (35) *is asymptotically stable if there exists a common positive definite matrix* P *such that*

$$\left(A_i - B_i F_j\right)^T P + P \left(A_i - B_i F_j\right) < 0, \; j > i \\ P > 0 \tag{37}$$

Note that the condition (37) is not linear because involves the multiplication of the variables P and $F'_j s$. Thus, in order to rewrite (37) in a linear manner, we multiply the inequality (37) on the left and right by P^{-1}, and we define a new variable $W = P^{-1}$, then proposition 4.2 can be rewritten as follows.

Proposition 4.3. *The continuous fuzzy system* (35) *is quadratically stable for some feedback gain* F_i *if there exists a common positive definite matrix* W *such that*

$$A_i W + W A_i^T - B_i Y_i - Y_i^T B_i^T < 0, \qquad\qquad i = 1, \dots r$$

$$A_i W + W A_i^T + A_j W + W A_j^T - B_i Y_j - Y_j^T B_j^T - B_j Y_i - Y_i^T B_j^T \leq 0, \; i < j \leq r \tag{38}$$

being $Y_i = F_i W$ *so that for* $W > 0$, *we have* $F_i = Y_i W^{-1}$

Using these LMI conditions, we establish the first controller design constraint, next we describe the second design restriction.

As dc-dc converter control signal corresponds to the incremental duty cycle, then the control signal is bounded in the interval $[-D, 1-D]$. In order to satisfy with this limitation, we constrain the control signal by the next proposition.

The satisfaction of the next proposition will assure that control signal $d(t)$ is inside the interval $[-D, 1-D]$ from starting condition $x(0)$ to the equilibrium point.

Proposition 4.4. *Assume that initial condition x(0) is known. The constraint* $\|d(t)\|_2 \leq \mu$ *is enforced at all times* $t \geq 0$ *if the LMIs (39) hold*

$$
\begin{bmatrix} 1 & x(0)^T \\ x(0) & \mathbf{W} \end{bmatrix} \geq 0,
$$
$$
\begin{bmatrix} \mathbf{W} & \mathbf{Y}_i^T \\ \mathbf{Y}_i & \mu^2 \mathbf{I} \end{bmatrix} \geq 0
\tag{39}
$$

where $\mathbf{W} = \mathbf{P}^{-1}$ *and* $\mathbf{Y}_i = \mathbf{F}_i \mathbf{W}$.

Also, it will be desirable a suitable transient performances of the closed loop system. The entire fuzzy system transient performances depends on the localizations of the poles of its linear systems corresponding to each rule. In our case, this poles are expressed in terms of decay rate introduced via exponential stability, which it can be seen as a special case of pole-placement on the closed-loop system.

Consequently, we impose that this poles must be inside a predetermined region as the one pictured in Fig. 7. Therefore, the design process will add the next proposition, adapted from (Tanaka & Wang, 2001).

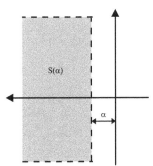

Fig. 7. $S(\alpha)$ region

Proposition 4.5. *The eigenvalues of* $\left(A_i - B_i F_j \right)$ *in each linear fuzzy system are inside the region* $S(\alpha)$ *if there exist a common positive definite matrix* $\mathbf{W}$ *such that*

$$
A_i \mathbf{W} + \mathbf{W} A_i^T - B_i \mathbf{Y}_i - \mathbf{Y}_i^T B_i^T + 2\alpha \mathbf{W} < 0, \qquad\qquad i = 1, \dots r
$$
$$
A_i \mathbf{W} + \mathbf{W} A_i^T + A_j \mathbf{W} + \mathbf{W} A_j^T - B_i \mathbf{Y}_j - \mathbf{Y}_j^T B_i^T - B_j \mathbf{Y}_i - \mathbf{Y}_i^T B_j^T + 4\alpha \mathbf{W} \leq 0, \; i < j \leq r
\tag{40}
$$

being $\mathbf{F}_i = \mathbf{Y}_i \mathbf{W}^{-1}$.

Between all the feasible set of feedback gains, the proposed algorithm finds the largest possible decay rate (α) of the state variables, satisfying the previous LMIs. Hence, the design procedure of the LMI Fuzzy control can be formulated by the following optimization algorithm.

$$
\begin{array}{ll}
max & \alpha \ subject\ to \\
\mathbf{W}, \mathbf{Y}_i & \\
i = 1, \ldots, r & (39), \ and \ (40)
\end{array} \tag{41}
$$

The solution of this optimization program with its corresponding LMIs will provide the set of feedback gains $F_{LMI-Fuzzy} = \{F_1, F_2, F_3, F_4\}$. The solution of this algorithm can be carried out by means of GEVP function in MATLAB LMI toolbox.

5. Design examples

This section shows two examples of LMI-based control applied to dc-dc converters. The first case presents the control design of a step-down converter working around equilibrium point. This example takes into account the same LMIs constraints of the algorithm (41). The second example proposes an LMI Fuzzy control for a step-up converter, allowing working at different operating point. Both examples are tested during a start-up and under load disturbances.

5.1 LMI control of a Buck converter

In this first example, we presents an LMI control approach applied to the problem of regulating the output voltage of the buck converter. The values of the converter parameter set are shown in Table 1. The nominal load of the converter is equal to 10 Ω, while supply voltage equal to 48 V. Consequently, the equilibrium point satisfying (7) is equal to $[i_L \ v_C] = [4.8 \ 24]^T$. The simulation prototype is designed to process less than 60 W corresponding to a load resistance $R = 10 \ \Omega$. The inductance and capacitance values and switching frequency have been selected to ensure low ripple level. In order to limit the control signal in the range $[-D, 1 - D]$, μ is set to 1500, since simulations show no saturation of the duty-cycle.

V_g	48V
$v_C(V_{ref})$	24V
L	200 μH
C	200 μF
R	10 Ω
D'	0.5 Ω
T_s	10 μ s

Table 1. Buck converter parameters

Once the parameters values of the converter and controller have been defined, the next step is to obtain the feedback gain vector. Thus, solving the optimization algorithm (41) for the system (11), by means of the LMI toolbox of MATLAB (Gahinet et al., 1995), the state-feedback controller obtained for the buck converter is

$$
\mathbf{F}_{Buck} = \begin{bmatrix} 0.0963 & 0.1133 & -319.8021 \end{bmatrix}
$$

with a decay rate of $\alpha = 3254$, which assures a maximum constant time of $1/3254$, and consequently a maximum settling time of $4 * (1/3254)$. In order to verify the behavior of the buck converter under the control law described above, numerical simulations have been carried out in MATLAB/Simulink, as shown in Fig.8.

Fig. 9 shows the transient simulation of the state variables and duty-cycle during start-up, in fact, represents a large signal perturbation around the equilibrium point of the state variables. It is remark that the settling time is smaller than 1.2 ms, and agrees with the decay rate obtained.

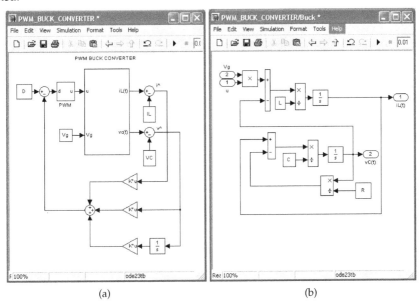

(a)   (b)

Fig. 8. Simulink diagram of a buck converter with state-feedback regulation. (a) Implementation diagram in MATLAB/Simulink. (b) Simulink model of the buck converter.

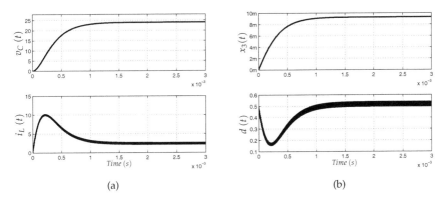

(a)   (b)

Fig. 9. Simulated response of the dc-dc buck converter during start-up. (a) Inductor current $i_L(t)$ and capacitor voltage $v_C(t)$. (b) Steady-state error $x_3(t)$ and duty-cycle $d(t)$.

Fig. 10 illustrates the system responses for step changes in the load current from 2.4 A to 4.4 A at $2ms$ and then returns to 2.4 A at $8ms$. It can be observed that the controller regulates the output voltage v_C smoothly at 24 V after a short transient period. It can also be observed that the duty-cycle does not exceed the limits of interval $[-D, 1-D]$. In the next subsection, the

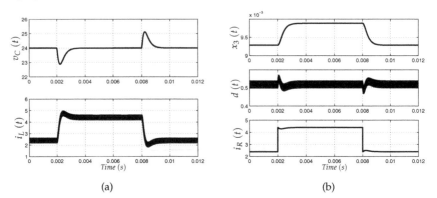

(a)   (b)

Fig. 10. Simulated response of the buck converter under a load step transient of 2 A.
(a) Inductor current $i_L(t)$ and capacitor voltage $v_C(t)$. (b) Steady-state error $x_3(t)$, duty-cycle $d(t)$ and load current i_R.

LMI Fuzzy controller design for a boost converter is described.

5.2 LMI Fuzyy control of a boost converter
In this subsection, we present the results of the design of the LMI Fuzzy controller applied to fuzzy model of the boost converter shown in subsection 3.1, whose parameter set is shown in Table 2. Consequently, the equilibrium state is given by $[i_L \ v_C] = [4.8 \ 24]^T$.

The design of the control law consists of solving the optimization algorithm (41) for the

V_g	12V
$v_C(V_{ref})$	24V
L	300 μH
C	300 μF
R	10 Ω
D'	0.5 Ω
T_s	20 μ s

Table 2. Boost converter parameters

four linear submodels of the fuzzy model. This submodels correspond to the vertices of the polytopic model of the boost converter in the region defined in Fig 6. Therefore, in order to ensure stability within the polytopic region during a start-up transition and disturbance, the polytopic region should be $[\hat{i}_{min} = 0, \hat{i}_{max} = 20] \times [\hat{v}_{min} = 0, \hat{v}_{max} = 10]$. To demonstrate the advantage of this Fuzzy approach, we will compare the LMI Fuzzy control with a LMI linear Control.

As in the previous subsection, the simulation prototype is designed to process less than 60 W, as well as the inductance and capacitance values and switching frequency are selected to ensure low ripple level. To maintain the control signal under the threshold limit value, μ is set to 350, for the two control designs. So, according to the optimization algorithm (41), the fuzzy state-feedback gains obtained via LMI Toolbox of Matlab are given follows:

$$\mathbf{F}_1 = \begin{bmatrix} 0.1737 \; 0.1019 \; -183.4507 \end{bmatrix}$$

$$\mathbf{F}_2 = \begin{bmatrix} 0.2737 \; 0.1871 \; -313.9974 \end{bmatrix}$$

$$\mathbf{F}_3 = \begin{bmatrix} 0.1814 \; 0.1157 \; -199.8689 \end{bmatrix}$$

$$\mathbf{F}_4 = \begin{bmatrix} 0.1877 \; 0.1149 \; -202.6875 \end{bmatrix}$$

The decay rate value obtained is 878, which assures a maximum settling time of $4 * (1/878)$. As mentioned above, to contrast the performance and robustness of the proposed control, we compare the LMI Fuzzy control law with a LMI linear law, which it presents the same optimization criteria (41). The resulting controller gain vector is

$$\mathbf{F}_{Boost} = \begin{bmatrix} 0.0895 \; 0.1018 \; -159.9759 \end{bmatrix}$$

with a decay rate of 1950, that assures a maximum settling time of $4 * (1/1950)$.
It can be observed that there exist differences between the decay rate obtained above. Next, we will show its properties during a start-up and in presence of load disturbances. Fig. 11 shows the simulation schematic of the boost converter with the LMI Fuzzy controller implemented in MATLAB/Simulink. Note that the MATLAB Function block is used to run the LMI Fuzzy

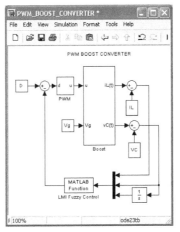

Fig. 11. Simulink implementation diagram of a boost converter with LMI Fuzzy regulation.

control on Simulink, which it is written by means of a code in the MATLAB Editor.
Fig. 12 illustrates the transient simulation of the boost converter during start-up. The waveforms depicted in the figure are the inductor current i_L, capacitor voltage v_C, steady-state error x_3 and duty-cycle $d(t)$. The response of the LMI linear contoller corresponds to dashed line, while the waveform of the LMI Fuzzy controller has been drawn with solid line. In Fig. 13, the converter reacts to large load disturbances. In this simulation the load current is initially 2.4 A. At $t = 2\ ms$, the current changes to 6.4 A, and at $t = 8\ ms$, it returns to its initial

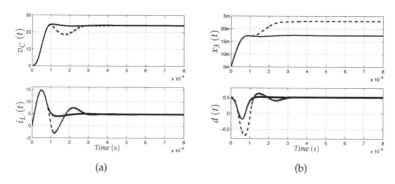

Fig. 12. Simulated responses of the dc-dc boost converter during start-up linearly controlled (dished) and fuzzy controlled (solid). (a) Inductor current $i_L(t)$ and capacitor voltage $v_C(t)$. (b) Steady-state error $x_3(t)$ and duty-cycle $d(t)$.

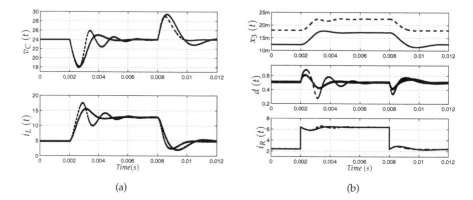

Fig. 13. Simulated responses of the boost converter under a load step transient of 4 A linearly controlled (dished) and fuzzy controlled (solid).
(a) Inductor current $i_L(t)$ and capacitor voltage $v_C(t)$. (b) Steady-state error $x_3(t)$, duty-cycle $d(t)$ and load current i_R.

value. It is worth noting that state variables and duty-cycle are better with the LMI Fuzzy controller (dashed line), since it maintains its stability properties under large disturbances, and despite that it is slower. The main advantage of this controller, is that it ensures robust stability in broad range of operation.

6. Conclusions

This chapter presents a LMI fuzzy controller design for dc-dc converters using MATLAB. The design methodology has been applied to a buck converter and to a boost converter where the control optimizes the decay rate of the state variables subject to a bound in the control effort. The methodology allows us to take into account the bilinear nature of the boost converter dynamics. We express the control objective and the bound as LMIs. The set of LMIs, which is solved by means of LMI Toolbox, provides the feedback gains.

The dynamical performances of LMI fuzzy controlled boost converter have been compared those of a linear-controlled boost considering the same design constraint. We have verified the closed-loop dynamic behavior using Simulink/MATLAB. The plots exhibit a perfect agreement with the design specifications. This design procedure ensures the stability of the converter in a wide region. On the contrary, a linear-controlled converter deteriorates its performances out of the operating point. The approach can be extended to more complex converters or other types of bilinear plants.

7. Acknowledgment

This work was partially supported by the Spanish Ministerio de Educación y Ciencia under grant DPI2010-16481

8. References

Boyd, S.; El Ghaoui, L.; Feron, E. & Balakrishnan, V. (1994). *Linear Matrix Inequalities in Systems and Control Theory*, ser. Studies in Applied and Numerical Mathematics, Philadelphia,PA:SIAM

Chilali, M. & Gahinet, P. (1996). H∞ Design with Pole Placement Constraints: An LMI Approach, *IEEE Trans. on Autom. Control.*, Vol. 42, No.3, (358-367)

Driankov, D.; Hellendoorn, H. & Reinfrank, M. (1993). *An introduction to Fuzzy Control*, Springer-Verlag, Germanny

Erickson, R.W. & Macksimovic, D. (2001). *Fundamental of Power Electronics, Second ed.*, 920 pages, Kluwer Academic Publisher, ISBN 0-7923-7270-0, USA

Gahinet, P.; Nemirovski, A.; Laub, A.J.; & Chilali, M. (1995). LMI Control Toolbox for Use With Matlab, *The MathWorks, Inc*, Vol. 3, No.1, (75-85)

He, Y. & Luo, F.L. (2006). Sliding-mode control for dc-dc converters with constant switching frequency, *IEE Proc.-Control Theory Appl.*, Vol. 153, No.1, (37-45)

Kawasaki, N.; Nomura, H. & Masuhiro, M. (1995). A new control law of bilinear DC-DC converters developed by direct application of Lyapunov, *IEEE Trans. Power Electron.*, Vol. 10, No.1, (318-325)

Korba, P.; Babuska, R.; Verbruggen, H.B. & Frank, P.M. (2003). Fuzzy Gain Scheduling: Controller and Observer Design Based on Lyapunov Method and Convex Optimization, *IEEE Trans. on Fuzzy Syst.*, Vol. 11, No.3, (285-298)

Kuang-Yow, L.; Jeih-Jang, L. & Chien-Yu, H. (2006). LMI-Based Integral Fuzzy Control of DC-DC Converters, *IEEE Trans. on Fuzzy Syst.*, Vol. 14, No.1, (71-80)

Lan, H.K & Tan, S.C (2009). Stability analysis of fuzzy-model-based control systems: application on regulation of switching dc-dc converter, *IET Control Theory and Appl.*, Vol. 3, No.8, (1093-1106)

Leyva, R.;Cid-Pastor, A.; Alonso, C.; Queinnec, I.; Tarbouriech, S. & Martínez-Salamero, L. (2001). Passivity-based integral control of a boost converter for large-signal stability, *IEE Proc.-Control Theory Appl.*, Vol. 153, No.2, (March) (139-146)

Middlebrook, R. & Cuk, S. (1976). A general unified approach to modeling switching-converter power stages, *in IEEE Power Electron. Special. Conf.*, (June)(18-34), Cleveland

Olalla, C.;Leyva, R.; El Aroudi, A. & Queinnec, I. (2009). Robust LQR Control for PWM Converters: An LMI Approach, *IEEE Trans. Ind. Electron.*, Vol. 56, No.7, (July) (2548-2558)

Olalla, C.;Leyva, R.; El Aroudi, A.; Garcés, P. & Queinnec, I. (2009). Robust LQR Control for PWM Converters: An LMI Approach, *IET Power Electron.*, Vol. 3, No.1, (75-85)

Sanders, S.R. & Verghese G.C.(1992). Lyapunov-based control for switched power converters, *IEEE Trans. Power Electron.*, Vol. 7, No.3, (17-24)

Takagi, T. & Sugeno, M. (1985). Fuzzy Identification of Systems and Its Applications to Modeling and Control, *IEEE Trans. on Syst., Man, and Cyber.*, Vol. 15, No.1, (January) (116-132)

Tanaka, K. & Wang, H.O. (2001). *Fuzzy Control Systems Design an Analysis*, Jhon Wiley & Sons, INC, New York

Torres-Pinzón, C.A. & Leyva, R. (2009). Fuzzy Control in DC-DC Converters: an LMI Approach,*in Proc. of the IEEE Annual Conf. on Ind. Electron., IECON'09*, (November)(510-515),Porto

12

MATLAB as Interface for Intelligent Digital Control of Dynamic Systems

João Viana da Fonseca Neto and Gustavo Araújo de Andrade
Federal University of Maranhão
Department of Electrical Engineering
Control Process Laboratory
Brazil

1. Introduction

Digital control systems have shown to the developers the features and their applications in a wide variety of plants. Tools that help the developer to promote a design methodology that is efficient and at the same time reliable, has gained ground in the market and attributions of control engineers. Tasks such as data acquisition system, control design and system implementation can become arduous if there are prerequisites for sensitivity and complexity of the controller for these tasks take time and performance of the developer which will entail additional costs to the final product. These tools provide the designer with the scientist and the smooth progress of their work role has important and necessary in many areas will be subject to this study. The integration of technologies to speed and lower costs as it relates the design phases can be observed with a proper exploration of the work tool and how knowledge of plant and control techniques that meet in a less costly the goal of being achieved whatever the difficulties of the project. The choice of a tool properly can be a deciding factor in a world where time and efficiency of processes is become extremely important because the applications are growing in scale and more complex, Moudgalya (2007), Andrade (2010).

Intelligent Systems has considerable performance in accordance with plans and small large and its design encompasses more robustness to the system as well as ease of expansion. The mathematical simplicity that fuzzy systems can present and adaptability of neural networks are adopted more frequently in the academy and the industry.

An approach of intelligent systems requires a systematic and efficient operation because one works with a data stream that needs a consistency so that the iterations will be where made all the decisions may have minimal accounting. A tool that can assist in the design of this requirement is most welcome in engineering projects for control system parameter becomes constant with time,S. Sumathi (2010).

The *MATLAB* software designers can provide facilities for development and interface with different technologies for data acquisition through its communication protocols such as Serial Interface, OPC, Ethernet and others. This work is mainly focused on a methodology design of digital control systems using as development platform and implementing in software *MATLAB*.

2. Digital control and Data Acquisition Systems

The Data Acquisition System (DAS)is a key part to the project and implementation of digital controllers for the nature of digital systems is based on sampled analog system, ie played by the analog system a digital computer and its Since the interface Digital - Analog system performs the control actions . The Figure 1 shows a diagram of a system digital control and its special features such as the pool Analog - Digital and Digital - Analogue, responsible for interfacing with the analog environment.

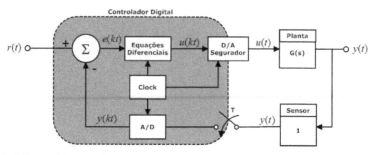

Fig. 1. Digital Control System Diagram

A digital control system is obtained from the reconstruction of analog signal contained in nature. This reconstruction is related mainly with the data acquisition system which is also involved modeling digital control system. Figure 2 illustrates the design of a system basic data acquisition of an industry.

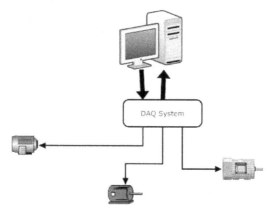

Fig. 2. DAQ System Diagram

The modern control concepts applied in the contemporary industry may be appropriated to the development of academic research activities. The introduction of a methodology parameters that specify and clarify the implementation of monitoring and control of dynamic systems.

In Figures 1 and 2 are shown at different levels, primary architectures to industrial control systems. In Figure 1 is exposed a system with minimal complexity, type SISO (Single Input - Single Output) that can occur in n times or a more complex system can be mapped as a black box system, where internal states of the process do not matter. In Figure 2 is noted, however, approach of discrete variables on the process that encompasses the entire plant worrying about sub stages.

In this work is explored a way to conceptualize these types of sound architecture in a way such that the system can be modeled and represented whatever its complexity, thus using a powerful tool when it comes to development concepts and analysis.

3. Discrete models of dynamic systems

To be held control of dynamic systems, it is necessary in this environment, the perception of some step that must be met for a procedure with minimum guarantees for the project. In the following sections will show important steps as ways to implement them by programming or graphical interface in $MATLAB$, Moudgalya (2007) and Charles L. Philips (1995).

3.1 Dynamic system identification tools

The identification of dynamic systems can be facilitated so as to make procedures the control design more efficient from the standpoint of technical feasibility and cost. processes of various types can be considered as chemical, mechanical or even behavior, used for macroeconomic modeling systems.

The use of tools that comply with the practicality of applying the concept and system design digital control is very suitable as mentioned before, so we introduce a way simple to obtain mathematical models of whatever the process, however in the case of linear or linearized process. To initiate an identification in the $MATLAB$ we can proceed in two ways and the designer must choose whichever is most convenient to your time and level of knowledge that it is your process or your plan.

In *Command Window* use the following command to open the graphical user interface the *Identification Toolbox*:

```
>> ident
```

will produce the screens shown in Figure 3, where you can begin the process of identification.

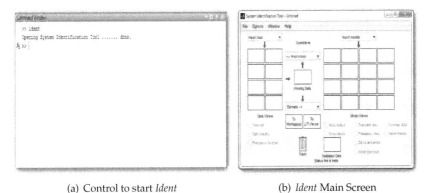

| (a) Control to start *Ident* | (b) *Ident* Main Screen |

Fig. 3. Opening The Identification Tool Box - $MATLAB$

On these screens you can start importing the measurement data on the system or even with knowledge in the previous system

The main tool for modeling dynamic systems to digital control is the *MATLAB* Identification Tool Box of, a feature that helps the designer to seamlessly and generates discrete polynomial transfer functions and the user without the need of programming the algorithms used for system identification. The *IDENT* from *MATLAB Graphical User Interface* is shown in Figures 4 and 3 and in this figure that can be seen are located to the left set of data and the right answer, ie the model to be obtained.

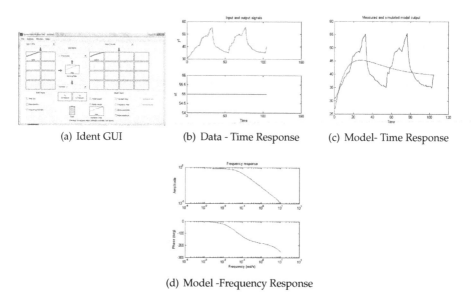

(a) Ident GUI   (b) Data - Time Response   (c) Model- Time Response

(d) Model -Frequency Response

Fig. 4. Results From The Identification Tool Box - MATLAB

Still in Figure 4 can observe that the user can define various aspects modeling systems such as filtering of data and type of modeling, as well as the analysis of response in time and frequency of the system model, Gene F. Franklin (1998).

Through this tool we can get two different ID type models in the output. The model based on parameters in the output shows a polynomial equation in discrete form

It should be added that among the numerous tools of identification, we will use polynomial will be the identification, because it gives us a response in discrete time, which makes this model implementable on digital computers. With the option to generate a polynomial model identification as described in Eq.1.

$$G(z) = \frac{Y(z)}{U(z)} = \frac{b_0 + b_1 z^{-1} + b_2 z^{-2} + \ldots b_n z^{-n}}{1 + a_1 z^{-1} + a_2 z^{-2} + \ldots a_n z^{-n}} \tag{1}$$

3.2 The plant modeling

The estimation of parameters of the transfer function of the plant is performed with the *Toolbox* Identification Systems *MATLAB*. Using the observations of voltage and temperature measurements, table,we can get the parameters of a *2nd* order transfer function.

In Figure 5 to represent the operation points thermal plant for a first evaluation of the algorithm, shows the temperature behavior from departure to variations in operating points.

The bands system operation are separated for purposes of calculation of the parameters of a model of second order. The band Operation of this plant is between 58^0 and $60^{\,0}$ as observed in Figure 5.

3.2.1 Computational and hardware setups

It is understood by *Hardware* setups and computational specifications of the hardware and and design specifications that are the model order and delay. Description of procedure for conducting the experiment are presented in next sections.

3.2.2 OE model

Using *Identification Toolbox* to estimate the parameters of the discrete model **OE** (Output-Error) operated in the delay is given by

$$T(t) = \frac{B(q)}{F(q)} w(t) + e(t) \tag{2}$$

where

$$A(q) = 1 - 1.52q^{-1} + 0.5336q^{-2}$$
$$B(q) = 0.7426q^{-1} - 0.7187q^{-2}$$

Considering the transfer function of the deterministic signal from the w input we have

$$\frac{T(t)}{w(t)} = \frac{B(q)}{F(q)} \tag{3}$$

3.2.3 The transfer function and polynomial form

The transfer function in Z plane is given by

$$\frac{W(z)}{V_a(z)} = \frac{B(z)}{F(z)} = \frac{0.7426z - 0.718}{z^2 - 1.52z + 0.5336} \tag{4}$$

The poles of the transfer function in Z, $pz_1 = 0.9697$ and $pz_1 = 0.5503$is the positive axis that divides the first and fourth quadrants. The zero is given by $z = 0.9678$ and is on top from one pole to the nearest two decimal places.

Applying the transformation C2D command of *Toolbox* Control gives the model transfer function continuously in the model time we have

$$\frac{T(s)}{V_a(s)} = \frac{B(s)}{F(s)} = \frac{0.9852s - 0.03224}{s^2 + 0.628s + 0.01837} \tag{5}$$

The poles of the transfer function at $s, pc_1 = -0.5973$and $pc_2 = -0.0308$. The zero at $zc = -0.0327$ nearly cancels the effect pole pc_2.

The *MATLAB scrip execution* has to read the temperature signals and actuator to estimate the parameters a mathematical model that represents the operating point system's thermal system.

```
Sys = OE (Data, [nb nf nk]
```

where
Data is the object containing the information input and output system;
nb is the order of the polynomial $B(q)$ from Equation 1;
nf is the order of the polynomial $F(q)$ from Equation 1;
nk is the input delay

We can also order the knowledge to perform analysis in continuous time by following the identification commands

```
M = idproc(type,value)
```

Thereby generating a frequency domain model type

$$G(s) = Kp\frac{1 + T_z s}{(1 + T_{p1}s)(1 + T_{p2}s)(1 + T_{p3}s)}e^{-T_d s} \tag{6}$$

Where the parameters of the function **idproc** are inherent in the system type, order and constant delay.
The graphs in Figure 5 are constructed in accordance with the instructions from design requirements . The first statement stores the vector *medt* values of temperature around the heat source (resistor) and the actuator speed ω. The third instruction is didactic and for implementation is not required to be codified.

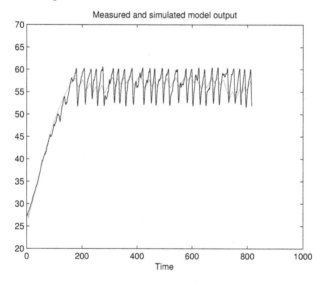

Fig. 5. Continuous Process Reaction Curve.

3.3 Model survey
The lifting of the method consists of parametric estimation conversion this model of transfer function in Z.

3.3.1 Model discrete time

The procedure for the identification of parameters of discrete time is encoded in the *script*, converting (describing) the discrete models in transfer function descriptions.
The Figure 5 shows the comparison of behavior temperature of the continuous model obtained by the process reaction curve

3.3.2 Transfer functions

The purpose of the transfer functions we generate the files contains models of the objects should be stored *OE* to conversion models.

3.3.3 Estimating parameters scripts

The establishment of a procedure for estimating parameters (connotation: scientific) or lifting of a model (connotation: engineering) presented in this section consists of three steps. The first step is the generation each measurement. The second step consists of estimating the parameters of functions transfer. The third step is the analysis of the model have the impulse response, Bode diagram and step.

3.4 A Platform to testing control systems

To validate our experiment we used a platform for experiments with micro digital circuits processed with the support of micro controllers that can be easily programmed using knowledge of language with *C* and a broad support to this type of application as in Ibrahim (2006),Lewis (2001) and Wilmshurst (2007).
Using the Microchip PIC micro controller family we can turn our platform to run on following code done in *C* programming language.

```
#device adc=10
#use delay(clock=4000000)
#fuses HS,NOWDT,PUT
#use rs232(baud=9600, xmit=PIN_C6,rcv=PIN_C7)
#include <mod_lcd.c>

main()
{
    long int value=0;
    float temp=0;
    int i=0;
    lcd_ini();
    setup_timer_2 (T2_DIV_BY_16, 61, 1);
    setup_ADC_ports (RA0_analog);
    setup_adc(ADC_CLOCK_INTERNAL );
    setup_ccp1(ccp_pwm);
    set_pwm1_duty ( 0 );
    setup_ccp2(ccp_pwm);
    set_pwm2_duty ( 0 );
    set_adc_channel(0);
    printf ("%%------------ DAQ - System ------------ \r\n");
    printf ("%%Temperature (žC) \r\n");
    while(true){
```

```
set_pwm1_duty(1023);
 delay_ms(100);
 value = read_adc();
    temp = ((5*(float) value)/(1024))*16.09;
    printf (" %f \r\n",temp);
    printf (lcd_write,"Temp = %f ",temp);
    lcd_write ('\f');

      if(temp>=60){
           set_pwm2_duty ( 1023 );
           }
      if(temp<=58){
      set_pwm2_duty ( 0 );
           }
 delay_ms(500);

  }
 }
```

The code shown above is the implementation of a system that simulates the temperature, in the form of *Hardware* a thermal system with relative temperature variation in responses to time much smaller.

The dynamics of this system is well demonstrated in Figure 6

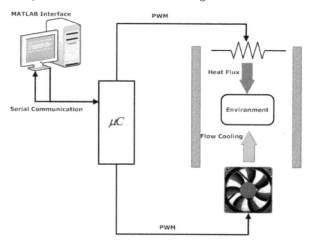

Fig. 6. A Diagram to System Hardware

Where the basis for the system of change of temperature in an open environment that is cooler acts as the system actuator. The control objective, as shown in the code is to keep a room temperature at a desired track with minimal accuracy in the output signal.

4. Implementing control systems on MATLAB

The *MATLAB* software provides support, form the implementation of acquisition system data to design a control system, which becomes possible with methods of identification and communication required in numerical methods implementation of a controller. This tool was incorporated for the purpose to help engineers and scientists in projects and systems design methods numeric, or for the resolution algorithms and systems simulation. In the following sections will be shown tools that are part of the suite of applications such as *MATLAB* concepts for implementation of digital control systems.

4.1 The serial interface

For the design of systems for data acquisition in *MATLAB*, an important tool are the protocols for data communications in environments that are common industries. The serial communication is known for its simplicity of connection and implementation in both hardware and software because there are a wide variety software and programming languages that provide libraries for development communication in serial protocol. In *MATLAB* the simplicity of applying this tool can be translated by code shown below

```
Serial_Obj = Serial('COM1');
fopen(Serial_Obj);
var_read = fscanf(Serial_Obj)
fprintf(var_read,'Data Receiveve');
fclose(Serial_Obj);
Delete(Serial_Obj);
```

With the above script you can communicate and receive data from an external device to your computer. With communication with the *external hardware* can open, using the following commands, send and receive data relevant to the control system

```
function send_data_tohard(data_ctrl,setpoint_ctrl)
fprintf(Serial_Obj,data_ctrl));
fprintf(Serial_Obj,setpoint_ctrl));
```

Therefore the system receives the data for the implementation of intelligent digital control system:

```
function receiv_data_fromhard(data_ctrl,data_error)
data_ctrl = fscanf(Serial_Obj,'data_ctrl');
data_error = fscanf(Serial_Obj,'data_error');
```

Always observing that the variable *Dataa_crtl* is used for timing and appropriateness of real-time system.

4.2 The user interface

The user interface development system shown in Figure 7 is used with supervisors and control environment of the platform.

Using the anointing of the environment development of **GUIDE** MATLAB can therefore obtain the convenience of the project environment be the same as the deployment environment

In the source code below is observed in connection with the generation via the serial port textbf GUID emph MATLAB.

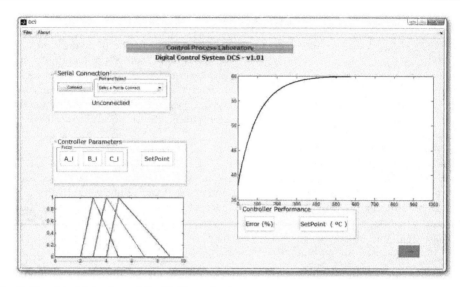

Fig. 7. Graphical Interface of the Platform System

```
function  Button_01_Callback(hObject, eventdata, handles, varargin)
Serial_Obj=serial('COM1','BaudRate',9600);
opcon2 =get(handles.menu_01,'Value');
opcon = get(handles.menu_01,'String');

switch opcon{opcon2}
    case 'COM1'
        Serial_Obj.Port='COM1';
    case 'COM2'
        Serial_Obj.Port='COM2';
    case 'COM3'
        Serial_Obj.Port='COM3';
    case 'COM4'
       Serial_Obj.Port='COM4';
    case 'COM5'
      Serial_Obj.Port='COM5';
    case 'COM6'
      Serial_Obj.Port='COM6';
    case 'COM7'
      Serial_Obj.Port='COM7';
    otherwise
        errordlg('Select a Valid Serial Port','Error')

end

fopen(Serial_Obj);
if Serial_Obj.Status ==open
```

```
set(handles.con_text,'String','Connected');
end
```

4.3 Real time control
Digital Control Systems has its roots in the interface with the analog world and thus the delay time this conversion to occur immediately. In real-time systems is a concern that the execution time of a given instruction does not exceed a predetermined threshold. Converging, the realtime systems are strictly necessary in digital control because it does necessary to guarantee instruction execution control U_c within the limit of sampling system T_s where a failure of this requirement may lead to instability as the plant design of discrete controllers is directly related T_s variable.

4.4 Implementing intelligent systems
The implementation of intelligent systems through *MATLAB* may well become a very profitable it facilitates the testing of new techniques that use features and tools already implemented in this software. Techniques computational intelligence can withdraw from the digital control system the important factor in the T_s, however the system still requires real time control. Each execution cycle lets you have the need to perform numerical derivatives and integrals and introducing a context of researching and mapping , which may require less computational effort. The diagram shown in Figure 8

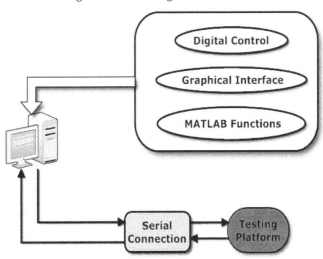

Fig. 8. Diagram of the General System

Itś possible conclude that with the development of both the hardware and software, these systems are likely to become the largest presence within the control and automation

4.4.1 A fuzzy method implementation
As described in Ross (2004),S. Sumathi (2010) and Andrade (2010) the commitment of systems based on fuzzy logic both in respect of the facility as implementation of policies that take into account not only the performance of closed loop of industrial process control as well as the

experience acquired human with the process that can be transferred directly to the core of the *Fuzzy Logic Controller(FLC)* with its implementation process described in Figure 9

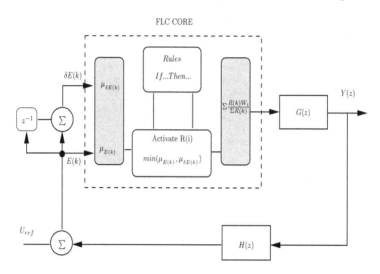

Fig. 9. Diagram of the General System

The consolidation of this type of system could provide designers with a feature not found on controllers classical, ie the aforementioned expertise. To use the Fuzzy controller is needed for the project prior knowledge on the implementation of systems based on fuzzy logic and can be found in Andrade (2010) and especially in Zadeh (1965). In *MATLAB* the design begins by checking the feasibility of the controller and can be done by graphical interface *Fuzzy Logic Toolbox* with a significant help from MathWorks (2010).
To open the *FLT (Fuzzy Logic Toolbox)* typed:

```
>>fuzzy
```

and the following screen will open
However the system to be implemented with *MATLAB* using the serial communication is necessary to implement the intelligent system in *script* and can be done as follows

```
error = data_ctrl;
NG(k)  = trimf(error, [a_i b_i c_i]);
NS(k)  = trimf(error, [a_i b_i c_i]);
ZR(k)  = trimf(error, [a_i b_i c_i]);
PS(k)  = trimf(error, [a_i b_i c_i]);
PB(k)  = trimf(error, [a_i b_i c_i]);
chang_error = data_ctrl;
NL(k)  = trimf(chang_error, [a_i b_i c_i]);
NS(k)  = trimf(chang_error, [a_i b_i c_i]);
ZR(k)  = trimf(chang_error, [a_i b_i c_i]);
PS(k)  = trimf(chang_error, [a_i b_i c_i]);
PL(k)  = trimf(chang_error, [a_i b_i c_i]);
```

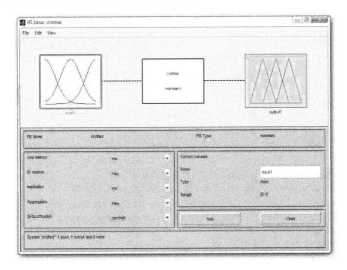

Fig. 10. The FLT Main Screen

Where *Negative Large, Negative Small, ZeRo, Positive Small* and *Positive Large* are linguistics vary based on experience. The system output can be given as shown in Figure 9 with a bank of rules based on Table 1 decision-making as an example

$Error \setminus changing_{Error}$	NL	NS	ZR	PS	PL
NL	PL	PL	PL	PL	NL
NS	PS	PS	PS	PS	NS
ZR	PS	ZR	ZR	NS	ZR
PS	NS	NS	NS	NS	PS
PL	NL	NL	NL	NS	PS

Table 1. The knowledge from the Rules of Decision System

And the controller output and results in a weighted sum that depends exclusively on the method chosen.

5. Conclusion

With the aid of this important tool can facilitate the development of applications to interface with and control devices industries. A overview of these tools has been shown here to that may be developed to greater diversity of applications according to the need of the designer. As an environment of the computational complex, *MATLAB* can provide solutions for engineering, physics and mathematics with the use of its functions basic and therefore leaving the search more efficient and less costly. This platform is an important and necessary tool, it can lead a project, with integration between *Software* and *Hardware*, for a safe convergence of results, thus integrating computational resources for simulation design and implementation from a direct single platform.

6. References

Andrade, G.A. Neto, J. L. L. (2010). A framework for modeling, digital control design and simulations of dynamic, *Computer Modelling and Simulation (UKSim), 2010 12th International Conference on*, IEEE Computer Society Digital Library.

Charles L. Philips, H. T. N. (1995). *Digital Control Systems: Analisys and Design*, third edition edn, Prentice Hall.

Gene F. Franklin, J. David Powell, M. L. W. (1998). *Digital Control of Dynamic Systems*, 3rd edn, Prentice Hall.

Ibrahim, D. (2006). *Microcontroller Based Applied Digital Control*, John Wiley and Sons.

Lewis, C. S. (2001). *Programming Microcontrollers in C*, 2nd edn, LLH Publishing.

MathWorks, T. (2010). *Fuzzy Logic Tool Box : User's Guide*.

Moudgalya, K. (2007). *Digital Control*, John Wiley and Sons.

Ross, T. J. (2004). *Fuzzy Logic With Engineering Applications*, 2nd edn, John Wiley and Sons.

S. Sumathi, S. P. (2010). *Computational Intelligence Paradigms: Theory and Applications Using MATLAB*, CRC Press.

Wilmshurst, T. (2007). *Designing Embedded Systems with PIC Microcontrollers*, Newnes.

Zadeh, L. A. (1965). Fuzzy sets, *Information and Control Proceedings* .

13

Design of PSO-Based Optimal/Tunable PID Fuzzy Logic Controller Using FPGA

Zeyad Assi Obaid[1], Saad Abd Almageed Salman[1], Hazem I. Ali[2],
Nasri Sulaiman[3], M. H. Marhaban[3] and M. N. Hamidon[3]

[1]College of Engineering University of Diyala
[2]Control Engineering Department University of Technology
[3]Faculty of EngineeringUniversity Putra Malaysia
[1,2]Iraq
[3]Malaysia

1. Introduction

Fuzzy Logic controllers have been successfully applied in a large number of control applications, with the most commonly used controller being the PID controller. Fuzzy logic controllers provide an alternative to PID controllers, as they are a good tool for the control of systems that are difficult to model. The control action in fuzzy logic controllers can be expressed with simple "if-then" rules (Poorani et al., 2005). Fuzzy controllers are more sufficient than classical controllers as they can cover a much wider range of operating conditions than classical Controllers. In addition, fuzzy controllers operate with noise and disturbances of a different nature. The common method for designing a fuzzy controller is to realize it as a computer program. Higher density programmable logic devices, such as the FPGA, can be used to integrate large amounts of logic in a single IC. The FPGA provides greater flexibility than ASIC, and can be used with tighter time-to-market schedules. The term programmable highlights the customization of the IC by the user. Many researchers have discussed the design of the hardware implementation of fuzzy logic controllers. A number was specialized for control applications, and aimed to get better control responses. These researches have concern using new techniques in fuzzy control, in order to get higher processing speed versus low utilization of chip resource (Jain et al., 2009 and Islam et al., 2007)

The hardware implementation of fuzzy logic controllers has many requirements, such as high-speed performance, low complexity and high flexibility (Leonid, 1997). With this type of application, and to provide these requirements, it is necessary to avoid various limitations and challenges. In deriving a practical PIDFC structure, it is desirable to reduce the number of inputs. In addition, it is difficult to formulate the fuzzy rules with the variable sum of error ($\sum e$), as its steady-state value is unknown for most control problems (Mann et al., 1999), (Hassan et al., 2007), (Obaid et al., 2009). Hence, it is necessary to design the FPGA-based PIDFC with fewer inputs and rules to get higher processing speed versus low utilization of chip resources. In addition, the design of digital fuzzy controllers has limitations concerning the structure. These include the restriction or limitation of the shapes of fuzzy sets implemented in the fuzzifier block, such as those in the controllers proposed in (Hassan et al., 2007) and (Seng et al., 1999). It is desirable to simplify the structure of the PIDFC controller to offer higher flexibility versus low-chip resources. The majority of PID fuzzy controller applications belong to the direct action (DA) type; here the fuzzy inference is used to compute the PID controller actions, not to tune the PID parameters (Mann et al., 1999). Therefore, it is necessary to design a tuning method inside the digital fuzzy chip, especially with the DA type, in order to scale the universe of discourse for the inputs/outputs variable in the PIDFC, and to obtain the best tuning case in the operational range. Changing the scaling gains at the input and output of PIDFC has a significant impact on the performance of the resulting fuzzy control system, as well as the controller's stability and performance (Leonid et al., 2000). Therefore, it is necessary to use an optimization method to calculate the optimal values of these gains. In recent years, several researchers have designed fuzzy controllers with different ranges of accuracy. Most of these controllers have 6-8 bits of accuracy (Poorani et al., 2005), (Tipsuwanpornet al., 2004), (Hassan et al., 2007), (Solano et al., 1997), (Gabrielli et al., 2009). This accuracy has a trade off with the speed of the process and it may affect the process behavior inside the digital fuzzy chip (Jantzen, 1998), (Ibrahim, 2004). Furthermore, increasing the accuracy will also increase the hardware complexity versus low-speed performance and vice versa. However, none have evaluated the same controller with different ranges of accuracy. Hence, it is necessary to find the best accuracy inside the digital chip that offers low hardware complexity versus high-speed performance. The aim of this chapter is to design a PIDFC that can efficiently replace other fuzzy controllers realized as a computer program, that have the ability to serve a wide range of systems with real-time operations. To achieve this aim, the following points are addressed:

Ref No.	Controller type	Optimization and tuning method	System Type
(Li and Hu , 1996)	PID with FIS	Tuned by FIS	Process control
(Tipsuwanpornet al., 2004)	Gain scheduling PID FC	Gain scheduling Tuning method	Level and temperature
(Poorani et al., 2005)	Specific FC 6-inputs, 1-output	No method	Speed control of electric vehicle
(Alvarez et al., 2006)	Optimal FC 2-inputs, 1-output	No method	Multi phase converter
(Gonzalez-Vazquez et al, 2006)	PD FC	No method	No system
(Khatr and Rattan, 2006)	Multi-layered PDFC	No method	Autonomous mobile robot
(Hassan et al., 2007)	PID FC	No method	Linear system
(Jain et al., 2009)	Optimal PID controller	Bacterial Foraging Optimization method	Inverted pendulum

Table 1. Summary of the Related FPGA-Based Controller in the Literature

1. To design a PIDFC with improved fuzzy algorithm that offers low implementation size versus high processing speed.
2. To aid the PIDFC with a tuning gains block inside the FPGA chip that makes the design able to accept PSO-based optimal scaling gains.
3. To design two versions of the proposed PIDFC. The first one is an 8-bits PIDFC, while the second one is a 6-bits PIDFC.
4. To test the proposed design with different plants models with a unity feedback control system.

Many researchers have discussed different approaches to the present fuzzy algorithms that offer high-processing speed and small chip size. Many of the fuzzy controllers implemented in the literature using FPGA, have many limitations and challenges with the structure, such as those in the shape of fuzzy sets implemented in the Fuzzifier block. This thesis will deal with some of these limitations. Table I lists the related FPGA-based controllers in the literature, highlighting the tuning and optimization methods used as well as the type of application and the type of controller.

2. PID fuzzy logic controller

A PID fuzzy controller is a controller that takes error, summation of error and rate of change of error (rate for short) as inputs. Fuzzy controller with three inputs is difficult and not easy to implement, because it needs a large number of rules and memory (Leonid, 1997). In the proposed design, if each input is described with eight linguistic values, then 8x8x8=512 rules will be needed. The PIDFC can be constructed as a parallel structure of a PDFC and a PIFC, and the output of the PIDFC is formed by algebraically adding the outputs of the two fuzzy control blocks (Leonid, 1997). In deriving a practical PIDFC structure, the following remarks are made (Hassan et al., 2007) (Mann et al., 1999), (Leonid, 1997), (Obaid et al., 2009): *Remark 1:* For any PIDFC, the error (e) is considered as the necessary input for deriving any PID structure. *Remark 2:* It is difficult to formulate control rules with the input variable sum-of-error $\sum e$, as its steady-state value is unknown for most control problems. To overcome the problem stated in remark 2, a PDFC may be employed to serve as a PIFC in incremental form, where a PD fuzzy logic controller, with summation at its output, is used instead of the PIFC (Hassan et al., 2007), (Obaid et al., 1999).

3. Particle swarm optimization

PSO is an evolutionary computation technique-based developed by Eberhart and Kennedy in 1995 (Wang et al., 2006). It was inspired by the social behavior of birds flocking or fish schooling, more specifically, the collective behaviors of simple individuals interacting with their environment and each other (Wang et al., 2006). PSO has been successfully applied in many areas: function optimization, artificial neural network training, fuzzy system control, and other areas where evolutionary computation can be applied. Similar to evolutionary computation (EC), PSO is a population-based optimization tool (Wang et al., 2006), (Allaoua et al., 2009). The system is initialized with a population of random solutions and searches for optima by updating generations. All of the particles have fitness values that are evaluated by the fitness function to be optimized, and have velocities that direct the flying of the particles (Wang et al., 2006). In a PSO system, particles change their positions by flying around in a multidimensional search space until computational limitations are exceeded.

The concept of the modification of a searching point by PSO is shown in Fig. 1 (Allaoua et al., 2009).

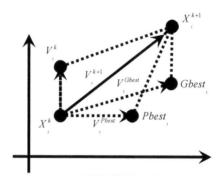

Fig. 1. Concept of the Modification of a Searching Point by PSO (Allaoua et al., 2009).

In the PSO algorithm, instead of using evolutionary operators such as mutation and crossover, to manipulate algorithms, for a d-variable optimization problem, a flock of particles are put into the d-dimensional search space with randomly chosen velocities and positions knowing their best values so far (Pbest) and the position in the d-dimensional space. The velocity of each particle, adjusted according to its own flying experience and the other particle's flying experience. For example, the i-th particle is represented as $xi = (xi, 1, xi, 2... xi, d)$ in the d-dimensional space. The best previous position of the i-th particle is recorded and represented as (Allaoua et al., 2009):

$$Pbesti = (Pbesti, 1, Pbesti, 2 ... Pbest\, i, d) \tag{1}$$

The index of best particle among all of the particles in the group is gbest$d$. The velocity for particle i is represented as $vi = (vi,1, vi,2, ..., vi,d)$. The modified velocity and position of each particle can be calculated using the current velocity and the distance from Pbest$i$, d to gbest$d$ as shown in the following formulas (Allaoua et al., 2009):

$$V_{i,m}^{(t+1)} = W.V_{i,m}^{(t)} + c_1 * rand\,()*(Pbest_{i,m} - X_{i,m}^{(t)}) + c_2 * rand\,()*(gbest_m - X_{i,m}^{(t)}) \tag{2}$$

$$X_{i,m}^{(t+1)} = X_{i,m}^{(t)} + V_{i,m}^{(t+1)} \; ; \quad i = 1, 2... n; \quad m = 1, 2... d \tag{3}$$

Where:
N: Number of particles in the group,
D: dimension,
t: Pointer of iterations (generations),
$V_{i,m}^{(t)}$: Velocity of particle I at iteration t, $V_d^{min} \le V_{i,m}^{(t)} \le V_d^{max}$
W: Inertia weight factor,
$c1, c2$: Acceleration constant,
$rand\,()$: Random number between 0 and 1
$X_{i,m}^{(t)}$: Current position of particle i at iterations,
Pbesti: Best previous position of i-th particle,
Gbest: Best particle among all the particles in the population.

4. The proposed PSO algorithm

The main aim of the PSO algorithm is to tune the controller parameters [Kp, Kd, Ki, Ko], by minimizing the cost function for minimum values in order to get the optimal gains value for these parameters. The target cost function is the integral square error (ISE), this is simple function and can easy represented in the fuzzy algorithm. The cost function (equation 4) is calculated by swapping the searching results in the local position with the minimum value of the function until reaching the best global search. In this case, the proposed PSO algorithm is 6-dimension in the population size for PIDFC (also can do it by 4-dimenssion), 3-dimension in the case of the PIFC and PDFC. This dimension belongs to the controller parameters, which represent the particle (X) inside the population space. These particles are explained in equations (5, 6 and 7) with i*th* iteration path. Note that during the search process the resulting gains were constrained by the interval [Xmin Xmax] to search with these limits in order to cover the range of the operational range (universe of discourse). Fig. 2 shows the flow chart of the proposed PSO algorithm.

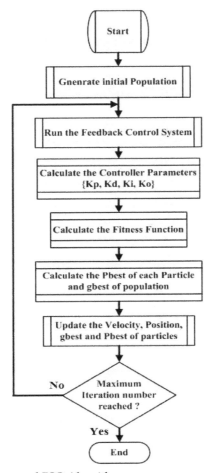

Fig. 2. Flowchart of the Proposed PSO Algorithm

$$ISE = \sum_{t=0}^{Maxiteration} (e(t))^2 \tag{4}$$

X(PIDFC)= [x(1) x(2) x(3) x(4) x(5) x(6)]=

[Kp Kd Ko + Kp Ki Ko]   , Dimension = 6

(5)

X(PIFC)= [x(1) x(2) x(3)]= [Kp Ki Ko]   , Dimension = 3   (6)

X(PDFC)= [x(1) x(2) x(3)]= [Kp Kd Ko]   , Dimension = 3   (7)

5. Block diagram of the PIDFC

The proposed controller accepts two signals, the first one is the plant output (y_p) and the second one is the desired output (y_d), both of them are digital signals, and deliver the control action signal as a digital output. It also accepts four 8-bit digital signals that represent the optimal gain parameters needed by the controller (K_p , K_d , K_i , and K_o). These parameters are used to aid the tuning block with optimal values of the scaling gains online with the digital FPGA chip. Other two (one-bit) signals have been used to select the type of the controller (PDFC, PIFC, or PIDFC) online with the chip. Fig. 3 shows the general block diagram of the controller chip in a unity feedback control system. In recent years, many of the digital fuzzy applications have different ranges of the accuracy. Most of them have 6-8 bits of accuracy (Poorani et al., 2005), (Tipsuwanpornet al., 2004), (Hassan et al., 2007), (Solano et al., 1997), (Gabrielli et al., 2009), (Obaid et al., 2009), (Obaid et al., 1999). This accuracy may affect the process behavior inside the digital fuzzy chip; also it has a trade off with the speed of the process (Leonid , 1997), (Jantzen, 1998), (Ibrahim, 2004). Therefore, it is necessary to find which range has better accuracy inside the digital chip. Two versions of the proposed PIDFC were designed, the first one is an 8-bit which uses 8 bits for each input/output variables. The second version is a 6-bit which uses 6 bits for each input/output variable. To make the discussion clear and general for the proposed controller in the following sections, symbol (q) will be used to represent the range of accuracy, (q=8) in the proposed 8-bits design, and (q=6) in the 6-bits version of the proposed design.

6. Structure of the PIDFC design

Generally, to represent PIDFC, it is required to design a fuzzy inference system with three inputs that represent the proportional, derivative, and integral components, and each one of them can have up to eight fuzzy sets. Therefore, the maximum number of the required fuzzy rules is 8^3=512 rules. To avoid this huge number of rules, the proposed controller was designed using two parallel PDFC to design the PIDFC as discussed earlier (Hassan et al., 2007), (Obaid et al., 2009), (Obaid et al., 1999). The second PDFC was converted to a PIFC by accumulating its output. Fig. 4 shows the structure of proposed PIDFC, where FIS refers to the fuzzy inference system with its three blocks, Fuzzifier, inference engine and defuzzifier. Both controllers, PDFC and PIFC, receive the same error signal. The structure of the single PDFC is discussed in the next sections. The main block in the PDFC is the fuzzy inference block which has two inputs ($e(n)$ and $\Delta e(n)$), one output (U(n)) fuzzy system of Mamdani type that uses singleton membership functions for the output variable. Initially, the two input signals are multiplied by a gain coefficient (K_p and K_d or K_p and K_i) before entering the fuzzy inference block. Similarly, the output of the fuzzy inference block is multiplied by a gain coefficient (K_o) (Hassan et al., 2007), (Obaid et al., 2009), (Obaid et al., 1999). At the same time, the output of the fuzzy inference block in the second PDFC is multiplied by a gain coefficient and then accumulated to give the output of the PIFC. Subsequently, both outputs of the PDFC and PIFC are added together to give the PIDFC output (u_{PID}). The final design works as a PDFC, PIFC, or PIDFC, depending on the two selection lines sw$_1$ and sw_0, which provide a more flexible design to cover a wide range of systems. The PIDFC is designed using two blocks of PDFC, and the main block in the proposed design is the PDFC block. The main components inside the PDFC block are: *Tuning-gain* block, *Fuzzifier* block, *inference engine* block, and *Defuzzifier* block.

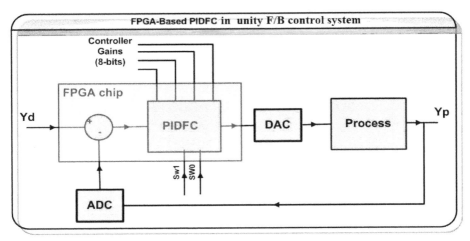

Fig. 3. Block Diagram of the PIDFC in a Unity Feedback Control System.

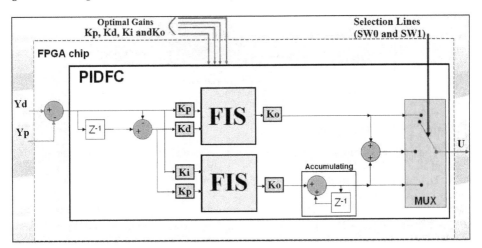

Fig. 4. Main structure of the Proposed Controller

Tuning-Gain Block

The tuning-gain block is used at each of the two inputs and also at the output of each PDFC block. This block receives and multiplies two inputs: the variable to be scaled (input or output) and its related gains, this implies the proposed tuning method via scaling the universe of discourse. An eight-bit latch was used at each Tuning-gain block to store the gain coefficient value received from one of the gain ports, depending on selection line values. The "*" operator was used in the VHDL files of the design to express a multiplication process just like a conventional language. This process has been designed at the *behavioral* level of abstraction in VHDL code, i.e. during the design synthesis process, if the library "*IEEE.std_logic_signed*" was included in the VHDL files (Hassan et al., 2007), (Obaid et al., 2009), (Obaid et al., 1999). Fig. 5 shows the Tuning-gain block with more details.

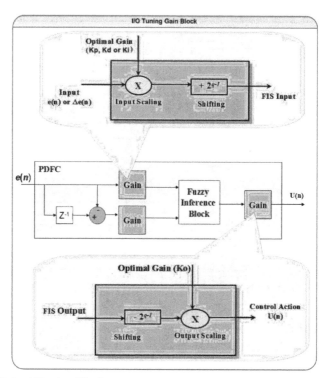

Fig. 5. Input/Output Tuning Block

Every "*" operator is synthesized to a *signed number multiplier* directly (Hassan et al., 2007), (Obaid et al., 2009), (Obaid et al., 1999). Fig. 6 shows the Tuning-gain block with more details. The fuzzy inference block in each PDFC can handle positive values only, and the error and its rate signals can have positive and negative values (Hassan et al., 2007), as the shifting process has been designed to convert the input variables range from $[-2^{q-1} \rightarrow 2^{q-1} - 1]$ to $[0 \rightarrow 2^{q} - 1]$. This process implies adding the number (2^{q-1}) to the input variable. This addition has been designed by inverting the last bit (MSB) of the input variable (Hassan et al., 2007), (Obaid et al., 2009), (Obaid et al., 1999). The shift process at the output has been designed using subtraction, instead of addition, to convert the range of the output variable from $[0 \rightarrow 2^q - 1]$ to $[-2^{q-1} \rightarrow 2^{q-1} - 1]$. This specification will increase the flexibility of the proposed design.

Fuzzifier Block

The overlapping degree (V) in the proposed design is two, which means that at each time instance there are two active, (have nonzero membership values), fuzzy sets for each input variable at maximum. The proposed fuzzification process has been designed using two fuzzifier blocks, one for each input variable. The fuzzifier block implies the fuzzification process by taking the input and producing four output values. These values represent the sequence numbers of the two active fuzzy sets (e1, e2 and de1, de2) and the membership degrees of the variable for each one of them (μe1, μe2 and μde1, μde2). The memory base was designed using ROM. The use of ROM is better than RAM when the programmability is directly achieved by the implementation techniques (as in the case of FPGA) (Barriga et al., 2006). The fuzzifier block was designed using memory based membership functions (MBMSF) (Solano et al., 1997), (Barriga et al., 2006). This method reduces the restrictions of the fuzzy set shapes, even it needs a smaller memory size than other method such as the arithmetic method. The memory model has been implemented with maximum possible membership values in the proposed design, where the maximum coded in p values is ($2^p - 1$), where p=4 bits in the 6-bits version of the PIDFC, and p=6 bits in the 8-bits version of the PIDFC. This dictates that the summation of membership values of two consecutive fuzzy set is always equal to ($2^p - 1$). Each word in the MBMSF is divided into two parts. The first part represents the sequence number of the active fuzzy set (3-bits, in both versions). Assigning 3 bits for the sequence number of the fuzzy sets, gives the controller flexibility to accept for each input variable for up-to 8 fuzzy sets. The second part of the memory word is p bits data word which represents the membership value of the input in the active fuzzy set. The total memory length for each input is equal to (2^q).

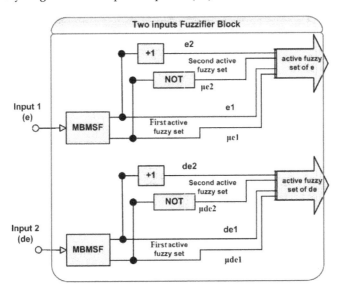

Fig. 6. Two Inputs Fuzzifier Block.

Inference Engine Block

The inference engine consists of three blocks: rule selector, rule memory, and minimum circuit as shown in Fig. 7. Different mechanisms have been used to minimize both the calculation time and the area of the fuzzy inference system; among the most interesting methods is the active rules selector concept (Hassan et al., 2007), (Solano et al., 1997), (Obaid et al., 2009), (Barriga et al., 2006), (Huang and Lai, 2005), (Obaid et al., 1999). This block uses the information from fuzzifier, which belongs to the active fuzzy sets to launch only active rules. This reduces the number of processed rules. Furthermore, by using an active rule selector, the number of rules to be processed will be reduced according to this equation (Hassan et al., 2007):

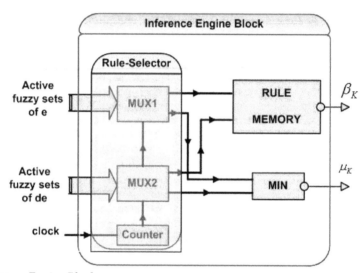

Fig. 7. Inference Engine Block

$$\text{Number of active rules} = V^m \tag{8}$$

Where m is the number of inputs, and V is the maximum number of overlapped fuzzy sets. In the proposed design, it is assumed that $m = 2$ and $V = 2$. Hence, the number of active rules at each time is: $V^m = 2^2 = 4$ rules. In each counter cycle, the membership degrees delivered from the two multiplexers are combined through the minimum circuit to calculate the applicability degree of the rule (μ_k), while the active fuzzy set sequence numbers are combined directly to address a rule memory location that contains the corresponding rule consequent (β_k). The rule memory is a ($2^{2\times3} \times q$) bits ROM, and each word in it represents the position of the output singleton membership functions of one rule.

Defuzzifier Block

The defuzzification process in the defuzzifier block has been designed using the *Centroid* method. The four main components that represent the proposed defuzzifier are: two accumulators, one multiplier, and one divider. The defuzzifier block accepts the information from the inference engine (four (μ_k), and four (β_k) each time), and produces an output (crisp set) to the output –tuning gain block, as shown in Fig. 8.

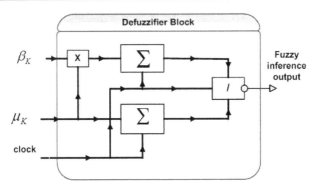

Fig. 8. Defuzzifier Block.

		NB	NM	NS	NZ	PZ	PS	PM	PB
		NB	NM	NS	NZ	PZ	PS	PM	PB
	NB	-1	-1	-1	-0.7	-0.7	-0.4	-0.1	0.1
	NM	-1	-1	-0.7	-0.7	-0.4	-0.1	0.1	0.1
	NS	-1	-0.7	-0.7	-0.4	-0.1	0.1	0.1	0.4
de	NZ	-0.7	-0.7	-0.4	-0.1	0.1	0.1	0.4	0.7
	PZ	-0.7	-0.4	-0.1	-0.1	0.1	0.4	0.7	0.7
	PS	-0.4	-0.1	-0.1	0.1	0.4	0.7	0.7	1
	PM	-0.1	-0.1	0.1	0.4	0.7	0.7	1	1
	PB	-0.1	0.1	0.4	0.7	0.7	1	1	1

Table 2. Fuzzy Rules.

The defuzzifier block was designed with two stages to reduce the memory size of the target device. Both accumulators are reset every four clock cycles to receive the next four active rules of the next input. Note that μ_k and β_k are delivered from the inference engine in series during four consecutive clock cycles, instead of being produced in parallel in one clock cycle. This will reduce the used area of the FPGA device, at the expense of increasing time interval between input latching and output producing (Hassan et al., 2007). However, during the design, whenever a trade off between area and speed is found, it is directed to optimize (reduce) area at the expense of speed reduction, since the maximum time delay caused by controller is still much less than the minimum sampling time in many control systems. Even less than other controllers proposed in the literature (Poorani et al., 2005), (Tipsuwanpornet al., 2004), (Hassan et al., 2007), (Obaid et al., 2009), (Alvarez et al., 2006), (Lund et al., 2006), (Obaid et al., 1999). Here, the multiplication process was designed at the *behavioral* level (the method used in the tuning-gain block). The only difference is that another library called "*IEEE.std_logic_unsigned*" must be used instead of the library "*IEEE.std_logic_signed*", to ensure that the produced multiplier after the synthesis process is an unsigned number multiplier (because the proposed fuzzy inference block can only handle positive numbers only) (Hassan et al., 2007), (Obaid et al., 2009). The group involves eight triangular membership functions for each input variable, eight singleton membership functions for output variable, and the rule table of 64 rules has been used in the proposed

PIDFC, as shown in Fig. 9 and Table II. The use of a singleton membership function is to increase the computation speed versus low complexity (Leonid , 1997). And also for the majority of applications, using singleton fuzzy sets is more sufficient (Ying, 2000).

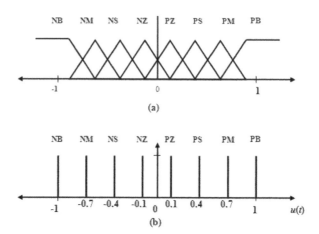

Fig. 9. (a) Inputs Membership Functions, (b) Output Membership Functions.

7. FPGA design considerations

The proposed device for the hardware implementation is the Virtex FPGAs family from Xilinx Company. Vertex FPGAs family is a useful device to the proposed design, it has internal RAM block. Virtex FPGAs consist of several large block memories. These complement the Look Up Table (LUT). This performance is very useful because the fuzzy system always needs large memory to store fuzzy sets information and rules table (Xilinx Company, 2009). The final design of the PIDFC has ($3*q + 36$) pins, four 8-bit input ports, two q-bits input ports and one q-bit output ports as well as 4 control signal pins, Table (III) lists the port names, sizes, and types.

Port name	Port size (bit)	Port type
Desired output	q	Input data
Plant output	q	Input data
Control action	q	Output data
K_p	8	Input data
K_d	8	Input data
K_i	8	Input data
K_o	8	Input data
sw1	1	Control signal
sw0	1	Control signal
Reset	1	Control signal
Clock	1	Control signal

Table 3. Port Names, Sizes, and Types Which Used In the Proposed Controller.

Note that the Reset signal does not change the contents of ROM or gain coefficients latches. However, the contents of ROM, as stated before can not be altered during the operation of the controller. The clock speed has a maximum frequency of 40 MH. This is necessary to cover a wide range of systems with a high sampling time.

8. Simulation environments

The Altera Quartus II 9.0 program was used to get the compilation and timing test results as well as the synthesized design. The ModelSim simulation program was also used for the purpose of simulation for all tests with the proposed design. The same design was designed in Matlab environments in order to make comparisons. The ModelSim stores the simulation data in text files, these files are used in Matlab and convert it to decimal vectors, which are used to plot the analog responses. Fig. 10 shows the Coding and Simulation environments used with the proposed design.

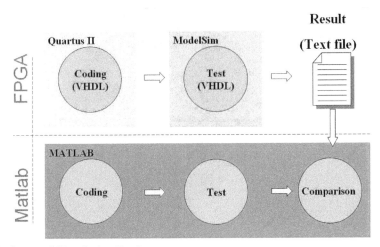

Fig. 10. Coding and Simulation Environments.

9. Timing analysis

The overall structure of the proposed PIDFC needs 16 clock cycles to complete one process. The input tuning-gain block needs one clock cycle. The fuzzification process needs one clock cycle. The inference engine needs four clock cycles to generate the four active rules consequent, $\beta_1, \beta_2, \beta_3, \beta_4$ and their corresponding applicability degrees $\mu_1, \mu_2, \mu_3, \mu_4$. Another four clock cycles are needed to calculate the terms $\sum_{k=1}^{4} \mu_k$ and $\sum_{k=1}^{4} \mu_k \times \beta_k$. Three of these four clocks are parallel to the four clocks of the inference engine, because the accumulation process starts after delivering the first rule consequent β_1 and its applicability degree μ_1. Subsequently, the division process starts and it takes eight clock cycles, which are split into two four-clock stages. The last clock cycle is needed to perform the output tuning-gain block.

10. Control surfaces test (comparison case study)

This test is performed to make sure that the fuzzy inference system used inside the FPGA-based controller (FBC) is working properly. This test involves generating the control surface using fuzzy sets and the rule shown in Fig. 9 and Table 2. This test has been used to make a comparison between both types of FBC with MSBC in order to evaluate the accuracy of the digital design implemented on FPGA with respect to the Matlab design. The control surfaces generated by MSBPD, 6FBC, MSBC and 8FBC are shown in Fig. 11 and Fig. 12. This surface reveals the effect of rounding and approximation processes (inside the FPGA design) on the result and also shows the accuracy of each version of the controller with respect to the Matlab-Based design. Generally, these statistics show that the surfaces generated by the fuzzy inference system of 8FBC are smoother than the surfaces generated by the fuzzy inference system of 6FBC with respect to MSBC, since the 8FBC has better accuracy and is adequate for this design.

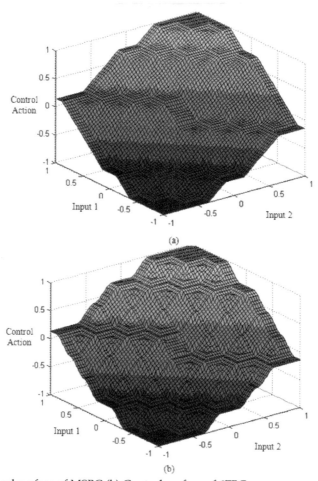

Fig. 11. (a) Control surface of MSBC (b) Control surface of 6FBC

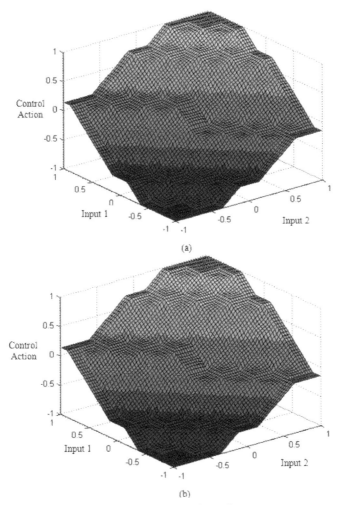

(a)

(b)

Fig. 12. (a) Control surface of MSBC (b) Control surface of 8FBC

11. The proposed controller with unity feedback control system

As mentioned before, the simplest and most usual way to implement a fuzzy controller is to realize it as a computer program on general purpose computers. Therefore, a comparison has been made between the simulation results of the two FPGA-based controller versions. The 6 bits FPGA-Based Controller (6FBC) and the 8 bits FPGA-Based Controller (8FBC), and the simulation results of the Software Base Controller designed using Matlab (MSBC). These comparisons are necessary to show that how FPGA-based design is close to Matlab-based design. The first level of this comparison was made using ModelSim as the test bench simulation before generating the results in a Text File. Subsequently, as explained before, these files were taken to the Matlab environment to do the comparison. The controllers

(6FBC, 8FBC, and MSBC) have been used in unity feedback control systems, and subjected to 0.5 step input. Mathematical models of five different plants have been used for this test. These consist of four case studies with linear systems and one case study with a nonlinear system. Each one of these plants has been designed in MATLAB software (for simulation in MATLAB), and also in non-synthesizable VHDL code (for simulation in ModelSim). Since each controller could serve as PDFC, PIFC, or PIDFC, a test was made for each one of these types. PSO was used to obtain the optimal values of the controller parameters that represent the tuning gains. Where the information of the proposed PSO algorithm is listed as follows: Population size: 100, W= [0.4 to 0.9], C1, C2=2, Iteration reached with every case is=1000 iteration path, and the particle searching range depends on the trial and is different in every case. All X-axes represent the time.

11.1 First order plant (first case study)

Many industrial processes such as level process can be represented by a first order model (Hu et al., 1999). Equation (9) shows the mathematical plant model (in s-plane). A discrete transfer function of this model has been obtained using the ZOH method, and the selected sampling period (T) is 0.1. Equation (10) shows the discrete transfer functions, (in z-plane). The searching range of the particle for this case ranges from [Xmin Xmax], and by using trial to reach the operational range with the universe of discourse. The optimal values of Kp, Kd, Ki, and Ko used in this test were selected using PSO; and listed in Table 4.

$$CS_1(s) = \frac{1}{s+1} \tag{9}$$

$$CS_1(z) = \frac{0.09516}{z - 0.9048}, T = 0.1 \tag{10}$$

Range of Particle X	Controller type	Gain type	Value
$0.0001 \le X \le 5$	PIDFC	K_p	4.5111
		K_d	0.8751
		K_i	4.6875
		K_o	0.5625
$0.0001 \le X \le 3.5$	PIFC	K_p	0.6875
		K_i	2.4375
		K_o	1.0212
$0.0001 \le X \le 15$	PDFC	K_p	13.7501
		K_d	0.6251
		K_o	0.5011

Table 4. Optimal Gains Values Used With Cs1.

Fig. 13 shows the test bench simulation results using ModelSim. This test is generated using non-synthesizable VHDL code, and the controller gives action at 0.3 μs. The 6FBC has the same procedure except the real data which has different values. ModelSim stores the results as digital data in a text file; this file is manipulated in Matlab environments to change the data to decimal before using it as a comparison. The closed loop responses with 0.5 step input are shown in Fig. 14. In Fig. 14-a, it seems that the response has a large study state error. This is because the controller is PDFC, this controller affects the transient response (rise time, overshoot), but has no effect on the steady state error (at most). When the PIFC is applied on the first order system, the error disappears, and the system is first order, since there is no overshoot in this system (Fig. 14-b). When the PIDFC is applied for this system, as shown in Fig. 14-c, the response has a fast rising time with zero overshoot and error. However, although the 6FBC can sometimes give a response close to the MSBC response, at most, the 8FBC has smoother responses to MSBC than the 6FBC. The response performance of the proposed controllers is listed in Table 5.

Controller type	Error	Over shoot	Rising time	Settling time
PDFC	0.025	0.0	0.89	0.1
PIFC	0.0	0.0	0.3	0.4
PIDFC	0.0	0.0	0.15	0.198

Table 5. Responses Performance of the Proposed 8fbc with Cs1.

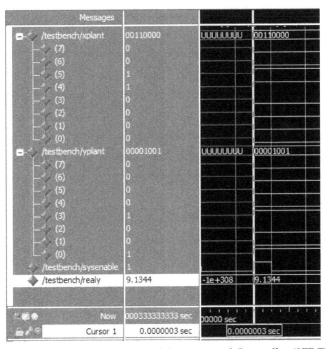

Fig. 13. Test Bench Results using ModelSim of the Proposed Controller (8FBC) with CS1 in unity Feedback Control system.

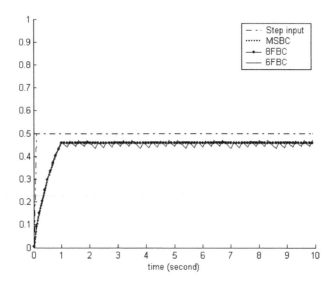

(a)

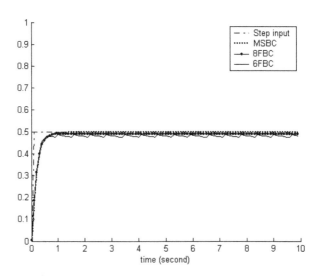

(b)

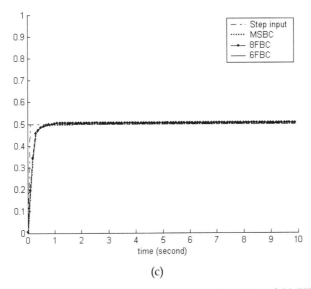

(c)

Fig. 14. First Order Linear Plant Controlled by (a) PDFC, (b) PIFC and (c) PIDFC.

11.2 Delayed first order plant (second case study)

The time delay occurs when a sensor or an actuator is used with a physical separation (Hu et al., 1999). Equation (11) shows the mathematical plant model (in *s-plane*). The discrete transfer functions of this model were obtained using the ZOH method, and the selected sampling period (T) is 0.1. Equation (12) shows the discrete transfer functions, (in *z-plane*). The searching range of the particle for this case is [Xmin Xmax], and by using trial to reach the operational range with the universe of discourse. The optimal values of K_p, K_d, K_i, and K_o used in this test were selected using PSO; and listed in Table 6.

Range of Particle X	Controller type	Gain type	Value
		K_p	1.4372
$0.0001 \le X \le 1.9$	PIDFC	K_d	1.687
		K_i	0.5625
		K_o	0.437
		K_p	0.501
$0.0001 \le X \le 1.9$	PIFC	K_i	1.5
		K_o	0.51
	PDFC	K_p	5
$0.0001 \le X \le 6$		K_d	0.125
		K_o	0.375

Table 6. Optimal Gains Values Used With CS2.

$$CS_2(z) = z^{-2} \times CS_1(z) \tag{11}$$

$$CS_2(z) = z^{-2} \times \left(\frac{0.09516}{z - 0.9048} \right) \quad , T = 0.1 \tag{12}$$

Fig. 15 shows the test bench simulation results using ModelSim. This test is generated in the same procedure as explained before. The controller gives action at 0.3 μs (Fig. 15), the delay with the systems affects the beginning of the real data (the response). The closed loop responses with 0.5 step input are shown in Fig. 16. In Fig. 16-a, again the response has a large study state error with the PDFC. When the PIFC is applied on the first order system (see Fig. 16-b), the error disappears with 8FBC. The 6FBC has a large steady state error, as the responses of the systems that use 8FBC are closer to the MSBC responses. When the PIDFC is applied for this system, as shown in Fig. 16-c, the response is close to the responses when using the PIFC. In all this, 8FBC has smoother responses to the MSBC than the 6FBC. The responses performance of the 8FBC are listed in Table 7.

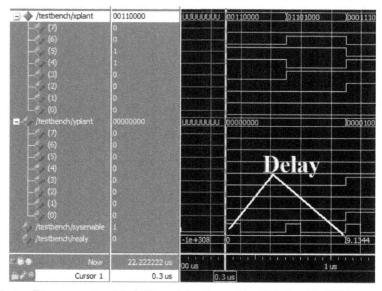

Fig. 15. Timing Diagram using ModelSim of the Controller (8FBC) with CS2 in unity Feedback Control system.

Controller type	Error	Over shoot	Rising time	Settling time
PDFC	0.11	0.01	1.12	1.2
PIFC	0.01	0.0	0.8	0.9
PIDFC	0.02	0.0	0.48	0.49

Table 7. Responses Performance of the Proposed 8fbc with CS2.

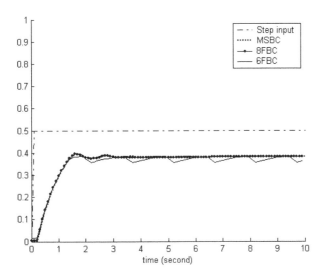

(a)

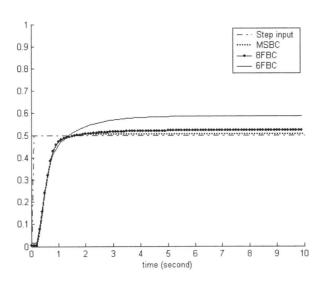

(b)

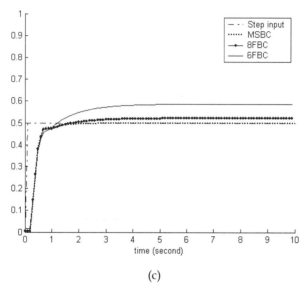

(c)

Fig. 16. Delayed first order linear plant controlled by(a) PDFC, (b) PIFC and (c) PIDFC.

11.3 Second order plant (third case study)

The position control of an AC motor process or temperature control can be represented by a second order model (Hu et al., 1999). Equation (13) shows the mathematical plant model (in s-plane). Discrete transfer functions of this model were obtained using the ZOH method, and the selected sampling period (T) is 0.2. Equation (14) shows the discrete transfer functions, (in z-plane). The searching range of the particle for this case is ranging as [Xmin Xmax], and by using trial to reach the operational range with the universe of discourse. The optimal values of K_p, K_d, K_i, and K_o used in this test were selected using PSO; and listed in Table 8.

$$CS_3(s) = \frac{1}{s^2 + 4s + 3} \tag{13}$$

$$CS_3(z) = \frac{0.01544\ z + 0.01183}{z^2 - 1.368\ z + 0.4493}\ , T = 0.2 \tag{14}$$

Fig. 17 shows the test bench simulation results using ModelSim for 8FBC; this test is generated using the same procedure as explained. The controller gives action at 0.3 µs (Fig. 17). This means the same action with CS1 and CS2, which represent the linear models. The closed loop responses with 0.5 step input are shown in Fig. 17. CS3 is a second order plant, and has a steady state error with non-controlled response. In Fig. 18-a, when PDFC is applied the overshoot is limited by the action of this controller, but the response still has a steady state error. When the PIFC is applied to this system (see Fig. 18-b), the error is disappears with 8FBC, and the system still has overshoot. The 6FBC has a rough and non-smooth response as can be seen in the control action figures where sharp spikes appear along the steady state part, while the responses of the systems that use 8FBC are closer to the MSBC responses. When the PIDFC is applied for this system, as shown in Fig. 18-c, the

8FBC response is close to the responses using MSBC, with zero error and little overshoot. The Responses Performance of the proposed 8FBC with CS3 is listed in Table 9.

Range of Particle X	Controller type	Gain type	Value
$0.0001 \leq X \leq 8.5$	PIDFC	K_p	5.0191
		K_d	7.101
		K_i	1.6875
		K_o	0.937
$0.0001 \leq X \leq 2$	PIFC	K_p	1.02
		K_i	1.812
		K_o	1.75
$0.0001 \leq X \leq 15$	PDFC	K_p	14.625
		K_d	6.021
		K_o	1.062

Table 8. Optimal Gains Values Used With CS3.

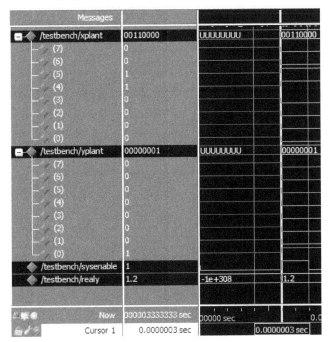

Fig. 17. Timing Diagram using ModelSim of the Controller (8FBC) with CS3 in unity Feedback Control system.

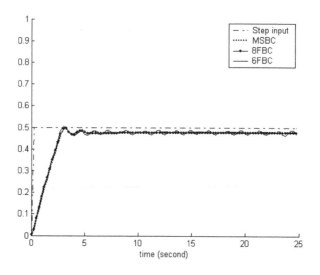

(a)

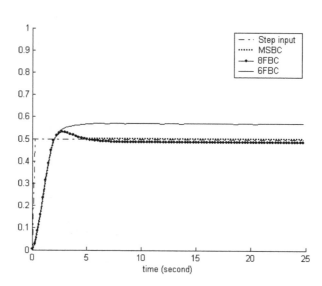

(b)

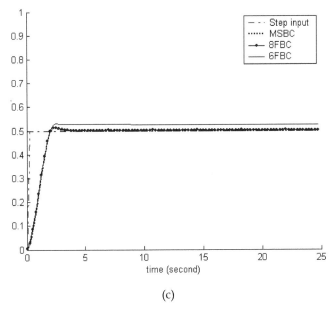

(c)

Fig. 18. Second order linear plant controlled by(a) PDFC, (b) PIFC and (c) PIDFC.

Controller type	Error	Over shoot	Rising time	Settling time
PDFC	0.02	0.02	2.1	2.3
PIFC	0.005	0.03	1.89	2
PIDFC	0.0	0.005	1.6	1.8

Table 9. Responses Performance of the Proposed 8fbc with CS3.

11.4 Delayed second order plant (fourth case study)

The time delay occurs when a sensor or an actuator are used with a physical separation (Hu et al., 1999). Equation (15) shows the mathematical plant model (in *s-plane*). Discrete transfer function of this model was obtained using the ZOH method, and the selected sampling period (T) is 0.2. Equation (16) shows the discrete transfer functions, (in *z-plane*). The searching range of the particle for this case is ranging as [Xmin Xmax], and by using trial to reach the operational range with the universe of discourse. The optimal values of K_p, K_d, K_i, and K_o used in this test were selected using PSO; and listed in Table 10.

$$CS_4(z) = z^{-2} \times CS_3 \tag{15}$$

$$CS_4(z) = z^{-2} \times \left(\frac{0.01544\ z + 0.01183}{z^2 - 1.368\ z + 0.4493} \right) ; T = 0.2 \tag{16}$$

Range of Particle X	Controller type	Gain type	Value
		K_p	2.11
$0.0001 \le X \le 8.5$	PIDFC	K_d	1.687
		K_i	0.5012
		K_o	0.375
$0.0001 \le X \le 2$	PIFC	K_p	0.253
		K_i	1.185
		K_o	1.251
$0.0001 \le X \le 15$	PDFC	K_p	7.18
		K_d	8.754
		K_o	0.503

Table 10. Optimal Gains Values Used with CS4.

Fig. 19 shows the test bench simulation results using ModelSim for 8FBC. This test is generated using the same procedure as explained before. The delay with the system only affects the value of the real data (response). The controller gives action at 0.3 μs. The closed loop responses with 0.5 step input are shown in Fig. 20. CS4 is the same model as CS3 but with delay. In Fig. 20-a, when the PDFC is applied, the overshoot is limited by the action of this controller, but the response has a large steady state error. In this case the 8FBC is very close to the MSBC while the 6FBC has a non-smooth response. When the PIFC is applied to

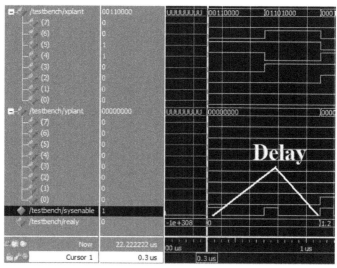

Fig. 19. Timing Diagram using ModelSim of the Controller (8FBC) with CS4 in unity Feedback Control system.

this system (see Fig. 20-b), the error disappears with the 8FBC with little overshoot. The 6FBC has a large steady state error while the responses of the systems that use 8FBC are closer to the MSBC responses. When the PIDFC is applied for this system, as shown in Fig. 20-c, the 8FBC response has better overshoot to the responses using MSBC, and is very close to the MSBC in the steady state response. The 6FBC has a long rising time with steady state error. The Responses Performance of the proposed 8FBC with CS4 is listed in Table 11.

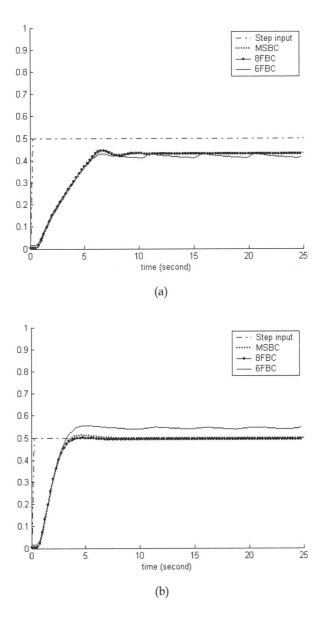

(a)

(b)

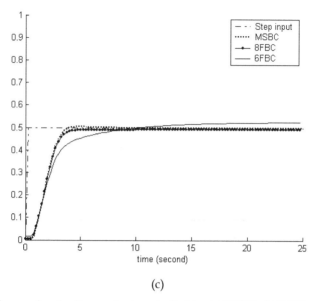

(c)

Fig. 20. Delayed second order linear plant controlled by (a) PDFC, (b) PIFC and (c) PIDFC.

Controller type	Error	Over shoot	Rising time	Settling time
PDFC	0.07	0.02	4.9	5.3
PIFC	0.0	0.0	2.3	2.4
PIDFC	0.0	0.0	2.4	2.5

Table 11. Responses Performance of the Proposed 8FBC with CS4.

11.5 Non-linear plant model (fifth case study)

A mathematical model of nonlinear plant (inverted pendulum) has been used to test the PIDFC with unity feedback control system; this model is characterized by Equation (17) and Equation (18) (Passino and Yurkovich, 1998).

$$CS_5 = \ddot{y} = \frac{9.8\sin(y) + \cos(y)\left[\dfrac{-\bar{u} - 0.25\dot{y}^2\sin(y)}{1.5}\right]}{0.5\left[\dfrac{4}{3} - \dfrac{1}{3}\cos^2(y)\right]} \tag{17}$$

$$\dot{\bar{u}} = -100\bar{u} + 100u \tag{18}$$

The first order filter on u to produce $\bar{u}$ represents an actuator. Assuming the initial conditions $y(0) = 0.1$ radians (= 5.73 deg.), $y'(0) = 0$, and the initial condition for the actuator state is zero. For simulation of the fourth-order, the Runge-Kutta method was used with an integration step size of 0.01 (Passino and Yurkovich, 1998), (Obaid et al., 1999). Again, this plant has been designed using MATLAB software (for simulation in MATLAB), and in

VHDL code (for simulation in ModelSim). A special package was designed in VHDL code to represent the trigonometric functions and fourth-order Runge-Kutta method, which are not available in Quartus II (or in ISE) standard libraries (Obaid et al., 1999). The searching range of the particle for this case is [Xmin Xmax], and by using trial to reach the proposed algorithm, the values of K_p, K_d, K_i, and K_o used in this test were selected using PSO. These values are listed in Table XII.

Range of Particle X	Controller type	Gain type	Value
		K_p	1.1012
		K_d	10.1103
$0.0001 \leq X \leq 11.5$	PIDFC	K_i	1.5013
		K_o	5.0032

Table 12. Optimal Gains Values Used With CS5.

Fig. 21 shows the test bench simulation results using ModelSim for 8FBC and the controller gives an output at 0.7 μs after the input latching (Fig. 21). The 6FBC has the same procedure in ModelSim and produces an output at 0.62 μs. The Responses Performance of the proposed controller with CS5 is listed in Table 13. Where the bound of the settling time of the pendulum to reach its initial position with the force applied to the cart is -0.02 and +0.02 with both versions. The first time of the pendulum reach s the initial position is listed as the rising time. When using a nonlinear system for testing, both versions (6FBC and 8FBC) provide generally good responses although there is some oscillation. One must not be deceived by the steady state error that appears in Fig. 22, as it represents less than 1% of the output range in the case of 6FBC and less than 0.5% of the output range, in the case of 8FBC. The absolute mean difference between the nonlinear plant response, using MSBC, and the

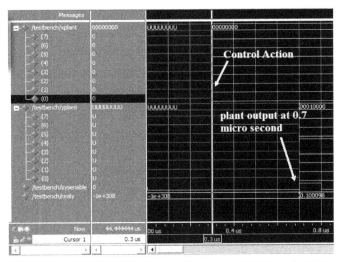

Fig. 21. Timing Diagram using ModelSim of the Controller (8FBC) with CS5 in unity Feedback Control system.

nonlinear plant response, using 6FBC is less than 0.017. The absolute mean difference between the nonlinear plant response, using MSBC, and the nonlinear plant response, using 8FBC is less than 0.006 as shown in Fig. 22. The experimental result is carried out by using the nonlinear inverted pendulum (the last case study CS5). The experimental data recorded to the inverted pendulum has been used in this test in unity feedback control system. This data has been recorded by Sultan (Sultan, 2006) to analyze, design & develop a control loop for the given inverted pendulum (with servomechanism). The pendulum reaches the initial position zero at 0.058 second with overshoot equal to 0.025 and undershoot equal to 0.02. Fig. 23 shows the experimental data simulation of the inverted pendulum with the PIDFC in 8-bit version. The controller (8FBC) provides a good control performance with respect to the simulation results of the same case as shown in Table 13.

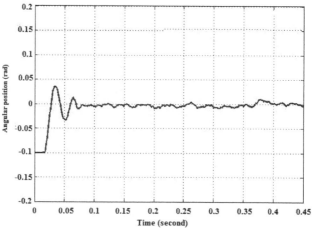

Fig. 23. Experimental data simulation of the PIDFC with the inverted pendulum in unity feedback control system.

Controller type	Error	Over Peak angle (rad)	Under Peak angle (rad)	Rising time	Settling time
6FBC	0.017	0.0	-0.01	0.13	0.1
8FBC	0.006	0.0	-0.01	0.13	0.1
6MSBC	0.0	0.018	-0.041	0.13	0.1
8MSBC	0.0	0.018	-0.041	0.13	0.1
Experimental case	0.0	0.025	0.024	0.029	0.058

Table 13. Responses Performance of the Proposed 8fbc with CS5.

12. Results comparison and discussion

The proposed design has been coded in Matlab environments as explained before. The aim of this test is to find to what extent the 6FBC and 8FBC responses are close to the MSBC responses with respect to the accuracy. In contrast to the 6FBC, the responses of the systems that use 8FBC are smooth (as MSBC responses). When the 6FBC or 8FBC is used as PIFC or

PIDFC, the system responses will settle at a value close to the response settling value of systems that use MSBC. The reason being the rounding error in the PI component, the proposed PIDFC consists of a PDFC and PIFC, the PIFC is a PDFC with a summation block at its output. This error could be positive or negative. Sometimes, during the summation process, the rounding error cancels itself. Commonly, in CS1 and CS2, it is clear that the responses have a steady state error with PDFC, because these systems do not have an overshoot, only a steady state error (no need to use PDFC), and this test is used to evaluate the multi structure in the proposed PIDFC. The absolute mean of differences between the MSBC and 6FBC was less than 0.07 with the linear systems and less than 0.017 with the nonlinear system, while the absolute mean of differences between MSBC and 8FBC was less than 0.017 with the linear systems and less than 0.006 with the nonlinear system. The proposed controller has good responses performance with respect to the classical controller proposed in the literature, and also better responses as compared it with other type of fuzzy PID controller.

CS1, CS2 and CS3 have been used in the work proposed in (Hu et al., 1999). In this work, Genetic algorithm (GA) based optimal fuzzy PID controller was used with new methodology (Matlab-based). Table 14 lists the comparison of the responses performance of this work with respect to the proposed PIDFC (8FBC) with CS1, CS2 and CS3. This comparison consists of rising time (Tr), settling time (Ts) and overshoot (OV). The proposed PSO-PIDFC with the linear cases CS1 and

CS2 have no overshoot and a short rising and settling time with respect to other types of controller designed in the literature with the same models. For the CS3, there is a 0.005 overshoot and short rising and settling time with respect to other types of controller designed in the literature with the same model. The proposed PSO-PIDFC with the nonlinear cases (CS5) have zero overshoot and 0.13, 0.1 rising and settling time respectively, while other types of controller with the same nonlinear model have an overshoot and longer rising and settling time. In CS5, a mathematical model of nonlinear plant (inverted pendulum) was used to test the controller with a unity feedback control system. This case has been used in (Jain et al., 2009), (Masmoudi et al., 1999) and (Jain et al., 1999) (Matlab-based) with different types of controllers. In (Jain et al., 2009), Bacterial Foraging (BF) algorithm was used for tuning the parameters of the PID controller for optimal performance, while (Jain et al., 1999) used a comparison between Evolutionary Algorithms namely Gas (Genetic Algorithms), and Swarm Intelligence i.e. PSO and BG. In (Jain et al., 1999) as there was no need to know the value of rising time as they used a reference input equal to zero. It is not considered by this author either. Therefore, a comparison is made with the proposed 8FB (PIDFC) with those presented in (Jain et al., 2009), (Masmoudi et al., 1999) and (Jain et al., 1999). This comparison is listed in Table 15. In the case of (Jain et al., 1999), PSO had the best responses with respect to the other methods proposed by this author, hence, we will compare with PSO and ISE only. Other comparison has been made to the proposed design with respect to FPGA chip resources. This comparison involves the utilization of the chip resources in the proposed FPGA-based PIDFC with respect to the other FPGA-based controllers proposed in the literature. It also involves a comparison with respect to the time required per one action with the maximum frequency. This comparison was made after compiling the design using the ISE program provided by Xilinx Company, because this tool provides a clear Report for the chip resources, even it was used by the authors in the literature. This comparison is listed in Table 16.

Case	Performance	Proposed FPGA-based PIDFC with PSO	GA - Fuzzy PID In (Hu et al., 1999)	GA -Optimal PID In (Hu et al., 1999)
	Tr (s)	0.19	0.16	0.2
CS1	Ts(s)	0.23	0.2	0.36
	OV	0.0	0.0	0.0039
	Tr (s)	0.48	0.16	0.38
CS2	Ts(s)	0.49	0.46	0.74
	OV	0.0	0.0051	0.0162
	Tr (s)	1.6	0.74	0.88
CS3	Ts(s)	1.8	2.34	1.34
	OV	0.005	0.0622	0.0107

Table 14. Performance Comparison of the PIDFC with the Work Proposed by Hu et al. In (Hu et al., 1999)

Performance	The proposed Controller In Experimental Case with CS5	The Proposed FPGA-based PIDFC With PSO	Optimal PID In (Jain et al., 2009) With BG	Fuzzy logic controller in (Masmoudi et al., 1999)	Optimal PD-PI In (Jain et al., 1999) With PSO
Ts (s)	0.058	0.1	0.4	0.21	2.4
Tr(s)	0.029	0.13	0.2	0.22	---
Peak angle (rad)	0.025	0.0	0.178	0.75	0.00127

Table 15. Performance Comparison of the PIDFC (8FBC) With Those Proposed In (Jain et al., 2009), (Masmoudi et al., 1999) and (Jain et al., 1999) By Using CS5.

References	Number of CLBs	Number of IOBs	Frequency	Time per action
PIDFC	494	68	40 MHz	0.3 µs
(Poorani et al., 2005)	757	39	8 KHz	41.1 ms
(Tipsuwanpornet al., 2004)	---	---	40.55 MHz	2.1 µs
(Hassan et al., 2007)	1394	61	40.245 MHz	0.421 µs
(Alvarez et al., 2006)	3492	51	100 MHz	1.4 µs
(Lund et al., 2006)	63	---	20 MHz	1 µs

Table 16. FPGA Chip Resources Comparison between the PIDFC and Other Type of Controllers Proposed In the Literature.

13. Conclusion

From the design and simulation results of the PIDFC, it can be concluded that: Higher execution speed versus small chip size is achieved by designing PIDFC with a simplified fuzzy algorithm as a parallel structure of PDFC and PIFC and also by designing PIFC by accumulating the output of the PDFC. These methods significantly reduce the number of rules needed. It also enables the controller to work as a PIFC, PDFC or PIDFC depending on two external signals to provide high-flexibilities with different applications. The controller needs 16 clock cycles to generate an output with a maximum clock frequency of 40 MHz. Therefore, the proposed controller will be able to control a wide range of systems with a high sampling rate. Higher flexibility versus good control performance is achieved by designing tuning-gains block at each input/output stage. This block involves a tuning by scaling the universe of discourse for the input/output variables (renormalization). This block makes the controller chip accept the PSO-based optimal scaling gains, and also enables the digital controller chip able to accept unsigned inputs. The PSO algorithm has better simulation results than other intelligent optimization methods proposed in the literature such as genetic algorithm. This block is very important and is useful for providing a best tuning case for the universe of discourse.

In addition, it makes the design applicable for different systems without requiring reprogramming the controller chip. Higher execution speed and small chip size versus acceptable accuracy is achieved by designing each one of the scaling gains as two parts: integer and fraction, and perform all mathematical operations using integer number algorithms, which are smaller in the implementation size than floating number algorithms, and even faster. Sufficient design accuracy can be achieved with 8FBC in Particular. 8FBC is superior to 6FBC since it presents higher accuracy versus moderately low target device utilizations. 8FBC was able to produce a control action in 0.3 μs after input latching (the computational time of the controller is 0.3 μs). The 8FBC produced responses approximately similar or better than the MSBC compared with the 6FBC or with the results in the literature. The absolute mean of differences between the responses of the 6FBC and the MSBC, was less than 4% of the output range, for the linear plants, and less than 0.5% of the output range for the nonlinear plant, while the absolute mean of differences between the responses of 8FBC and the MSBC, was less than 1% of the output range, for the linear plants, and less than 0.3% of the output range for the nonlinear plant. Both versions showed some error at the steady state part of the response when serving as PIFLC or PIDFLC because of the accumulation of the rounding error at the summation block. This error depends on the rounding error; therefore it becomes larger when using the 6FBC than when using 8FBC. As a result, the proposed controller could be used to control many industrial applications with high sampling time. Its small size versus high speed makes it a good choice for other applications, such as robots. It is hoped that some future work could settle down the feasibility of the suggestions: Increasing the number of the first part of the fuzzy set in the MBMSF inside the fuzzifier block more than (3-bits) could make the design accept more than 8 fuzzy sets at each input. Increasing the number of bits of the entire design may be useful in decreasing the error in the PIFC component (in some cases) of the controller at the expense of increasing design area and processing time.

14. Acknowledgment

The authors would firstly like to thank God, and all friends who gave us any help related to this work. Other Appreciation goes to the Assist chancellor amend to Diyala University-Iraq

(Prof. Dr Amer Mohammed Ibrahim) and the Dean of Collage of Engineering-Diyala University- Iraq (Assist. Prof. Dr. Adel Khaleel Mahmoud). Further appreciation goes to My Colleagues Mr. Waleed Fawwaz and Mrs. Areej Sadiq for their wide help and support. Finally, a heartfelt thank to our families and home countries.

15. References

Poorani, S., Priya, T.V.S.U., Kumar, K.U., and Renganarayanan, S., (2005) "*FPGA Based Fuzzy Logic Controller for Electric Vehicle*," Journal of the Institution of Engineers, Singapore, Vol. 45 Issue 5.

Jain, T., Patel, V., Nigam and M.J., "*Implementation of PID Controlled SIMO Process on FPGA Using Bacterial Foraging for Optimal Performance*," International Journal of Computer and Electrical Engineering, Vol. 1, No. 2, p: 1793-8198, June.

Tipsuwanporn, V., Intajag, S. and Krongratana, V., (2004) "*Fuzzy Logic PID Controller Based on FPGA for Process Control*," Proceedings of IEEE International Symposium on Industrial Electronics, Vol. 2, May 4-7, page(s):1495-1500.

Karasakal, O., Yesl, E., Guzelkaya, M. and Eksin, I., (2005) "*Implementation of a New Self-Tuning Fuzzy PID Controller on PLC*," Turk J Elec Engin, Vol.13, NO.2.

Hassan, M.Y., and Sharif, W.F., (2007) "*Design of FPGA based PID-like Fuzzy Controller for Industrial Applications*," IAENG International Journal of Computer Science, Vol. 34 Issue 2, November.

Kim, D., (2000) "*An Implementation of Fuzzy Logic Controller on the Reconfigurable FPGA System*," IEEE Transactions on Industrial Electronics, Vol. 47, No. 3, p: 703- 715, June.

Solano, S.S., Barriga, A., Jimenez, C.J and Huertas, J.L., (1997) "*Design and Application of Digital Fuzzy Controllers*", Proceedings of Sixth IEEE International Conference on Fuzzy Systems (FUZZ-IEEE'97), Vol. 2, July 1-5, page(s):869-874.

Islam, S., Amin, N., Bhuyan, M.S, Zaman, M., Madon, B. and Othman, M., (2007) "*FPGA Realization of Fuzzy Temperature Controller for Industrial Application*", WSEAS Transactions on Systems and Control, Volume 2, Issue 10, p: 484- 490, October.

Mann, G.K.I., Hu, B.G. and Gosine, R.G., (1999) "*Analysis of Direct Action Fuzzy PID Controller Structures*", IEEE Transactions on Systems, Man, and Cybernetics — Part B: Cybernetics, Vol. 29, No. 3, p: 371 – 388, June.

Seng, T.L., Khalid, M. and Yusuf, R., (1999) "*Tuning of a Neuro-Fuzzy Controller by Genetic Algorithm*", IEEE Transactions on Systems, Man, and Cybernetics — Part B: Cybernetics, Vol. 29, No. 2, P: 226- 236, April.

Leonid, R., Ghanayem, O. and Bourmistrov, A., (2000) "*PID plus fuzzy controller structures as a design base for industrial applications*", Engineering Applications of Artificial Intelligence, Elsevier Science Ltd, 13, p: 419-430.

Leonid, R. (1997). *Fuzzy Controllers*, first edition, Newnes.

Gabrielli, Gandolfi, E. and Masetti, M., (2009) "*Design of a Very High Speed Fuzzy Processor by VHDL Language*", Physics Department University of Bologna, URL:http://www.bo.infn.it/dacel/papers/96_03_parigi_EDTC.pdf. Accessed on 4 October 2009.

Jantzen, J., (1998) "*Design of Fuzzy Controllers*". Technical University of Denmark, and Department of Automation, reports no 98-H 869 (soc), 19 Aug.

Ibrahim, A.M., (2004) "*Fuzzy Logic for Embedded Systems Applications*", USA, Elsevier Science.

Obaid, Z.A., Sulaiman, N. and Hamidon, M.N., (2009) *"Developed Method of FPGA-based Fuzzy Logic Controller Design with the Aid of Conventional PID Algorithm"*, Australian Journal of Basics and Applied Science, Vol. 3(3), P: 2724-2740.

Ying, H., (2000) *"Fuzzy Control and Modeling, Analytical Foundations and Applications"*, Institute of Electrical and Electronic Engineers Inc., USA.

Wang, J., Zhang, Y. and Wang, W., (2006) *"Optimal design of PI/PD controller for non-minimum phase system"*, Transactions of the Institute of Measurement and Control, Vol. 28 No. 1, p: 27-35.

Allaoua, B., Gasbaoui, B. and Mebarki, B., (2009) "Setting Up PID DC Motor Speed Control Alteration Parameters Using Particle Swarm Optimization Strategy", Leonardo Electronic Journal of Practices and Technologies, Issue 14, p: 19-32, January-June 2009.

Barriga, A., Sanchez-Solano, S., Brox, P., Cabrera, A., and Baturone, I., (2006) *"Modeling and implementation of Fuzzy Systems Based on VHDL"*, International Journal of Approximate Reasoning, Elsevier Inc, Vol. 41, p: 164–178.

Huang, S.H. and Lai, J.Y., (2005) *"A High Speed Fuzzy Inference Processor with Dynamic Analysis and Scheduling Capabilities"*, IEICE Transaction Information & System., Vol. E88-D, No.10 October.

Alvarez, J., Lago, A. and Nogueiras, A., (2006) *"FPGA Implementation of a Fuzzy Controller for Automobile DC-DC Converters"* Proceeding of IEEE International Conference on Field Programmable Technology, December, page(s): 237-240.

Lund, T., Aguirre, M. and Torralba, A., (2004) "Fuzzy Logic Control via an FPGA: A Design using techniques from Digital Signal Processing", Proceedings of IEEE International Symposium on Industrial Electronics, vol. 1, May 4-7, page(s): 555- 559.

Sultan, KH., *"Inverted Pendulum, Analysis, Design and Implementation"* IIEE Visionaries Document Version 1.0, Institute of Industrial Electronics Engineering, Karachi, Pakistan. [Available online at] Matlab Central File Exchange http://www.Mathworks.com.

Xilinx Company. 2009. Virtex 2.5 V Field Programmable Gate Arrays, Data Sheet DS003, URL www.xilinx.com. Accessed on 2009.

Hu, B.G., Mann, G.K. and Gosine, R.G, (1999) *"New Methodology for Analytical and Optimal Design of Fuzzy PID Controllers"*, IEEE Transactions on Fuzzy Systems, Vol. 7, No. 5, pp. 521-539, October.

Passino, K.M., and Yurkovich, S., (1998) *"Fuzzy Control*, Addison-Weslwey Longman Inc., USA.

Masmoudi, N., Hachicha, M. and Kamoun, L., (1999) *"Hardware Design of Programmable Fuzzy Controller on FPGA"*, Proceedings of IEEE International Fuzzy Systems Conference Proceedings, August 22-25, page(s):1675-1679.

Jain, T. and Nigam, M.J., (2008) *"Optimization of PD-PI Controller Using Swarm Intelligence"*, Journal of Theoretical and Applied Information Technology, Page: 1013-1018, 2008.

Obaid, Z.A., Sulaiman, N., Marhaban, M.H. and Hamidon, M.N. (2010), "Implementation of Multistructure PID-like Fuzzy Logic Controller using Field Programmable Gate Array" IEICE Electronics Express, Vol. 7 No. 3, P: 132-137, 10 February.

Li J. and Hu B.S., (1996) "The Architecture of Fuzzy PID Gain Conditioner and its FPGA Prototype Implementation", Proceedings of the Second International Conference on ASIC, October 21-24, page(s):61-65.

Khatr, A. P., and Rattan, K.S., (2006) "Implementation of a Multi-Layered Fuzzy Controller on an FPGA", Annual meeting of the North America, by IEEE Fuzzy Information Processing Society, Page(s): 420- 425.

J.L. Gonzalez-vazquez, O. Castillo and L.T. Aguilar-bustos, "A Generic Approach to Fuzzy Logic Controller Synthesis on FPGA", Proceedings of IEEE international conference on fuzzy systems, 2006, page(s): 2317 – 2322.

Gonzalez-Vazquez, J.L., Castillo, O. and Aguilar-bustos, L.T., (2006) "A Generic Approach to Fuzzy Logic Controller Synthesis on FPGA", Proceedings of IEEE international conference on fuzzy systems, page(s): 2317 – 2322.

14

Cascaded NPC/H-Bridge Inverter with Simplified Control Strategy and Superior Harmonic Suppression

Tom Wanjekeche, Dan V. Nicolae and Adisa A. Jimoh
Tshwane University of Technology
South Africa

1. Introduction

In recent decades the electric power systems has suffered significant power quality problems caused by the proliferation of non linear loads, such as arc furnace lighting loads adjustable ac drives etc., which causes a large amount of characteristic harmonics, low power factor and significantly deteriorates the power quality of the distribution system (Benslimane, 2007; Franquelo et. al., 2008; Gupta et al., 2008). The increasing restrictive regulations on power quality have significantly stimulated the development of power quality mitigation equipments. For high power grid connected systems, the classical two level or three level converters topology are insufficient due to the rating limitations imposed by the power semiconductors (Holmes & McGrath, 2001; Koura et al., 2007). Hence considerable attention has been focused on multilevel inverter topologies. This important multilevel technology has found widespread application in medium and high voltage electric drives, renewable energy – grid interface, power conditioning, and power quality application (Lai & Peng, 1996; Peng et al., 1996; Rodriguez et al., 2002; Sinha & Lipo, 1996; Tolbert et al., 1999).

Multilevel converters offer several advantages compared to their conventional counterparts (Manjrekar & Lipo, 1988, 1998, 200; Corzine & Familiant, 2002; Lund et. al., 1999; Sneineh et. al., 2006; Park et. al., 2003; Zhang et al., 2002; Ding et. al., 2004; Duarte et al., 1997; Rojas &. Ohnishi, 1997). By synthesizing the AC output terminal voltage from several voltage levels, staircase waveforms can be produced, which in their turn approach the sinusoidal waveform with low harmonic distortion, thus reducing filters requirements. However the several sources on the DC side of the converter make multilevel technology difficult to control by the need to balance the several DC voltages. For the class of multilevel inverter called diode clamped, if a higher output voltage is required one of the viable methods is to increase the number of inverter voltage levels. For Neutral Point Clamped (NPC) inverter voltage can only be increased up to five level beyond which DC voltage balancing becomes impossible. For single Phase H Bridge inverter, an increase in the number levels leads to increase in the number of separate DC sources, thus the proposed hybrid model is developed by combining the NPC and H- bridge topologies (Wu et al., 1999).

A lot of research has been done on single phase H- Bridge inverter where each inverter level generate three different voltage outputs, $+V_{dc}$, 0, and $-V_{dc}$ by connecting the dc source to the ac output using different combinations of the four switches of the Bridge (Peng et al., 1996). There has also been more emphasis on modeling and control of a five level NPC/H-bridge inverter without cascading the bridge (Cheng & Wu, 2007). This fails to address the principle of realizing a general cascaded n- level NPC/H-Bridge. It is on this need of realizing a higher voltage output with simplified control algorithm that this book chapter proposes a simplified control strategy for a cascaded NPC/H-bridge inverter with reduced harmonic content. Because of the modularity of the model only two cascaded cells which gives a 9 level cascaded NPC/H-bridge inverter is considered. The new control strategy is achieved by decomposing the nine level output into four separate and independent three-level NPC PWM output. By combining the three- level NPC PWM back to back using DC sources and properly phase shifting the modulating wave and carrier a simplified control strategy is achieved with reduced number of components. The control strategy is applied on cascaded NPC/H-bridge inverter that combines features from NPC inverter and cascaded H-Bridge inverter. For higher voltage applications, this structure can be easily extended to an n- level by cascaded NPC/H-Bridge PWM inverters.

The article starts by developing a control algorithm based on novel phase shifted PWM technique on the proposed inverter model. This is done on a two cell of the cascaded model to realize nine level voltage output. A theoretical harmonic analysis of the model with the proposed control algorithm is carried out based on double Fourier principle. Spectral characteristics of the output waveforms for all operating conditions are studied for a five-level and nine- level voltage output. Theoretical results are verified using MATLAB simulation.The results shows that the spectrum can be made to only consist of the multiples of fourth order for a five level and with proper phase shift combination, a multiple of eighth order is achieved for nine level voltage output. The results are compared with those of a conventional multicarrier PWM approach; it is shown that with the proposed phase shifted PWM approach, the inverter exhibits reduced harmonic content are present. Finally the article compares the components count of the the model with the convetional cascaded H-bridge inverter, it is clealry shown that the proposed model requires a lesser number of separate dc sources as compared to conventional cascaded H-bridge inverter.

2. System topology and switching technique

2.1 Main system configuration

Fig 1 shows the circuit configuration of the proposed nine- level cascaded NPC/H-Bridge PWM inverter which consists of two legs for each cell connected to a common bus. Four active switches, four freewheeling diodes and two diodes clamped to neutral are adopted in each leg. The voltage stress of all the eight power switches is equal to half of DC bus voltage. The power switches in each leg are operated in high frequency using phase shifted PWM control technique to generate the three voltage levels on the ac terminal to neutral voltage point

The building block of the whole topology consists of two identical NPC cascaded cells. The inverter phase voltage V_{an} is the sum of the two cascaded cells, i.e.,

$$V_{an} = V_{01} + V_{02} \tag{1}$$

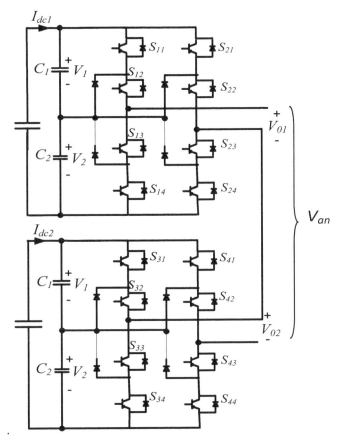

Fig. 1. Schematic diagram of the proposed cascaded NPC/H-bridge inverter model

Assuming that the two capacitor voltages on the DC bus voltage are equal, five different voltage levels $+2Vdc$, $+V_{dc}$, 0, $-V_{dc}$ and $-2V_{dc}$, are generated on the ac terminal V_{01} which consist of two legs. Same applies to V_{02} fig. 2 shows the switching model for a nine- level output [6]. This implies that by cascading two NPC/H-Bridge inverters (V_{01} and V_{02}) and properly phase shifting the modulating wave and carriers, a nine- level PWM output is achieved. The number of output voltage levels is given by

$$m = 4N + 1 \tag{2}$$

Where N is the number of series connected NPC/H-Bridges. The topology is made up of four three level legs and each leg has four active switches and four freewheeling diodes.

2.2 System operation
Most of the past research on modeling of cascaded multilevel inverter has concentrated on realizing a switching model of conventional H- bridge inverter without giving a guideline

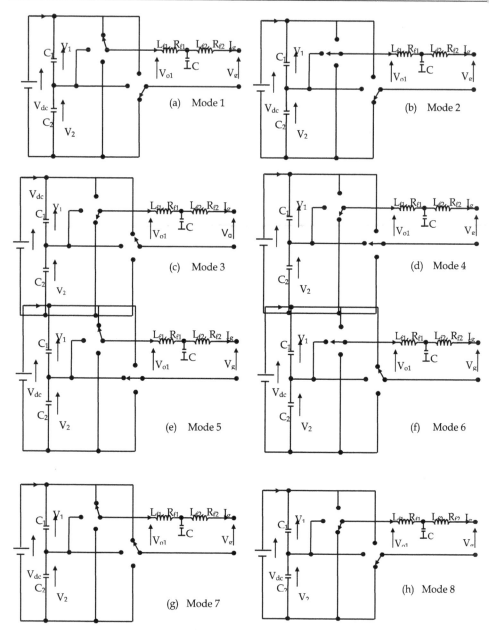

Fig. 2. Operating modes of one cell of NPC/H-Bridge inverter

on how one can get operating modes of cascaded NPC/H-bridge inverter and hence obtain a valid model for the topology. This section analyses eight valid operating modes of one cell of the proposed topology. The following assumptions are made in the modeling and analysis process:

- All components (power switches and capacitors) are ideal.
- The DC- link capacitors V_1, V_2, V_3 and V_4 have the same capacitance.
- PV cells supplies constant and equal voltages to the four DC link capacitors.
- The reference phase voltage is assumed to be a constant value during one switching period.

Figure 3 shows the operation modes for one NPC/H-bridge cell from the 9-level inverter. In mode 1 the power switches S_{11} & S_{12} and S_{23} & S_{24} are turned on to supply voltage at the output of first NPC/H-bridge cell that is equal to $V_{01} = V_1 + V_2$. The capacitors C_1 and C_2 are discharged as they supply power to the utility as shown in figure 2 (a). The modes 2 to 8 are as shown in figures 2 (b) to 2 (h) respectively. In mode 2 the output voltage is $V_{01} = V_2$, in mode 3: $V_{01} = -(V_1 + V_2)$, in mode 4: $V_{01} = -V_2$, in mode 5: $V_{01} = V_1$, in mode 6: $V_{01} = -V_1$: in mode 7: $V_{01} = 0$ and in mode 8: $V_{01} = 0$.

Based on the analysis of the operation model, the state variable equation for the proposed inverter can be estimated. To prevent the top and bottom power switched in each inverter leg from conducting at the same time, the constraints of power switches can be expressed as:

$$S_{i1} + S_{i3} = 1; \; S_{i2} + S_{i4} = 1 \} \tag{3}$$

Where i = 1, 2. Let's define the switch operator as: $T_1 = S_{11}$ & S_{12} ; $T_2 = S_{13}$ & S_{13} ; $T_3 = S_{21}$ & S_{22} $T_4 = S_{23}$ & S_{24}. The four valid expressions are given by:

$$T_1 = \begin{cases} 1 \; if \; both \; S_{11} \; \& \; S_{12} \; are \; ON \\ 0 \; Otherwise \end{cases} \tag{4}$$

$$T_2 = \begin{cases} 1 \; if \; both \; S_{13} \; \& \; S_{14} \; are \; ON \\ 0 \; Otherwise \end{cases} \tag{5}$$

$$T_3 = \begin{cases} 1 \; if \; both \; S_{21} \; \& \; S_{22} \; are \; ON \\ 0 \; Otherwise \end{cases} \tag{6}$$

$$T_4 = \begin{cases} 1 \; if \; both \; S_{23} \; \& \; S_{24} \; are \; ON \\ 0 \; Otherwise \end{cases} \tag{7}$$

From fig. 4 taking two legs for each cell to be a and b, the equivalent switching function are:

$$K_a = \begin{cases} 1 \; if \; T_1 = 1 \\ 0 \; if \; S_{12} \; 1 \\ -1 if \; T_2 = 1 \end{cases} \; \& \; K_b = \begin{cases} 1 \; if \; T_3 = 1 \\ 0 \; if \; S_{22} \; 1 \\ -1 if \; T_4 = 1 \end{cases} \tag{8}$$

Using equation (3 - 7), a switching state and corresponding voltage output V_{ol} can be generated as shown in table 1 which clearly indicates that there are 8 valid switching states; From table 1, the voltage V_{01} generate by the inverter can be expressed as:

$$V_{01} = V_a + V_b \tag{9}$$

For the control technique stated above; the voltage level for one leg of the cell is given as:

K_a	K_b	T_1	T_2	S_{12}	T_3	T_4	S_{21}	V_a	V_b	V_{01}	Mode
1	-1	1	0	1	0	1	0	V_1	$-V_2$	$V_1+ V_2$	1
0	-1	0	0	1	0	1	0	0	$-V_2$	V_2	2
-1	0	0	1	0	0	0	1	0	V_2	$-V_2$	3
1	0	1	0	1	0	0	1	V_1	0	V_1	4
0	1	0	0	1	1	0	1	$-V_1$	0	$-V_1$	5
1	1	1	0	1	1	0	1	V_1	V_1	0	6
-1	-1	0	1	1	0	1	1	V_2	V_2	0	7
-1	-1	0	1	0	1	0	1	V_2	V_1	$-V_1- V_2$	8

Table 1. Switching States and Corresponding Voltage(s) for One Cell of NPC/H-bridge Inverter

$$V_a = K_a\left(\frac{K_a+1}{2}\right)V_1 - K_a\left(\frac{K_a-1}{2}\right)V_2 \tag{10}$$

Similarly for the second leg the expression is given by (11)

$$V_b = K_b\left(\frac{K_b+1}{2}\right)V_1 - K_b\left(\frac{K_b-1}{2}\right)V_2 \tag{11}$$

S_{11}	S_{12}	S_{21}	S_{22}	S_{31}	S_{32}	S_{41}	S_{42}	V_{01}	V_{02}	V_{an}
0	0	0	0	0	0	0	0	0	0	0
0	0	0	1	0	0	0	0	$-V_{dc}$	0	$-V_{dc}$
0	0	0	1	0	0	0	1	$-V_{dc}$	$-V_{dc}$	$-2V_{dc}$
0	0	0	1	0	0	1	1	$-V_{dc}$	$-2V_{dc}$	$-3V_{dc}$
0	0	0	1	0	1	0	0	$-V_{dc}$	V_{dc}	0
0	0	0	1	1	1	0	0	$-V_{dc}$	$2V_{dc}$	V_{dc}
0	0	1	1	0	0	0	0	$-2V_{dc}$	0	$-2V_{dc}$
0	0	1	1	0	0	0	0	$-2V_{dc}$	$-V_{dc}$	$-3V_{dc}$
0	0	1	1	0	0	1	0	$-2V_{dc}$	$-2V_{dc}$	$-4V_{dc}$
0	0	1	1	0	1	0	0	$-2V_{dc}$	V_{dc}	$-V_{dc}$
0	0	1	1	1	1	0	0	$-2V_{dc}$	$2V_{dc}$	0
0	1	0	0	0	0	0	0	V_{dc}	0	V_{dc}
0	1	0	0	0	0	0	1	V_{dc}	$-V_{dc}$	0
0	1	0	0	0	0	1	1	V_{dc}	$-2V_{dc}$	$-V_{dc}$
0	1	0	0	0	1	0	0	V_{dc}	V_{dc}	$2V_{dc}$
0	1	0	0	1	1	0	0	V_{dc}	$2V_{dc}$	$3V_{dc}$
1	1	0	0	0	0	0	0	$2V_{dc}$	0	$2V_{dc}$
1	1	0	0	0	0	0	1	$2V_{dc}$	$-V_{dc}$	V_{dc}
1	1	0	0	0	0	1	1	$2V_{dc}$	$-2V_{dc}$	0
1	1	0	0	0	1	0	0	$2V_{dc}$	V_{dc}	$3V_{dc}$
1	1	0	0	1	1	0	0	$2V_{dc}$	$2V_{dc}$	$4V_{dc}$
1	1	1	1	1	1	1	1	0	0	0

Table 2. Switching scheme for one phase leg of a nine level cascaded NPC/H- bridge inverter

From equation (9), the voltage output for one cell of the model can be deduced as;

$$V_{01} = \frac{K_a - K_b}{2}(V_1 + V_2) + \frac{K^2_a - K^2_b}{2}(V_1 - V_2)$$ (12)

For the compound nine level inverter let's assume that $V_1 = V_2 = V_3 = V_4 = V$, the switching states are as shown in Table 2.

For a nine level cascaded NPC/H-bridge inverter, there are 22 valid switching states though two of the switching states are short circuits and thus cannot compensate the DC capacitor as current do not pass through either of the four DC- link capacitors.

3. Mathematical analysis

Most of the past research on modeling of cascaded multilevel inverter has concentrated on realizing a switching model of conventional H- bridge inverter without giving a guideline on how one can get operating modes of cascaded NPC/H-bridge inverter and hence obtain a valid model for the topology. This section analyses eight valid operating modes of one cell of the proposed topology and proposes an equivalent circuit for the topology.

The following assumptions are made for deriving the mathematical model of the cascaded H-bridge inverters.

- The grid is assumed to be AC current source,
- The power losses of the whole system are categorized as series loss and parallel loss. The series loss and interfacing inductor loss are represented as equivalent series resistance (ESR). Parallel losses are represented as shunt connected resistances across the dc-link capacitors.

The differential equations describing the dynamics of the coupling inductor between the NPC/H-bridge inverter and the grid of the model shown in fig. 1 can be derived as:

$$\begin{cases} L_{f1}\dfrac{di_{fx}}{dt} = -V_{cx} - i_{fx}R_{f1x} + \delta_{1x}V_1 + \delta_{2x}V_2 \\ L_{f2}\dfrac{di_{sx}}{dt} = -V_{cx} - i_{sx}R_{f2x} - V_{sx} \end{cases}$$ (13)

According to Kirchhoff's law, the currents flowing into the dc link capacitors C_1 and C_2 can be expressed as:

$$\begin{cases} i_{C1} = C_1\dfrac{dV_1}{dt} = \delta_{1x}i_{fx} + \dfrac{V_1}{R} + \dfrac{V_2}{R} \\ i_{C2} = C_2\dfrac{dV_2}{dt} = -\delta_{2x}i_{fx} + \dfrac{V_1}{R} + \dfrac{V_2}{R} \\ i_{CX} = C_f\dfrac{dV_{fx}}{dt} = i_{fx} - i_{sx} \\ C_1\dfrac{dV_1}{dt} - C_2\dfrac{dV_2}{dt} = \delta_3 i_{fx} \end{cases}$$ (14)

The equations (13) and (14) can be rearranged as:

$$\begin{cases} \dfrac{di_{fx}}{dt} = \dfrac{R_{f1x}}{L_{f1}} - \dfrac{V_{cx}}{L_{f1}} + \dfrac{\delta_{1x}V_1}{L_{f1}} + \dfrac{\delta_{2x}V_2}{L_{f1}} \\[2mm] \dfrac{di_{sx}}{dt} = \dfrac{V_{cx}}{L_{f2}} - \dfrac{R_{f1}}{L_{f2}} - \dfrac{V_{sx}}{L_{f2}} \\[2mm] \dfrac{dV_1}{dt} = \dfrac{\delta_{1x}i_{fx}}{C_1} - \left(\dfrac{V_1}{RC_1} + \dfrac{V_2}{RC_1} \right) \\[2mm] \dfrac{dV_2}{dt} = \dfrac{\delta_{2x}i_{fx}}{C_2} - \left(\dfrac{V_1}{RC_2} + \dfrac{V_2}{RC_2} \right) \\[2mm] \dfrac{dV_f}{dt} = \dfrac{i_{fx}}{C_f} - \dfrac{i_{sx}}{C_f} \\[2mm] \delta_3 i_{fx} = C_1 \dfrac{dV_1}{dt} - C_2 \dfrac{dV_2}{dt} \end{cases} \qquad (15)$$

Equation (16) can be written in the format of:

$$Z\dot{x} = Ax + B \qquad (16)$$

Capacitor current, inverter current and utility line current and DC- Link capacitors are taken as state variables:

$$x = [i_{fx}\ i_{sx}\ V_c\ V_1\ V_2]^T \qquad (17)$$

$$Z = \begin{bmatrix} L_{f1} & 0 & 0 & 0 & 0 \\ 0 & L_{f2} & 1 & 0 & 0 \\ 0 & 0 & C & 0 & 0 \\ 0 & 0 & 0 & C_1 & 0 \\ 0 & 0 & 0 & 0 & C_2 \end{bmatrix} \qquad (18)$$

$$B = [0 - V_s\ 0\ 0\ 0]^T \qquad (19)$$

Matrix A depends on each operating mode as such
- For $V_{01} = +V_2$

$$A_1 = \begin{bmatrix} -R_{f1} & 0 & -1 & 0 & 1 \\ 0 & -R_{f2} & 1 & 0 & 0 \\ 1 & -1 & 0 & 0 & 0 \\ 0 & 0 & 0 & R^{-1}R^{-1} \\ -1 & 0 & 0 & R^{-1}R^{-1} \end{bmatrix} \qquad (20)$$

- For $V_{01} = -V_2$

$$A_5 = A_1^T \qquad (21)$$

- For $V_{01} = +V_1$

$$
A_2 = \begin{bmatrix}
-R_{f1} & 0 & -1 & 1 & 0 \\
0 & -R_{f2} & 1 & 0 & 0 \\
1 & -1 & 0 & 0 & 0 \\
-1 & 0 & 0 & R^{-1} & R^{-1} \\
0 & 0 & 0 & R^{-1} & R^{-1}
\end{bmatrix}
\tag{22}
$$

- For $V_{01} = -V_1$

$$
A_6 = A_2^{\,T}
\tag{23}
$$

- For $V_{01} = 0$

$$
A_4 = \begin{bmatrix}
-R_{f1} & 0 & -1 & -1 & -1 \\
0 & -R_{f2} & 1 & 0 & 0 \\
1 & -1 & 0 & 0 & 0 \\
-1 & 0 & 0 & 0 & 0 \\
-1 & 0 & 0 & 0 & 0
\end{bmatrix}
\tag{24}
$$

Considering the same assumption made earlier that the dc link capacitors have the same capacitance $C_1 = C_2 = C$ which implies $V_1 = V_2 = V_{dc}/2$, the state space equation (17) can be simplified to:

$$
Z'\dot{x} = A'x + B'
\tag{25}
$$

With

$$
x = [i_{fx}\ i_{sx}\ V_c\ V_{dc}\,/\,2]^T
\tag{26}
$$

$$
Z' = \begin{bmatrix}
L_{f1} & 0 & 0 & 0 \\
0 & L_{f2} & 1 & 0 \\
0 & 0 & C & 0 \\
0 & 0 & 0 & C_T
\end{bmatrix}
\tag{27}
$$

$$
B = [0\ V_s\ 0\ 0\ 0]^T
\tag{28}
$$

$$
A' = \begin{bmatrix}
-R_{f1} & 0 & -k & k \\
0 & -R_{f2} & k & 0 \\
k & -1 & 0 & 0 \\
-k & 0 & 0 & 0
\end{bmatrix}
\tag{29}
$$

Where k depends on the operating mode and can take five different values: 1. 0.5 0, -05, -1.

For a three phase system, V_s is replaced $V_s(\cos\omega_o t)$, $V_s(\cos\omega_o\text{-}2\pi/3)$ and $V_s(\cos\omega_o\text{+}2\pi/3$. similarly the Z, A and B matrices are expanded accordingly to three phase. Where V_s is the grid voltage.

3.1 Harmonic analysis of a nine level cascaded NPC/H-bridge inverter

Having realized a nine- level output from the a cascaded 9- level model, it is important to theoretically investigate its harmonic structure and show how harmonic suppression is achieved. Based on the principle of double Fourier integral (Holmes & Thomas, 2003). the first modulation between triangular carrier v_{cr1}, and the positive sinusoidal waveform a naturally sampled PMW output $V_p(t)$ of equation (30). Where M is the modulation index, V_{dc} is the DC link voltage of the PWM inverter and J_n is the nth order Bessel function of the first kind. Using v_{cr2} which is the same carrier but displaced by minus unity, the naturally sampled PWM output V_n is as given in equation (31)

$$V_p(t) = \begin{cases} \dfrac{V_{dc1}}{2} + \dfrac{V_{dc1}M}{2}\cos\omega_s t + \dfrac{2V_{dc1}}{\pi}\sum\limits_{m=1}^{\infty}\dfrac{1}{m}J_0(m\dfrac{\pi}{2}M) \\[2ex] \sin m\dfrac{\pi}{2}\cos\omega_s t + \dfrac{2V_{dc1}}{\pi}\sum\limits_{m=1}^{\infty}\sum\limits_{\substack{n=-\infty \\ n\neq 0}}^{\infty}\dfrac{1}{m}J_n \\[2ex] (m\dfrac{\pi}{2}M)\sin(m+n)\dfrac{\pi}{2}\cos(n\omega_c t + n\omega_s t) \end{cases} \tag{30}$$

$$V_n(t) = \begin{cases} \dfrac{V_{dc1}}{2} - \dfrac{V_{dc1}M}{2}\cos\omega_s t - \dfrac{2V_{dc1}}{\pi}\sum\limits_{m=1}^{\infty}\dfrac{1}{m}J_0(m\dfrac{\pi}{2}M) \\[2ex] \sin m\dfrac{\pi}{2}\cos\omega_s t + \dfrac{2V_{dc1}}{\pi}\sum\limits_{m=1}^{\infty}\sum\limits_{\substack{n=-\infty \\ n\neq 0}}^{\infty}\dfrac{1}{m}J_n \\[2ex] (m\dfrac{\pi}{2}M)\sin(m+n)\dfrac{\pi}{2}\cos(n\omega_c t + n\omega_s t) \end{cases} \tag{31}$$

The output of leg 'a' is given by $V_a(t) = V_p(t) - V_n(t)$ which is:

$$V_a(t) = \begin{cases} V_{dc1}\cos(\omega_s t) + \dfrac{4V_{dc1}}{\pi}\sum\limits_{m=2,4,6}^{\infty}\sum\limits_{n=\pm 1\pm 3\pm 5}^{\infty}\dfrac{1}{m}J_n \\[2ex] (m\dfrac{\pi}{2}M)\cos(m\omega_c t + n\omega_s t) \end{cases} \tag{32}$$

The output of leg 'b' is realized by replacing ω_s with $\omega_s + \pi$ and using v_{cr2} which is same as phase displacing v_{cr1} by minus unity which gives

$$V_b(t) = \begin{cases} -V_{dc1}\cos(\omega_s t) - \dfrac{4V_{dc1}}{\pi}\sum\limits_{m=2,4,6}^{\infty}\sum\limits_{n=\pm 1\pm 3\pm 5}^{\infty}\dfrac{(-1)^{m+n}}{m}J_n \\[2ex] (m\dfrac{\pi}{2}M)\cos(m\omega_c t + n\omega_s t) \end{cases} \tag{33}$$

From equations (32) and (33), it can be clearly deduced that that odd carrier harmonics and even sideband harmonics around even carrier harmonic orders are completely eliminated. Five- level obtained by taking the differential output between the two legs and is given by (35). Similarly the output between the other two legs of the second cell of the hybrid model is achieved by replacing ω_s with $\omega_s + \pi$ and ω_c with $\omega c + \pi/4$ which gives another five level inverter for equation given by equation (34)

$$V_{01}(t) = \begin{cases} 2V_{dc1}\cos(\omega_s t) + \dfrac{8V_{dc1}}{\pi} \displaystyle\sum_{m=4,8,12}^{\infty} \displaystyle\sum_{n=\pm1\pm3\pm5}^{\infty} \dfrac{1}{m} J_n \\[4mm] (m\dfrac{\pi}{2}M)\cos(m\omega_c t + n\omega_s t) \end{cases} \tag{34}$$

$$V_{02}(t) = \begin{cases} -2V_{dc1}\cos(\omega_s t) - \dfrac{8V_{dc1}}{\pi} \displaystyle\sum_{m=4,8,12}^{\infty} \displaystyle\sum_{n=\pm1\pm3\pm5}^{\infty} \dfrac{(-1)^{\frac{m}{4}+n}}{m} J_n \\[4mm] (m\dfrac{\pi}{2}M)\cos(m\omega_c t + n\omega_s t) \end{cases} \tag{35}$$

Equations (34) and (35) clearly show that for five- level inverter, the proposed control strategy has achieved; Suppression of carrier harmonics to multiples of four; Elimination of even side harmonics around multiples of four carrier harmonics of Multiples of four carrier harmonics. Finally the output for a nine level is achieved differentiating the output voltage between the two cells of the five level cells and this is given by equation (36). It can be concluded that for a cascaded N-level inverter the carrier harmonic order is pushed up by factor of $4N$ where N is the number of cascaded hybrid inverters. The output voltages and spectral waveforms to confirm the validation of the control strategy using this approach of double Fourier transform will be discussed later.

$$V_{an}(t) = \begin{cases} 4V_{dc1}\cos(\omega_s t) + \dfrac{8V_{dc1}}{\pi} \displaystyle\sum_{m=8,16,24}^{\infty} \displaystyle\sum_{n=\pm1\pm3\pm5}^{\infty} \dfrac{1}{m} J_n \\[4mm] (m\dfrac{\pi}{2}M)\cos(m\omega_c t + n\omega_s t) \end{cases} \tag{36}$$

4. Proposed hybrid control method

The above section has illustrated in general the switching technque for one cell of the cascaded NPC/H-bridge model, because of the modularity of the model, two cells will be considered for modulatin and analysis in this section.For the two cells an improved strategy for realizing nine level output is proposed in this book chapter. The article uses the principle of decomposition where each leg is treated independently and gives a three level output (Naderi &. Rahmati, 2008).
Positive and negative legs are connected together back to back and they share the same voltage source V_{dc}. PD modulation is used for achieving three level output (Rodriguez et al., 2002). To achieve a five level PWM output two triangular carriers V_{cr1} and V_{cr2} in phase but vertically disposed and modulating wave phase shifted by π are used. The multilevel converter model is modulated using phase shifted PWM technique as illustrated in fig. 3

and 4 for the two NPC/H-Bridge cells. Finally a nine- level PWM output is achieved by using the same two carriers but phase shifted by π/4 and modulating wave phase shifted by π as shown in fig. 5. This is a simple control strategy that can be easily implemented in a digital signal processor. The switching states for one phase leg of a nine- level NPC/H-bridge inverter is shown in table 2, as can be seen there several redundant states which can be utilized in DC voltage balance, this is not within the scope of this paper.

The control strategy has two advantages as compared to multicarrier PWM approach (Holmes & McGrath, 2001). First for an N-level cascaded NPC/H-bridge PWM inverter, we can use a switching frequency of 4N times less to achieve the same spectrum as multicarrier approach. This has an advantage of reducing the switching losses, which is an important feature in high power application. Secondly the multicarrier PWM approach requires 8 carriers to achieve nine level output, but the proposed control strategy requires only one carrier phase shifted by (N-1)π/4 where N is the number of series connected NPC/H-Bridge inverter.

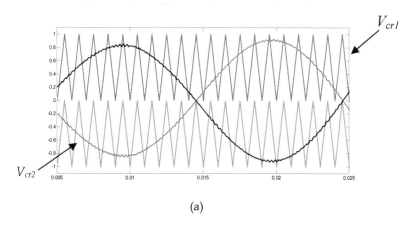

(a)

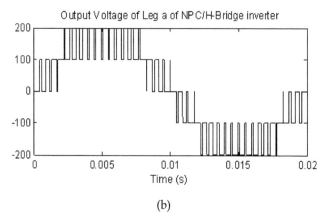

(b)

Fig. 3. (a) PWM scheme and (b) output voltage waveform for one cell of NPC/H-Bridge inverter

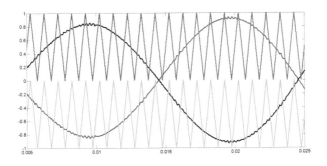

(a)

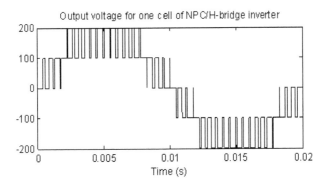

(b)

Fig. 4. (a) Phase shifted PWM scheme and (b) output voltage waveform for the second cell of cascaded NPC/H-Bridge inverter

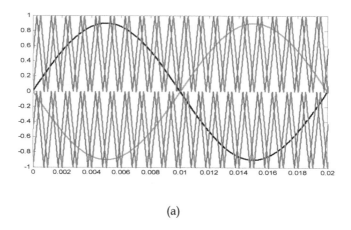

(a)

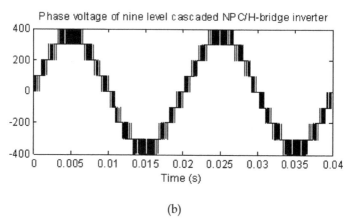

(b)

Fig. 5. (a) PWM scheme and (b) output voltage waveform for a nine level cascaded NPC/H-Bridge inverter

5. MATLAB simulation

Part of the Matlab simulation has already been carried out in section 4 to investigate the proposed phase shifted PWM control technique. In order verify that a nine- level output is achieved by cascading two NPC/H-Bridge PWM inverter and properly phase shifting the carrier and the modulating wave, a model as shown in fig. 6 was developed and simulated in MATLAB. The control strategy to minimize harmonics was designed and developed in MATLAB as shown in fig. 7 (wanjekeche et.al., 2009). It is assumed that the dc voltage input for each module is E = 100V. The inverter operates under the condition of $f_m=50HZ$, $m_f=20$ for a five level output and $m_a=0.9$. The device switching frequency is found from $f_{sw,dev}= m_f/2$ X $f_m=500HZ$

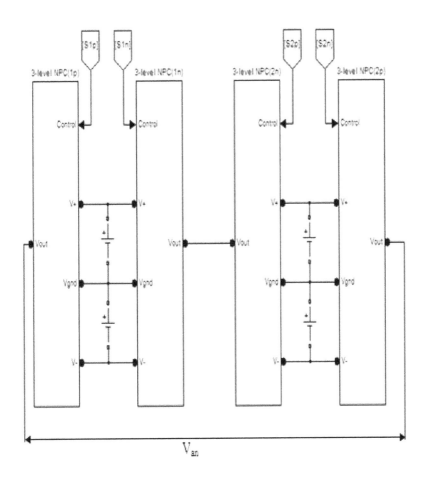

Fig. 6. Four legs of a nine-level cascaded NPC/H-bridge inverter

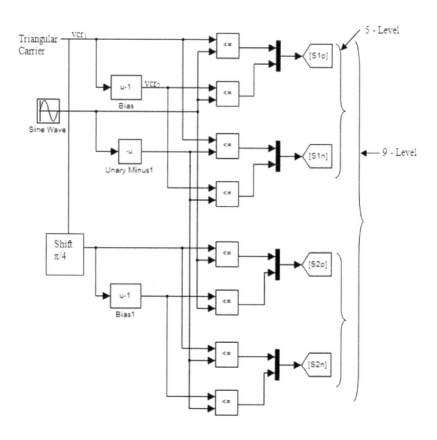

Fig. 7. Control strategy for a nine-level cascaded NPC/H-bridge inverter

5.1 Simulation results and discussion

Five- level inverter output are shown in figs.8, 9 and 10 for various switching frequency. Fig.8 shows the simulated waveform for the phase voltage V_{01} of the NPC/H-Bridge PWM inverter and its harmonic content. The waveform V_{01} is a five voltage levels, whose harmonics appear as sidebands centered around $2m_f$ and its multiples such as $4m_f$, $6m_f$. This simulation verifies analytical equation (34) which shows that the phase voltage does not contain harmonics lower than the 31st, but has odd order harmonics (i.e. $n=\pm1\pm3\pm5$) centered around $m=4, 8, 12$. Figs. 9 & 10 shows five- level NPC/H-Bridge inverter output for device inverter switching frequency of 1000HZ and 200HZ respectively.

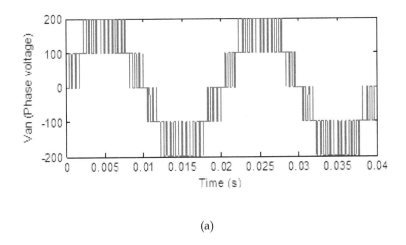

(a)

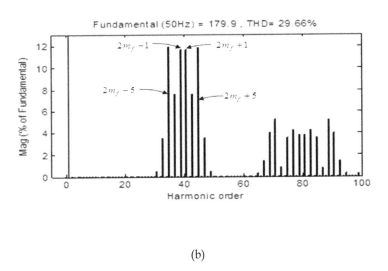

(b)

Fig. 8. (a) Waveform and (b) Spectrum for a five level NPC/H-Bridge inverter phase voltage (f_m=50HZ, $f_{sw,dev}$=500HZ, m_f=20, m_a=0.9)

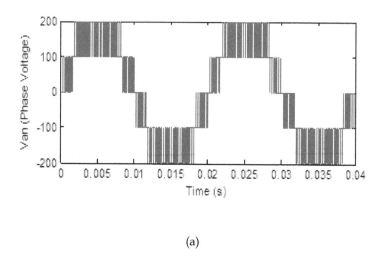

(a)

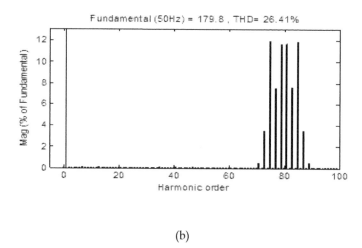

(b)

Fig. 9. (a) Waveform and (b) Spectrum for a five level NPC/H-Bridge inverter phase voltage
(f_m=50HZ, $f_{sw,dev}$=1000HZ, m_f=40, m_a=0.9)

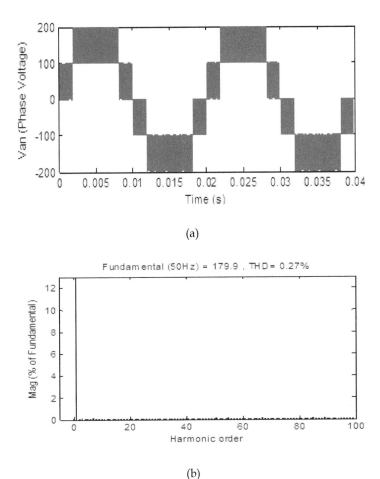

(a)

(b)

Fig. 10. (a) Waveform and (b) Spectrum for a five level NPC/H-Bridge inverter phase voltage (f_m=50HZ, $f_{sw,dev}$=2000HZ, m_f=80, m_a=0.9

Fig. 11 shows the waveform of the phase voltage of a nine level NPC/H-Bridge PWM inverter. It has sidebands around $4m_f$ and its multiples, this shows further suppression in harmonic content. This topology operates under the condition of f_m=50HZ, m_f=40 and m_a=0.9. The device switching frequency is found from $f_{sw,dev}$= $m_f/4$ X f_m=500HZ. This simulation verifies analytical equation (36) which shows that the phase voltage does not contain harmonics lower than the 67th, but has odd order harmonics (i.e. n=±1±3±5) centered around m=8, 16, 32. As can be seen from fig. 12, a switching frequency of 1KHZ which fits most of high power switching devices has a THD of 0.18% this makes the topology a perfect fit for most high power application such as utility interface power quality control and Medium Voltage drives.

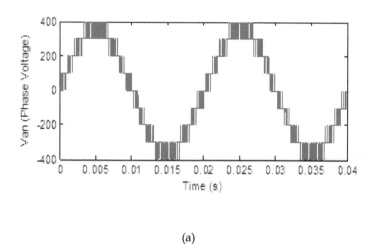

(a)

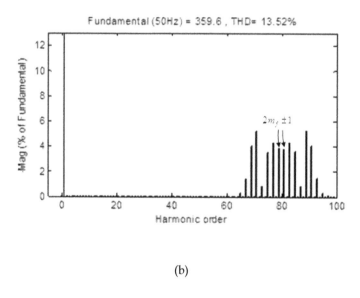

(b)

Fig. 11. (a) Waveform and (b) Spectrum for a nine- level cascaded NPC/H-Bridge inverter phase voltage (f_m=50HZ, $f_{sw,dev}$=500HZ, m_f=40, m_a=0.9)

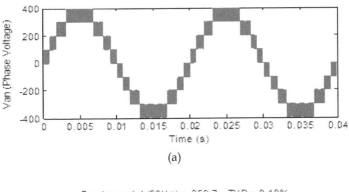

(a)

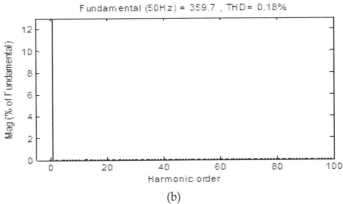

(b)

Fig. 12. (a) Waveform and (b) Spectrum for a nine- level cascaded NPC/H-Bridge inverter phase voltage (f_m=50HZ, $f_{sw,dev}$=1000HZ, m_f=80, m_a=0.9)

6. Comparison of the proposed control technique with conventional PWM multicarrier approach

As can be seen from fig. 1, to achieve the same voltage levels N for each phase, only $(N-1)/4$ separate dc sources are needed for one phase leg converter of the cascaded NPC/H-bridge model, whereas $(N-1)/2$ separate voltage voltages is need for cascaded H –bridge inverter. Thus for an n- cascaded NPC/H-bridge inverter, the number of separate DC sources S is given by:

$$S = \frac{N-1}{4} \tag{37}$$

Table 3 shows comparison on the number of components for various multilevel inverters, cascaded NPC/H-bridge inverter requires 16 switching devices just as the other topologies but used only two carriers for any level of voltage output. For comparison between the two cascaded inverters it is readily shown in table 4 that the NPC/H-bridge inverter has an advantage of realizing the same voltage level as cascaded H-bridge inverter with a half number of separate DC sources which is more expensive as compared to clamping diodes.

Topology / No. of Components	Diode clamped	Flying capacitor	Cascaded H- bridge	Cascaded NPC/H-bridge
Switching devices	16	16	16	16
Clamping diodes	56	·0	0	8
Flying capacitors	0	56	0	0
Carriers	8	8	4	2
Separate cells	0	0	4	2
Separate dc sources	1	0	4	2

Table 3. Component comaprison for different multilevel inverters for nine level voltage output

Topology / No. of Components	Cascaded H- bridge	Cascaded NPC/H-bridge
Switching devices	2N-1	2N-1
Clamping diodes	0	N-1
Flying capacitors	0	0
Carriers	(N-1)/2	2
Separate cells	(N-1)/2	(N-1)/4
Separate dc sources	(N-1)/2	(N-1)/4

Table 4. Component comaprison for different multilevel inverters for nine level voltage output

6.1 Comparison of the MATLAB simulation results of the two PWM control methods

To clearly investigate the superiority of the model under the proposed PWM control technique, Matlab simulation results was carried out on a cascaded NPC/H-bridge nine level inverter model under the conditions of f_m=50HZ, fc =1000Hz and m_a=0.9.

With the proposed Phase – shifted PWM technique, there is further harmonic suppression as shown in fig. 13 (b), as compared to conventional PWM Phase shifted approach. This is clearly illustrated in fig. 13 (a) where Phase Disposition and Phase shifted PWM modulation strategy is adopted (Jinghua & Zhengxi, 2008). This is beacuse with conventional PWM multicarrier approach, optimum harmonic cancellation is achieved by phase shifting each carrier by $(i-1)\pi/N$ (Holmes & Thomas, 2003). where i is the ith converter, N is the number of series – connected single the multicarrier PWM approach requires 8 carriers to achieve nine level output, but the proposed control strategy requires only one carrier phase shifted by $(N-1)\pi/4$ as stated in section 4.1(Wanjekeche et al., 2009).

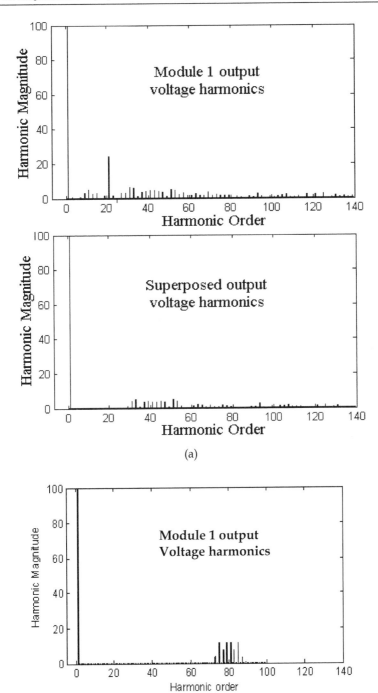

(a)

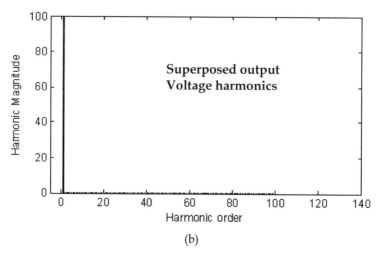

(b)

Fig. 13. Spectra voltage waveforms of NPC/H-bridge topology using (a) conventional multicarrier phase shifted PWM approach (b) proposed phase shifted PWM approach

7. Conclusion

In this chapter it has been demonstrates with proper modeling of the converter, the operating characteristic and the control technique to be applied on the model can be easily found. This can be used to develop standard model for cascaded NPC/H-bridge inverter which is currently not available.

The article has developed an improved topology that can be used to achieve a nine- level NPC/H-Bridge PWM inverter. It has been clearly shown that five level NPC/H-Bridge inverter that has been proposed by many researchers gives a higher THD which is not acceptable in most high and medium power application unless a filter is used. And since there is limited research on cascaded this important hybrid model, the chapter has developed a novel phase shifted PWM control technique that was tested on a two cell cascaded NPC/H-bridge model. In the proposed control technique it has been shown that by properly phase shifting both the modulating wave and the carrier, a nine- level voltage output can be achieved with a reduced harmonic content. With a THD of 0.18% without a filter, this makes the control strategy for a cascaded nine level NPC/H-bridge inverter a good option for medium and high power application such as utility interface and medium drives.

The simulation results obtained clearly verifies the analytical equations from double Fourier transform, showing that a nine- level output has multiples of eighth- order cross modulated harmonics. From the mathematical analysis it has been shown that cross modulated harmonics for a generalized m- level cascaded NPC/H-Bridge inverter is a multiple of $4N$ where N is the number of series connected NPC/H-Bridge inverter

And finally the superiority of the proposed phase shifted PWM control technique is validated by comparing its waveform spectra with that of the conventional phase shifted PWM technique and it was shown the inverter exhibits reduced harmonic content

8. References

Benslimane, T. (2007). Open Switch Faults Detection and Localization Algorithm for Three Phase Shunt Active Power Filter based on Two Level Voltage Source Inverter," *Electronics and Electrical Engineering Conference* 2(74), pp. 21- 24, ISSN 1392 -1215

Franquelo, L.G.; Rodriquez, J.; Leon, J.I.; Kouro, S.; Portillo, R. & Prats, M.A.M. (2008). The Age of Multilevel Converters Arrives, *IEEE Industrial Electronics Magazine*, pp. 28- 39, ISSN 1932-4529

Gupta, R.; Ghosh, A. & Joshi, A. (2008). Switching Characteristics of Cascaded Multilevel Inverter Controlled Systems, *IEEE Transactions on Industrial Electronics*, vol.55, no.3, pp. 1047- 1058, ISSN: 0278-0046

Holmes, D.G. & McGrath, B.P. (2001). Opportunities for harmonic cancellation with carrier-based PWM for two – level and multilevel cascaded inverters, *IEEE Transaction on Industrial Applications*, vol. 37, no. 2, pp.547 – 582, ISSN 0093-9994, August 2002

Kouro, S.; Rebolledo J. & Rodriquez J. (2005). Reduced switching frequency modulation algorithm for high power multilevel inverters, *IEEE Transaction on Industrial Electronics,* vol.54, no.5, pp. 2894- 2901, ISBN 0-7803-9033-4, January 2006

Lai, J. S. & Peng, F. Z. (1995). Multilevel Converters - A New Breed of Power Converters," *IEEE Transactions on Industry Applications*, vol. 32, no. 3, pp. 509-517, ISBN 0-7803-3008-0 August 2002

Peng, F. Z.; Lai, J. S.; McKeever, J. W. & VanCoevering, J. (1996). A Multilevel Voltage-Source Inverter with Separate DC Sources for Static Var Generation, *IEEE Transactions on Industry Applications*, vol. 32, no. 5, pp. 1130-1138, Aug. 2002. ISBN: 0-7803-3008-0

Rodriguez, J.; Lai, J. S. & Peng, F. Z. (1995). Multilevel Inverters: Survey of Topologies, Controls, and Applications, *IEEE Transactions on Industry Applications*, vol. 49, no. 4, pp. 724-738, ISSN 0278-0046

Sinha, G. & Lipo, T. A. (1996). A Four Level Rectifier-Inverter System for Drive Applications, *IEEE-IAS Conference Record*, pp. 980-987, ISBN 0-7803-3544-9, August 2002

Tolbert, L. M.; Peng, F. Z. & Habetler, T. (1999). Multilevel Converters for Large Electric drives, *IEEE Trans. Ind. Application*, vol.35, pp. 36-44, ISSN 0093-9994, August 2002

Manjrekar, M.D. & Lipo, T.A. (1988). A hybrid multilevel inverter topology for drive applications, *IEEE APEC*, pp. 523-529, ISBN 0-7803-4340-9, August 2002

Manjrekar, M.D. & Lipo, T.A. (1998). A generalized structure of multilevel power converter, *Proc. IEEE PEDS*, 62-67, ISBN 0-7803-4879-6

Manjrekar, M.D. & Lipo, T.A. (2000). Hybrid multilevel power conversion system: A competitive solution for higher power application, IEEE *Transaction on Industry Application*, Vol. 36, no. 3, pp. 834-841, ISSN 0093-9994, August 2002

Corzine, K. & Familiant, Y. (2002). A new cascaded multilevel H- bridge drive, *IEEE Trans on Power Electronics*, Vol. 17, no.1, pp. 125-131, ISSN 0885-8993

Lund, R. et. al., (1999). Control strategies for hybrid seven level inverter, *EPE Conference Proceedings*

Sneineh, A.A.; Wang, M. W. & Tian, K. (2006). A new topology for capacitor clamp cascaded multilevel converters, *IEEE –IPEMC*, pp. 1-5, ISSN 1-4244-0448-7, February 2009

Park J. et. al., (2003). A new single phase 5 – level PWM inverter employing a deadbeat control scheme, *IEEE Transaction on Power Electronics*, vol.18, no.3, pp. 831-843, ISSN 0885-8993

Zhang, L.; Watkins, S.J. & Shepherd, W. (2002). Analysis and control of multilevel flying capacitor inverter, *IEEE CIEP*, pp. 66-71, ISBN 0-7803-7640-4, August 2003

Ding, K. et. al., (2004). A novel hybrid diode clamp cascade multilevel converter for high power application, *IEEE Transaction on Industry Application, 39th IAS Annual Meeting*, 820-827, ISBN 0-7803-8486-5

Duarte, J.L.; Jullicher, P.J.M.; Offringa L.J.J. & Groningen, W.D.H. (1997). Stability analysis of multilevel converters with imbricated cells, *EPE Conference Proceedings*, pp. 168-174.

Rojas, R. & Ohnishi, T. (1997). PWM control method with reduced of total capacitance required in a three- level inverter, *COBEP Conference Proceedings*, pp. 103-108

Wu, C.M.; Lau W.H. & Chung, H. (1999). A five-level neutral-point-clamped H-bridge PWM inverter with superior harmonics suppression: A theoretical analysis, *ISACS '99, proceedings of the 1999 IEEE international symposium*, vol. 5, pp.198-201

Cheng, Z. & Wu, B. (2007). A novel switching sequence design for five-Level NPC/H-Bridge inverters with improved output voltage spectrum and minimized device switching frequency, *IEEE Transactions on Power Electronics*, vol. 22 no.6, 2138 – 2145, ISSN 0885-8993

Naderi, R. & Rahmati, A. (2008). Phase shifted carrier PWM technique for general cascade inverters, *IEEE Transactions on power electronics*, vol. 23, no.3, pp.1256-1269, ISSN 0885-8993

Jinghua, Z. & Zhengxi, L. (2008). Research on hybrid modulation strategies based on general hybrid topology of multilevel inverter, *International symposium on power electronics and electric drives, automation and motion (SPEEDAM)*, pp. 784 – 788, ISBN 978-1-4244-1663-9

Holmes, D.G. & Thomas, A.L. (2003). *Pulse Width Modulation for Power Converters –principles and practices*, IEEE press series, A John Wiley & Sons inc. publication, ISBN: 978-0-471-20814-3, 445 Hoes Lane, Piscataway NJ 0885

Wanjekeche, T. Jimoh, A.A. & Nicolae, D.V. (2009). A Novel Multilevel 9- level inverter based on 3 – level NPC/H-Bridge topology for Photovoltaic application" *international review of electrical engineering*, Vol. 4, No.5, ISSN 1827- 6679

Wanjekeche, T. Nicolae, D.V. & Jimoh, A.A. (2009). A Cascaded NPC/H-bridge inverter with simplified control strategy and minimum component count, *IEEE – Africon*, pp. 1-6, ISBN 978-1-4244-3918-8

15

A Fuzzy Finite Element Method Programmed in MATLAB for the Analysis of Uncertain Control Systems of Structures

Angel L. Morales[1], Jem A. Rongong[2] and Neil D. Sims[2]
[1]*Universidad de Castilla - La Mancha*
[2]*The University of Sheffield*
[1]*Spain*
[2]*United Kingdom*

1. Introduction

Vibration is an important aspect of many engineering systems. In most cases, such vibration is undesirable and requires attenuation or control, which explains the huge quantity of vibration control techniques that can be found in the literature. Nevertheless, sometimes all this knowledge is not enough to guarantee the success in this purpose. Model inaccuracies or parameter uncertainty are unavoidable in all relevant practical application and not only can they degrade the performance of an otherwise well-designed control system, but they may also lead to instability and even structural failure.

For these reasons, robustness is of crucial importance in control-system design. Although always being appreciated, it was not until late 1970s when a theory capable to explicitly handle the robustness issue in feedback design was developed: the H_∞ optimal control theory (Zames, 1981; Zames & Francis, 1983). This optimization approach is well developed and we can even find a full *Robust Control Toolbox* in MATLAB which, in collaboration with the *Control System Toolbox*, let us identify worst-case scenarios and generate optimal controllers so that the stability and good performance of the plant is ensured (Gu et al., 2005).

Obviously, the H_∞ optimal control theory shows some disadvantages, like the high level of mathematical understanding needed to apply them successfully and the fact that it sometimes leads to potentially very conservative results (Gu et al., 2005). Indeed, even when a solution via H_∞ techniques is eventually found, the process may have been too expensive in terms of designer's time and the sensitivity to the uncertainty sources is not analyzed. These motivations make us think that a straightforward possibilistic methodology for simulating and analyzing the uncertainty propagation in control system would be a very valuable, complementary and time saving tool.

This work focuses on how MATLAB can supply suitable tools in order to manage uncertainty propagation in finite element models of structures from the point of view of fuzzy arithmetic. More specifically, we will describe a methodology fully programmed in MATLAB in order to deal with uncertain control systems of vibrating structures and we will illustrate the application of this approach to a case study.

In order to develop this work we need to integrate two different problems: the calculation of the dynamic response of a vibrating structure via finite element models and the study of the uncertainty propagation via fuzzy arithmetic. Both problems can be solved using MATLAB code obtaining very good results in terms of accuracy and computational cost.

The motivation behind this work is threefold: firstly, it is meant to show how MATLAB provides suitable functions and specialized toolboxes in order to study the static or dynamic response of a controlled structure via finite elements and control theory; secondly, it demonstrates the suitability of MATLAB to solve uncertainty propagation problems through fuzzy arithmetic minimizing the computational cost; and thirdly, it illustrates the application of a Fuzzy Finite Element procedure, which integrates these two tools, with a specific case study.

The chapter is organized in the following way: Section 1 has summarized the aims and concerns of the chapter; Section 2 deals with dynamic analysis of structures with active damping by means of the *OpenFEM Toolbox* and the *Control System Toolbox* of MATLAB; Section 3 discusses the different types of uncertainty and how they could be analyzed using fuzzy arithmetic programmed in MATLAB; Section 4 describes a Fuzzy Finite Element procedure in MATLAB in order to study the propagation of uncertain parameters in control systems of structures; Section 5 shows a case study in which the Fuzzy Finite Element procedure is tested; Section 6 deals with the main conclusions of this work; and finally the acknowledgements and references included through the text are included.

2. Dynamic analysis and control of structures

2.1 Finite Element analysis and the OpenFEM Toolbox

The study of the dynamic behaviour of a structure can be carried out by means of finite element analysis. Among all the different possibilities to solve finite elements problems, in this chapter we focus on the use of a specific toolbox of MATLAB: the *OpenFEM Toolbox* (Balmes et al., 2009).

It is an open-source toolbox for finite element analysis within the matrix computing environment MATLAB. The software is developed in collaboration between Macs and the SDTools Company and it is distributed under a GNU Lesser General Public License, that is, a free software license which also allows the user to make modifications in the code. Performing finite element analysis within a matrix computing environment is of considerable interest, in particular as regards the ease of new developments, integration of external software, portability, post-processing, etc. This relatively young software is already quite successful in the finite element community as it is proven by the about 300 downloads per month (OpenFEM, 2011).

Though the toolbox architecture includes graphical user interfaces for visualization, analysis and animation of results, the powerful of this toolbox does not lie in this fact but in the standard and advanced methods which are implemented. Moreover, the provided functions are open and can be easily extended to suit particular needs of the user (Balmes et al., 2009), as it is our case.

Let us consider a vibrating structure. The first step in order to carry out its finite element analysis consists in discretizing the structure. The mesh nodes, elements which join the nodes, material properties, element properties and any additional information such as boundary conditions, loads, etc., are stored in a *struct* class variable which defines the model of the multi degree of freedom vibrating structure which is governed by the next set of equations of motion

$$M\ddot{x} + C\dot{x} + Kx = f \tag{1}$$

where M, K and C are the mass, the stiffness and the damping matrices, respectively, x the vector of displacements of all the degrees of freedom of the structure and f a general vector of forces. Matrices M and K arise from the finite element analysis of the structure whereas C is usually obtained under the hypothesis of Rayleigh damping.

Both in the state space approach and in the transfer function approach, working with physical coordinates is not practical because of the usually high number of degrees of freedom. Thus, a change of variables into modal coordinates is suggested. In addition, in this way the problem can be restricted to the bandwidth of interest, neglecting the high frequency dynamics of the system. After the computation of modes via finite element analysis one obtains the natural frequencies of the modes and the matrix of the mode shapes Φ. After performing the change of variables $x = \Phi z$, where z is the vector of modal coordinates and Φ is normalized in such a way that the modal mass matrix is the identity matrix, the governing equations in modal coordinates read

$$\ddot{z} + 2\zeta\Omega\dot{z} + \Omega^2 z = \Phi^T f \qquad (2)$$

where Ω and ζ define the diagonal matrices of natural frequencies and damping factors.

Finally, the software also provides several commands related to the definition of the actuators and sensors or, strictly speaking, the input force influence vector L_u and the sensor influence vector L_y, both of them required for the definition of either the transfer function or the state space matrices.

The finite element models which are obtained with this toolbox can be used to solve both static and dynamic problems, the results of which being ready to be plotted or post-processed under any other MATLAB toolbox. In this work, we blended these commands which those corresponding to the *Control System Toolbox*.

2.2 Active damping and the Control System Toolbox

The *Control System Toolbox* provides a collection of matrix-based functions, usually expressed as M-files, for the topic of control engineering. The control systems may be modelled as transfer functions, zero-pole-gain or even using the state space approach, which allows the designer to apply classic techniques as well as modern techniques. However, it is not our purpose to study thoroughly this topic, so we will concentrate on briefly reviewing, as an example, one of the most common active control techniques of structures (Preumont, 2002): active damping with collocated piezoelectric pairs via Positive Position Feedback, which, in the end, will be the case study discussed in Section 5.

The transfer function of the multi degree of freedom vibrating structure obtained via modal expansion reads

$$G(\omega) = \frac{X(\omega)}{F(\omega)} = \sum_{n=1}^{\infty} \frac{\Phi_n \Phi_n^T}{\omega_n^2 + 2j\omega\zeta_n\omega_n - \omega^2} \qquad (3)$$

where Φ_n, ω_n and ζ_n are the mode shape, the natural frequency and the damping ratio for the nth mode of vibration, respectively. The same model based upon the first N modes of vibration leads to the expression

$$\hat{G}(\omega) \approx \sum_{n=1}^{N} \frac{\Phi_n \Phi_n^T}{\omega_n^2 + 2j\omega\zeta_n\omega_n - \omega^2} \qquad (4)$$

where the residual term due to the contributions of the truncated nodes has been neglected. Combining the equations for the surface-bonded actuator and sensor (Dosch et al., 1992; Sims et al., 2005) and Equation 4 which governs the structural dynamics, we obtain the frequency response function between the voltage V_a applied to the actuator and the voltage V_s at the output of the charge amplifier of the sensor

$$H(\omega) = \frac{V_s(\omega)}{V_a(\omega)} = k_a k_s \sum_{n=1}^{N} \frac{L_u^T \Phi_n \Phi_n^T L_y}{\omega_n^2 + 2j\omega \zeta_n \omega_n - \omega^2} \tag{5}$$

where k_s and k_a are the sensor gain and the actuator gain, respectively.

As far as the Positive Position Feedback scheme is concerned, it is appropriate for a structure equipped with strain actuators and sensors (Preumont, 2002). The objective of a Positive Position Feedback controller is to use a second order filter to improve the roll-off of the control system, allowing high frequency gain stabilization. The implementation of this control system is given by the following equations

$$\begin{aligned}
M\ddot{x} + C\dot{x} + Kx &= L_u u \\
y &= L_u^T x \\
\ddot{v} + \beta_f \dot{v} + \Omega_f^2 v &= y \\
u &= -Gv
\end{aligned} \tag{6}$$

where u is the control force acting on the structure through the influence vector L_u, y is the difference of slope between the ends of the sensor, $G = \text{diag}(g_i)$ is the positive gain matrix, and v is the output of the second order filter defined by the matrices $\beta_f = \text{diag}(2\zeta_f \omega_f)$ and $\Omega_f^2 = \text{diag}(\omega_f^2)$. Note that the fact that the same localization vector (L_u) rules the actuator and sensors is a consequence of collocation.

The transfer function of the controller (a second order low pass filter) can be written as follows

$$gD(w) = g \frac{\omega_f^2}{\omega_f^2 + 2j\omega \zeta_f \omega_f - \omega^2} \tag{7}$$

This compensator has both advantages and drawbacks. On the one hand, the open-loop transfer function has a roll-off of -40dB/decade, larger in comparison to Direct Velocity Feedback (-20dB/decade), which may decrease the risk of destabilizing high frequency dynamics. On the other hand, there is a stability limit which is reached when the open-loop static gain is equal to 1, this fact being independent of the damping (Preumont, 2002).

Once the open loop transfer functions of the plant and the regulator are defined, they can be used in the *Control System Toolbox* as *transfer function* class variables. Then, the desired active damping can be obtained by selecting the proper gain g of the regulator. In order to do this, several techniques can be used such as Bode Diagram Design, Root Locus Design, Nichols Plot design, etc.

Finally, the *Control System Toolbox* also provides valuable functions in order to analyze the stability and performance in terms of stability margins, time responses or the position of the closed loop poles and zeros in the pole-zero map. They will be used in our Fuzzy Finite Element methodology as fuzzy outputs in order to analyze the behaviour of the uncertain control system.

3. Uncertainty and fuzzy arithmetic

In the literature, the use of the term uncertainty is slightly ambiguous. In order to establish the nomenclature for the ensuing description, the reader is referred to the terminology proposed in (Oberkampf et al., 2004).

On the one hand, we will use the term aleatory uncertainty to describe the inherent variation associated with the physical system or the environment under consideration. These sources of uncertainty can be represented as randomly distributed quantities, usually in terms of probability distribution functions. Typical examples of this kind of uncertainty are manufacturing tolerances, environmental effects, properties of non-uniform materials or any other identifiable disturbances. On the other hand, epistemic uncertainty derives from some level of ignorance of the system or the environment in any activity of the modelling process. In this case, its definition stresses the lack of knowledge as the origin of this uncertainty. Thus, unlike aleatory uncertainty, a mathematical representation of epistemic uncertainty has proven to be much more of a challenge since it is subjective and based on some expert opinion to a certain extent. Typical examples of epistemic uncertainties are some models for boundary conditions, simplified models for joints, models for material damping or unpredictable model changes due to ageing, loading, etcetera.

Uncertainty propagation in dynamic systems has been a very frequent topic in the literature, which has been tackled from two different points of view (De Gersem et al., 2005): *probabilistic* and *possibilistic* approaches. Probabilistic approaches, such as the well-known Monte Carlo Simulation method, investigate the influence of aleatory uncertainties, this method being particularly suitable for finite element models with certain uncertainties. Possibilistic approaches are complementary to probabilistic approaches, since not only are they able to describe problems of aleatory uncertainties to a certain extent, yet without statistical interpretation, but they can also handle problems where incomplete information (epistemic uncertainty) is available. We consider that computationally expensive "brute-force" probabilistic methods are not worthwhile in most cases, where an intuitive worst-case scenario provides enough information. Thus, a possibilistic method in terms of fuzzy arithmetic will be the tool that we develop and propose in order to simulate and analyze uncertainty propagation in control systems.

Fuzzy arithmetic has been used by various researchers as a technique for propagating uncertainty or variability through complex engineering models. The origins of this approach can be found in the theory of Fuzzy Sets (Zadeh, 1965). In contrast to the classical set theory, the elements of a fuzzy set are assigned a degree of membership to the set, which is referred to as the membership level μ. The core of the set is defined as the subset of elements for which $\mu = 1$, whilst the support is the subset for which $\mu > 0$. A fuzzy number is a fuzzy set that is convex and normal, and whose membership function is piecewise continuous.

The issue of performing mathematical operations on fuzzy numbers instead of on conventional numbers can be a challenge rather than a trivial problem. In fact, the Fuzzy Arithmetic processes are usually performed by decomposing the fuzzy numbers into a number of intervals given by the α-cuts at the α-levels μ_i, $(i = 0, 1, \ldots, m)$ with

$$\mu_i = \frac{i}{m} \tag{8}$$

Then, a interval analysis via interval arithmetic can be carried out separately to each membership level μ_i.

For monotonic problems this process may be trivial, since the maxima or minima of the inputs will lead to the maxima or minima for the output. Conversely, for non-monotonic problems this is no longer the case (Sims et al., 2010). In addition, the Standard Fuzzy Arithmetic may become problematic and lead to different results for the same problem depending on the form in which the solution procedure is applied, as can be seen in the examples gathered in (Hanss, 2002). In short, the application of Standard Fuzzy Arithmetic usually leads to overestimate results to a lesser or greater extent and alternative methods must be employed.

The Transformation Method, introduced in (Hanss, 2002), represents a special implementation of Fuzzy Arithmetic that avoids the undesired overestimation which usually arises when Fuzzy Arithmetic is reduced to interval computation. A later efficient implementation of this method was carried out in (Klimke, 2003), taking advantage of the matrix computing environment of MATLAB and providing enhanced features such as fast processing of discretized fuzzy numbers through multi-dimensional arrays, elimination of recurring permutations, automatic decomposition of models, treatment of single occurrences of variables through interval arithmetic and a monotonicity test based on automatic differentiation. Nevertheless, we have to note that the fuzzy parameters are restricted to convex fuzzy numbers when using the Transformation Method.

Specially relevant for an efficient implementation of the Transformation Method is the elimination of recurring permutations. The decomposition scheme of this method sometimes produces recurring points which in the end generate recurring permutations. By removing these recurring permutations from the evaluation procedure one could save a very valuable computation time. Indeed, we could even try to reuse as many points for different α-cuts as possible by selecting only inner points which have already occurred in a higher-level α-cut. For symmetric triangular membership functions, the obtained discretization is identical to the original formulation, but for other arbitrarily shaped membership functions, the distribution of the points is less regular, but of similar density (see Figure 1). However, for the same number of α-cuts, the less regular distribution of the inner points results in less accurate results compared to the original formulation.

The number of permutations r by using this efficient implementation of the Transformation Method is given by the following equation

$$r = m^n + (m+1)^n \tag{9}$$

where $m + 1$ is the number of α-cuts and n is the number of fuzzy parameters. As proven in (Klimke, 2003), the new scheme provides a valuable improvement in terms of computational cost unless the number of α-cuts is too large compared to the number of fuzzy inputs. If that was the case, one could disregard the removing of recurring permutations in favour of more accurate results.

4. Fuzzy Finite Element procedure in MATLAB

The fuzzy theory has led to the development of Fuzzy Finite Element methods as that described in (De Gersem et al., 2005; De Munck et al., 2008; Moens & Vandepitte, 2005) for analyzing the propagation of uncertainties in the Frequency Response Functions of a dynamic system. When using this methodology, the uncertainties in the model parameters can be taken into account by fuzzy numbers with their shape obtained from experimental data or assumed from expert knowledge. Then, the numerical procedure for the implementation of these Fuzzy Finite Element methods consists of a sequence of Interval Finite Element procedures based on a general strategy for computing the fuzzy result from operations on fuzzy operands, i.e. the α-sublevel or α-cuts technique.

Figure 1 clarifies this procedure. This technique subdivides the membership range into a number of α-cuts. At each level, the intersection with the membership function of the input uncertainties results in an interval. Based on these input intervals for all uncertain parameters, an interval analysis can be performed obtaining the interval of the output variables at the considered α-cut. Strictly speaking, the interval analysis for a specific α-cut consists in running all the finite elements calculations corresponding to all the possible permutations among input variables at said level and choosing the lower and upper bound of the required output

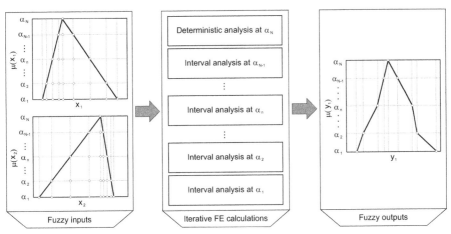

Fig. 1. Scheme of the numerical procedure to perform a Fuzzy Finite Element analysis using four α-cuts.

variables. Note that if $\mu = 1$, the interval analysis degenerates into the deterministic analysis. Finally, the membership functions of the required output variables are assembled from the interval results at all sublevels.

The Fuzzy Finite Element analysis is based on the results of a previous deterministic design of the control system. The control engineer must set the control parameters and gains of the regulator in order to accomplish all the features required for the active damping in terms of both stability and performance. After this process, which is usually easier and faster than other complex control techniques such as those derived from H_∞ control, the Fuzzy Finite Element analysis will simulate the behaviour of the control system when some parameters are considered uncertain. This method is not a robust designing technique but a possibilistic method which tests whether the deterministic design is robust enough to keep the closed loop behaviour of the structure inside the allowable bounds for its stability and performance features.

The set of calculations which are carried out at each permutation of input values is compound of these steps:

Step 1: Finite Element calculations via the *OpenFEM Toolbox*

Step 2: Closed loop simulation of the control system via the *Control System Toolbox*

Step 3: Analysis of stability and performance via fuzzy variables such as stability margins or active damping.

The method chosen for carrying out the interval fuzzy arithmetics was the efficient implementation of the Transformation Method proposed in (Klimke, 2003). Nevertheless, we have included some modifications which will be introduced in the ensuing.

The first modification lies in the fact that Klimke's MATLAB script is made under the assumption that the fuzzy output is the result of evaluating an analytical expression. In our case, we need to replace the evaluation of such analytical function (*inline* class) with a list of MATLAB commands which develops the aforementioned steps. This also allows us to include the possibility of achieving several fuzzy outputs instead of only one. The second modification was not necessary but it endows the method with enhance capabilities. It consists on using *cell* class arrays instead of *double* class arrays to define the fuzzy outputs, so an extra field may be included where information about each iteration is stored (for instance, the exact value of the fuzzy inputs at each permutation). Figures 2 and 3 show the MATLAB implementation of the efficient Transformation Method after modifying the Klimke's implementation. Note that the MATLAB implementation of the external function in Figure 3 only shows an example corresponding to the evaluation of a test function. In our case, this function would contain all the required commands which carry out the three foregoing calculating steps.

In order to prove the validity of our modified version of the Klimke's Transformation Method, a comparative fuzzy analysis was run. We took as a reference one example found in (Klimke, 2003) where the test function $f(x_1, x_2) = \cos(\pi x_1)x_2$ is subjected to the triangular fuzzy inputs

```
function [fzr]=gtrmrecur_modif(varargin)
% Angel L. Morales, 2011.
% FZR=GTRMRECUR_MODIF(FZ1,FZ2,...,FZN) calls the general transformation
% method implemented by Klimke in 2003 with extended capabilities.
% The function allows N fuzzy numbers in alpha-cut representation.
% An accompanying function called GTRMRECUR_EXTERNAL_FCN is required.
fzin=varargin;
n = nargin;
m = size(fzin{1},1) - 1;
indices.subs = {};
indices.type = '()';
fzr = cell(m+1,2);
for k = 1:2
t = (floor((m+2-k)/2)+rem(m+2-k,2))*2-2+k;
for i = 1:n
c = reshape(fzin{i}(end+1-k:-2:1,:)',t+2-k,1);
c = c(3-k:end);
repvec = t*ones(1,n);
repvec(i) = 1;
x{i} = repmat(shiftdim(c,1-i),repvec);
end
s = k;
z_cell_matrix=gtrmrecur_external_fcn(x);
for j = m+2-k:-2:1
indices.subs(1:n) = {1:s};
w = reshape(subsref(z_cell_matrix,indices),s^n,1);
wc = zeros(size(w));
for cont=1:length(wc) wc(cont)=w{cont}{2}; end;
[none,pos_min]=min(wc); fzr{j,1} = w{pos_min};
[none,pos_max]=max(wc); fzr{j,2} = w{pos_max};
s = s + 2;
end
end
for j = m:-1:1
if fzr{j+1,1}{2}>=fzr{j,1}{2}; fzr{j,1}=fzr{j,1}; else fzr{j,1}=fzr{j+1,1}; end
if fzr{j+1,2}{2}>=fzr{j,2}{2}; fzr{j,2}=fzr{j+1,2}; else fzr{j,2}=fzr{j,2}; end
end
```

Fig. 2. MATLAB implementation of the efficient Transformation Method after modifying Klimke's script.

```
function [z_cell_matrix]=gtrmrecur_external_fcn(x)
% Angel L. Morales, 2011.
% Z_CELL_MATRIX=GTRMRECUR_EXTERNAL_FCN(FZ1,FZ2,...,FZN) calls the function
% which executes the commands in order to obtain the fuzzy output.
% It is called during the execution of FZR=GTRMRECUR_MODIF(FZ1,FZ2,...,FZN)
func = inline('cos(pi.*x1).*x2');
x_vector=cell(size(x));
for cont=1:length(x)
    x_vector{cont} = reshape(x{cont},numel(x{cont}),1);
end
iterations=length(x_vector{1});
z_cell=cell(1,2); z_cell_array=cell(1,iterations);
for iteration=1:iterations
    x1=double(x_vector{1}(iteration));
    x2=double(x_vector{2}(iteration));
    z_cell{1}=[x1 x2];
    z_cell{2}=feval(func,x_vector{1}(iteration),x_vector{2}(iteration));
    z_cell_array{iteration}=z_cell;
end
z_cell_matrix=reshape(z_cell_array,size(x{1}));
```

Fig. 3. Example of the MATLAB function called by the modified Transformation Method which contains the commands for the obtention of the fuzzy output

$\tilde{p}_1 = \langle 2.5, 2.5, 2.5 \rangle_{\text{TFN}}$ and $\tilde{p}_2 = \langle 3, 2, 2 \rangle_{\text{TFN}}$, in accordance to the nomenclature proposed in (Dubois & Prade, 1980). The fuzzy output obtained with the modified version clearly matched the results obtained with the original version. Nevertheless, an unavoidable loss of computational efficiency arose.

Our modified version results more time-consuming because of the different way in which the simulated function is handled, as it can be seen in Table 1. In the original version, the *inline* class analytical expression can be executed only once with the array containing all the required permutations of fuzzy inputs at a time. In the modified version, the expression is evaluated separately at each permutation as it would be the case when a control system is simulated with several MATLAB commands. The elapsed time during these operations is called t_{fcn}. As far as the obtention of the fuzzy output as a *cell* array instead of as a *double* array, this fact does not add any noticeable increase of computational cost but it does lead to heavier variables and higher memory requirements. The elapsed time during these operations is called t_{max}. In all the cases, the loss of efficiency is acceptable with regard to the benefits they provide, specially considering that the elapsed time in any finite element simulation may be on the order of seconds and it has much more restrictive memory requirements.

5. A case study of uncertainty propagation

Consider an aluminium plate in free conditions, the dimensions and material properties of which are detailed in Table 2. The finite element model of this plate was carried out by means of the *OpenFEM Toolbox* of MATLAB (Balmes et al., 2009). After defining the mesh, the matrices of mass (M) and stiffness (K) which define the undamped model were obtained. The eigenvalue problem can then be solved, the natural frequencies and mode shapes being shown in Figure 4. The damping matrix (C) is constructed considering a structural damping of $\xi_i = 0.6\%$ in all the modes.

The piezoelectric actuator and sensor, the properties of which are detailed in Table 3, are collocated in the centre of the plate. As described in (Dosch et al., 1992; Sims et al., 2005), the piezoelectric actuator and sensor may be modelled as a beam which provides bending moments at its ends and measures a voltage proportional to the difference of slope of its ends. Due to collocation, the localization vectors of actuator (L_u) and sensor (L_y) are identical and equal to

$$L_u^T = L_y^T = (0, \ldots, -1, 0, \ldots, 1, 0, \ldots, 0) \tag{10}$$

	Original	Modified
t_{tot} (s)	0.047	0.344
t_{tot} (%)	100.00	100.00
t_{fcn} (s)	0.016	0.313
t_{fcn} (%)	34.04	90.99
t_{max} (s)	0.000	0.000
t_{max} (%)	0.000	0.000
t_{oth} (s)	0.031	0.031
t_{oth} (%)	65.96	9.01
Weight (bytes)	336	8568

Table 1. Efficiency comparison between the original and the modified Klimke's implementation. The total time (t_{tot}), the time for evaluating the analytical expression (t_{fcn}), the time for calculating the maxima and minima of the output fuzzy number (t_{max}) and the time for other calculations (t_{oth}) are shown. The weight means the size in bytes of the output fuzzy variable.

Width (*mm*)	300.00
Length (*mm*)	500.00
Thickness (*mm*)	3.00
Young's modulus (GPa)	72.00
Poisson's coefficient	0.30
Density (kg/m^3)	2700.00
Structural damping (%)	0.60

Table 2. Geometries and material properties of the plate.

Width (*mm*)	40
Length (*mm*)	100
Thickness (*mm*)	0.250
d_{33} (m/V)	$0.30 \cdot 10^{-9}$
d_{31} (m/V)	$-0.15 \cdot 10^{-9}$
e_{31} (N/Vm)	-7.5
k_{33}	0.7
Young's modulus (GPa)	50
Maximum traction (MPa)	80
Maximum compression (MPa)	600
Maximum electric Field (V/mm)	2000
Density (kg/m^3)	7600
Maximum strain	Brittle
Maximum temperature (C)	80°C - 150°C

Table 3. Geometries and material properties of the piezoelectric (Preumont, 2002).

where the non-zero values are placed in the position corresponding to the active rotational degree of freedom of the nodes in which the piezoelectric is located.

As described in the Section 2.2, a Positive Position Feedback control strategy designed with the *Control System Toolbox* of MATLAB is to be used. Figure 5 presents the root locus of the control system after tuning the second order filter parameters (ξ_f and ω_f) so that the first flexible mode of vibration become actively damped. After the tuning process ($\xi_f = 0.9$ and $\omega_f = 900$ rad/s), the next step consists of selecting the control gain which most approaches

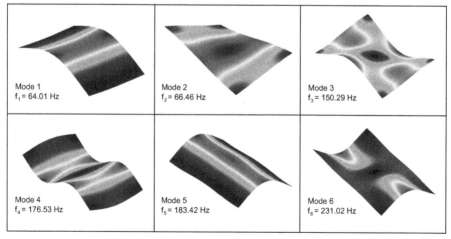

Mode 1
f_1 = 64.01 Hz

Mode 2
f_2 = 66.46 Hz

Mode 3
f_3 = 150.29 Hz

Mode 4
f_4 = 176.53 Hz

Mode 5
f_5 = 183.42 Hz

Mode 6
f_6 = 231.02 Hz

Fig. 4. Mode shapes and natural frequencies for the plate in free conditions.

the maximum damping of the first vibration mode ($\xi_{1,max}$). In this particular case, a gain of $g = 0.200$ entails a selected damping coefficient of $\xi_{1,sel} = 88.30\%$. Figure 5 also shows the characteristic stability limit of the Positive Position Feedback control systems and the fact that only the first and the fifth modal shapes seem to be controllable in the view of the wide loops going from the poles to the zeros (Preumont, 2002).

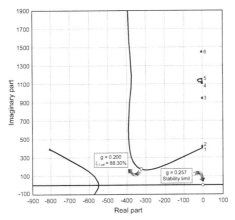

Fig. 5. Root locus of the control system after tuning the second order filter parameters to the first flexible mode of vibration ($\xi_f = 0.9$ and $\omega_f = 900$ rad/s).

In the proposed case study the collocated pair of actuator and sensor are subjected to uncertainty. More precisely, the position of the centre of both the actuator and sensor are considered to be uncertain parameters. Additionally, another source of uncertainty corresponding to the structural damping of the plate is included as this is known to be uncertain in practice. Thus, we have a total of five different fuzzy numbers: $\tilde{x}_a$ (position "x" of the centre of the actuator), $\tilde{y}_a$ (position "y" of the centre of the actuator), $\tilde{x}_s$ (position "x" of the centre of the sensor), $\tilde{y}_s$ (position "y" of the centre of the sensor) and $\tilde{\xi}$ (structural damping). The membership functions of these fuzzy parameters, assuming that they are both symmetric and triangular, can be seen in Figure 6.

After applying the Fuzzy Finite Element algorithm described in Section 4 one can obtain several fuzzy outputs which describe the stability and performance of the control system. In fact, it is possible to choose those variables which better fit the effects which one is interested in. In this particular case, the following are calculated:

$\tilde{G}$ Gain margin.

$\tilde{P}$ Phase margin.

$\tilde{\xi}_{1,max}$ Maximum damping coefficient of the first mode.

$\tilde{\xi}_{1,sel}$ Selected damping coefficient of the first mode.

The gain margin $\tilde{G}$ is the increase in the system gain when the phase is -180 that will result in a marginally stable system with intersection of the $-1 + j0$ point on the Nyquist diagram. The phase margin $\tilde{P}$ is the amount phase shift of the system at unity magnitude that will result in a marginally stable system with intersection of the $-1 + j0$ point on the Nyquist diagram. The maximum damping coefficient $\tilde{\xi}_{1,max}$ is the highest damping achievable in the first mode loop independently of the selected gain, whilst the selected damping coefficient $\tilde{\xi}_{1,sel}$ is the

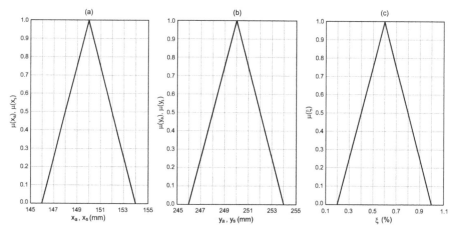

Fig. 6. Membership functions of the input fuzzy numbers: (a) coordinates of the centre of the actuator ($\tilde{x}_a$ and $\tilde{x}_s$), (b) coordinates of the centre of the sensor ($\tilde{y}_a$ and $\tilde{y}_s$) and (c) structural damping of the plate ($\tilde{\zeta}$).

damping that the control systems provides at the value of gain selected in the deterministic case. Clearly, the gain and phase margins can be used to quantify controller stability, whilst the damping ratios serve to quantify performance and reliability.

The membership functions of these variables are shown in Figure 7. We observe that the uncertainty considered may lead to a both better and worse behaviour of the control system in comparison to the considered deterministic situation.

Another possibility for obtaining a global view of the whole control system lies in plotting its root locus for different α-sublevels or α-cuts. In particular, we show in Figure 8 the root locus for two different values of the membership. Although the fourth mode has not been

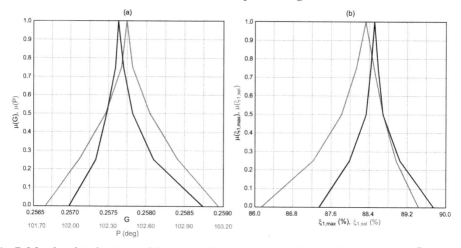

Fig. 7. Membership function of the output fuzzy numbers: (a) stability indicators ($\tilde{G}$ in black color and $\tilde{P}$ in gray color) and (b) performance indicators ($\tilde{\zeta}_{1,max}$ in black color and $\tilde{\zeta}_{1,sel}$ in gray color).

specifically analyzed via fuzzy variables, we can note that its zero crosses the imaginary axis and becomes unstable for some values of the gain. Note that zeros are essentially related to mode shapes of the structure, which tend to be more sensitive to the parameter uncertainty than the natural frequencies. This fact warns us that a higher gain level may lead to instability of the fourth mode when actively damping the first, which can be detected easily by means of including new fuzzy variables in the analysis such as the maximum real part of the closed loop poles.

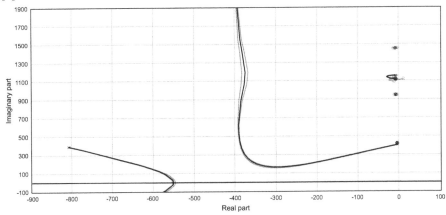

Fig. 8. Root locus of the control system for two different α-cuts: $\mu = 1$ (black) and $\mu = 0$ (grey).

6. Conclusion

In this chapter we have shown the suitability of the matrix computing environment MATLAB to solve control problems of structures via finite element analysis and root locus design and how these two issues have been blended and integrated into a Fuzzy Finite Element methodology for the analysis and simulation of uncertain control of structures.

The Fuzzy Finite Element procedure has been described. The approach relies on the α-cut technique which subdivides the membership range into a number of α-levels. The fuzzy arithmetic is based upon an efficient implementation in MATLAB code for the Transformation Method. This implementation has been modified and improved with some enhanced features. This methodology has been shown to be applicable to a realistic case study related to structural control using a Positive Position Feedback technique and piezoelectric actuators and sensors. In the light of the obtained results, the proposed procedure may prove useful to other analysis involving any other control technique or uncertainty source. In addition, the efficient implementation obtained due to MATLAB programming allows us to achieve high accuracy results together with low computational costs.

Finally, further research may be carried out in this topic. Firstly, a more efficient implementation of the Transformation Method can be found when using *cell* arrays instead of *double* arrays or when considering multiple fuzzy outputs. Secondly, the Transformation Method also allows a sort of sensitivity analysis which should be included in the MATLAB implementation in order to endow our method with extended capabilities. Thirdly, and in-depth comparison between this possibilistic methodology and the robust H_∞ optimal control theory must be carried out in order to identify more precisely the situations in which one method stand out from the other.

7. Acknowledgment

The authors are grateful for the support received from the "Ministerio de Educación" of the Spanish government through the "Programa Nacional de Movilidad de Recursos Humanos del Plan Nacional de I-D+i 2008-2011" and from the EPSRC through grant reference EP/D078601/1.

8. References

Balmes, E., Bianchi, J.-P. & Leclére, J.-M. (2009). *Structural Dynamics Toolbox for use with MATLAB: User's guide*.

De Gersem, H., Moens, D., Desmet, W. & Vandepitte, D. (2005). A fuzzy finite element procedure for the calculation of uncertain frequency response functions of damped structures: Part 2 - numerical case studies, *Journal of Sound and Vibration* 288: 463–486.

De Munck, M., Moens, D., Desmet, W. & Vandepitte, D. (2008). A response surface based optimisation algorithm for the calculation of fuzzy envelope frfs of models with uncertain properties, *Computers & Structures* 86: 1080–1092.

Dosch, J. J., Daniel, D. J. & Garcia, E. (1992). A self-sensing piezoelectric actuator for collocated control, *Journal of Intelligent Material Systems and Structures* 3: 166–185.

Dubois, D. & Prade, H. M. (1980). *Fuzzy sets and systems : theory and applications*, Mathematics in science and engineering, Academic Press, New York.

Gu, D.-W., Petkov, P. H. & Konstantinov, M. M. (2005). *Robust control design with MATLAB*, Springer, London.

Hanss, M. (2002). The transformation method for the simulation and analysis of systems with uncertain parameters, *Fuzzy Sets and Systems* 130: 277–289.

Klimke, A. (2003). An efficient implementation of the transformation method of fuzzy arithmetic, (IANS), extended preprint 2003/009, *Technical report*, University of Stuttgart.

Moens, D. & Vandepitte, D. (2005). A fuzzy finite element procedure for the calculation of uncertain frequency-response functions of damped structures: Part 1 - procedure, *Journal of Sound and Vibration* 288: 431–462.

Oberkampf, W. L., Helton, J. C., Joslyn, C. A., Wojtkiewicz, S. F. & Ferson, S. (2004). Challenge problems: uncertainty in system response given uncertain parameters, *Reliability Engineering & System Safety* 85: 11–19.

OpenFEM (2011).
URL: *http://support.sdtools.com/gf/project/openfem*

Preumont, A. (2002). *Vibration control of active structures: An introduction*, Kluwer Academic, Dordrecht.

Sims, N. D., Bayly, P. V. & Young, K. A. (2005). Piezoelectric sensors and actuators for milling tool stability lobes, *Journal of Sound and Vibration* 281: 743–762.

Sims, N. D., Manson, G. & Mann, B. (2010). Fuzzy stability analysis of regenerative chatter in milling, *Journal of Sound and Vibration* 329: 1025–1041.

Zadeh, L. A. (1965). Fuzzy sets, *Information and Control* 8: 338–353.

Zames, G. (1981). Feedback and optimal sensitivity: Model reference transformations, multiplicative seminorms and approximate inverses, *IEEE Transactions on Automatic Control* 26: 301–320.

Zames, G. & Francis, B. A. (1983). Feedback, minimax sensitivity and optimal robustness, *IEEE Transactions on Automatic Control* 28: 585–601.

Permissions

The contributors of this book come from diverse backgrounds, making this book a truly international effort. This book will bring forth new frontiers with its revolutionizing research information and detailed analysis of the nascent developments around the world.

We would like to thank Dr. ir. Clara M. Ionescu, for lending her expertise to make the book truly unique. She has played a crucial role in the development of this book. Without her invaluable contribution this book wouldn't have been possible. She has made vital efforts to compile up to date information on the varied aspects of this subject to make this book a valuable addition to the collection of many professionals and students.

This book was conceptualized with the vision of imparting up-to-date information and advanced data in this field. To ensure the same, a matchless editorial board was set up. Every individual on the board went through rigorous rounds of assessment to prove their worth. After which they invested a large part of their time researching and compiling the most relevant data for our readers. Conferences and sessions were held from time to time between the editorial board and the contributing authors to present the data in the most comprehensible form. The editorial team has worked tirelessly to provide valuable and valid information to help people across the globe.

Every chapter published in this book has been scrutinized by our experts. Their significance has been extensively debated. The topics covered herein carry significant findings which will fuel the growth of the discipline. They may even be implemented as practical applications or may be referred to as a beginning point for another development. Chapters in this book were first published by InTech; hereby published with permission under the Creative Commons Attribution License or equivalent.

The editorial board has been involved in producing this book since its inception. They have spent rigorous hours researching and exploring the diverse topics which have resulted in the successful publishing of this book. They have passed on their knowledge of decades through this book. To expedite this challenging task, the publisher supported the team at every step. A small team of assistant editors was also appointed to further simplify the editing procedure and attain best results for the readers.

Our editorial team has been hand-picked from every corner of the world. Their multi-ethnicity adds dynamic inputs to the discussions which result in innovative outcomes. These outcomes are then further discussed with the researchers and contributors who give their valuable feedback and opinion regarding the same. The feedback is then collaborated with the researches and they are edited in a comprehensive manner to aid the understanding of the subject.

Apart from the editorial board, the designing team has also invested a significant amount of their time in understanding the subject and creating the most relevant covers. They scrutinized every image to scout for the most suitable representation of the subject and create an appropriate cover for the book.

The publishing team has been involved in this book since its early stages. They were actively engaged in every process, be it collecting the data, connecting with the contributors or procuring relevant information. The team has been an ardent support to the editorial, designing and production team. Their endless efforts to recruit the best for this project, has resulted in the accomplishment of this book. They are a veteran in the field of academics and their pool of knowledge is as vast as their experience in printing. Their expertise and guidance has proved useful at every step. Their uncompromising quality standards have made this book an exceptional effort. Their encouragement from time to time has been an inspiration for everyone.

The publisher and the editorial board hope that this book will prove to be a valuable piece of knowledge for researchers, students, practitioners and scholars across the globe.

List of Contributors

Fikri Serdar Gökhan
Gazikent University, Faculty of Engineering and Architecture, Department of Electrical and Electronic Engineering, Gaziantep, Turkey

Damian Trif
Babes-Bolyai University of Cluj-Napoca, Romania

Alain Hébert
École Polytechnique de Montréal, Canada

João Eduardo da Silva Pereira, Janete Pereira Amador and Angela Pellegrin Ansuj
Federal University of Santa Maria, Brazil

Krasimira Stoilova and Todor Stoilov
Institute of Information and Communication Technologies, Academy of Sciences, Bulgaria

Woo Nam Lee and Jong Bae Park
Konkuk University, Korea

Kelly Bennett
U.S. Army Research Laboratory, Sensors and Electron Devices Directorate, Adelphi, MD, U.S.A

James Robertson
Clearhaven Technologies LLC, Severna Park, MD, U.S.A

Abbas Mahmoudabadi
PhD Candidate, Technical and Engineering Faculty, Payam-e-Noor University & General Director of Traffic Safety Department, Road Maintenance and Transportation Organization, Tehran, Iran

Arezoo Abolghasem
Transportation Engineer, Road Maintenance and Transportation Organization, Tehran, Iran

Shahram Javadi
Islamic AZAD University, Central Tehran Branch, Iran

Damir Sumina, Neven Bulić, Marija Mirošević and Mato Mišković
University of Zagreb/Faculty of Electrical Engineering and Computing, Croatia
University of Rijeka, Faculty of Engineering, Croatia
University of Dubrovnik/Department of Electrical Engineering and Computing, Croatia

Carlos Andrés Torres-Pinzón and Ramon Leyva
Department of Electronic, Electrical and Automatic Control Engineering, Rovira i Virgili University, Tarragona, Spain

João Viana da Fonseca Neto and Gustavo Araújo de Andrade
Federal University of Maranhão, Department of Electrical Engineering, Control Process Laboratory, Brazil

Zeyad Assi Obaid and Saad Abd Almageed Salman
College of Engineering University of Diyala, Iraq

Hazem I. Ali
Control Engineering Department, University of Technology, Iraq

Nasri Sulaiman, M. H. Marhaban and M. N. Hamidon
Faculty of Engineering, University Putra Malaysia, Malaysia

Tom Wanjekeche, Dan V. Nicolae and Adisa A. Jimoh
Tshwane University of Technology, South Africa

Angel L. Morales
Universidad de Castilla - La Mancha, Spain

Jem A. Rongong and Neil D. Sims
The University of Sheffield, United Kingdom

Printed in the USA
CPSIA information can be obtained
at www.ICGtesting.com
JSHW011504221024
72173JS00005B/1193